WE, THE ROBOTS?

*Regulating Artificial Intelligence and
The Limits of The Law*

我们，机器人？

Simon Chesterman
［澳］陈西文——著

游传满 费秀艳——译

人工智能监管及其法律局限

北京大学出版社
PEKING UNIVERSITY PRESS

著作权合同登记号　图字：01-2023-2933

图书在版编目(CIP)数据

我们，机器人？：人工智能监管及其法律局限/(澳)陈西文著；游传满，费秀艳译. —北京：北京大学出版社，2024.6

ISBN 978-7-301-35038-6

Ⅰ. ①我… Ⅱ. ①陈… ②游… ③费… Ⅲ. ①人工智能—科学技术管理法规—研究 Ⅳ. ①D912.170.4

中国国家版本馆 CIP 数据核字(2024)第 096177 号

This is a simplified Chinese translation of the following title published by Cambridge University Press：WE，THE ROBOTS？ Regulating Artificial Intelligence and the Limits of the Law (ISBN978-1-009-04831-6)

@ Simon Chesterman 2021

This simplified Chinese translation edition for the People's Republic of China (excluding Hong Kong SAR，Macau SAR and Taiwan) is published by arrangement with the Press Syndicate of the University of Cambridge，Cambridge，United Kingdom.

ⓒ Peking University Press 2024

This simplified Chinese translation edition is authorized for sale in the People's Republic of China (excluding Hong Kong SAR，Macau SAR and Taiwan) only. Unauthorized export of this simplified Chinese translation edition is a violation of the Copyright Act. No part of this publication may be reproduced or distributed by any means，or stored in a database or retrieval system，without the prior written permission of Cambridge University Press and Peking University Press. Copies of this book sold without a Cambridge University Press sticker on the cover are unauthorized and illegal.

本书封面贴有 Cambridge University Press 防伪标签，无标签者不得销售。

书　　　名	我们，机器人？——人工智能监管及其法律局限 WOMEN，JIQIREN？——RENGONG ZHINENG JIANGUAN JIQI FALÜ JUXIAN
著作责任者	[澳]陈西文(Simon Chesterman)　著 游传满　费秀艳　译
责 任 编 辑	孙维玲
标 准 书 号	ISBN 978-7-301-35038-6
出 版 发 行	北京大学出版社
地　　　址	北京市海淀区成府路 205 号　100871
网　　　址	http://www.pup.cn　新浪微博：@北京大学出版社
电 子 邮 箱	zpup@pup.cn
电　　　话	邮购部 010-62752015　发行部 010-62750672 编辑部 021-62071998
印 刷 者	三河市博文印刷有限公司
经 销 者	新华书店 965 毫米×1300 毫米　16 开本　24.5 印张　296 千字 2024 年 6 月第 1 版　2024 年 6 月第 1 次印刷
定　　　价	79.00 元

未经许可，不得以任何方式复制或抄袭本书之部分或全部内容。

版权所有，侵权必究

举报电话：010-62752024　电子邮箱：fd@pup.cn

图书如有印装质量问题，请与出版部联系，电话：010-62756370

中译本推荐序

在这个人工智能技术快速迭代、应用场景不断拓展的时刻，人类社会正站在一个前所未有的历史节点上，面临前所未有的挑战和机遇。

作为人工智能技术与产业大国，我国近年来在人工智能监管制度供给上取得了显著成就。特别是自2017年《新一代人工智能发展规划》发布以来，中国在人工智能发展与安全建设方面，已经形成了全链条、多层次、较为完善的法律规范体系。从《民法典》到《网络安全法》等基本法律，再到《数据安全法》和《个人信息保护法》等专门规范，《互联网信息服务算法推荐管理规定》《互联网信息服务深度合成管理规定》《生成式人工智能服务管理暂行办法》等部门规章，以及《国家新一代人工智能标准体系建设指南》《人工智能——机器学习系统技术要求》等行业指南和标准，为人工智能的健康发展提供了坚实的制度保障。

时下，欧盟、美国等出台法典式的《人工智能法》《犹他州人工智能政策法》，又引起了中国当前是否需要制定颁布类似的"人工智能法"的广泛讨论。《国务院2023年度立法工作计划》已经明确预备提请全国人大常委会审议人工智能法草案，而一些学者也已提出多份相对完整的人工智能立法建议稿。与此同时，也有观点认为，鉴于人工智能技术本身的飞速变动以及对政策合成谬误制约产业创新的忧虑，目前在立法方面应采取更为审慎的态度，《十四届全国人大常委会立法规划》未将人工智能法列入立法规划也在一定程度上反映了立法机关的谨慎。

陈西文教授（Simon Chesterman）所著《我们，机器人？——人工智能监管及其法律局限》（We, the Robots? Regulating Artificial Intelligence and the Limits of the Law）一书，不仅为我们提供了从历史与国际视角对人工智能法律监管问题的深入分析，更为中国乃至全球人工智能治理理论研究与政策发展贡献出宝贵的智慧和见解。

陈教授是国际公法、冲突治理、法律科技等领域的权威学者。他的学术旅程始于澳大利亚墨尔本大学。本科学习期间，他获得包括澳大利亚维多利亚州最高法院奖在内的诸多奖项，还担任国际知名期刊《墨尔本大学法律评论》的学生编辑。在以一等荣誉获得墨尔本大学法律与文学双学位之后，他获得罗德奖学金资助，前往英国牛津大学深造，在著名国际法学者伊恩·布朗利（Ian Brownlie）教授的指导下获得国际法博士学位。

在2006年获聘纽约大学法学教授并出任纽约大学法学院新加坡项目主任之前，陈教授曾在多家国际组织工作，包括担任国际和平学会（International Peace Academy）高级研究员，担任国际危机组织（International Crisis Group）纽约办公室联合国关系主任，以及在联合国人道主义事务协调厅驻南斯拉夫办事处、卢旺达问题国际刑事法庭等组织工作。这些丰富的一线工作经历为他积累了深厚的国际法和国际关系实践经验，并推动了他在国际法、全球治理领域的学术研究。

2012年至2022年，陈教授担任新加坡国立大学法学院院长，在任期间他对学院进行了多项影响深远的改革，包括丰富课程设置、增设研究中心以及优化国际师生比例。在他的领导下，新加坡国立大学法学院在国际排名中显著提升，成为全球顶尖的法学院之一。除此之外，陈教授还创办了《亚洲国际法》（Asian Journal of International Law）等期刊，发起成立了全球法学院联盟等组织，为全世界法学教育和研究做出了重要贡献。

陈教授著作等身，目前已经出版了二十多部著作，发表了上百篇学术论文，内容涵盖国际法、冲突治理、人工智能、数据保护、法律教育等多个领域。早在 2001 年，陈教授就在牛津大学出版社出版专著《正义战争还是正义和平：人道主义干预与国际法》（Just War or Just Peace? Humanitarian Intervention and International Law），探讨了人道主义干预的法律依据和道德争议，就国际社会面对大规模人权侵害提出了相应的法律和政治应对措施。

陈教授的丰硕成果，不仅在学术界产生广泛的影响，更在实践中推动着地区与全球的数据立法与人工智能政策的发展。陈教授是新加坡数据保护委员会（Data Protection Advisory Committee）专家委员，也是新加坡国家人工智能核心计划（AI Singapore）高级主任；他还经常作为专家顾问，为联合国撰写全球治理方面的报告，包括 2023 年由联合国人工智能顾问组（AI Advisory Body）发布的《中期报告：以人为本的人工智能治理》（Interim Report：Governing AI for Humanity）。

本书是陈教授有关国际治理与人工智能规范的集大成之作。本书从比较法与历史的维度深入探讨了人工智能法律监管问题，以及传统法律体系在应对这一新兴技术时的局限性，比如人工智能的法律主体地位与法律责任分配问题，并提出了一系列创新性的制度和政策建议。

　　本书中译本的出版，无疑为我们提供了一个重要的参考和借鉴。它不仅能使我们更好地理解人工智能法律监管的必要性和紧迫性，更可以帮助我们在立法过程中避免政策合成谬误，实现规则制定的科学性和前瞻性。此外，本书特别强调了亚洲法域的实践经验对于人工智能国际治理协同的重要性。这对于中国而言无疑是一个重要的启示。作为亚洲乃至全球的重要力量，中国在人工智能治理上的责任和作用不容忽视。我相信，随着本书的传播和影响，通过广泛学习和借鉴国际经验，结合自身国情和发展阶段持续探索和实践，中国完全有能力在人工智能治理理论研究和政策创新上迈向新的高度，为全球人工智能治理贡献中国智慧和中国方案。

　　是为序。

郭　雳
北京大学法学院院长、教授
2024 年 6 月

中 译 本 序

目前，人工智能（Artificial Intelligence，AI）的迭代发展可谓日新月异。世界各国有识之士在探讨如何充分发挥人工智能价值贡献的同时，也在努力探寻如何减少或降低人工智能对社会、经济、政治、法律各方面带来的风险冲击。讨论的关注焦点多集中在美国科技巨头的产业创新，比如谷歌的 Gemini、微软和 OpenAI 的 ChatGPT，或者欧盟监管机构的制度创新，比如最近通过的《人工智能法》（AI Act）。与此同时，中国企业在人工智能模式创新与应用生态发展上也扮演着日益重要的作用，中国政府在如何创造性地引导与规范人工智能方面也变得更加积极有为。

特别是生成式人工智能的出现，使得这些讨论变得更具紧迫性与现实性。过去，许多人认为人工智能的短期影响主要体现在算法推荐系统和人脸图像识别上。而其中的突出风险体现在偏见与歧视、无益建议以及身份盗用上。然而，2016 年美国总统大选中出现的各种问题，说明人工智能很可能在更大范围内被用来操纵普罗大众。现如今，随着新型人工智能，诸如 ChatGPT、Gemini、Ernic Bot（文心一言）、Tongyi Qianwen（通义千问）等大语言模型（Large Language Model，LLM）的产生与应用，还出现了更多重要的治理规范命题。

其中，侵犯知识产权可能是它们的"原罪"，因为大语言模型多是在海量数据上进行训练的，而这些海量数据就包括盗版侵权作品，以及被分享以供阅读但未经授权复制的信息数据。这是输入端的问题。除此之外，输出端的所有权问题也存在极大争议。大多数国家目前还不承认计算机对其生成内容在知识产权法律体系中的所有权，尽管中国最近的判例已经部分支持了此类所有权。

这些法律规范问题可能在根本上影响到知识经济（knowledge economy）对于社会发展转型变革的影响。"知识工作者"（knowledge worker）是现代管理学之父彼得·德鲁克（Peter Drucker）在1959年为非传统问题解决者创设的专有名词，他们是"以思考为生"的职业人士，他们通过分析和创作的专业能力赚取收入——此类分析与创作是ChatGPT等大语言模型可以在几乎零时间成本与零资金成本的情况下完成的。如今，此类职业人士迫切地想知道大语言模型是否会在不久的将来取代他们的工作。

鉴于以上诸种原因，我非常荣幸地向中文读者呈献我早前于剑桥大学出版社出版的《我们，机器人？——人工智能监管及其法律局限》一书的中译本。此中译本的出版可谓正逢其时。我本人长期在新加坡生活和工作，时常觉得本地关于人工智能治理的讨论偏于狭隘和肤浅。所谓偏于狭隘，我的意思是讨论由少数声音主导——特别是美国和西欧的声音，虽然偶尔也涉及中国。所谓偏于肤浅，我的意思是讨论往往局限于治理原则等形而上学的问题。

希望此中译本的面世，能为如何促进人工智能治理与监管更广泛、更深入的讨论贡献我的绵薄之力。借此中译本，我也衷心期待能够与中文理论界和实务界同仁在人工智能领域进行更直接的交流和探讨。正如我在前言部分的结尾所写的，拙著很可能无法提供所有答案。但我希望它能帮助我们共同努力，以寻找和确定问题所在。

我要借此机会，再次感谢在英文致谢中列出的同事与家人。当然，此中译本能在这么短的时间内与中文读者见面，还需要感谢游传满和费秀艳两位学者夜以继日的付出。特别是传满，早在英文版本的写作过程中，我们就对人工智能的司法应用和数据保护等议题开展过探讨。

"借你们文采飞渡，此书得以横跨语言之桥！"①

最后，我还要感谢北京大学出版社的孙维玲女士及其同事们，以及剑桥大学出版社的 Joe Ng 及其众多同事们。

陈西文
（Simon Chesterman）
于新加坡
2024 年 3 月 12 日

---

① 此句为原作者借助人工智能辅助工具写作的中文，英文为："Through your literary talents, the book can cross the bridge of language."——译者注

全书概要

我们应该规范人工智能吗？我们能做到吗？

从自动驾驶汽车到高频交易再到算法决策，我们的生活、工作和娱乐越来越依赖于人工干预逐渐让位、退出的人工智能系统。这些高速、自主和不透明的智能系统带来了巨大的好处，但也带来了诸多重大风险。

本书研究了法律如何处理监管人工智能，以及还需要哪些额外的规则和制度——包括人工智能在自我监管中可能发挥的作用。

本书借鉴了世界各地主要法域的制度样本和规范案例，前瞻性地总结并提出如何管理风险、画定红线和维护公共权力合法性的规制模式。尽管人工智能系统超越传统法律规制界限的前景似乎还很遥远，但是，这些规制措施不仅在短期内具有现实的规范意义，即使将来进入通用人工智能甚或超级人工智能时代，这些规制模式也将具有指导意义。

序　言

　　人工智能正在改变现代生活。从自动驾驶汽车到高频交易再到算法决策，我们的生活、工作和娱乐方式越来越依赖于人工干预逐渐让位、退出的人工智能系统。由于迭代变化的速度和对监管限制创新的谨慎，以及人工智能对传统监管范式提出的理论和实际挑战，对人工智能的有效监管也变得越发具有难度。这些挑战包括现代计算系统的速度、某些人工智能系统的自主性以及日益增加的不透明性。本书研究了如何使现有法律工具适应新环境，以及还需要哪些额外的规则和制度——包括人工智能能够和应该在自我监管中发挥怎样的作用。

　　目前，这一领域的大多数工作都集中在律师、他们的潜在客户或机器本身的活动上。本书则侧重于那些试图规范这些活动的人，以及人工智能系统给政府和更广泛的治理体系所带来的困难。本书没有以特定的行为者或活动为起点，而是强调了人工智能对有效的监管范式本身带来的结构性问题。本书的重要贡献之一，是从三个视角来区分不同的监管困境：如何规范管理由新技术衍生的风险的现实性问题，是否将某些社会功能让渡于人工智能系统承担的伦理道德问题，以及当公共机构将其权力委托给算法时的合法性问题。

本书的核心论点是，人工智能时代的监管是公共规制（public control），它需要各国政府的积极参与。同时，人工智能的特性——高速性、自主性、不透明性——也使得任何一个国家都无法单独面对。在正常情况下，国际法和国际机构可以发挥协调作用，就像在从大规模杀伤性武器到气候变化和大流行病管控等领域一样。然而，由于种种原因，那些处于人工智能发展前沿的国家往往是最不愿意让国际法和国际机构限制其经济发展和政治独立的国家。结果是，目前具有制定全球人工智能规范最大影响力的国家，也是最不愿意这样做的国家。

通过从公法和国际法的视角来探讨这些问题，本书提供了如何管理风险、画定红线和维护公共权力合法性的经验教训。尽管人工智能超越传统法律规制界限的前景似乎还很遥远，但这些规制措施不仅在短期内具有现实规范意义，即使将来进入通用人工智能甚或超级人工智能时代，这些规制模式也将具有指导意义。

致　　谢

写作可能是一段孤独的心路旅程，但很少是可以一个人独自走完的。

我要感谢我的诸多同事，包括库马拉林加姆·阿米瑞塔林加姆（Kumaralingam Amirthalingam）、达米安·查尔默斯（Damian Chalmers）、陈荣（Tracey Evans Chan）、钟慧明（Denise Cheong）、加布里埃尔·甘（Gabriel Gan）、米里亚姆·戈尔德比（Miriam Goldby）、安德鲁·哈尔平（Andrew Halpin）、克里斯蒂安·霍夫曼（Christian Hofmann）、胡颖（Hu Ying）、阿里夫·贾马尔（Arif Jamal）、金正宇（Jeong Woo Kim）、许金连（Koh Kheng Lian）、邱泉源（Kenneth Khoo）、尚提尼·K. 克里希南（Shantini J Krishnan）、帕维特拉·克里希纳斯瓦米（Pavitra Krishnaswamy）、刘君灏（Lau Kwan Ho）、李义腾（Lee Yee Teng）、梁嘉韵（Emma Leong）、林友良（Brian Y Lim）、林浩康（Lim How Khang）、林方前（Mark Lim）、林琳（Lin Lin）、伯顿·王（Burton Ong）、詹姆斯·佩纳（James Penner）、妮可·卢汉（Nicole Roughan）、尼维迪塔·S（Nivedita S）、丹尼尔·森（Daniel Seng）、莎伦·谢（Sharon Seah）、亚历克·斯通·斯威特（Alec Stone Sweet）、陈家兴（David

Tan)、陈文炜（Patrick Tan）、陈忠星（Tan Zhong Xing）、汉斯·基奥（Hans Tjio）、乔尔·特拉克特曼（Joel Trachtman）、雅各布·特纳（Jacob Turner）、乌马坎斯·瓦罗蒂尔（Umakanth Varottil）、约瑟芬·瓦拉特（Josefine Wallat）、弗拉斯塔·瓦拉特（Vlasta Wallat）、魏铭声（Wee Meng Seng）、瑞安·怀伦（Ryan Whalen）、克里斯蒂安·威廷（Christian Witting）、黄志梁（Wong Chee Leong）、杨子健（Yeong Zee Kin）、游传满（You Chuanman）、尼科·扎克特（Nico Zachert）以及在本书写作过程中提出宝贵建议的几位匿名审稿人。

本书的部分内容，之前在新加坡国立大学法学院、李光耀公共政策学院，新加坡创新机构（SG Innovate），物联网亚洲（the Internet of Things Asia），TechLaw. Fest，加拿大麦吉尔大学法学院，英国埃克塞特大学，英国国际法和比较法研究所，以及其他论坛的演讲中分享、探讨过，特此感谢。在新加坡国立大学，我要感谢詹妮·田（Jenny Thian）的帮助，她在我的日程安排上专门空出了宝贵的写作时间，她写的日程备注非常简洁，就两字："写作"！我还要感谢黄倩薇（Violet Huang）、尤金·刘（Eugene Lau）、王凯骏（Ong Kye Jing）、叶珈庆（Yap Jia Qing）等研究助理提供的宝贵协助。当然，本书若有谬误和遗漏之处，都归咎于我本人。

本书的部分内容，此前也以论文形式发表在学术期刊上，包括 Artificial Intelligence and the Problem of Autonomy，(2020) 1 *Notre Dame Journal on Emerging Technologies* 210; Artificial Intelligence and the Limits of Legal Personality，(2020) 69 *International & Comparative Law Quarterly* 819; "Move Fast and Break Things": Law, Technology, and the Problem of Speed,

(2021) 33 *Singapore Academy of Law Journal* 5; Through a Glass, Darkly: Artificial Intelligence and the Problem of Opacity, (2021) 69 *American Journal of Comparative Law* (forthcoming)。感谢相关出版单位允许我再次使用这些内容。

最后,也是最重要的,感谢我亲爱的 M、V、N 和 T:他们是我灵感的来源,也是我各种天马行空构想的内测用户(beta testers)。此书献给他们!

英文缩写列表

中文全称	英文全称	简称
自动驾驶系统	Automated Driving System	ADS
自动驾驶系统实体	Automated Driving System Entity	ADSE
人工智能	Artificial Intelligence	AI
高级目标定位与致命性自动化系统（美国）	Advanced Targeting and Lethality Automated System (United States)	ATLAS
首席执行官	Chief Executive Officer	CEO
近程武器系统	Close-in Weapon System	CIWS
国家信息与自由委员会（法国）	Commission Nationale de l'Informatique et des Libertés [National Commission on Informatics and Liberty] (France)	CNIL
替代性制裁的罪犯管理分析	Correctional Offender Management Profiling for Alternative Sanctions	COMPAS
美国国防高级研究计划局	Defense Advanced Research Projects Agency (United States)	DARPA
脱氧核糖核酸	Deoxyribonucleic Acid	DNA
美国司法部	Department of Justice (United States)	DOJ
数据保护影响评估	Data protection Impact Assessment	DPIA
欧洲专利局	European Patent Office	EPO
欧盟	European Union	EU
美国联邦贸易委员会	Federal Trade Commission (United States)	FTC
美国政府问责办公室	Government Accountability Office (United States)	GAO

(续表)

中文全称	英文全称	简称
通用数据保护条例（欧盟）	General Data Protection Regulation (European Union)	GDPR
全球人工智能伙伴关系	Global Partnership on AI	GPAI
高频交易者	High-frequency Trader	HFT
国际原子能机构	International Atomic Energy Agency	IAEA
国际人工智能机构（假设性）	International Artificial Intelligence Agency (hypothetical)	IAIA
互联网名称与数字地址分配机构	Internet Corporation for Assigned Names and Numbers	ICANN
国际红十字会	International Committee of the Red Cross	ICRC
简易爆炸装置	Improvised Explosive Device	IED
电气和电子工程师协会	Institute of Electrical and Electronics Engineers	IEEE
国际法委员会	International Law Commission	ILC
政府间气候变化专门委员会	Intergovernmental Panel on Climate Change	IPCC
国际标准化组织	International Organization for Standardization	ISO
国际电信联盟	International Telecommunication Union	ITU
远程反舰导弹	Long Range Anti-ship Missile	LRASM
金融工具市场指令二（欧盟）	Markets in Financial Instruments Directive II (European Union)	MiFID II
核不扩散条约	Nuclear Non-Proliferation Treaty	NPT
国家交通委员会（澳大利亚）	National Transport Commission (Australia)	NTC
经济合作与发展组织	Organisation for Economic Co-operation and Development	OECD
私营军事和安全公司	Private Military and Security Company	PMSC
汽车工程师协会	Society of Automotive Engineers	SAE
联合国	United Nations	UN
美国专利商标局	United States Patent and Trademark Office	USPTO

（续表）

中文全称	英文全称	简称
波动率指数（芝加哥期权交易所）	Volatility Index (Chicago Board Options Exchange)	VIX
世界卫生组织	World Health Organization	WHO
世界知识产权组织	World Intellectual Property Organization	WIPO
可解释人工智能	Explainable Artificial Intelligence	XAI

目录
CONTENTS

前　言 // i

第Ⅰ部分　人工智能带来的挑战

第 1 章　高速性 // 003

1.1　信息的全球化　// 007

1.2　高频交易　// 011

1.3　竞争法　// 016

1.4　高速度衍生的问题　// 020

第 2 章　自主性 // 024

2.1　自动驾驶汽车与风险管理　// 027

2.2　杀手机器人与外包服务的伦理问题　// 040

2.3　算法决策及其合法性　// 051

2.4　自主性的问题 // 059

第 3 章　不透明性 // 062

　　3.1　劣质决策 // 067

　　3.2　不可接受的决策 // 070

　　3.3　不合法决策 // 077

　　3.4　不透明性带来的问题 // 084

第 Ⅱ 部分　监管人工智能的工具

第 4 章　法律责任 // 089

　　4.1　风险管控 // 092

　　4.2　不可委托职责 // 107

　　4.3　政府固有职能和外包的局限性 // 117

　　4.4　法律责任的局限性 // 121

第 5 章　法律人格 // 123

　　5.1　可踢之躯？// 127

　　5.2　我思故我在？// 139

　　5.3　管控超级智能 // 154

　　5.4　法律人格的局限性 // 159

第 6 章　透明原则 // 163

　　6.1　一般理论 // 166

　　6.2　实践经验 // 172

　　6.3　立法规定 // 182

　　6.4　透明原则的局限性 // 191

第Ⅲ部分　可　能　性

第 7 章　新规则 // 201

  7.1　为什么（不）监管？// 207

  7.2　何时监管 // 211

  7.3　如何监管 // 217

  7.4　规则前景 // 225

第 8 章　新机构 // 229

  8.1　行业标准 // 233

  8.2　全球红线 // 239

  8.3　国家责任 // 257

  8.4　机构前景 // 263

第 9 章　由人工智能进行监管？ // 266

  9.1　法律自动化 // 270

  9.2　法律作为数据 // 279

  9.3　法律作为编码 // 282

  9.4　监管前景 // 286

结论　我们，机器人？ // 290

参考文献 // 295

索　引 // 339

译后记 // 348

前　　言

关于人工智能及其对人类的潜在影响的担忧已经伴随我们半个多世纪了。这个词是在1956年达特茅斯学院的一次研讨会上进入人们视野的。早期的人工智能研究探讨过一些主题，比如证明逻辑定理、推断化学样品的分子结构以及玩飞镖等游戏。十几年后，斯坦利·库布里克（Stanley Kubrick）的电影《2001年：太空漫游》展现了一个经典场景，即机器人被赋予推翻人类判断的权力：哈尔9000（HAL 9000）以令人毛骨悚然的平静声音解释为什么一艘前往木星的航天器的任务比机组人员生命更重要。

在随后的几十年里，人工智能和与之相关的恐惧都在迅速发展蔓延。尽管很多发明都伴随着对新技术影响的担忧，但人工智能领域的不同之处在于，一些最严厉的技术危险警告来自对该领域最了解的人，比如埃隆·马斯克、比尔·盖茨和斯蒂芬·霍金等人。其中，许多担忧与"泛人工智能""强人工智能"有关：一个可以执行人类所能完成的任何智力任务的系统，无疑也会带来有关非生物体自我认知和意识本质之类的复杂问题。

上述非生物体将自己的优先事项置于人类优先事项之上的可能性并非微不足道,但本书的重点是"弱人工智能"带来的更紧迫的挑战,此类人工智能系统可以将认知功能应用于通常由人类承担的特定任务。① 一个相关的术语是"机器学习",这是人工智能的一个子集,指的是计算机在没有明确指令的情况下自我优化的能力。② 例如,阿尔法狗元(AlphaGo Zero)程序只是被输入众所周知的极为复杂的围棋规则;利用这些基本规则信息,阿尔法狗元通过机器学习自我优化,开发了新的对弈策略,建立了对战人类棋手的绝对优势。③

人工智能与法律方面的学术成果汗牛充栋,已有几十本专著、数千篇文章以及至少两个专门的期刊。④ 除了关于什么可能

---

① 有关如何恰当定义人工智能的讨论,请参见 Stuart J Russell and Peter Norvig, *Artificial Intelligence:A Modern Approach* (3rd edn, Prentice Hall 2010) 1-5。大体上有四种定义方法:行为像人类(著名的图灵测试)、思考像人类(模拟认知行为)、理性思考能力(基于逻辑主义传统)和理性行为能力(罗素和诺维格所推崇的理性代理人,因为它不依赖于对人类认知的特定理解或对理性思维构成的详尽模型)。关于图灵测试,请参见本书第 5 章的引言。

② 这个过程可能是有人类监督指导,也可能是没有人类监督指导,还可能是通过自我强化过程进行,参见 Kevin P Murphy, *Machine Learning:A Probabilistic Perspective* (MIT Press 2012),第 2 页。有关人类参与与否、和其他人工智能模型的讨论,详见本书第 2 章第 2.3 节;有关机器学习中偏差的讨论,详见本书第 3 章第 3.2.1 节。

③ David Silver, *et al*, 'Mastering the Game of Go Without Human Knowledge' (2017) 550 *Nature* 354。该程序的后续迭代版本 MuZero,甚至没有被输入围棋和其他游戏的规则。参见 Julian Schrittwieser, *et al*, 'Mastering Atari, Go, Chess, and Shogi by Planning with a Learned Model' (2020) 588 *Nature* 604。

④ *Artificial Intelligence and Law* (Springer, 1992-); *RAIL:The Journal of Robotics, Artificial Intelligence & Law* (Fastcase, 2018-)。

被定义为"机器人意识"的推测性文献外,① 大多数研究阐述人工智能系统的最新发展②、对法律行业实际的或潜在的影响③以及

---

① See generally Nick Bostrom, *Superintelligence*: *Paths*, *Dangers*, *Strategies* (OUP 2014); Mark O'Connell, *To Be a Machine*: *Adventures Among Cyborgs*, *Utopians*, *Hackers*, *and the Futurists Solving the Modest Problem of Death* (Granta 2017); David J Gunkel, *Robot Rights* (MIT Press 2018). 关于人工智能系统的法律人格,可参见 Samir Chopra and Laurence F White, *A Legal Theory for Autonomous Artificial Agents* (University of Michigan Press 2011); Gabriel Hallevy, *When Robots Kill*: *Artificial Intelligence Under Criminal Law* (Northeastern UP 2013); John Frank Weaver, *Robots Are People Too*: *How Siri*, *Google Car*, *and Artificial Intelligence Will Force Us to Change Our Laws* (Praeger 2014); Gabriel Hallevy, *Liability for Crimes Involving Artificial Intelligence Systems* (Springer 2015); Visa AJ Kurki and Tomasz Pietrzykowski (eds), *Legal Personhood*: *Animals*, *Artificial Intelligence and the Unborn* (Springer 2017). 进一步阅读可参见本书第 5 章第 5.3 节。

② 这一领域近年的著作包括:Ryan Calo, A Michael Froomkin, and Ian Kerr (eds), *Robot Law* (Edward Elgar 2016); Patrick Lin, Keith Abney, and Ryan Jenkins (eds), *Robot Ethics 2.0*: *From Autonomous Cars to Artificial Intelligence* (OUP 2017); Woodrow Barfield and Ugo Pagallo (eds), *Research Handbook on the Law of Artificial Intelligence* (Edward Elgar 2018); Marcelo Corrales, Mark Fenwick, and Nikolaus Forgó (eds), *Robotics*, *AI and the Future of Law* (Springer 2018); Markus D Dubber, Frank Pasquale, and Sunit Das (eds), *The Oxford Handbook of Ethics of AI* (OUP 2020); Martin Ebers and Susana Navas (eds), *Algorithms and Law* (CUP 2020); Thomas Wischmeyer and Timo Rademacher (eds), *Regulating Artificial Intelligence* (Springer 2020).

③ See, eg, Richard Susskind, *The Future of Law*: *Facing the Challenges of Information Technology* (OUP 1996); Richard Susskind, *The End of Lawyers? Rethinking the Nature of Legal Services* (OUP 2008); Dory Reiling, *Technology for Justice*: *How Information Technology Can Support Judicial Reform* (Leiden UP 2010); Richard Susskind, *Tomorrow's Lawyers*: *An Introduction to Your Future* (OUP 2013); Kevin D Ashley, *Artificial Intelligence and Legal Analytics*: *New Tools for Law Practice in the Digital Age* (CUP 2017); Richard Susskind, *Online Courts and the Future of Justice* (OUP 2019); Simon Deakin and Christopher Markou (eds), *Is Law Computable? Critical Perspectives on Law and Artificial Intelligence* (Hart 2020).

由特定技术引起的规范性问题——自动驾驶汽车①、自主武器系统②、算法运用治理③等。其他很多论述,则与更广泛的数据、隐私保护领域或更普遍的法律和技术领域相重叠。

  该类文献中的大部分内容往往集中在法律从业者、其潜在客户或机器本身的活动上。④ 相比之下,本书重点关注的是那些努力监管以上活动的主体,以及人工智能系统给政府及其相关治理带来的挑战。本书不是以具体的行为者或活动为出发点,而是强调人工智能给有效监管带来的结构性冲击。

---

① See, eg, James M Anderson, *et al*, *Autonomous Vehicle Technology: A Guide for Policymakers* (RAND 2014); Markus Maurer, *et al* (eds), *Autonomous Driving: Technical, Legal and Social Aspects* (Springer 2016); Hannah YeeFen Lim, *Autonomous Vehicles and the Law: Technology, Algorithms, and Ethics* (Edward Elgar 2018).

② See, eg, Nehal Bhuta, *et al* (eds), *Autonomous Weapons Systems: Law, Ethics, Policy* (CUP 2016); Alex Leveringhaus, *Ethics and Autonomous Weapons* (Palgrave Macmillan 2016); Stuart Casey-Maslen, *et al*, *Drones and Other Unmanned Weapons Systems Under International Law* (Brill 2018); Wolff Heintschel von Heinegg, Robert Frau, and Tassilo Singer (eds), *Dehumanization of Warfare: Legal Implications of New Weapon Technologies* (Springer 2018).

③ Christopher Steiner, *Automate This: How Algorithms Came to Rule Our World* (Penguin 2012); Frank Pasquale, *The Black Box Society: The Secret Algorithms That Control Money and Information* (Harvard UP 2015); Cathy O'Neil, *Weapons of Math Destruction: How Big Data Increases Inequality and Threatens Democracy* (Broadway Books 2016).

④ 其他一些研究关注的是人工智能和机器对传统私法体系的挑战。参见 Ugo Pagallo, *The Laws of Robots: Crimes, Contracts, and Torts* (Springer 2013); Jacob Turner, *Robot Rules: Regulating Artificial Intelligence* (Palgrave Macmillan 2019); Mark Chinen, *Law and Autonomous Machines: The Co-Evolution of Legal Responsibility and Technology* (Edward Elgar 2019); Ryan Abbott, *The Reasonable Robot: Artificial Intelligence and the Law* (CUP 2020); Matthew Lavy and Matt Hervey, *The Law of Artificial Intelligence* (Sweet & Maxwell 2020); Dominika Ewa Harasimiuk and Tomasz Braun, *Regulating Artificial Intelligence: Binary Ethics and the Law* (Routledge 2021).

本书选择"监管"(regulation)一词，也是经过深思熟虑的。① 根据不同的语境，"监管"一词的外延不仅包括对各类具体行为的管控，还包括政府制定的各类法律规则。在美国，"监管"往往被认为是一种附加于自由市场的额外负担；在学术领域，"监管"被其视为对私人自主权的侵犯或者一项合作。② 总体而言，大部分的"监管"研究讨论的是特定的监管者可以和应该在经济和政治活动中扮演的不同角色。

当前而言，本书的重点将放在对人工智能一系列活动的官方监管上，主要涉及两个维度。③ 第一，监管的实施。可能通过规则、标准或其他手段，包括政府指导下的自我监管。第二，这种监管是由一个或多个政府机构实施的。这些监管机构可能是行政部门、立法机构、司法机构或其他政府或政府间实体，这种监管形式的合法性在于其与政府机构的联系——无论这种联系多么松散。这种监管的重点在于避免发生反面情况，即避免由于人工智能系统实施监管而导致那些通常会受到监管的活动不在任何公共实体的有效管辖范围内。当然，"监管"并不一定是狭义上的纯粹通过法律进行、以制裁为后盾的国家命令。④ 本书定义的"监

---

① Barry M Mitnick, *The Political Economy of Regulation: Creating, Designing, and Removing Regulatory Forms* (Columbia UP 1980); Anthony Ogus, *Regulation: Legal Form and Economic Theory* (Hart Publishing 2004); Robert Baldwin, Martin Cave, and Martin Lodge (eds), *The Oxford Handbook of Regulation* (OUP 2010).

② Tony Prosser, *The Regulatory Enterprise: Government, Regulation, and Legitimacy* (OUP 2010) 1-6.

③ Cf Philip Selznick, 'Focusing Organizational Research on Regulation' in Roger Noll (ed), *Regulatory Policy and the Social Sciences* (University of California Press 1985) 363.

④ John Austin, *The Province of Jurisprudence Determined* (first published 1832, CUP 1995) 18-37.

管",还包括经济激励措施,如税收或补贴、专业机构的认可或认证、其他市场机制。①

从这一语境衍生出一个问题,即人工智能系统本身能够在监管中发挥多大作用。② 本书的一个核心主张是,监管的首要责任必须由政府承担,这包括消极和积极两方面的含义。就消极方面而言,在短期内,政府不应该将固有的政府职能外包给它们无法控制的实体(比如人工智能系统)。③ 就积极方面而言,随着人工智能的发展,未来如何有效管控人工智能相关风险,将需要国际层面的通力合作和协调。但是,政府承担首要的监管责任并不意味着排他性责任。科技公司在确定标准方面已经发挥了极大的作用;而随着人工智能系统变得更加复杂,其作用无疑会进一步加强。而如何保证这些标准得到政府公权力的认可,将决定这些标准的合法性以及作为监管体系一部分的有效性。

本书是为全球读者而写的。此前绝大部分此类著作几乎完全依托于欧洲和美国的法律。当然,考虑到这些地域的经济重要性,以及它们在建立全球技术标准方面直接或间接的巨大影响力,这种偏好也是可以理解的。欧洲、美国的制度也提供了极为有趣的比较:人权问题决定了欧洲的应对方式,而商业市场逻辑则在美国占据了主导地位。然而,中国在人工智能领域已经是或

---

① Robert Baldwin, Martin Cave, and Martin Lodge, *Understanding Regulation: Theory, Strategy, and Practice* (first published 1999, 2nd edn, OUP 2011) 3.

② See Lawrence Lessig, *Code: Version 2.0* (first published 1999, Basic Books 2006).

③ See generally Simon Chesterman and Angelina Fisher (eds), *Private Security, Public Order: The Outsourcing of Public Services and Its Limits* (OUP 2009).

不久即将成为具有支配地位的参与者。① 因此，本书也关注中国特色的监管进路，以及如何平衡人工智能的产业领先地位与国内法律规范相对滞后的关系。本书重点关注的另一个法域是亚洲的新加坡。长期以来，新加坡一直努力将自己塑造为法治模范以大量吸引海外投资。与数据保护法的情况一样，② 新加坡政府也已明确将人工智能监管目标定为吸引和鼓励人工智能产业创新与投资。③

迄今为止，有关人工智能监管的讨论非常缺乏这种公法视角，特别是国际法和国际机构的作用几乎完全被排除在讨论之外。④ 本书的研究建立在作者过去对危机时期政府管控的研究基础之上，包括人道主义干预和政府过度管理，⑤ 以及在应对恐怖主义时政府将安全业务外包给私人主体、情报机构权力扩张等。⑥ 目前，虽然人工智能可能还没有构成和上述问题相当的系统性挑

---

① 参见腾讯研究院、中国信通院互联网法律研究中心：《人工智能：国家人工智能战略行动抓手》，中国人民大学出版社 2017 年版；Kai-Fu Lee, *AI Superpowers: China, Silicon Valley, and the New World Order* (Houghton Mifflin Harcourt 2018).

② Simon Chesterman (ed), *Data Protection Law in Singapore: Privacy and Sovereignty in an Interconnected World* (2nd edn, Academy Publishing 2018).

③ Model Artificial Intelligence Governance Framework (2nd edn) (Personal Data Protection Commission, 2020).

④ 有关目前已有的各种全球性、非约束性框架的讨论，请参见本书第 7 章引言部分。

⑤ Simon Chesterman, *Just War or Just Peace? Humanitarian Intervention and International Law* (OUP 2001); Simon Chesterman, *You, The People: The United Nations, Transitional Administration, and State-Building* (OUP 2004).

⑥ Simon Chesterman and Chia Lehnardt (eds), *From Mercenaries to Market: The Rise and Regulation of Private Military Companies* (OUP 2007); Simon Chesterman, *One Nation Under Surveillance: A New Social Contract to Defend Freedom Without Sacrificing Liberty* (OUP 2011).

战,但与此类问题相关的风险管控、画定红线和公共权力合法性的研究成果,对人工智能监管极具借鉴意义。如果人工智能大规模威胁真的出现,这些经验将更为重要。

章节概要

本书是围绕以下几组问题展开讨论的:我们应该如何理解被宽泛地描述为"人工智能系统"的技术给监管带来的挑战?哪些监管工具可以应对这些挑战以及它们的局限性是什么?我们还需要什么样的规则、制度、主体来促进人工智能带来增益,同时最大限度地减少不良影响?

本书的第一部分将监管面临的挑战分为三大类。

第 1 章,讨论高速性问题。自从计算机在 20 世纪 60 年代广泛应用以来,数据处理的效率就引发了监管关注。这从隐私保护方面很容易理解。名义上被公开的数据,比如离婚诉讼,长期以来一直通过纸质记录的"实质性隐蔽"而受到保护。① 当这样的材料在政府办公室只有一份纸质复件时,熟人或雇主找到它的机会是微乎其微的。然而,当它被计算机数字化,并最终可以通过互联网进行搜索时,"实质性隐蔽"消失了。如今,从证券监管到竞争法,高速算力对已有监管模式构成极大挑战,而这仅仅是因为股票交易、比较和调整价格这些合法活动以比以前设想的更快速度运行所导致的。另外,这些问题很多是实践方面的挑战,而非概念性挑战,并且更多产生于技术层面而不是人工智能层面。然而,目前采取的诸如通过熔断机制来停止交易等减缓决策

---

① *United States Department of Justice v. Reporters Committee for Freedom of the Press*,489 US 749,762 (1989)。

速度的方案,并不足以解决高速率的人工智能系统所带来的问题。

第 2 章提出了一种新的类型划分,从三个维度来检视人工智能系统自主性引发的监管问题:管控新技术相关风险的实际困难,由机器完全承担某些功能的伦理问题,以及政府机构将其权力下放给算法时的合法性问题。其挑战是,人工智能系统的自主性日益增强,暴露出以人类为中心的监管制度的漏洞。然而,令人惊讶的是,人们很少关注"自主性"的含义,以及其与这些制度漏洞的关系。自动驾驶汽车和自主武器系统是被研究最多的例子,但相关问题也出现在分配资源、确定私营或政府部门项目资格的算法中。

第 3 章分析人工智能日益增加的不透明性问题。随着计算机程序变得越来越复杂,非专业人员理解它们的能力不断下降。公司为追求专有利益保护可能在程序中植入"不透明"。尽管通过向专家求助或命令相关公司披露内部工作,可以理解这些系统的运行情况。然而,新一代的人工智能系统可能天生就是不透明的:某些机器学习技术很难甚至不可能以人类能够理解的方式进行阐释。当作出决定的过程与决定结果一样重要时,就更需要监管机构的关注。例如,一个判决算法可能对一类被定罪的人产生一项貌似"公正"的判决。然而,除非这些判决结果对每个被告人的公正性都能在法庭上得以阐释,否则将面临法律程序上的质疑。另一个已经引发担忧的情况是,人工智能系统可能掩盖或产生歧视性的做法或结果。

当然,这只是人工智能带来的部分挑战。其他即将面临的挑战包括:大部分劳动力可能被取代,以及通用人工智能可能质疑

我们，机器人？
人工智能监管及其法律局限

"智能机器人"的权利。① 另外，本书并不寻求研究人工智能在社会中发挥巨大作用时的广泛伦理影响，更不会探究网络空间、虚拟世界等领域的监管问题。② 同样，本书也不会试图完全涵盖人工智能对区块链或分布式账本技术的潜在影响。③ 本书的目的较为务实，即通过以上部分挑战中发现的问题来审视现有监管模式的漏洞，同时检验我们已有的监管工具是否能够填补这些漏洞。

本书第二部分主要探讨应对这些挑战的监管工具。

第 4 章探究如何改造现有的法律，通过划分责任归属应对新兴技术带来的挑战。法律制度通常设法遏阻可识别的自然人或法人主体从事特定形式的行为，或将特定行为产生的损失分配给这些主体。责任可能是直接的，也可能是间接的，关键问题是如何理解人工智能系统的作为和不作为。鉴于人工智能系统的复杂性，人们已经提出了新的归责方法，包括产品责任、代理和因果关系的特殊应用。更为重要但研究较少的是，保险在补偿损害和

---

① Christopher Steiner, *Automate This: How Algorithms Came to Rule Our World* (Penguin 2012); Frank Pasquale, *The Black Box Society: The Secret Algorithms That Control Money and Information* (Harvard UP 2015); Cathy O'Neil, *Weapons of Math Destruction: How Big Data Increases Inequality and Threatens Democracy* (Broadway Books 2016).

② See, eg, F Gregory Lastowka, *Virtual Justice: The New Laws of Online Worlds* (Yale UP 2010); Andrew Sparrow, *The Law of Virtual Worlds and Internet Social Networks* (Gower 2010); Jacqueline Lipton, *Rethinking Cyberlaw: A New Vision for Internet Law* (Edward Elgar 2015); Andrew Murray, *Information Technology Law: The Law and Society* (3rd edn, OUP 2016); Paul Lambert, *Gringras: The Laws of the Internet* (5th edn, Bloomsbury 2018); Lilian Edwards (ed), *Law, Policy, and the Internet* (Hart 2019); Roxana Radu, *Negotiating Internet Governance* (OUP 2019); Frank Pasquale, *New Laws of Robotics: Defending Human Expertise in the Age of AI* (Belknap Press 2020).

③ See, eg, William J Magnuson, *Blockchain Democracy: Technology, Law, and the Rule of the Crowd* (CUP 2020); Fabian Schär and Aleksander Berentsen, *Bitcoin, Blockchain, and Cryptoassets* (MIT Press 2020).

构建行动激励方面可以发挥什么样的作用。另一种进路是限制逃避责任的能力，可借鉴关于外包和禁止转移某些刑事责任方面的研究，特别是借鉴公共部门行使自由裁量权方面的研究。

随着人工智能系统以更大的自主性运行，它们自身可能被追究法律责任的观点已经日渐获得认可。从表面上看，赋予人工智能系统某种形式的独立法律人格的想法似乎很有吸引力。然而，第 5 章的分析认为，这种进路可能过于草率，且极难操作。它过于草率，因为它将多种多样的技术不恰当地归入单一法律类别；它极难操作，因为它隐含或明确地包含拟人化的谬论，即人工智能系统最终将以前面提到的"机器人自主意识"的方式拥有完全的法律人格。尽管这样的通用人工智能在未来很可能出现，也极有必要采取预防措施，但这于当下的监管却并不是最契合的。

作为限制人工智能相关风险的手段，另一监管工具的底层逻辑是可预见性。第 6 章探析了透明原则和与之相关的"可解释性"概念的阐述方式，尤其是欧盟的"解释权"，以及开发者对可解释人工智能（Explainable Artificial Intelligence，XAI）的追求。这些都比赋予人工智能系统法律人格的论点更有前景意义。但是，随着人工智能系统展现出连编写其程序的程序员都难以理解的能力，透明原则的局限性已经开始显现。这导致监管机构不得不让步，转而寻求对不利决策的解释，而不是决策过程本身的透明度。这种"回顾式"（backward-looking）监管手段依赖于人们获知自己已经受到伤害，问题是人们有时并不知晓自己已经受到伤害，因此，应当辅之以影响评估、审计和监察员等前瞻性监管手段。

本书的最后部分探讨了解决现有监管工具和监管机构不足所需的新的规则和机构。

正如前面几章所示，现有的规范经过适当的解释后，能够应对人工智能带来的诸多挑战，但不能应对全部挑战。第 7 章首先概述了国家、行业和政府间组织提出的指南、框架和原则。各方的努力已经使人们就可能用于治理人工智能的六条原则达成广泛共识，但在如何实施这些原则或者说是否有必要实施这些规范方面，人们所投入的精力要少得多。这一章的重点并不在于探讨增加规范数量，而是聚焦于为什么监管是必要的，什么时候应该进行监管改革，以及在实践中如何运作。法律改革的两个具体领域涉及人工智能的武器化和受害化。其中，针对通用人工智能的法律将会特别困难，因为它们面临着许多"未知的未知数"，不受控或不受限的人工智能可能远比致命自主武器系统带来更严重的威胁。此外，对于越来越具有生命特征的机器，需要禁止某些伤害机器的行为，这可能与虐待动物法相类似。

每个政治团体对人工智能的法律改革问题找到的答案可能各不相同，但在不久的将来，一个更大的威胁是人工智能系统所引发的危害将并不限于一个司法管辖区，事实上可能无法将其与特定司法管辖区相关联。这并不是网络安全中的新问题，但不同国家的监管方式将对有效监管构成障碍，而人工智能系统的高速性、自主性和不透明性更加剧了这种障碍。出于上述原因，全球需要某种程度的集体行动，或者至少是协作。可以借鉴监管全球公域的经验，以及从国际层面取缔某些产品（如武器和毒品）和活动（如奴隶制和儿童色情观光业）的行动中吸取教训。这里提出的论点是，在公共控制的意义上，监管需要各个国家的积极参与。为了协调这些行动并执行全球"红线"，第 8 章提出了一个假想的国际人工智能机构（IAIA），该机构以第二次世界大战后为促进核能和平使用同时阻止或遏制核能武器化或引发其他有害影响目的所创建的机构为模型。

第 9 章讨论的是，挑战法律秩序的人工智能系统也可能至少提供部分解决方案。在这里，中国作为规范人工智能系统行为规则尚不完善的国家之一，却在法庭使用人工智能技术方面走在了前列。然而，这是一把双刃剑，因为它的使用意味着一种工具主义的法律观，诉讼当事人被视为手段而非目的。这反过来又引发了关于法律和权威本质的基本问题：从根本上说，法律是否可以被还原为可以优化人类状况的代码，或者它是否必须继续成为一个争议和政治场所，并与本身对公众负责的机构密不可分地联系起来。对于所提出的许多问题，理性答案就足够了；但对于其他问题，答案是什么可能并不重要，重要的是如何和为什么形成答案，以及受影响的人群是否可以对其后果进行问责。

预防还是创新？

监管的核心问题是对不必要的遏制创新的预防措施进行平衡。例如，新加坡政府的一份报告强调了人工智能衍生的风险，但得出的结论是："目前没有一个国家对人工智能系统的刑事责任出台具体规则。如果贸然成为此类规则的全球先行者，可能损害我们新加坡对人工智能领域顶级行业参与者的吸引力。"①

这些担忧是有根据的。与其他研究领域一样，过于严格的监管可能直接扼杀创新，或是将创新推向其他地区。然而，如果不

---

① Penal Code Review Committee（Ministry of Home Affairs and Ministry of Law，August 2018）29. 在中国，国务院颁布的人工智能发展规划中包括在 2025 年前建立完善的人工智能法律法规的计划，参见《国务院关于印发新一代人工智能发展规划的通知》（国发（2017）35 号）。

能适时引入法律工具，就有可能让以盈利为目的的市场主体围绕他们自身利益塑造经济结构，最后将使得监管者难以跟上节奏。这在信息技术领域的创新与监管中显得尤其突出。例如，以脸书（Facebook）为代表的社交媒体巨头，在数据保护法仍处于起步阶段时，就将大量用户个人数据商业化。① 同样，优步（Uber）和其他现在被称为"共享经济"或"'零工'经济"的先行者，在保护工人或维持用工标准的规则出台之前就充分利用了平台资源。② 正如佩德罗·多明戈斯（Pedro Domingos）曾经指出的：人们往往担心计算机会进化得太聪明从而接管世界；但其实，真正的问题是，即使现在的计算机还很愚蠢，也已经接管了世界。③

目前，许多关于人工智能和法律的研究似乎都没找准对焦点，或者对焦过远，模糊了与科幻小说的界限；或者对焦过近，跟在人工智能技术之后亦步亦趋。当然，这种现实主义和夸张想象之间的复杂关系，此前也体现在人工智能本身的发展历史上。"人工智能的冬天"一词，就是用来描述对人工智能不切实际的期待和现实之间的不匹配。④ 事实上，早在1956年人工智能这一学科在达特茅斯大学诞生时，这一点就很明显。为了资助这次研讨会，约翰·麦卡锡（John McCarthy）和三位同事写信给洛克

---

① Shoshana Zuboff, *The Age of Surveillance Capitalism: The Fight for a Human Future at the New Frontier of Power* (Public Affairs 2019).

② Jeremias Prassl, *Humans as a Service: The Promise and Perils of Work in the Gig Economy* (Oxford University Press 2018).

③ Pedro Domingos, *The Master Algorithm: How the Quest for the Ultimate Learning Machine Will Remake Our World* (Basic Books 2015) 286.

④ 据此，有些研究人士认为，人工智能的每一项成就都伴随着对真正智能的重新定义校正。道格拉斯·霍夫施塔特（Douglas Hofstadter）简洁地总结了拉里·泰斯勒（Larry Tesler）归纳的一个定理："人工智能就是尚未完成的事物。"参见 Douglas R Hofstadter, *Gödel, Escher, Bach: An Eternal Golden Braid* (Basic Books 1979) 601。

菲勒基金会（Rockefeller Foundation），提出了以下温和的建议。

  我们建议在 1956 年夏天对人工智能进行为期 2 个月的 10 人研究……这项研究将基于如下猜想进行：学习的每个方面或智能的任何其他特征，原则上都可以被精确地描述，以至于可以用机器来模拟它。我们将试图找到如何使机器使用语言，形成抽象和概念，解决留给人类的（那些）种种问题，并不断自我演化迭代。我们认为，如果一个精心挑选的科学家小组能够在一个夏天里精诚合作，共同研究这些问题，就可以在其中一个或多个问题上取得重大进展。①

  在随后的几十年里，人们对人工智能的热情和恐惧起起伏伏。在 1956 年达特茅斯研讨会几年后的《巴黎评论》（Paris Review）采访中，巴勃罗·毕加索（Pablo Picasso）令人难忘地认为新的机械大脑毫无用处，"它们只能给你答案，"他嘲笑道。②鉴于世界各国都在努力利用人工智能的经济潜力，同时尽量避免可能的伤害，本书不可能是关于人工智能监管话题的最后定论。但是，通过研究挑战的性质、现有工具的局限性以及一些可能的解决方案，我们希望确保至少在提出正确的问题。

---

  ① J McCarthy, et al, A Proposal for the Dartmouth Summer Research Project on Artificial Intelligence (31 August 1955).

  ② William Fifield, 'Pablo Picasso: A Composite Interview' (1964) 32 *Paris Review* 37, 62.

第 I 部分

人工智能带来的挑战

第1章

高　速　性

2010年5月6日（星期四），纽约金融市场如往常一样开市。《华尔街日报》有一条报道警告说，希腊可能出现经济混乱；欧盟和国际货币基金组织（IMF）正在拼凑一揽子救助方案。在华尔街，由于担忧欧洲债务问题，道琼斯工业平均指数（一种市值指数，以下简称"道琼斯指数"）前一天下跌了近60点，收盘报10868点。

纽约证券交易所开盘铃响时，预计股市会继续下跌。英国即将到来的选举和即将发布的就业报告加剧了市场不确定性。在华盛顿特区，美国参议院正在讨论一项金融监管法案——这是为了防范类似三年前次贷危机所引发的危机的持续努力。交易开始后，正如人们预期的，道琼斯指数继续下滑。一些交易员将资金转移到黄金上，长期以来黄金被视为经济低迷时期的避风港。这些都不是特别不寻常的事：市场既可能上涨也可能下跌。

然而，有一个品种却在上涨，那就是芝加哥期权交易所的首字母缩写为"VIX"的波动率指数，该指数是度量期权指数与基础股票价格差异的——本质上，它衡量的是交易员押注价格在一段时间内变动的程度。理论上讲，VIX出现较高的数字意味着市场可能发生大幅上升或下降，故 VIX 指数也被称为"恐慌指数"。2010 年 5 月 6 日那个星期四上午，VIX 指数上涨了 20% 以上。交易员们安慰自己，这仍然远低于 2007—2008 年全球金融危机期间的高点。

然而，当天下午 2:32，市场开始崩盘。在短短 15 分钟内，道琼斯指数下跌了近 1000 点，相当于其价值的 1/10，这是其历史上单日跌幅最大的一次。长期以来被视为市场最稳定的蓝筹股之一的宝洁公司（Proctor & Gamble）股价下跌了逾 1/3。咨询公司埃森哲的价值基本上归零，其股价从 40 美元暴跌至 1 美分。没有人能解释为什么短短几分钟，市场价值会蒸发掉超过 1 万亿美元。在纽约证券交易所的交易大厅，交易员们或大声叫喊，或目瞪口呆地看着屏幕上闪烁的卖出指令，电话铃声此起彼伏。国家经济委员会主任劳伦斯·萨默斯（Lawrence Summers）被叫出了会议室。在白宫，财政部部长蒂姆·盖特纳（Tim Geithner）匆忙向总统巴拉克·奥巴马简报上述已被称为"黑色星期四"的情况。

然后，同样迅速的是，市场回升了。

在 90 秒内，市场跌幅收复了一半。到下午 3 点，大多数股票的价格已经基本恢复到之前的水平。关键监管机构的报告用朴实的文字描述："交易以更有序的方式恢复。"[①] 当天收盘时，道琼斯指数比前一天收盘时下跌了 347 点，跌幅为 3.2%，意味着这是一次调整，而非灾难。

---

① Findings Regarding the Events of May 6, 2010 (US Commodity Futures Trading Commission and US Securities & Exchange Commission, 30 September 2010) 9. See also Mary L Schapiro, Examining the Causes and Lessons of the May 6th Market Plunge (US Securities and Exchange Commission, 20 May 2010).

在接下来的几周里，分析师和监管者努力解释那半小时内发生了什么。有人猜测是一个交易员无意中触发了宝洁股票的大规模抛售，这被称为"胖手指理论"。但随后，人们的注意力很快转向了交易算法。经过五个月的调查，政府报告得出结论，一家共同基金试图抛售大量期货合约，引发了"闪电崩盘"。执行该出售的高频交易员（HFT）在不到一秒钟的时间内购买和出售股票和期权，无法找到传统买家，反而将期权卖给其他HFTs。这产生了报告中所称的"烫手山芋"效应，同样的操作和交易在计算机程序之间快速传递。在14秒内，完成超过2.7万份此类合约，占总交易量的近一半。

信息技术速度的提高是本书讨论的人工智能系统的关键组成部分。摩尔定律的著名预言是，处理速度将继续增加，大约每两年翻一番，这种趋势已经持续了半个世纪。[1] 尽管有迹象表明增速正在放缓，但效率越来越高的机器意味着数据存储和计算能力的边际成本正趋近于零。[2] 这些系统日益复杂，尽管通用人工智能目前仍停留在科幻小说领域，但狭义人工智能的现实应用已经大大超越了人类的认知能力。正如2010年纽约证券交易所"闪电崩盘"所表明的，这些系统运行速度之快，人类可能难以控制。

本章主要探讨速度带来的监管挑战。尽管本书的重点是人工智能，但许多数字经济的变革实际上与数据处理的速度和效率有关，而非真正的认知能力或"智能"本身。然而，在面对21世纪不断变化的实践时，速度的确给20世纪社会制定的法律带来

---

[1] Robert F Service, 'Chipmakers Look Past Moore's Law, and Silicon' (2018) 361 (6400) *Science* 321.

[2] Jeremy Rifkin, *The Zero Marginal Cost Society: The Internet of Things, the Collaborative Commons, and the Eclipse of Capitalism* (St. Martin's Press 2014).

了问题。本章将对其中的三个问题进行分析。

第一，也是最为人所熟知的，数据在世界范围内流动的速度消除了距离的障碍。网络和互联网法律现已成为独立的子学科，在规范网络行为方面涉及复杂的数字管辖权和实践问题。[①] 这些结构特征与日益复杂的软件相结合，从保护知识产权到打击"假新闻"都给潜在监管者带来困难。

第二，我们回到 2010 年纽约证券交易所"闪电崩盘"事件及应对高频交易的努力上。理论上，执行交易的算法受到与发起交易的人类经纪人相同的监管。然而，由于这些算法的运行速度可能快速导致市场混乱或被操纵，因此交易所已经开始探讨如何减缓它们的速度。此外，还有一个更大的争论是，基于计算机的交易不仅改变了市场文化，而且改变了市场的本质。

第三，数据处理速度问题涉及竞争法，也被称为"反垄断法"。数字经济为消费者提供了以前传统市场中无法想象的规模和速度的信息获取途径。然而，零售商也能获取这些甚至更多信息，他们可以使用定价软件来最大化利润。过去，反竞争行为需要证明行为主体在价格操纵或滥用市场支配地位方面达成共识。如今，价格调整的速度意味着，市场参与者在没有任何意图的情况下，甚至在没有他们的计算机程序之间进行正式协

[①] See, eg, F Gregory Lastowka, *Virtual Justice: The New Laws of Online Worlds* (Yale UP 2010); Andrew Sparrow, *The Law of Virtual Worlds and Internet Social Networks* (Gower 2010); Jacqueline Lipton, *Rethinking Cyberlaw: A New Vision for Internet Law* (Edward Elgar 2015); Andrew Murray, *Information Technology Law: The Law and Society* (3rd edn, OUP 2016); Paul Lambert, *Gringras: The Laws of the Internet* (5th edn, Bloomsbury 2018); Lilian Edwards (ed), *Law, Policy, and the Internet* (Hart 2019); Roxana Radu, *Negotiating Internet Governance* (OUP 2019); Frank Pasquale, *New Laws of Robotics: Defending Human Expertise in the Age of AI* (Belknap Press 2020).

调的情况下，可能发生默契共谋。从个别方面来看，这些挑战指出了在全球化世界中对信息技术进行监管的实际障碍。而当这些问题结合在一起，特别是与具有自主性、不透明的人工智能系统相结合时，显示出这些系统可能以无法控制、无法阻止或无法检测的方式运行的危险。

单独来看，这些挑战表明在全球化世界中，信息技术监管面临实际障碍。当它们与具有自主性、不透明的人工智能系统相结合时，这些系统可能存在以无法控制、无法停止或无法检测的方式运行的危险。

1.1　信息的全球化

互联网本身结构中包含速度带来的最基本困难之一就是信息的全球化。几乎可以从地球上的任何地方即时访问数据并将其在全球范围内传播的能力，给基于领土边界的法律制度带来了明显的局限性。这些局限性并非概念上的，而是实际上的，需要跨法域的协调。关于协调以监管人工智能的更大问题将在本书第 8 章中讨论。在这里，讨论将仅限于简要介绍几个足以解释这个问题的例子。

例如，知识产权保护一直受到制作复制品能力的威胁。模拟技术（如录音机、复印机）被数字技术取代，从根本上改变了复制的经济性：劳动密集型的制作复制品的任务实际上不花费成本且无距离限制地分享音乐和其他内容。[1] 诉讼和立

---

[1]　实际上，各种社交媒体平台正是通过"助推"用户积极分享不是他们自己创建的内容，来鼓励这种复制行为。参见 David Tan,'Fair Use and Transformative Play in the Digital Age' in Megan Richardson and Sam Ricketson (eds), *Research Handbook on Intellectual Property in Media and Entertainment* (Edward Elgar 2017) 102。

法变更①导致大多数媒体平台采纳了版权政策和下架程序,②而其他一些媒体平台则完全关闭。③生产商和分销商研发了技术手段来限制复制,但一定程度的盗版通常被视为正常商业成本。④

与未经授权使用知识产权一样,互联网也为非法传播违禁材料提供了便利。信息在全球范围内传播的速度经常使遏制信息的努力受挫,同时也挑战了旨在阻止或惩罚侵权或犯罪行为的法律规定。⑤事实上,试图在一个法域内禁止某种材料可能只会提高其知名度,而不能限制其在其他法域内的可获得性。同样,这并不是什么新鲜事:20世纪80年代,彼得·赖特(Peter Wright)的有关其军情五处职业生涯的丑闻回忆录在英国被禁,在禁令最终解除之前,这一法律行动几乎肯定会提高该书全球销售额。⑥

---

① Notably the Digital Millennium Copyright Act (DMCA) 1998, Pub L No 105-304 (US).

② 例如,2020年,Facebook每月删除超过40万条因侵犯版权而被举报的内容。更多信息请参见 Daniel Seng, 'The State of the Discordant Union: An Empirical Analysis of DMCA Takedown Notices' (2014) 18 *Virginia Journal of Law & Technology* 369。

③ *AMG Records Inc v Napster Inc*, 239 F3d 1004 (9th Cir, 2001). See also Joseph Menn, *All the Rave: The Rise and Fall of Shawn Fanning's Napster* (Crown 2003).

④ Luis Aguiar, Jörg Claussen, and Christian Peukert, 'Catch Me If You Can: Effectiveness and Consequences of Online Copyright Enforcement' (2018) 29 *Information Systems Research* 656; P Jean-Jacques Herings, Ronald Peeters, and Michael S Yang, 'Piracy on the Internet: Accommodate It or Fight It? A Dynamic Approach' (2018) 266 *European Journal of Operational Research* 328.

⑤ Lord Anthony Grabiner, 'Sex, Scandal and Super-Injunctions—The Controversies Surrounding the Protection of Privacy' (2012) 45 *Israel Law Review* 537.

⑥ Laurence Zuckerman, 'How Not to Silence a Spy: Banned in Britain, an Agent's Memoirs Become Big-Selling News', *Time* (17 August 1987). See Peter Wright, *Spycatcher: The Candid Autobiography of a Senior Intelligence Officer* (Viking 1987).

近年来,像维基解密(WikiLeaks)这样的组织纷纷将分类分销纳入其运营模式。①

信息流速度所带来的困难的另一个例子是现代"假新闻"现象。② 恶意谣言在网络上传播的能力早已被认为是一个问题,因为它与欺凌和扭曲股票价格有关,而2016年美国大选引发了人们对其可能被用于更大的政治目的的担忧。③ 与分享受保护或禁止的材料一样,假新闻的传播速度并非人工智能引起的问题。然而,与新技术相关的新发展包括自动生成的内容和所谓的"深度伪造"——虚假内容,如经过篡改的图片和视频,很难与真实材料区分开来。④

政府应对假新闻现象的努力主要集中在试图纠正或遏制它。德国⑤、法国⑥、马来西亚⑦和新加坡⑧的立法允许公共机构有权要求社交媒体网站在规定的时间内对特定材料进行纠正或删除。一些国家则采取其他方法,强调用户对内容的责任,要求用户实

---

① Stephen ME Marmura, *The WikiLeaks Paradigm*: *Paradoxes and Revelations* (Palgrave 2018).

② Brian McNair, *Fake News*: *Falsehood*, *Fabrication and Fantasy in Journalism* (Routledge 2018). 当然,假信息的传播像人类社会本身一样古老。

③ Report on the Investigation into Russian Interference in the 2016 Presidential Election (Mueller Report) (Department of Justice, March 2019) vol 1, 14-29.

④ Zack Whittaker, 'US Lawmakers Warn Spy Chief that "Deep Fakes" Are a National Security Threat', *TechCrunch* (13 September 2018).

⑤ Netzdurchsetzunggesetz(NetzDG)[Network Enforcement Act] 2017 (Germany).

⑥ Loi organique no 2018-1201 du 22 décembre 2018 relative à la lutte contre la manipulation de l'information 2018 (France); Loi no 2018-1202 du 22 décembre 2018 relative à la lutte contre la manipulation de l'information 2018 (France). 法国法律仅在选举期间有效。

⑦ Anti-Fake News Act 2018 (Malaysia).

⑧ Protection from Online Falsehoods and Manipulation Act 2019 (Singapore).

名注册，限制用户广泛分享信息的能力以及对用户发布的内容进行直接审查。中国在新浪微博和微信上就采用了以上三种方法。①

社交媒体平台长期以来都否认对其托管的内容负有责任。2016 年美国总统大选期间，个人数据被出售给剑桥分析公司的事件曝光后，脸书（Facebook）、推特（Twitter）等平台采取一系列措施，努力加强对假新闻传播的控制。具体包括删除违反社区规定的账户，优先显示好友和家人的帖子而不是发布者和企业的帖子，以及雇佣事实核查员为新闻提供背景信息。2018 年，推特删除了数千万个涉嫌造假的账户。在印度，因 WhatsApp 传播的虚假信息而引发的暴力事件导致该通信应用在 2019 年对消息转发的数量进行限制。2020 年，关于新冠病毒感染疫情和美国总统选举方面的虚假信息传播危害更大。

尽管最乐观的监管者都不相信假新闻会在短期内消失，但深度伪造和看似真实的机器人账户等创新技术显示，人工智能系统在加剧这个问题的同时，或许也能为解决这个问题提供方法。②然而，根本问题似乎在于人类。正如美国麻省理工学院对十年间

---

① Ronggui Huang and Xiaoyi Sun, 'Weibo Network, Information Diffusion and Implications for Collective Action in China' (2014) 17 *Information, Communication & Society* 86; Huiquan Zhou and Quanxiao Pan, 'Information, Community, and Action on Sina-Weibo: How Chinese Philanthropic NGOs Use Social Media Authors' (2016) 27 VOLUNTAS: *International Journal of Voluntary and Nonprofit Organizations* 2433; James Griffiths, *The Great Firewall of China: How to Build and Control an Alternative Version of the Internet* (Zed Books 2019).

② Georgios Gravanis, et al, 'Behind the Cues: A Benchmarking Study for Fake News Detection' (2019) 128 Expert Systems with Applications 201; Hoon Ko, et al, 'Human-Machine Interaction: A Case Study on Fake News Detection Using a Backtracking Based on a Cognitive System' (2019) 55 *Cognitive Systems Research* 77. 另请参见本书第 9 章第 9.3 节。

推特发布内容的研究所示,假新闻比真实新闻更具新颖性,激发的情感也更为强烈。谎言比真相传播得更快,而传播这些谎言的正是人类,而不是机器人。①

全球信息的全球化使得比任何时候都更多的人掌握了比人类历史上任何时候都更多的知识。在许多专制政权中,由于信息难以遏制,互联网发挥了解放的作用。然而,这些促成这一现象的结构,同时也是遏制专有、诽谤或其他有害材料的障碍。随着人工智能系统在生成内容方面发挥更大的作用,通过数据本地化、过滤或以其他方式减缓信息流动的遏制努力将有可能破坏数字经济的基础,并且最多只是针对快速发展的问题进行短期补救。

1.2 高频交易

在高频交易领域,速度带来了不同的实际问题,其中的算法买卖股票或衍生品,目的是在大量交易中获得微小利润。一个对速度重视的体现是,美国一家总部位于芝加哥的公司斥资 3 亿美元铺设了一条通往新泽西州的专用光纤电缆,目的是将数据从办公室传输到证券交易所的时间缩短 3 毫秒。② 据估计,高频交易如今在美国和欧洲市场的交易量中占据了约一半。③ 尽管在美国

---

① Soroush Vosoughi, Deb Roy, and Sinan Aral, 'The Spread of True and False News Online' (2018) 359 (6380) *Science* 1146.

② Michael Lewis, *Flash Boys: A Wall Street Revolt* (WW Norton 2014) 7-22; Megan Woodward, 'The Need for Speed: Regulatory Approaches to High Frequency Trading in the United States and the European Union' (2011) 50 *Vanderbilt Journal of Transnational Law* 1359.

③ See generally Irene Aldridge and Steven Krawciw, *Real-Time Risk: What Investors Should Know About FinTech, High-Frequency Trading, and Flash Crashes* (Wiley 2017).

以此获取利润似乎已达到顶峰,但亚洲市场被认为在高频交易方面具有很大的增长潜力。①

高频交易(HFT)的支持者认为,它们通过增加在任何给定时刻的买方和卖方数量,为市场提供流动性,同时有助于价格发现。② 然而,由于这些程序运行速度如此之快,它们也可能增加价格波动性并破坏市场稳定。例如,在2010年闪电崩盘事件中,美国监管机构当时得出结论,高频交易可能并非导致崩盘的原因,但它们至少加剧了崩盘的后果。③ 作为回应,交易限制或"熔断机制"(circuit breakers)得到了扩展。这些机制是在1987年的黑色星期一崩盘事件之后引入的,旨在防止股票市场因人们的恐慌而出现抛售潮。如果市场下跌幅度达到一定百分比,④ 交易可能暂停一段时间或暂停当天剩余时间。监管机构希望这样的暂停能给投资者"更多时间获取信息并作出理性决策"。⑤

---

① Hao Zhou and Petko S Kalev,'Algorithmic and High Frequency Trading in Asia-Pacific, Now and the Future'(2019) 53 *Pacific-Basin Finance Journal* 186; Guo Li,'Regulating Investment Robo? Advisors in China: Problems and Prospects'(2020) 21 *European Business Organization Law Review* 69.

② Jonathan Brogaarda, et al,'High Frequency Trading and Extreme Price Movements'(2018) 128 *Journal of Financial Economics* 253, 254. Cf James Upson and Robert A Van Ness,'Multiple Markets, Algorithmic Trading, and Market Liquidity'(2017) 32 *Journal of Financial Markets* 49; Donald MacKenzie,'"Making", "Taking", and the Material Political Economy of Algorithmic Trading'(2018) 47 *Economy and Society* 501; Brian M Weller,'Does Algorithmic Trading Reduce Information Acquisition?'(2018) 31 *Review of Financial Studies* 2184.

③ Findings Regarding the Events of May 6, 2010 (n 1) 45-48. Cf Andrei Kirilenko, et al,'The Flash Crash: High-Frequency Trading in an Electronic Market'(2017) 72 *Journal of Finance* 967.

④ 直到1997年,阈值都是根据下降的数值来设定的。

⑤ Yong H Kim and J Jimmy Yang,'What Makes Circuit Breakers Attractive to Financial Markets? A Survey'(2004) 13 *Financial Markets, Institutions & Instruments* 109, 121.

根据纽约证券交易所 2010 年开始实施的规则，如果道琼斯指数在下午 2 点 30 分之前相对季度基准指数下跌 10%，交易将暂停半小时；如果在下午 2 点之后下跌 20% 或以上，市场将完全关闭。在 2010 年闪电崩盘事件之后，这些规则被修订为涵盖五分钟内上涨或下跌超过 10% 的特定股票。① 2011 年，全市场阈值得到了收紧，如果标准普尔 500 指数（包括 500 家大型上市美国公司）相对于每日基准下跌 7%，而非每三个月设置一次的基准，交易将被暂停。②

其他国家也纷纷效仿。③ 在欧盟，金融工具市场指令二（MiFID Ⅱ）现在对高频交易（以及更普遍的算法交易）设定了限制，增加了隐喻性的"减速带"，以防止无序交易并减少市场波动。④ 经授权的交易者还必须披露，如何运作他们的算法以及由谁来控制等信息。交易数据必须保留，并提供建模的途径，同时标记异常订单和设定价格及成交量阈值，一旦超过该阈值就会

---

① Securities Exchange Act Release No 62252 (Securities and Exchange Commission, 10 June 2010). See also E Wes Bethel, et al, 'Federal Market Information Technology in the Post Flash Crash Era: Roles for Supercomputing' (2012) 7 (2) *The Journal of Trading* 9.

② Recommendations Regarding Regulatory Responses to the Market Events of May 6, 2010 (Joint CFTC-SEC Advisory Committee, 18 February 2011); Notice of Proposed Rule Change Related to Trading Halts Due to Extraordinary Market Volatility (Securities and Exchange Commission, Release No 34-65425; File No SR-ISE-2011-61, 28 September 2011).

③ 新加坡与中国香港，分别在 2014 年、2016 年引入类似的熔断机制。参见 David R Meyer and George Guernsey, 'Hong Kong and Singapore Exchanges Confront High Frequency Trading' (2017) 23 *Asia Pacific Business Review* 63。

④ Directive 2014/65/EU of the European Parliament and of the Council of 15 May 2014 on Markets in Financial Instruments and Amending Directive 2002/92/EC and Directive 2011/61/EU 2014 (EU).

触发熔断机制。①

欧盟法律强调，与市场恐慌有关的高频交易与人类情绪引发的市场抛售显然并非一回事。最初的熔断机制为作出"理性"决策提供了时间。这并不是高频交易的缺陷。②或许正因如此，纽约证券交易所现在强调，尽管它采用了"尖端、超快速的技术，但我们相信没有什么能代替人类的判断和责任"。

任何试图限制高频交易行为的尝试都面临着它们是否以及如何应得到特殊待遇的问题。③从原则上讲，高频交易具有与其他投资者相同的信息获取能力，并以相同的基础进行交易。迄今为止，大多数监管努力都集中在限制与其在短时间内进行大量交易的能力相关的市场破坏和操纵上。实际上，速度也带来了信息不对称：抢先处理和交易信息的能力具有明显的优势。因此，一些高频交易者直接订阅新闻和市场数据源，以便在名义上的"公共"数据发布后几乎立即进行交易并获得先发优势。④尽管这并非非法行为，但前纽约州总检察长埃里克·施耐德曼（Eric Schneiderman）仍

---

① Tilen Čuk and Arnaud van Waeyenberge, 'European Legal Framework for Algorithmic and High Frequency Trading (Mifid 2 and MAR) A Global Approach to Managing the Risks of the Modern Trading Paradigm' (2018) 9 *European Journal of Risk Regulation* 146.

② 的确，有证据表明，算法交易的存在可以使人类交易员的行为更加理性。参见 Mike Farjama and Oliver Kirchkampb, 'Bubbles in Hybrid Markets: How Expectations About Algorithmic Trading Affect Human Trading' (2018) 146 *Journal of Economic Behavior & Organization* 248。

③ Steven R McNamara, 'The Law and Ethics of High-Frequency Trading' (2016) 17 *Minnesota Journal of Law*, Science & Technology 71.

④ 尤其是当系统能够预测其他大额订单并抢先一步时，这一点尤为正确。参见 Florian Gamper, Is High Frequency Trading Fair? The Case of Order Anticipation (NUS Centre for Banking & Finance Law, CBFL-WP-FG03, 2016)。

将其称为"内幕交易 2.0"。①

一种方法是,通过设置减速带和其他减缓高频交易速度的手段以降低这种优势。② 另一种方法是,限制交易者提前获取市场数据。③ 更激进的想法包括改变交易所对时间本身的思考方式。其中一项建议是,用频繁的批量拍卖取代当前将时间视为连续单位的订单系统。交易将不再按接单顺序进行,而是以离散的时间间隔执行,如每 1/10 秒执行一次。这将减少在下单时缩短毫秒时间的动力以及由此产生的市场扭曲。④

还有一个区别点在于,是否能够以及应该强制高频交易用户在自己的投资策略上比人类交易员更透明地公开他们的算法,比如欧盟现在就要求这样做。特殊对待的理由通常也与市场可能发生的破坏和操纵有关。然而,有一种观点认为,算法和高频交易不仅改变了交易的方式,还改变了市场的运作方式。从理论上讲,在交易所大厅执行交易的经纪人与那些使用鼠标点击和算法的经纪人一样,要遵守相同的基本合同和证券监管规则。然而,

---

① James J Angel and Douglas M McCabe, 'Insider Trading 2.0? The Ethics of Information Sales' (2018) 147 *Journal of Business Ethics* 747. See also Walter Mattli, *Darkness by Design: The Hidden Power in Global Capital Markets* (Princeton UP 2019).

② Edwin Hu, Intentional Access Delays, Market Quality, and Price Discovery: Evidence from IEX Becoming an Exchange (US Securities and Exchange Commission, Division of Economic and Risk Analysis Working Paper, 7 February 2018).

③ Gaia Balp and Giovanni Strampelli, 'Preserving Capital Markets Efficiency in the High-Frequency Trading Era' (2018) *University of Illinois Journal of Law, Technology & Policy* 349, 388-92.

④ Eric Budish, Peter Cramton, and John Shim, 'The High-Frequency Trading Arms Race: Frequent Batch Auctions as a Market Design Response' (2015) 130 *Quarterly Journal of Economics* 1547.

在实践中，转向基于计算机的交易已经改变了市场文化以及监管空间。① 除了金融市场的正常波动之外，这还增加了类似于2010年闪电崩盘危机的风险。例如，2012年，券商骑士资本集团（Knight Capital）使用的一个程序出错，导致近50亿美元的损失，实际上意味着该公司的倒闭。②

一个更有说服力的解释是，额外的披露不仅是为了促进稳定和阻止操纵，而且首先是为了实现监管。这一点在德国最为明显，德国超越了欧盟的规定，要求交易员标记由算法生成的订单，以便它们可以与人类订单区分开来，并确定相关的算法。③ 正如我们所看到的，对透明度的渴望在人工智能的其他领域也得到了体现，尽管"可解释性"的界限可能已经逼近。④

1.3 竞争法

与人工智能相关的信息加速流动的一个特殊案例是它对竞争

---

① Marc Lenglet and Joeri Mol, 'Squaring the Speed of Light? Regulating Market Access in Algorithmic Finance' (2016) 45 *Economy and Society* 201; Ann-Christina Lange, Marc Lenglet, and Robert Seyfert, 'Cultures of High-Frequency Trading: Mapping the Landscape of Algorithmic Developments in Contemporary Financial Markets' (2016) 45 *Economy and Society* 149.

② Sandeep Yadav, 'Operational Risk—A Case of Knight Capital', *Newstex Global Business* (13 July 2015).

③ 德国2013年《高频交易法》（Hochfrequenzhandelsgesetz［High Frequency Trading Act］）对《证券交易法》（Börsengesetz［Stock Exchange Act］）和《股票交易法》（Wertpapierhandelsgesetz［Securities Trading Act］）等进行了修订，要求对算法交易进行额外报告。这和要求对"卖空订单"进行单独标注——无论是由人类还是算法执行——有相似之处。参见 Nathan Coombs, 'What Is an Algorithm? Financial Regulation in the Era of High-Frequency Trading' (2016) 45 *Economy and Society* 278, 279.

④ 参见本书第6章。

法所带来的挑战。数据分析的崛起使企业变得更加高效，并为企业增长创造了新的机会。然而，反竞争行为也存在明显的潜在可能。

只要资本主义存在，市场的特点就是买方和卖方关注价格，并根据供求关系调整价格。这些价格曾经印在商店的商品上，改变它们可能是一个需要几周的时间才能实施的决定。实际上，一些通过投币式机器出售的商品价格几十年保持不变。例如，在美国，从1886年到1959年，一瓶可口可乐的售价一直是五美分。[①]

如今，价格的变化以毫秒为单位。动态定价已成为零售、旅游、体育和娱乐行业的常态。有时，这种做法所依赖的算法会产生奇怪的结果，比如彼得·劳伦斯（Peter Lawrence）的书《果蝇的形成》（*The Making of a Fly*）在亚马逊的售价曾一度达2400万美元（另加3.99美元的运费）。[②] 然而，总体来说，数字市场可以提高价格透明度，降低消费者的搜索成本，这对竞争是有益的。消费者可以比较不同零售商的价格，从而选择更便宜的选项或要求更优质的服务。[③] 但是，实际情况却更为复杂。[④]

不同法域的反垄断或竞争法禁止反竞争协议和协同行为。一

---

① Daniel Levy and Andrew T Young, '"The Real Thing": Nominal Price Rigidity of the Nickel Coke, 1886-1959' (2004) 36 *Journal of Money, Credit, and Banking* 765.

② Ariel Ezrachi and Maurice E Stucke, 'Artificial Intelligence & Collusion: When Computers Inhibit Competition' (2017) *University of Illinois Law Review* 1775, 1781.

③ Nicolas Petit, 'Antitrust and Artificial Intelligence: A Research Agenda' (2017) 8 *Journal of European Competition Law & Practice* 361.

④ See Ariel Ezrachi and Maurice E Stucke, *Virtual Competition: The Promise and Perils of the Algorithm-Driven Economy* (Harvard UP 2016) 27-33; Julie E Cohen, *Between Truth and Power: The Legal Constructions of Informational Capitalism* (OUP 2019).

个世纪前，这可能意味着召集竞争对手公司的高管聚集在烟雾缭绕的房间，如一个世纪前埃尔伯特·加里（Elbert Gary）邀请美国钢铁制造商到华尔道夫酒店的一系列晚宴，请他们"坦率地、自由地……告诉对方他们的价格、给员工支付的工资以及……所有与他们的业务有关的信息"①。如今，可获得的数据已经大大增加。如果数据是历史性的，或者是与消费者和政府机构共享的，则这种数据没有问题。②然而，随着数据变得可用并可以实时进行分析，公司是否有意识地决定披露定价信息可能变得无关紧要。

确定名义上的竞争对手是否存在共谋也存在类似的问题。当竞争对手之间存在共同政策，对政策的遵守受到监督，并且对偏离政策的行为进行惩罚时，它们之间就建立了共谋均衡。然而，由于企业越来越多地使用价格监测算法来跟踪竞争对手的行动，这些算法本身可能趋向于形成这样的"政策"。例如，如果一种商品的价格立即被竞争对手匹配，就没有动力降低价格——实际上，算法可能得出平行提高价格的反应是理性的结论。然而，在没有直接或间接沟通证据的情况下，很难证明共谋的存在。如果算法本身是专有的或者异常复杂，那么这可能是不可能的。③

这些并非纯粹的理论问题。2015年，美国司法部指控了通过亚马逊市场销售海报策划价格操纵计划的实施者。该计划涉及一

---

① William H Page, 'The Gary Dinners and the Meaning of Concerted Action' (2009) 62 *Southern Methodist University Law Review* 597.

② See, eg, WONG Chun Han, *et al*, Data: Engine for Growth-Implications for Competition Law, Personal Data Protection and Intellectual Property Rights (Competition and Consumer Commission of Singapore, 16 August 2017).

③ Kay Firth-Butterfield, 'Artificial Intelligence and the Law: More Questions than Answers?' (2017) 14 (1) *Scitech Lawyer* 28.

种算法，该算法在线收集竞争对手的定价信息并采用卖家的定价规则。美国司法部在新闻稿中指出：

> 我们不会容忍反竞争行为，无论该种行为是发生在烟雾缭绕的房间里还是通过复杂的定价算法在互联网上进行。美国消费者有权在网络和实体商店中都享受自由公平的市场环境。①

事实上，这是网络反竞争行为中较为简单的形式之一。在其背后是精心设置算法的人类共谋者，他们的目的正是削弱那些虚拟卡特尔垄断之外的竞争对手。更复杂的情况还有，竞争对手采用类似的算法，在没有正式协调的情况下设定类似的价格。在没有人类意图的情况下，这是否构成反竞争行为？更为困难的问题是：处理整个市场数据的算法是否会以难以检测或不可能检测的方式操纵价格？②

监管机构敏锐地意识到了其中的困难。2016年，经济合作与发展组织（OECD）的一份背景文件警告称，找到防止自学算法之间共谋的方法可能是竞争法执法者迄今为止面临的最大挑战之一。③一位美国联邦贸易委员会成员指出："我们谈论的是一种非人类的决策速度。而所有的经济模型都是基于人类的动机以及我

---

① Former E-Commerce Executive Charged with Price Fixing in the Antitrust Division's First Online Marketplace Prosecution (Department of Justice, 6 April 2015).

② Maurice E Stucke and Ariel Ezrachi, 'Antitrust, Algorithmic Pricing, and Tacit Collusion' in Woodrow Barfield and Ugo Pagallo (eds), *Research Handbook on the Law of Artificial Intelligence* (Edward Elgar 2018) 624 at 626-31.

③ Big Data: Bringing Competition Policy to the Digital Era (OECD, DAF/COMP (2016) 14, 27 October 2016) 24.

们认为人类会理性作出的决策。在一些市场中,这种学习并不一定都适用。"①

算法的默契共谋引发了一个担忧,竞争法希望避免的损害之一即为高价,但没有相应的补救措施。与高频交易的情况类似,一个建议是通过在价格调整中引入时滞来施加人为的延迟。② 另一种选择可能是仔细审查价格,以确定给定的利润率是否过高,这是一项烦琐且可能毫无意义的工作。正如欧洲委员会所承认的,随着算法的运作更加独立,它们的决策将与为实现"更可预测、更易管理和更加可控的技术"而设计的监管框架发生冲突。③

1.4 高速度衍生的问题

"快速行动,打破陈规"是脸书早期的座右铭,旨在鼓励开发者大胆冒险尝试。2012 年脸书上市时,该口号出现在办公室

---

① David J Lynch, 'Policing the Digital Cartels', *Financial Times* (9 January 2017).

② Paolo Siciliani, 'Tackling Algorithmic-Facilitated Tacit Collusion in a Proportionate Way' (2019) 10 *Journal of European Competition Law & Practice* 31, 34.

③ Commission Staff Working Document on the Free Flow of Data and Emerging Issues of the European Data Economy [European Commission, SWD (2017) 2, 10 January 2017] 43. 一个相对乐观的观点是与难以有效监管人类之间的默示合谋进行比较。在没有通谋的情况下,对于看似合理的行为(如在对自己的产品进行定价时考虑竞争对手的定价)很难归责。对于算法监管,至少理论上可以直接禁止那些含有竞争对手关联依赖性代码设置的算法。参见 Kenneth Khoo and Jerrold Soh, 'The Inefficiency of Quasi-Per Se Rules: Regulating Information Exchange in EU and US Antitrust Law' (2020) 57 *American Business Law Journal* 45. 关于默示合谋和其他反垄断行为,参见 Lawrence A Sullivan, Warren S Grimes, and Christopher L Sagers, *The Law of Antitrust, An Integrated Handbook* (3rd edn, West 2014) 255-56.

的海报上，并出现在马克·扎克伯格写给投资者的信中。① 随着时间的推移，这句话逐渐被广泛接受，成为适用于技术颠覆的口头禅，被无数硅谷效仿者奉为圭臬。然而，随着脸书的成熟以及由此产生的潜在危害的增长，这个口号逐渐失宠。②

这里讨论的速度主要涉及处理能力和连接性，而非创新，但对于被称为"第四次工业革命"的数字经济，也将面临类似的考验。③ 人们早已清楚，这样的速度可能给监管带来挑战。本章分析了三个与人工智能系统公共监管相关的典型领域，这些领域皆已发生此类挑战。信息全球化展示了在速度战胜距离的互联世界中，遏制问题行为的难度。高频交易存在着一种危险，即当事态失控时，其决策的速度可能挫败人类阻止决策的努力。在竞争法中，算法之间的默契共谋带来了这样一种现实可能性：由人类实施就会违法的行为，如果由机器实施，就可能无法被发现。

这些问题——人工智能系统的处理速度，可能使某些类型的危害变得无法遏制、无法阻止或无法检测。这同样适用于本书中讨论的许多其他领域。解决这些问题的一种方法是放慢一切：对数据进行本地化和分隔化，为交易算法引入人为延迟，阻碍数字

---

① Form S-1 Registration Statement of Facebook, Inc. (United States Securities and Exchange Commission, 1 February 2012).

② Jonathan Taplin, *Move Fast and Break Things: How Facebook, Google, and Amazon Cornered Culture and Undermined Democracy* (Little, Brown 2017); Hemant Taneja, 'The Era of "Move Fast and Break Things" Is Over', *Harvard Business Review* (22 January 2019).

③ See, eg, Klaus Schwab, *The Fourth Industrial Revolution* (Crown 2017).

市场的运转。① 这种方法可能是继续依赖为人类设计并在人类时间尺度上运作的监管工具的唯一途径,但却可能破坏那些系统本身的价值。

问题是,这种方法是不可持续的。无论是否接受人工智能系统处理能力将永远增长的预测,放缓或停止它的可能性在短期内都是遥不可及的。因此,新的规则和新的监管机构将是必需的,人工智能系统本身在调查和维护法律方面也需要承担一定的角色。这些将在第三部分中进行探讨。

暂时而言,这些任务仍然由人类来执行。在 2010 年 5 月的闪电崩盘之后,前文提到的监管报告受到批评,因为它将市场崩溃归咎于一个无意引发崩盘的大型共同基金。② 除了随后采取的各种安全措施——熔断机制、减速带等,对崩盘原因的调查仍在继续。随着调查的深入,人们的关注焦点从恶意算法转向了一个恶意交易员身上。

在差不多五年后,一名总部位于伦敦的交易商因参与导致股灾而被捕。美国司法部提起的刑事指控指责纳温德·辛格·萨拉奥(Navinder Singh Sarao)利用自动交易程序操纵市场进行"欺诈":提供价值 2 亿美元的虚假赌注,推动价格下跌,修改了 1.9 万次,然后在交易完成前取消。随着市场的下跌,该交易商出售了期货合约,然后以较低价格买回;当市场开始恢复时,他买入

---

① 例如,国际红十字会呼吁在冲突区部署的人工智能系统以"人类速度"而非"机器速度"运行。参见 Artificial Intelligence and Machine Learning in Armed Conflict: A Human-Centred Approach (International Committee of the Red Cross, 6 June 2019) 7.

② Findings Regarding the Events of May 6, 2010 (n 1) 14. 这家基金后果据说是瓦德尔-里德金融公司(Waddell & Reed)。

期货合约并以更高的价格出售。① 他被引渡到美国，并承认自己从市场操纵中非法获利约4000万美元的罪行。

起诉书引用了他发出的电子邮件，其中他要求为一个现成的交易程序提供技术支持，以便他可以"通过一次点击"在不同价格上输入"多个订单"，并添加"关闭即取消功能"，以便在订单完成前取消订单。② 被英国媒体称为"豪恩斯洛的猎犬"的萨拉奥后来自己也被骗走了几乎全部的非法所得，这在某种程度上可以说是因果报应。作为认罪协议的一部分，他继续协助美国监管机构起诉其他市场滥用行为的人。③

2010年闪电崩盘背后的软件并非失控的算法，相反软件忠实地执行了萨拉奥所要求的任务。因此，虽然这种崩盘暗示了交易算法可能造成的危害，但这次崩盘本身几乎不能归咎于算法。然而，在下一个要讨论的领域，计算速度不仅加快执行人类的决策，而且完全取代了这些决策。

---

① Futures Trader Charged with Illegally Manipulating Stock Market, Contributing to the May 2010 Market 'Flash Crash' (Department of Justice, 21 April 2015).

② *United States of America v. Navinder Singh Sarao*: Criminal Complaint (United States District Court, Northern District of Illinois, Eastern Division, 15 CR 75, 11 February 2015, paras 15-16.

③ 萨拉奥后来被判在他父母位于豪恩斯洛的家中监视居住一年——他又回到了他最初犯罪的那个卧室。

第 2 章
自 主 性

2018年3月的一个漆黑的星期天夜晚，伊莱恩·赫茨伯格（Elaine Herzberg）走下亚利桑那州坦佩市（Tempe，Arizona）米尔（Mill）大道上的一条装饰性绿化带，准备穿越这条四车道马路。当时刚过晚上10点，这名49岁的无家可归的妇女推着一辆装满购物袋的自行车。正当她即将抵达马路对面时，一辆以每小时70公里的速度行驶的优步测试车从右侧撞上了她。赫茨伯格被送往医院，但因伤势过重不治身亡，成为历史上第一位因自动驾驶汽车导致的行人死亡者。

撞上赫茨伯格的沃尔沃XC90配备有前置和侧置摄像头、雷达和激光雷达（光探测和测距）以及导航传感器和集成计算与数据存储单元。美国国家交通安全委员会的一份报告得出结论，该车辆检测到了赫茨伯格女士，但软件将其先后识别为未知物体、汽车，然后又将其识别为具有不确定未来行驶路径的自行车。在碰撞前的一秒多钟，人工智能系统判断需要紧急刹车，但为了减少"汽车异常行为"的可能性，紧急刹车功能此前已被停用。[①]

---

① Preliminary Report Highway HWY18MH010（National Transport Safety Board，24 May 2018）.

至今，那天晚上米尔大道上究竟发生了什么还不完全清楚。优步将其测试车辆从美国四个城市撤离，但八个月后，它们又重新上路，不过现在限速为每小时40公里，且不得在夜间或雨天行驶。

现代人工智能系统的一个关键特点是能够在无人干预的情况下运行。人们通常说这样的系统是"自主运行"的。在此，有必要首先区分自动化和自主驾驶。许多汽车具有自动化功能，如巡航控制系统，可用于调节车速。这些功能由驾驶员监督，驾驶员始终保持对车辆的主动控制并可在必要时进行干预。在这种情况下，"自主"意味着车辆本身能够在无须驾驶员输入的情况下作出决策，实际上也可能根本没有"驾驶员"。

导致赫茨伯格死亡的车辆是在自主运行状态下行驶的，但车内并非空无一人。坐在驾驶座上的是优步雇佣的安全驾驶员拉斐尔·瓦斯克斯（Rafaela Vasquez）。尽管系统并非只在需要时警醒安全驾驶员采取行动，但她仍有责任在必要时进行干预。警方后来认定，瓦斯克斯女士在事故发生前的20分钟里，很可能一直在观看流媒体视频，似乎是电视歌唱比赛节目《好声音》的一集。系统数据显示，就在撞击前刻，她确实伸手去抓方向盘，并在撞到行人后约一秒钟后踩下刹车。在车辆停下后，瓦斯克斯女士拨打了911求助电话。

那么，在此类事件中，谁应该承担责任：优步？"驾驶员"？制造车辆控制人工智能系统的公司？车辆本身？还是无人能负责？① 大多数观察者认为，必须有人要为行人的死亡负责，但很难判定其他各方的责任分配。这表明，有必要更明确地界定责任

---

① 也有一种观点认为，已故的赫茨伯格女士自身也可能有部分责任。

的判断标准。随着具有不同自主程度的系统变得越来越复杂和普遍,这一需求将变得更为迫切。

尽管自主性被视为人工智能系统的一个单一品质,但本章提出一个自主性的类型学,强调三个不同领域的监管挑战,这些领域中的人工智能系统呈现出不同程度的自主行为。①

第一个也是最突出的领域是自动驾驶汽车。在有限情况下,某些交通方式早已在没有人为操控的情况下运行,如飞机在巡航时使用自动驾驶仪、自动驾驶的轻轨列车。然而,随着自主程度的提高,以及自动驾驶汽车和公共汽车等交通工具与其他道路使用者的互动,有必要考虑现有的关于损害赔偿责任的规定是否需要调整,以及是否需要审查假定驾驶员在场的刑事法律。多个法域已经在尝试进行监管改革,以实现预期的安全和效率效益并且不使道路使用者面临不必要的风险或未分配损失。

第二个例子是自主武器。自动驾驶汽车和公交车引发了关于法律责任和损害赔偿的问题,而致命的自主武器系统则提出了关于将生死决定权转移到非人类过程的独特伦理问题。在这种背景下,对自主性的担忧不仅集中在如何管理风险上,还涉及是否应该在任何情况下都允许自主性。

第三类自主实践较不显眼,但却更为普遍:算法决策。许多常规决策都受益于计算机的处理能力。在类似的事实应该导致类似处理的情况下,算法可能产生公平和一致的结果。然而,当决策影响个体的权利和义务时,自动化决策过程可能将人类主体纯粹当作手段而非目的对待。

正如本书前言中所指出的,这些主题中每一个的讨论都可写

---

① 针对性的监管方案,如新的分配责任机制、人工智能是否可以具有法律人格,将分别在本书第4、5章进行讨论。

成皇皇巨著。① 本部分的目标并不是试图对其技术层面进行完整的研究，而是测试现有监管结构在更一般意义上处理自主性的能力。这些例子揭示了人工智能系统自主决策的不同关注点，而非单一问题：与新技术相关的风险管理的实际挑战，某些决策是否应由机器作出的伦理问题，以及当公共权力机关将其权力下放给算法时产生的合法性差距。

2.1　自动驾驶汽车与风险管理

现代交通法律通常假定有驾驶员、飞行员或船长在场。在某些情况下，这点是毋庸置疑的。例如，在某些法域，"船舶"被定义为"有人驾驶"的船只。② 但更多情况下，这是隐含的——要么是因为法律是在假定任何交通工具都有负责人的情况下制定的，要么是因为在没有可识别个体的情况下，如果发生民事侵权或犯罪行为，就没有人可以追究责任。③ 例如，1968 年《维也纳道路交通公约》规定，道路上的每辆行驶车辆都"应当有驾驶员"。④

不同程度的自动驾驶汽车实验可以追溯到几十年前，但直到 2010 年代，真正意义上的自动驾驶汽车才正式上路行驶，成为更

---

① 参见本书前言第 4 页注释 1—3。
② Robert Veal and Michael Tsimplis, 'The Integration of Unmanned Ships into the Lex Maritima' (2017) *Lloyd's Maritime and Commercial Law Quarterly* 303, 308-14.
③ 这不仅限于机械车辆。例如，在某些法域，马匹在骑手在场时会被视为道路运输法定义下的"车辆"。参见 Brenda Gilligan, *Practical Horse Law: A Guide for Owners and Riders* (Blackwell Science 2002) 106-12。
④ Convention on Road Traffic, done at Vienna, 8 November 1968, in force 21 May 1977, art 8.

为现实的图景。随着技术的发展，更精确地定义"自动驾驶"变得非常有必要。2013 年，美国交通部发布了一项关于自动驾驶车辆发展的政策，其中包括五个自动化级别。① 美国汽车工程师协会（SAE）在次年发布了一份自己的报告，提出了六个自动化级别，同时还参考了德国联邦公路研究所的研究成果。② SAE 的报告后又更新了两次，最近一次是在 2018 年，六个自动化级别现在已成为行业标准。③

在零级别（无自动化）中，人类驾驶员完全控制并执行所有驾驶功能；在五级别（全自动化）中，车辆完全自主运行，无须任何人工干预。在这两个极端之间，越来越多的控制权被赋予驾驶系统。其中，一级代表通过定速巡航等技术进行驾驶员辅助，即使驾驶员仍然控制车辆，也能保持速度。实际上，这意味着驾驶员需要将双手放在方向盘上。在二级中，部分自动化可能使车辆能够控制加速、刹车和转向，但驾驶员必须监视驾驶环境。尽管这有时被描述为"解放双手"模式，但驾驶员必须随时准备恢复对车辆的控制。

三级，有条件自动化，标志着一个转折点。此时，驾驶系统主要负责监控环境并控制车辆；人类驾驶员可以将注意力转移到其他地方，但在需要干预时应作出回应。四级，高度自动化，无须人类驾驶员响应干预请求，并有能力在人类不接管控制车辆的情况下阻停车辆。三级有时被描述为"眼离"路面，而四级则俗

---

① US Department of Transportation Releases Policy on Automated Vehicle Development (Department of Transportation, 30 May 2013).
② Taxonomy and Definitions for Terms Related to On-Road Motor Vehicle Automated Driving Systems (Society of Automotive Engineers, 2014).
③ Taxonomy and Definitions for Terms Related to On-Road Motor Vehicle Automated Driving Systems (revised) (Society of Automotive Engineers, 2018).

称为"心离"。在五级自动化下，车辆完全不需要人类干预，因此五级被描述为"方向盘可有可无"。

在法律责任归属方面，二级和三级之间的拐点尤为重要，尽管二级结束和三级开始的界线可能并不总是明确的。从理论上讲，本章开头描述的优步试验车辆属于二级车辆，但其"驾驶员"似乎表现得像是三级车辆。这种差异突显了自动化程度提高的一个重大风险：虽然"驾驶员"的存在满足了法律上的虚构，如果需要随时准备接管车辆的人在场，但现实情况是，不积极参与驾驶任务的人（即双手离开方向盘时）不太可能长时间保持在紧急情况下作为备用驾驶员所需的注意力水平。① 出于这个原因，一些汽车制造商已宣布计划完全跳过 SAE 三级。②

许多观察家认为，自动驾驶汽车最终将比人类驾驶员更安全，并最终取代他们。③ 目前，全球每年有超过一百万人死于交通事故，其中绝大多数死亡是由驾驶员失误造成的。④ 随着自动驾驶汽车越来越普及，继续依赖"存在驾驶员"这一虚构可能与交通现实脱节。英国法律委员会的一份讨论文件提出了"负责使

---

① Raja Parasuraman and Dietrich Manzey, 'Complacency and Bias in Human Use of Automation: An Attentional Integration' (2010) 52 *Human Factors* 381.

② Paresh Dave, 'Google Ditched Autopilot Driving Feature After Test User Napped Behind Wheel', *Reuters* (31 October 2017); 'Why Car-Makers Are Skipping Sae Level-3 Automation?', *M14 Intelligence* (20 February 2018).

③ See, eg, Tracy Hresko Pearl, 'Fast & Furious: The Misregulation of Driverless Cars' (2017) 73 *New York University Annual Survey of American Law* 24, 35-39. Cf Hannah YeeFen Lim, *Autonomous Vehicles and the Law: Technology, Algorithms, and Ethics* (Edward Elgar 2018) 1-2（认为自动驾驶车辆的安全性能被夸大太多）.

④ See, eg, Road Traffic Injuries (World Health Organization, 7 February 2020).

用的用户"的概念，即在特定情况下可能需要接管车辆的人。①在真正的驾驶员和纯粹的乘客之间的这种中间步骤有助于增加对责任灰色地带的关注，但它并不能解决一旦发生交通事故所引起的法律责任问题。

2.1.1 民事责任

在民事责任方面，如赔偿因自己受伤的他人的义务，现有法律规定在很大程度上可以适用于自动驾驶汽车。目前，如果有人因为粗心驾驶而碾过你的脚，司机可能需要为你的医疗费用买单。如果你的脚是因燃油箱存在缺陷发生爆炸而受伤，那么汽车制造商可能需要承担责任。保险有助于更有效地分担这些成本，许多法域已经要求提供最低保险额度或者通过提供强制保险来解决交通事故导致的个人伤害责任问题，不再涉及过错问题。追索侵权行为、产品责任和法定保险要求将解决与自动驾驶汽车相关的大部分损害问题。②

在过失方面，一个初步的问题是是否有人对可能受到伤害的人承担保护义务。一般来说，汽车驾驶员对其他道路使用者负有注意义务。③ 在 SAE 零级、一级和二级中，这种注意义务显然适用。在某些情况下，驾驶员的雇主也可能承担这种义务。例如，在本章开篇所述的案件发生后，优步与赫茨伯格女士的家人达成一项未公开的和解协议，优步默认责任。然而，在三级和四级

---

① Automated Vehicles: A Joint Preliminary Consultation Paper (Law Commission, Consultation Paper No 240; Scottish Law Commission, Discussion Paper No 166, 2018), para 1.42.

② 参见本书第 4 章第 4.1 节。

③ Robert M Merkin and Jeremy Stuart-Smith, *The Law of Motor Insurance* (Sweet & Maxwell 2004) 186-88.

中，即使"驾驶员"被认定有注意义务，但由于汽车制造商承担控制驾驶责任，因此"驾驶员"所承担的注意义务标准也会降低。① 在五级中，可能根本没有驾驶员。

本书第4章将探讨的一个关键问题是，如何确定人工智能系统（在这种情况下指自动驾驶汽车）的行为责任。尽管有可能该系统本身具有足够的法律人格，能够实施侵权行为，② 但更可能的情况是，民法下的潜在问责空白将由产品责任和强制性法律填补。2015年，沃尔沃公司首席执行官宣布沃尔沃瑞典公司将对其汽车在自动驾驶模式下发生的事故承担全部责任，引发了轩然大波。③ 然而，这种做法有些虚伪，因为各个法域已经通过产品责任法对制造商施加了高标准的注意义务。

民事责任归属的复杂性在于，自动驾驶汽车中可能有许多存在缺陷的独立组件，特别是各种传感器——尽管这些问题属于实际上而非概念上的困难。同样，黑客干扰人工智能系统软件从而导致汽车失事的可能性对于确定法律责任构成新的挑战，但这与未知人员割断传统汽车刹车线的情况并无本质区别。④ 考虑到自动驾驶汽车中网络安全问题的可预见性，一方面，合理的防护措施包括驾驶员的注意义务（如更新软件）和制造商（提供合理的

---

① Jonathan Morgan, 'Torts and Technology' in Roger Brownsword, Eloise Scotford, and Karen Yeung (eds), *The Oxford Handbook of Law, Regulation, and Technology* (OUP 2017) 522 at 538。这里的"制造商"认定，有可能会因参与自动驾驶汽车的生产和维护的不同阶段而稍显复杂，但这些情况在传统的产品责任认定中并不是全新问题。另参见本书第4章第4.1.3节。

② 本书第5章讨论了这种可能性。

③ Jim Gorzelany, 'Volvo Will Accept Liability for Its Self-Driving Cars', *Forbes* (9 October 2015).

④ Daniel A Crane, Kyle D Logue, and Bryce C Pilz, 'A Survey of Legal Issues Arising from the Deployment of Autonomous and Connected Vehicles' (2017) 23 *Michigan Telecommunications and Technology Law Review* 191, 248-49.

防范病毒和黑客的保护）所承担的注意义务。① 另一方面，严格责任标准的实施将明确制造商采取充分的预防措施的责任。一个更具挑战性的例子是，车辆的所有者或驾驶员本人对自动驾驶汽车进行改装而导致事故。例如，无视安全驾驶设置或修改最高时速设定。如果法律没有涵盖这种情况，那么可以像在其他案例中那样，按照共同过失分摊责任。② 如果交通业务模式发生变化，如将车辆视为一种可使用而非可拥有的服务，则可能需要进一步调整。③

因此，在确保道路安全和效率方面的潜在优势不以不公平或不成比例的风险分配为代价方面，自动驾驶汽车提出了重要挑战。就民法如何分配这些风险而言，可能需要对法律进行修改以反映责任从驾驶员向制造商和软件提供商的转移，但基本的法律概念是合理的。④

2.1.2 刑法

与民法不同的是，刑法更多关注的是为了制止和惩罚目的而分配责任，而非分摊成本。道路交通的监管在很大程度上依赖于

---

① See Araz Taeihagh and Hazel Si Min Lim, 'Governing Autonomous Vehicles: Emerging Responses for Safety, Liability, Privacy, Cybersecurity, and Industry Risks' (2019) 39 *Transport Reviews* 103.

② See generally Vadim Mantrov, 'A Victim of a Road Traffic Accident Not Fastened by a Seat Belt and Contributory Negligence in the EU Motor Insurance Law' (2014) 5 *European Journal of Risk Regulation* 115; Noah M Kazis, 'Tort Concepts in Traffic Crimes' (2016) 125 *Yale Law Journal* 1131, 1139-41; James Goudkamp and Donal Nolan, 'Contributory Negligence in the Twenty-First Century: An Empirical Study of First Instance Decisions' (2016) 79 *Modern Law Review* 575.

③ James Arbib and Tony Seba, Rethinking Transportation 2020-2030: The Disruption of Transportation and the Collapse of the Internal-Combustion Vehicle and Oil Industries (RethinkX, 2017).

④ 参见本书第 4 章第 4.1.3 节。

刑法，其中大部分道路交通犯罪针对的是机动车辆的人类驾驶员。这些责任不仅包括驾驶员应对车辆的速度和行驶方向负责，还包括车辆的适用性以及驾驶员自身的驾驶适应性。驾驶员还可能需要有充足的保险、报告事故，并在某些情况下控制乘客的行为（如要求儿童系上安全带）。① 确定道路交通责任涉及的驾驶员可以通过推定车辆登记的人名来辅助。例如，如果车辆被测速摄像头拍到，除非责任能够指向他人，否则登记的人就可能被推定为责任人。②

由于驾驶员的关键地位，许多允许自动驾驶汽车上路的法域最初要求必须有人类"驾驶员"在驾驶座并保持警觉。2018 年 4 月，美国亚利桑那州州长签署行政命令，批准首批真正意义上的自动驾驶汽车在该州的开放道路上行驶。该命令规定，交通违章或车辆违规行为引发的其他处罚将归于"测试或操作完全自动驾驶汽车"的人。③ 但实际上，在各种自动驾驶汽车中仍然保留备用驾驶员。同月，美国加利福尼亚州（以下简称"加州"）机动车管理局修改了州法规，允许申请自动驾驶测试许可。④ 在无人类备用驾驶员在场的情况下，需要有持有相应驾照的远程操作员"持续监督车辆的动态驾驶任务执行"。⑤ 其他法域也同样将"驾驶员"的概念扩展到了被认为负责车辆的远程操作员，尽管他们

---

① Automated Vehicles: A Joint Preliminary Consultation Paper (Law Commission, Consultation Paper No 240; Scottish Law Commission, Discussion Paper No 166, 2018), para 7.1.

② See, eg, Road Traffic Act 1961 (Cap 276, 2004 Rev Ed, Singapore) s 81 (1B).

③ Executive Order 2018-04: Advancing Autonomous Vehicle Testing and Operation; Priotizing Public Safety 2018 (Arizona), para 3 (c).

④ Autonomous Vehicles in California (California Department of Motor Vehicles 2018).

⑤ Testing of Autonomous Vehicles 2018 13 CCR § 227.02 (California).

并未坐在车内。①

新加坡和美国亚利桑那州一样，为真正的自动驾驶汽车制定了规定，这些汽车不需要"人类操作员的积极物理控制或监控"。② 在德国，经修订的道路交通法允许使用相当于 SAE 三级的自动驾驶技术，但要求驾驶员在任何时候都保持"精神警觉"，并在需要时或在"明显情况"要求时接管车辆。③

2018 年，中国制定了自动驾驶测试法规，详细规定了作为交通违法责任人的备份驾驶员所需承担的个人责任，同时要求测试实体必须在中国注册，并具备足够的民事赔偿能力以补偿可能发生的人身和财产损失。④ 中国是一个重要的法域，自 2009 年以来已经超过美国成为全球最大的汽车市场。⑤ 非标准道路标志仍然是一个问题，增加了自动驾驶系统的训练时间。而这些限制可能为更宽容的监管体系、较低的诉讼水平以及迅速接受新技术并愿意承担更高风险的态度所抵消。中国政府已经在 14 个城市设立了自动驾驶测试区，其中最大的区域位于北京和上海。与此同时，阿里巴巴、百度和腾讯等公司也在这方面进行了大量投资。

就前文提到的 SAE 级别而言，相关法域的刑法通常继续假定，没有车辆的自主运行级别会超过二级，驾驶员需要持续对车辆的操作承担责任。⑥ 随着自动驾驶技术的发展，这种立场将变

---

① See, eg, Experimenteerwet zelfrijdende auto's 2018 (Netherlands)（荷兰法律允许无人驾驶汽车在公共道路上行驶，但是必须有人类操作员远程控制它们）.

② Road Traffic (Amendment) Act 2017 (Singapore).

③ Strassenverkehrsgesetz (StVG)［Road Traffic Act］1909 (Germany), §1b.

④ 中国《智能网联汽车道路测试管理规范（试行）》(2018)。

⑤ Luca Pizzuto, et al, How China Will Help Fuel the Revolution in Autonomous Vehicles (McKinsey Center for Future Mobility, 2019).

⑥ 亚利桑那州的行政命令，极为罕见地明确规定了四级和五级自动驾驶。参见 Arizona Executive Order 2018-04, para 1 (d).

得难以维系。

首先需要了解的是，现行某些法律可能导致某些形式的自动驾驶从本质上被视为非法。例如，要求汽车具有"驾驶员"或者禁止无人看管车辆等强制性规定，与完全自动驾驶出租车服务不相容。① 除非改变对人类驾驶员的要求，否则无辜的乘客可能被追究自动驾驶车辆出现错误的责任。这不仅不公平，而且可能阻碍公众对自动驾驶技术的接受。②

美国各州针对自动驾驶汽车的问题尝试了不同的解决方案。第一种方法是继续关注车内的驾驶人或者远程操控人，如亚利桑那州和加州。③ 目前为止，这仍然是在明确允许自动驾驶汽车在公共道路上行驶的各个法域中最常见的法律立场。第二种方法是针对车辆的"操作者"，类似于英国法律委员会提议的"负责使用的用户"。④ 在美国佐治亚州，这意味着"导致"车辆移动的人。⑤ 第三种方法是让车辆所有者承担责任。这是美国得克萨斯州采用的方法。⑥

第四种方法是将"自动驾驶系统"（ADS）本身定义为"驾驶员"，目前只有美国田纳西州采用了这一定义。同时，该州还

---

① See, eg, Road Vehicles (Construction and Use) Regulations 1986 (UK), reg 107.

② Michael Cameron, Realising the Potential of Driverless Vehicles: Recommendations for Law Reform (New Zealand Law Foundation, 2018) 9.

③ Executive Order 2018-04: Advancing Autonomous Vehicle Testing and Operation; Priotizing Public Safety 2018 (Arizona), para 3 (c); Autonomous Vehicles in California (California Department of Motor Vehicles, 2018); Testing of Autonomous Vehicles 2018 13 CCR § 227.02 (California).

④ Automated Vehicles: A Joint Preliminary Consultation Paper (Law Commission, Consultation Paper No 240; Scottish Law Commission, Discussion Paper No 166, 2018), para 1.42.

⑤ Official Code of Georgia Annotated § 40-1-1 (38) (2017).

⑥ Texas Transportation Code § 545.453 (a) (1) (2017).

在2017年州法典修正案中将"人"的定义扩大为"自然人、公司、合伙企业、协会、法人或从事自动驾驶系统的人"。① 但是，这个定义仅适用于关于机动车辆的专门法律规范，似乎尚未适用于民事责任或刑事制裁。其他法域的法律改革机构，尤其是澳大利亚和英国，提出了"自动驾驶系统实体"（ADSE）的概念，但这是指负责车辆的法律实体，而非一种新的法人类别。②

一个更乌托邦的愿景是，自动驾驶汽车在驾驶技术上可能远远优于人类驾驶员，以至于根本不需要考虑刑事责任。这看似不现实，但的确引发了道路交通法律的功能以及惩罚违法行为的目的等问题。道路交通法的两个基本目标是提高道路安全和维护道路秩序。③ 正如澳大利亚国家交通委员会（NTC）所指出的，现行的处罚措施旨在影响人类驾驶员的行为。违反规则的个人可能受到惩罚，其驾驶执照可能被暂停或吊销。就自动驾驶汽车而言，罚款和监禁可能不如将执法视为训练系统的反馈环节的一部分更为合适。具体可以采取改进通知和可执行承诺的形式来提高安全性。④ 在更严重的情况下，撤销自动驾驶汽车在道路上行驶

---

① Tennessee Code Annotated §55-8-101 (2017) (emphasis added).

② Changing Driving Laws to Support Automated Vehicles (Policy Paper) (National Transport Commission, May 2018), para 1.5; Automated Vehicles: A Joint Preliminary Consultation Paper (Law Commission, Consultation Paper No 240; Scottish Law Commission, Discussion Paper No 166, 2018), para 4.107.

③ Sally Cunningham, *Driving Offences: Law, Policy and Practice* (Routledge 2008) 1-6.

④ Changing Driving Laws to Support Automated Vehicles (Policy Paper) (National Transport Commission, May 2018), para 8.2.1. See also Automated Vehicles: A Joint Preliminary Consultation Paper (Law Commission, Consultation Paper No 240; Scottish Law Commission, Discussion Paper No 166, 2018), paras 7.33-7.34. 当然，这将取决于某一违规行为发生的原因。例如，如果违规是由于驾驶员/操控员的人工操作导致的，那么传统的处罚机制可以适用。

的授权可能足以保护其他道路使用者，而如果有证据表明其行为构成刑事犯罪，则可以对相关自然人或法人实施传统的处罚措施。

关于是否以及如何"惩罚"人工智能系统本身的更广泛问题将在第 5 章中讨论。① 就目前的问题而言，有趣的是，在适用于自动驾驶汽车时，刑法摒弃了德性论的色彩，转而倾向于工具主义：违法行为可能被视为需要调试的错误，而不是需要纠正的道德缺陷。②

2.1.3 伦理

自动驾驶汽车最终可能比人类驾驶员更为优秀，这引发了许多关于它们在极限情况下（如即将发生的车祸）应如何应对的猜测。人类驾驶员通常要达到"合理驾驶员"的标准。③ 例如，如果一个孩子突然跑到马路上，为了避开他或她而突然转向可能违反了交通规则，但不太可能受到起诉。相比之下，为了避开老鼠而突然转向可能无法被原谅。④ 自动驾驶汽车反应更迅速，但缺乏指导人类行为的道德指南。这种道德指南必须通过编程或经验来学习。⑤

---

① 参见本书第 5 章第 5.1.2（b）节。
② 参见本书第 9 章第 9.3.2 节。
③ Jeffrey K Gurney, 'Imputing Driverhood: Applying a Reasonable Driver Standard to Accidents Caused by Autonomous Vehicles' in Patrick Lin, Keith Abney, and Ryan Jenkins (eds), *Robot Ethics 2.0: From Autonomous Cars to Artificial Intelligence* (OUP 2017) 51.
④ See Filippo Santoni de Sio, 'Killing by Autonomous Vehicles and the Legal Doctrine of Necessity' (2017) 20 *Ethical Theory and Moral Practice* 411.
⑤ Ivó Coca-Vila, 'Self-Driving Cars in Dilemmatic Situations: An Approach Based on the Theory of Justification in Criminal Law' (2018) 12 *Criminal Law and Philosophy* 59.

伦理学家提出的电车难题就是能说明可能出现的两难困境的一个常见的示例。一辆单车厢的火车正朝着五个人驶去，将会撞死他们全部。如果拉动一个操纵杆，火车将被转移到侧线，但会撞死另一个人。你会拉动这个杆吗？尽管许多人会这样做，但这个问题并没有"正确"的答案。当面临类似的情境，即五个人将死去，唯一能阻止火车的方法是将一个人撞倒在火车轨道上时，大多数人往往会犹豫。第一个情景反映了一种功利主义方法，关注行为的后果（一死对比五死）。第二种情况不同，因为我们直觉上知道将一个人推向死亡是错误的——尽管仍然是在一个人和五个人死亡之间作出选择。①

麻省理工学院的研究人员开发了一个名为"道德机器"（Moral Machine）的系统，提供了一些可能遇到的自动驾驶汽车的情境。例如，如果牺牲两名乘客可以拯救五名行人，是否应该这样做？如果行人在横穿马路时犯规了，或者他们是罪犯呢？在现实生活中，更快的反应时间意味着刹车几乎肯定是最好的选择，但在实验目的中，我们需要假设刹车失灵、车辆无法停止。在一种不同寻常的抽样方法中，研究人员放弃了标准的学术调查方法，转而使用"病毒式在线平台"——这带来了自我选择问题，但使他们能够从世界各地数百万人那里收集数据。②

这项研究发现，全球范围内都有的一个普遍倾向是，人们更愿意牺牲动物的生命以挽救人类的生命，也偏向于挽救更多人的

---

① See generally David Edmonds, *Would You Kill the Fat Man? The Trolley Problem and What Your Answer Tells Us About Right and Wrong* (Princeton UP 2013); Thomas Cathcart, *The Trolley Problem; or, Would You Throw the Fat Guy Off the Bridge? A Philosophical Conundrum* (Workman 2013).

② Edmond Awad, *et al*, 'The Moral Machine Experiment' (2018) 563 *Nature* 59, 63.

生命，特别是年轻人的生命。前者与德国自动化和联网驾驶伦理委员会提出的规则一致，而后者则直接违背了禁止根据年龄等个人特征进行区分的要求。① 在关于这项研究的访谈中，其中一位共同作者被问及结果中透露的隐含偏见，即优先挽救专业人士而非无家可归者、健康人而非肥胖者、狗而非罪犯等问题时他回答道："这表明我们不应该完全把决策交给普罗大众。"②

应该注意的是，在实践中上述"困境情况"都过于简单化。它们提出了仅有两种结果的错误二分法，即假定在两个结果中只有一个结果是正确的，而在任何实际道路事件中，现实情况都有许多可能的结果。③ 特别是在汽车必须要么牺牲乘客、要么撞死行人的情况下，这种情况尤其明显。梅赛德斯-奔驰公司的高管们表示，在任何情况下他们都将优先考虑车内乘客的生命安全。④ 发表在《科学》杂志上的一篇论文支持这种商业决策：虽然许多人理论上赞成自动驾驶车辆牺牲一名乘客来拯救其他人，但在实践中，他们不太可能购买或乘坐这样编程方式的汽车。⑤

监管机构往往从一般意义上强调安全的重要性，但并没有对自动驾驶车辆在极限情况下需要作出的具体选择发表意见。在人类驾驶员仍占主导地位的道路上，合理驾驶员的标准将继续存

---

① Christoph Luetge, 'The German Ethics Code for Automated and Connected Driving' (2017) 30 *Philosophy & Technology* 547.

② Caroline Lester, 'A Study on Driverless-Car Ethics Offers a Troubling Look Into Our Values', *New Yorker* (24 January 2019) (quoting Azim Shariff).

③ Tom Michael Gasser, 'Fundamental and Special Legal Questions for Autonomous Vehicles' in Markus Maurer, et al (eds), *Autonomous Driving: Technical, Legal and Social Aspects* (Springer 2016) 523 at 533-34.

④ Michael Taylor, 'Self-Driving Mercedes-Benzes Will Prioritize Occupant Safety over Pedestrians', *Car and Driver* (8 October 2016).

⑤ Jean-François Bonnefon, Azim Shariff, and Iyad Rahwan, 'The Social Dilemma of Autonomous Vehicles' (2016) 352 (6293) *Science* 1573.

在，自动驾驶车辆也将以此为衡量标准。如果未来自动驾驶汽车占据了主导地位，则可能需要制定新的标准，并相应地从驾驶员技能的许可转向产品安全的认证。

2.2 杀手机器人与外包服务的伦理问题

自动驾驶车辆引发了人们对它们如何适应现有民事和刑事责任模式的担忧，以及人工智能系统应该如何在即将发生的撞车等生死关头中作出决策的问题。从很多方面来看，这些都是可以通过技术改进和监管调整来解决的问题。相比之下，真正的自主武器系统的前景已经引发了呼吁暂停或彻底禁止的声音。①

从某种意义上说，这是不理性的。就像自动驾驶车辆有望减少驾驶员因驾驶失误造成死亡和伤害一样，减少战场上的失误和过激行为可能降低战争的人道成本。任何情况下，许多"愚蠢"的装置已经被"自动化"了。例如，杀伤性地雷或简易爆炸装置（IED）无须额外的人类控制就能运作，尽管它不具有选择性的瞄准能力。红外制导导弹也是一个例子，这种武器在发射时按照一个程序行动，但在实质上并没有选择性。沿着这一谱系进一步发展的是一代新的远程反舰导弹（LRASMs），它们在发射时有着目标参数，但能够在这些参数范围内搜索和识别敌方战舰。

与自动驾驶车辆一样，自主武器系统的关键区别在于系统决

---

① Losing Humanity: The Case Against Killer Robots (Human Rights Watch, 2012); Michael Press, 'Of Robots and Rules: Autonomous Weapon Systems in the Law of Armed Conflict' (2017) 48 *Georgetown Journal of International Law* 1337, 1344.

策的独立程度。根据美国国防部的定义，自主武器系统是指一旦启动，可以在没有进一步人类干预的情况下选择和攻击目标的系统。① 同样，国际红十字会（ICRC）强调，在这种情况下，自主性应该集中在选择和攻击目标这些关键功能上，而不是在移动或导航上。②

对于纯粹的防御性系统，人们关注较少。例如，美国海军的"菲兰克斯近程武器系统"（Phalanx CIWS）于20世纪70年代首次部署在舰船上，作为防御海上攻击的最后一道防线。③ 陆基弹道导弹防御系统也具有不同程度的自动化，其中最引人注目的是美国的"爱国者导弹"和以色列的"铁穹"，它们可以识别和试图摧毁火箭弹和炮弹。④ 朝鲜半岛非军事区已经部署了哨兵枪等固定式杀伤武器，但其真实自主程度尚存争议。⑤

进攻性自主武器尚未广泛部署，但这一技术正在快速发展。各种无人驾驶飞行器，或称"无人机"，具有独立目标定位的能力；有些还能够建议攻击目标和攻击角度，尽管决定是否交战仍然由其操作员负责。⑥ 其他陆基和海基作战飞行器也已研制成功，

---

① Autonomy in Weapon Systems (Department of Defense, Directive Number 3000.09, 21 November 2012). 这包括允许人类手动操作的系统。

② Towards Limits on Autonomy in Weapon Systems (International Committee of the Red Cross, 9 April 2018).

③ 类似的系统包括俄罗斯的 Kaftan CIWS 和中国的 730 型 CIWS（近程炮）。

④ See, eg, Michael J Armstrong, 'Modeling Short-Range Ballistic Missile Defense and Israel's Iron Dome System' (2014) 62 *Operations Research* 1028.

⑤ Ian Kerr and Katie Szilagyi, 'Evitable Conflicts, Inevitable Technologies? The Science and Fiction of Robotic Warfare and IHL' (2018) 14 *Law, Culture and the Humanities* 45, 52.

⑥ Kenneth Anderson and Matthew Waxman, Law and Ethics for Autonomous Weapon Systems: Why a Ban Won't Work and How the Laws of War Can (Hoover Institution, 2013) 4.

具有不同程度的自主性。通常情况下，这些武器都是遥控的，但是有时会出现惊人的报道，称杀手机器人在实战中部署，如 2007 年美国在伊拉克试验的"SWORDS"机枪坦克系统。①

十二年后的 2019 年，美国陆军在推出"高级目标定位和致命自动化系统"（ATLAS）的供应商招标请求时引发了争议。最初的公告表示，希望开发具有"至少比当前手动过程快 3 倍的获取、识别和攻击目标的能力"的作战车辆。② 在新闻头条宣布五角大楼即将将其坦克变成"人工智能驱动的杀人机器"的时候，该公告被修改以强调国防部对武器系统自主性政策没有发生变化。该政策规定，自主武器系统必须允许指挥官和操作员对使用武力进行"适当水平的人为判断"。③

许多评论人士认为，在战场上实现越来越高程度的自主性是不可避免的，自主武器系统对人类的优势也是不可避免的。④ 然而，人们普遍认为，扣动扳机的手指必须是血肉之躯，而不是金属和硅，这与道路交通中的自主性争论有着本质区别。

2.2.1 国际人道主义法

与本书审视的许多法律体系相比，国际人道主义法明确规定

---

① Noah Shachtman, 'First Armed Robots on Patrol in Iraq (Updated)', *Wired* (2 August 2007). 特种武器观察侦察侦测系统（SWORDS）本质上是一个改造过的遥控排爆装置。

② Industry Day for the Advanced Targeting and Lethality Automated System (ATLAS) Program (Department of the Army, Solicitation Number: W909MY-19-R-C004, 11 February 2019).

③ Autonomy in Weapon Systems (Department of Defense, Directive Number 3000.09, 21 November 2012), para 4a.

④ 例如，早在 2001 年，美国国会就设定了目标，要求到 2010 年实现 1/3 的作战飞机无人驾驶，到 2015 年实现 1/3 的地面作战车辆无人驾驶。参见 Floyd D Spence National Defense Authorization Act for Fiscal Year 2001 2000, Pub L No 106-398 (US), s 220。

其适用于新兴技术。这项规定采取马顿斯条款的形式,以1899年海牙和平会议上提出该条款的俄罗斯代表的名字命名。以下文本被写入《战争法与惯例公约》的序言中:

> 在颁布更完整的战争法典之前,缔约方认为有必要声明,在他们通过的规则未包括的情况下,平民和交战方仍然受国际法原则的保护和支配,这些原则和规定源于文明国家之间建立的习俗惯例、人道主义法律和公众良知的要求。①

随着时间的推移,原本是打破僵局而引入的这一文本逐渐被赋予更重要的意义,有时被视为创造新法的渊源,而不是在不确定情况下适用的解释工具。② 例如,当国际法院被要求考虑威胁或使用核武器的合法性时,它援引马顿斯条款——现在被确立为《日内瓦公约第一附加议定书》第1(2)条,明确规定"人道主义法的原则和规则"适用于这些武器,尽管缺乏专门的条约规定。③

然而,将这些原则和规则应用于新技术并非易事。有时有人认为,计算机不应该被赋予作出生死决策的权力,因为可能出现"无数种可能的情景"。④ 这是反对自主武器系统自主权的较温和

---

① Convention (Ⅱ) with Respect to the Laws and Customs of War on Land and Its Annex: Regulations Concerning the Laws and Customs of War on Land (1899 Hague Regulations), done at The Hague, 29 July 1899, preamble.

② Antonio Cassese, 'The Martens Clause: Half a Loaf or Simply Pie in the Sky?' (2000) 11 *European Journal of International Law* 187, 212-14.

③ *Legality of the Threat or Use of Nuclear Weapons* (Advisory Opinion) [1996] ICJ Rep 226 (International Court of Justice), para 87.

④ Shaking the Foundations: The Human Rights Implications of Killer Robots (Human Rights Watch, 2014).

的论点之一，因为其根本担忧不在于人工智能系统对无数种可能情景的反应能力，而在于人类能否事先编程它们。实际上，一些评论人士认为，与人类相比，人工智能系统可能更有能力遵守战争法规则。① 与必须接受训练的人类不同，自主武器系统可以在这些编程的规则下行动，并被要求不带感情色彩地执行它们。许多战争罪行不是由于有意违反交战规则而产生的，而是由于疲劳、恐惧或愤怒——这正是机器所能够避免的特质。②

另一组担忧涉及一个非常现实的可能性，即一台真正意义上的通用人工智能系统可能认为人类是其敌人。③ 自主武器系统转而攻击其创造者的前景是人工智能威胁的更为生动和引人注目的形象之一，这在《终结者》系列电影中得到了体现和表达。虽然战场上还没有发生这样戏剧性的事件，但自主武器系统误伤友军事件已有发生，这些系统出现了目标定位错误或攻击友方飞行器的情况。

在某些情况下，参与人工智能系统开发的人员表示根本不想参与军事项目。当谷歌参与美国国防部的"麻文项目"（Project Maven）被曝光后，成千上万员工联名写信，要求谷歌退出该项

---

① See, eg, Kenneth Anderson, Daniel Reisner, and Matthew Waxman, 'Adapting the Law of Armed Conflict to Autonomous Weapon Systems' (2014) 90 *International Law Studies* 386, 411; Pedro Domingos, *The Master Algorithm: How the Quest for the Ultimate Learning Machine Will Remake Our World* (Basic Books 2015) 280.

② Ronald C Arkin, 'The Case for Ethical Autonomy in Unmanned Systems' (2010) 9 *Journal of Military Ethics* 332; Kenneth Anderson and Matthew C Waxman, 'Debating Autonomous Weapon Systems, Their Ethics, and Their Regulation Under International Law' in Roger Brownsword, Eloise Scotford, and Karen Yeung (eds), *The Oxford Handbook of Law, Regulation, and Technology* (OUP 2017) 1097 at 1108-10.

③ 参见本书第5章第5.3节。

目并承诺公司及其承包商永远不会开发"战争技术"。① 尽管这可能是谷歌员工自负的表现,毕竟谷歌是一家口号为"不作恶"的公司,② 但这种"愤慨"已显而易见于自主武器系统争论的许多方面。③

2.2.2 人类不参与?

许多担忧表达的核心是,脱离对杀人对象的选择,则会削弱应伴随此类决策的道德困境。④ 有人可能认为,这也适用于其他"模糊痕迹"军事行动——从对付不特定目标的巡航导弹到在军营里操作无人机的操作员。⑤ 然而,真正的自主武器系统的区别在于,除了物理上不在战场上之外,将生死决策交给算法还意味着人类操作员也可能在心理上缺席。⑥ 在2018年向联合国大会发表的讲话中,联合国秘书长安东尼奥·古特雷斯谴责了这一前景在"道义上是不可接受的"。⑦

---

① "麻文项目"(Project Maven)专注于计算机视觉,使用机器学习从运动或静止的图像中提取关注目标对象。参见 Cheryl Pellerin, Project Maven to Deploy Computer Algorithms to War Zone by Year's End (Department of Defense, 21 July 2017)。

② Ken Auletta, *Googled: The End of the World as We Know It* (Penguin 2009) 20; Steven Levy, *In the Plex: How Google Thinks, Works, and Shapes Our Lives* (New York 2011) 144.

③ Helen Nissenbaum, 'Protecting Privacy in an Information Age: The Problem of Privacy in Public' (1998) 17 *Law and Philosophy* 559, 583.

④ See, eg, Wendell Wallach, *A Dangerous Master: How to Keep Technology from Slipping Beyond Our Control* (Basic Books 2015) 213-34.

⑤ Cf Jean Baudrillard, *The Gulf War Never Happened* (Polity Press 1995).

⑥ Christof Heyns, 'Autonomous Weapons Systems: Living a Dignified Life and Dying a Dignified Death' in Nehal Bhuta, *et al* (eds), *Autonomous Weapons Systems: Law, Ethics, Policy* (CUP 2016) 3 at 4.

⑦ António Guterres, 'Address to the General Assembly' (United Nations, New York, 25 September 2018).

关于致命性武力，经常有人认为，使用致命性武力的决定应该由人类作出，并且应该事后能追究那个人的责任。这种观点基于战争本身是一种与人类密切相关的制度。正如迈克尔·沃尔泽（Michael Walzer）所观察到的那样：

> 战争最重要的特征之一是陷入其中的男男女女不仅是受害者，也是参与者。这一点区别于人类的其他灾难。我们都倾向于让他们对自己的行为负责。①

如果自主武器系统得到普及，战争成本可能降低，在工业化国家中已经受到技术和物质约束的情况下降低的甚至更多。争论继续指出，这种系统与人类对手的并置，其冷酷的逻辑与致命的恐惧将继续侵蚀人类的平等和尊严。② 它还暗示了自主武器竞赛的可能进展：一旦一方部署了这样的系统，就很难再有理由派遣人类士兵与之作战。③

在国际层面上，反对自主武器系统的态度往往与国家实力呈反比例关系。少数几个国家支持全面禁止条约，但若没有拥有先进技术和军事能力的国家的参与，则这种禁止最多只是一种姿态而已。例如，中国政法大学军事法研究所的学者们认为，拥有先

---

① Michael Walzer, *Just and Unjust Wars: A Moral Argument with Historical Illustrations* (3rd edn, Basic Books 2000) 15.
② Nehal Bhuta, Susanne Beck, and Robin Geiβ, 'Present Futures: Concluding Reflections and Open Questions on Autonomous Weapons Systems' in Nehal Bhuta, et al (eds), *Autonomous Weapons Systems: Law, Ethics, Policy* (CUP 2016) 347 at 355-56.
③ Leonard Kahn, 'Military Robots and the Likelihood of Armed Conflict' in Patrick Lin, Keith Abney, and Ryan Jenkins (eds), *Robot Ethics 2.0: From Autonomous Cars to Artificial Intelligence* (OUP 2017) 274 at 283.

进人工智能技术的国家应该发挥"示范"作用。他们进一步提出，使用"完全自主"武器系统的军事指挥官或文职官员应该承担违反国际人道主义法所产生的个人责任。[①]

目前正在进行的讨论包括武器审查和可能的"有意义的人为控制"要求。《日内瓦公约第一附加议定书》第 36 条规定，"研究、开发、获取或采用新武器、新战争方法和新战争手段"的缔约方应当确定其使用是否违反国际法。联合国政府专家组也认为，这是该领域的潜在指导原则。[②] 尽管有人认为该第 36 条反映了习惯国际法，但国际红十字会认为，审查新武器在任何情况下都是必要的，是履行国际法义务的"忠实和负责任"的一部分。[③] 美国在《日内瓦公约第一附加议定书》生效前三年就引入了类似的程序，并在 20 世纪 90 年代拒绝研制致盲激光武器。[④]

对武器是否违反国际法的判定往往集中在其是否本质上具有不区分靶对象的特性，或是否会造成不必要的痛苦或过分伤害。尽管有人认为自主武器系统必然是不区分靶对象的，因为它们缺乏识别战斗人员和评估其他人类意图所需的人类特征，而这些都

[①] Li Qiang and Xie Dan, 'Legal Regulation of AI Weapons Under International Humanitarian Law: A Chinese Perspective', *ICRC Humanitarian Law & Policy Blog* (2 May 2019).

[②] Report of the 2018 Session of the Group of Governmental Experts on Emerging Technologies in the Area of Lethal Autonomous Weapons Systems, UN Doc CCW/GGE. 2/2018/3 (2018), para 26 (d).

[③] A Guide to the Legal Review of New Weapons, Means and Methods of Warfare: Measures to Implement Article 36 of Additional Protocol I of 1977 (International Committee of the Red Cross, January 2006) 4.

[④] Kenneth Anderson and Matthew Waxman, Law and Ethics for Autonomous Weapon Systems: Why a Ban Won't Work and How the Laws of War Can (Hoover Institution, 2013) 10. See The Defense Acquisition System (Department of Defense, Directive Number 5000.01, 9 September 2020), s 1.2 (v).

是这种系统的感知和分析能力所面临的实际挑战。① 同样，有人认为机器将无法区分失去能力或投降的敌人和合法目标，因此将导致不必要的痛苦。这同样是一个可以克服的问题，或许类似于自动驾驶汽车在人类司机和行人中间导航时面临的一些挑战。②

在自主武器系统的背景下，更重要的不是机器的能力，而是人类的缺席。国际红十字会在2018年发布了一份声明，强调人类参与的重要性——并非因为人类在识别或理解其他人方面具有更高的能力，而是为了深入探讨是否应使用武力的道德困境，以及使用武力者应承担的责任。③

尽管对完全禁止自主武器存在抵制，但要求"有意义的人类控制"的呼声却越来越高，尽管这种控制可能与真正的自主武器系统不一致。目前，最低限度的共识似乎是可能禁止那些一旦启动就无法中止任务的全自主武器。至少在目前这个阶段，即使在敌对行动结束后，真正"无人参与"的机器仍然在运行，这似乎足以抵消它们在战场上可能带来的任何好处。④

2.2.3 雇佣兵的经验教训

与在人工智能系统监管的许多其他方面一样，人们往往将自

---

① Ryan Poitras, 'Article 36 Weapons Reviews & Autonomous Weapons Systems: Supporting an International Review Standard' (2018) 34 *American University International Law Review* 465, 486-89.

② Cf Noel Sharkey, 'Staying in the Loop: Human Supervisory Control of Weapons' in Nehal Bhuta, *et al* (eds), *Autonomous Weapons Systems: Law, Ethics, Policy* (CUP 2016) 23 at 24-27.

③ Towards Limits on Autonomy in Weapon Systems (International Committee of the Red Cross, 9 April 2018). See also Artificial Intelligence and Machine Learning in Armed Conflict: A Human-Centred Approach (International Committee of the Red Cross, 6 June 2019) 7-10.

④ Amitai Etzioni and Oren Etzioni, 'Pros and Cons of Autonomous Weapons Systems', *Military Review* (May-June 2017) 71, 79-80. 关于"人类完全脱离决策回路"和其他决策范式的讨论，请参见本章第2.3节。

主武器系统带来的问题视为独特的全新问题，而忽略可以从其他引发类似担忧的活动中吸取经验教训的可能性。特别是，可以从过去三十年来将作战能力外包给雇佣兵而非机器的战争监管努力中汲取经验教训。

对现代雇佣兵及其同类公司——私营军事和安全公司（PMSCs）的警惕，特别是对他们使用致命性武力的能力的警惕，源于一种信念：这样的决策应该在一个不仅包括法律，还包括政治和道德问责的框架内进行。① 如今，"常识"认为，对暴力的控制和使用应该局限于国家。但并非始终如此。例如，教皇至今仍由一支始建于 1502 年的瑞士私人部队保护。雇佣兵在过去是可接受的，这种观念在我们的语言中依然存在。例如，"自由职业者"一词现在意味着临时工，但在历史上它实际上指的是拥有长矛的自由代理人。②

有趣的是，雇佣兵的受欢迎程度或受鄙视程度取决于军事技能和军事数量重要性的变化，其中一个主要影响因素是新兴技术。两个世纪前，火枪的引入大大缩短了培训一名有效士兵所需的时间，结果导致数量远比质量更重要。在这种情况下，国家征兵提供了一种更有效的组建一支庞大的军队的方法。这些军事和经济变革随后又在政治和文化上得到强化，使得雇佣兵在 19 世纪"过时"。依赖雇佣兵很快被视为不仅效率低下，而且不值得信任：一个国家的人民不为国家而战，说明这个国家缺乏爱国

---

① See Simon Chesterman and Chia Lehnardt (eds), *From Mercenaries to Market: The Rise and Regulation of Private Military Companies* (OUP 2007).

② See generally Sarah Percy, *Mercenaries: The History of a Norm in International Relations* (OUP 2007).

者；那些出于爱国以外的原因而战的人往往缺乏道德。①

20世纪雇佣兵对非洲的颠覆作用导致了人们努力全面禁止雇佣军。1989年的一项条约试图做到这一点，但由于签名不足和定义问题而搁浅。雇佣兵被定义为"主要出于谋求私利而参与敌对行动的人"。② 由于难以证明其动机，一位学者甚至建议，在公约框架下被定罪的任何人都应被枪决，包括他的律师。③

这个建议与瑞士政府和国际红十字会领导的一项倡议形成鲜明对比，后者并未对雇佣兵追究刑事责任，而是强调国家的持续性义务。一系列政府间会议促成了《蒙特勒文件》的起草，该文件以日内瓦湖畔的小镇命名，政府专家们于2008年9月在此召开了为期三天的会议。该文件强调国际法下国家义务的不可转移性，包括对外包活动的持续责任，并禁止将某些活动完全外包。④

因此，更好且更有用的区分，也是与本书的讨论相关的是，某些职能具有"固有政府性质"，不能转移给承包商、机器或其他任何人。这一概念将在本书第4章中进一步探讨。⑤

---

① Deborah Avant, 'From Mercenary to Citizen Armies: Explaining Change in the Practice of War' (2000) 54 *International Organization* 41; Deborah Avant, *The Market for Force: The Consequences of Privatizing Security* (CUP 2005).

② International Convention Against the Recruitment, Use, Financing, and Training of Mercenaries (Convention on Mercenaries), 4 December 1989, in force 20 October 2001, art 1 (1) (b).

③ Geoffrey Best, quoted in David Shearer, *Private Armies and Military Intervention* (OUP 1998) 18.

④ The Montreux Document on Pertinent International Legal Obligations and Good Practices for States Related to Operations of Private Military and Security Companies During Armed Conflict (Swiss Federal Department of Foreign Affairs & International Committee of the Red Cross, 17 September 2008).

⑤ 参见本书第4章第4.3节。

2.3　算法决策及其合法性

人工智能系统的自主行为不仅限于其与现实世界的物理互动。尽管自动驾驶汽车和杀手机器人让人联想到机器的独立形象，但支撑这种自主性的是收集数据和作出具有更广泛应用的决策的能力。随着越来越多的商业和政府活动转移到网络，大量日常任务可以在没有人类参与的情况下完成。现在越来越多的决策实际上是由算法作出的，这些算法要么直接得出结论性的决定，要么提出一个可能被名义上负责的人类毫不犹豫地接受的决策建议。[①]

与自动驾驶汽车的情况一样，算法决策自主性也有必要区分不同等级。这里常用的一个比喻是，人类处于参与、监督或完全不参与决策过程的"循环"中。一个极端是完全由人类决策，没有计算机的支持。回顾前面讨论的 SAE 自动驾驶汽车等级，这相当于零级自动驾驶。[②] "人在循环之中"是指系统支持的决策，如系统提供选项或建议，但由人类作出积极决策。这可能对应于 SAE 一级或二级自动驾驶（"手握方向盘"）。"人在循环之上"表示人类可以监督过程并在必要时进行干预，对应于 SAE 三级或四级自动驾驶。[③] "人在循环之外"意味着过程在最少或不需要

[①]　Cf Tarleton Gillespie, 'Algorithm' in Benjamin Peters (ed), *Digital Keywords: A Vocabulary of Information Society and Culture* (Princeton UP 2016) 18 at 26.

[②]　参见本书第 2 章第 2.1 节。

[③]　Austin Graham, et al, 'Formalizing Interruptible Algorithms for Human Over-the-Loop Analytics' (2017 IEEE International Conference on Big Data (Big Data), Boston, MA, 2017).

人类干预的情况下进行，类似于SAE五级自动驾驶。①

不同的算法决策过程，也可以类比于演绎推理和归纳推理的过程。第一种决策形式是应用人类预先编程的规则。最基本的应用包括简单的计算，如自动结账时的杂货账单汇总，又如应用一组变量来确定政府福利的资格或贷款的利率。这种基于规则的决策并非真正的"自主"。后一种决策形式是依据历史数据、借用算法工具进行推断或预测，如机器学习。② 随着这些工具变得越来越复杂，理解或解释决策背后的原因可能引发不透明性问题，这将在本书第3章中进行探讨。本章重点关注的是这些算法工具得出结论的自主性，因为这个过程不能直接归因于人类主体。

算法构建的方式也很重要。对于基于规则的处理，需要对这些规则进行解释。如果它们是基于法律规定的，如"如果满足条件A和B，则得出结论C"，那么这可能并不成为问题。然而，法律很少如此简单。③ 例如，在澳大利亚，2015年一个名为"自动债务索偿系统"（Robo-debt）的项目试图计算并收回因福利超额支付而产生的债务。尽管它系统地应用了规则，但这些规则是法律中复杂条款的不完整转录，导致大约1/5的人被错误送达债务

---

① Cf Natasha Merat, et al, 'The "Out-of-the-Loop" Concept in Automated Driving: Proposed Definition, Measures and Implications' (2019) 21 *Cognition, Technology & Work* 87. See also Karen Yeung, 'Algorithmic Regulation: A Critical Interrogation' (2018) 12 *Regulation & Governance* 505, 508 (developing a taxonomy of algorithmic regulation).

② 这个过程可能有也可能没有人类参与监督，还可能通过强化算法实现。Kevin P Murphy, *Machine Learning: A Probabilistic Perspective* （MIT Press 2012) 2. 关于"人在循环之中"和其他模型的讨论，请参见本书第2章第2.3节相关内容；关于机器学习矫正问题的讨论，请参见本书第3章第3.2.1节相关内容。

③ 参见本书第9章第9.1.1节。

通知。① 在机器学习的情况下，人工智能系统依赖的数据本身可能可靠也可能不可靠，这个话题将在下一章讨论。②

在许多情况下，使用算法支持或替代人类决策是无争议的。除了提高效率，自动化处理还有助于确保一致性和可预测性。事实上，在某些情况下，它可能比人类决策中经常出现的任意性更为可取——无论这种随意性是由于概念限制、粗心还是腐败造成的。与此同时，将决策责任让渡给机器可能引发其他问题，从潜在的歧视到缺乏正当程序或程序公平等，其中存在着如何行使自由裁量权以及是否有些决策不应仅由机器独立作出等问题。这类似于关于自主武器的争论。

2.3.1 合同与知识

如今，从在线购物到与聊天机器人争论物品未送达或有瑕疵等问题，大量的日常商业交易无须人工干预就可以进行。在高交易量且低风险的领域，自动化决策过程的推动力最大。除了在线购物外，这种趋势还扩展到了诸如小额贷款、零售保险和招聘筛选等领域，不同程度的自动化提升了企业的效率。③ 同时，越来越多的企业使用自动化纠纷解决系统。④

在这个领域，很多旨在限制自动化处理的影响的监管干预举措都是由欧洲主导的。这些努力旨在防止自动化侵犯权利——如

---

① See Monika Zalnieriute, Lyria Bennett Moses, and George Williams, 'The Rule of Law and Automation of Government Decision-Making' (2019) 82 *Modern Law Review* 425, 446.

② 参见本书第 3 章第 3.2 节。

③ Stefanie Hänold, 'Profiling and Automated Decision-Making: Legal Implications and Shortcomings' in Marcelo Corrales, Mark Fenwick, and Nikolaus Forgó (eds), *Robotics, AI and the Future of Law* (Springer 2018) 123 at 127-28.

④ 参见本书第 9 章第 9.1 节。

果相关决策是由人类作出的,这种方式将是不允许的。在本节中,我们仅关注算法自主性所带来的新挑战。

就像自动驾驶汽车的情况一样,涉及算法的大多数民法问题可以适用现有的法律和原则来解决。然而,当这些方法应用于新的事实模式时,有时可能产生奇怪的结果。例如,对算法交易软件的依赖增加,可能导致计算机程序之间达成的交易超出其初始参数的现象。这种合同的有效性并不复杂,[①] 尽管高频交易可能给实施带来实际挑战,正如本书第 1 章中讨论的那样。

与自主性直接相关的问题出现在 2019 年新加坡国际商事法庭审理的一起案件中。当事一方的平台公司 Quoine 和平台用户 B2C2 做市商通过算法程序,执行涉及加密货币比特币和以太坊的交易,交易价格根据外部市场信息确定。该案涉及 7 笔交易,案件的焦点在于,Quoine 使用的软件出现缺陷后,导致其以 250 倍的市场汇率执行了价值约 1200 万美元的交易。Quoine 声称这是一个错误,并试图撤销交易以挽回损失。B2C2 认为撤销订单是违约行为,而 Quoine 则辩称依据单方面错误原则,该合同是无效或可撤销的。

在普通法下,如果另一方知道错误,单方面错误可以使合同无效。[②] 如果无法证明对方确实知道错误,但可以证明他或她应该知道,那么根据公平原则,合同可能是可撤销的。[③] 在本案中,

---

① See Faye Fangfei Wang, *Law of Electronic Commercial Transactions: Contemporary Issues in the EU, US and China* (2nd edn, Routledge 2014).

② John Cartwright, 'Unilateral Mistake in the English Courts: Reasserting the Traditional Approach' (2009) *Singapore Journal of Legal Studies* 226.

③ Yeo Tiong Min, 'Unilateral Mistake in Contract: Five Degrees of Fusion of Common Law and Equity' (2004) *Singapore Journal of Legal Studies* 227, 231-33.

至关重要的是法官认定有关计算机程序无法"知道"任何事情:

> 本案中的算法程序是确定性的,它们只做它们被编程要做的事情,没有自己的思想。它们按照预先设定的方式运行。它们不知道为什么要这么做,也不知道导致它们以这种方式运行的外部事件是什么。①

在本案中,知识问题取决于 B2C2 软件的原始程序员,而他不可能知道 Quoine 后来的错误。因此,Quoine 应向 B2C2 支付损害赔偿。②

这一裁决与现行法律相一致,但法官谨慎地局限于本案的事实,指出法律可能需要随着技术的发展而发展——尤其是在未来计算机被认为具有"自主意识"的情况下。③ 然而,他显然认为这是一个渐进的过程,他引用并赞同英国最高法院布里格斯勋爵(Lord Briggs)在前一年作出的一份裁决中发表的相当乐观的声明:"法庭擅长识别企业的管理思想,当需要时,毫无疑问能够为机器人做同样的事情。"④

知识在刑法中也起着一定的作用。另一个关于自主决策的奇特案例是"随机暗网购物者",这是两位瑞士艺术家的创意产物。

---

① B2C2 Ltd v. Quoine Pte Ltd [2019] SGHC (I) 3 (Singapore International Commercial Court), para 208.

② Ibid., paras 210, 221-222。上诉法院维持了这一决定,其中多数意见强调,算法的决策性特征是法院分析本案的核心。参见 Quoine Pte Ltd v. B2C2 Ltd [2020] SGCA (I) 2 (Singapore Court of Appeal), paras 97-128。

③ B2C2 Ltd v. Quoine Pte Ltd [2019] SGHC (I) 3 (Singapore International Commercial Court), para 206.

④ Warner-Lambert Co Ltd v. Generics (UK) Ltd. [2018] UKSC 56, para 165.

这是一个自动在线购物机器人，每周拥有高达 100 美元的比特币购物预算，随机选择并从暗网购买物品邮寄到展览空间。当圣加仑警方注意到这个机器人在互联网未编入索引的部分购买了一包摇头丸时，一个有趣的法律难题产生了。整个展览被扣押，但公诉人后来认定该事件"属于艺术范畴"，并在不起诉的情况下处理了毒品。

在本书第 4 章中，我们将更详细地讨论自主过程的责任问题，而人工智能系统本身是否应承担责任将在第 5 章中讨论。目前值得注意的是，在私营部门，算法过程自主性出现的问题比公共部门要少。

2.3.2　自动化处理

与私营部门一样，许多政府也通过自动化寻求效率。不同之处在于，公共权力的行使通常不仅要求结果的效率，还要求其过程的合法性。

在某些公共机构的决策中，立法明确要求人类决策者的参与。例如，根据英国《税收管理法》，缴税通知可由"委员会官员"签发。① 据此，被控逾期报税而被起诉的纳税人可以其收到的通知是计算机生成的、没有签名甚至没有姓名为由提出异议。而法官则会认为，上述规定的措辞要求该决定由"一个真实的'有血有肉'的官员"作出，而不是由（税务局）作为一个集体机构来作出，也不是计算机化的决策。② 尽管这样的决策本身并非非法，但在这种情况下，至少需要一名可识别的公职人员来作

---

① Taxes Management Act 1970 (England)，s 8.
② *Peter Groves v. The Commissioners for Her Majesty's Revenue & Customs* (*Appeal number*：TC/2017/09024) (15 June 2018) (First-Tier Tribunal Tax Chamber).

出判断。

同样地，在大多数法域，司法职能必须由法庭的人类官员执行。尽管在中国，在线争议解决在小额索赔法庭越来越普遍，预测算法也越来越多地协助法官办案，并且类似的系统也在美国、欧洲和其他地区进行测试，但短期内法官不太可能被机器人取代。① 至于中期，我们将在本书第9章中分析这个问题。

针对某些形式的算法决策，欧洲提供了最强大的保护措施。早在1978年，法国就通过了一项法律，禁止仅基于描述个人"特征或个性"的数据的自动处理的行政和私人决策。② 尽管葡萄牙③和西班牙④也颁布了类似的法律，但直到1995年欧盟《数据保护指令》颁布之前，这些法律仍然是特例。该指令要求欧盟成员国赋予个人在诸如"工作表现、信用状况、可靠性、行为等"领域不受基于自动处理数据评估的决策制约的权利。这种处理只有在个人要求的合同关系中或者采取适当措施保障合法利益（如允许个人"陈述他的观点"）的情况下才被允许。另外一个例外是，通过法律授权的处理同时还包括保障个人合法利益的措施。⑤

2016年欧盟《通用数据保护条例》（GDPR）扩大了自动化处理的可能性，也增加了可用的保护措施。除了合同安排外，明

---

① 参见本书第3章第3.3.2节。

② Loi no 78-17 du 6 janvier 1978 relative à l'informatique, aux fichiers et aux libertés 1978 (France), art 2.

③ Lei no 10/91, Lei da Protecção de Dados Pessoais face à Informática 1991 (Portugal), art 16.

④ Ley Orgánica 5/1992, de 29 de octubre, de regulación del tratamiento automatizado de los datos de carácter personal 1992 (Spain).

⑤ 关于欧盟在个人数据处理和数据自由流动方面对个人的保护，参见欧盟《数据保护指令》第15条。

示同意也可以成为自动化处理的依据。然而，任何一种依据都要求保护利益的措施不仅仅是提供"陈述意见"的机会，还包括获得"人工干预"以质疑决策的权利。①

本书第 6 章将讨论《通用数据保护条例》是否创造了一种"解释权"，即要求说明某个特定决策是如何作出的能力。② 在当前语境下，值得关注的是禁止纯粹的自动化决策的理由以及允许这种自动化决策的情况。

早期的论点侧重于个体对自己的重要决策产生影响的需求，以及防止在面对计算机批准的结果时放弃人类对这些决策的责任。③ 纯粹的自动化处理的保障措施本可以被完全禁止，如要求采用"人在循环之中"的方法，在作出决策之前需要人的干预。然而这是不现实的，因为这实际上会使许多普遍存在的做法变得不合法。这种方法还可能变得无效，因为例行的人类参与批准计算机提示的结果很快就会演变为橡皮图章或"准自动化"。④

总的来说，对于基于合同或明示同意的私人活动和基于法律授权的公共活动，要采取"适当措施"保护个人的权利和利益，要让人们清楚地知道，只要其权利或利益受到侵犯，就会有补救措施，特别是当决策基于不允许的歧视形式时。⑤ 对于基于合同

---

① General Data Protection Regulation 2016/679（GDPR）2016（EU），art 22.
② 参见本书第 6 章第 6.3.1 节。
③ Lee A Bygrave, 'Automated Profiling: Minding the Machine—Article 15 of the EC Data Protection Directive and Automated Profiling' (2001) 17 *Computer Law & Security Review* 17, 18.
④ Ben Wagner, 'Liable, but Not in Control? Ensuring Meaningful Human Agency in Automated Decision-Making Systems' (2019) 11 *Policy & Internet* 104.
⑤ 参见本书第 3 章第 3.2 节。

或同意的决策,则显然与质疑决策的能力以及确保可以向人类提出这样的质疑息息相关。①

算法决策因此构成与自动驾驶汽车的功利主义方法的有趣对比,其中关注的是安全性和问责制的问题,以及对自主武器的规范方法——是否应该允许作出生死决策的伦理问题。在自动化处理的情况下,如果通过保护权利和利益(在某些情况下明确包括将自己的关切提交他人的权利)来确保这些决策的合法性,那么机器作出的决策是可以容忍的。

2.4 自主性的问题

真正的人工智能系统自主性使得人类长期以来的一些基本假设,即法规来源、手段和目的受到质疑。② 然而,正如我们所见,这个问题以不同的方式出现。自动驾驶汽车的出现暴露了道路责任和刑事法律制度中的漏洞,这些是要最终通过修改相关规则来解决的实际问题。这种修改的复杂性不容忽视,但管理风险的目标基本上是无争议的。相比之下,自主武器系统引发了不同的伦理问题——不是机器如何适应我们的法律范式,而是是否允许这样的决策。至于算法决策,至少对于一些影响个人权利和义务的决策,存在将人类作为手段而非目的对待的风险。不同于自动驾驶汽车和自主武器系统,这里的关注点在于没有人类参与的决策的合法性。

---

① Cf Antoni Roig, 'Safeguards for the Right Not to Be Subject to a Decision Based Solely on Automated Processing (Article 22 GDPR)' (2017) 8 (3) *European Journal of Law and Technology*.

② 这包括人类行为的法律建构,如公司法律体系。参见本书第 5 章第 5.1 节。

这三种类型的关注点——实用性、道德性、合法性，是审视、应对人工智能更大挑战所需的监管工具的有用途径，包括那些目前还未能预见的挑战。管理风险、保护道德边界和维护公共权威的合法性提供了三种策略，以确保人工智能的好处不会带来无法接受的代价。

然而，在每种情况下，成本的性质的计算方法是不同的。最小化伤害的实际问题反映了功利主义成本效益分析的计算方法。明确、不可谈判的伦理问题表明了义务伦理学的基于责任的伦理。相比之下，公共权威的合法性涉及政治理论的问题。这里的目标不是调和这些截然不同的讨论，而是强调"自主性"这个表面简单的概念的复杂性。①

"自主性"（autonomy）一词的历史本身就体现了一些复杂性。从词源学角度来看，"autonomy"一词来源于希腊语"autonomía"，由"autos"（自身）和"nomos"（法律）组成；其最初的用途几乎完全局限于政治领域，表示具有独立立法权的市民社区。② 直到18世纪，康德将这个概念应用于人类，提出道德要求一种个体自我治理的形式——作为理性生物，我们自己立定道德法则。③ 如今，"自主性"一词还用于表示个人自主性，意味着一个人根据自己的欲望和价值观行事。④

---

① Cf Mike Ananny, 'Toward an Ethics of Algorithms: Convening, Observation, Probability, and Timeliness' (2016) 41 *Science, Technology, & Human Values* 93.

② John M Cooper, 'Stoic Autonomy' in Ellen Frankel Paul, Fred D Miller, Jr, and Jeffrey Paul (eds), *Autonomy* (CUP 2010) 1.

③ Jerome B Schneewind, *The Invention of Autonomy: A History of Modern Moral Philosophy* (CUP 1997) 483.

④ James Stacey Taylor, 'Autonomy' in Gregory Claeys (ed), *Encyclopedia of Modern Political Thought* (Sage 2013) 57.

这些含义都无法完全对应于此处讨论的人工智能系统。尽管通常以这些系统的"自主性"来描述它们自主决策的能力，但它们并没有在任何有意义的意义上具有"欲望"或"价值观"，也不是康德所理解的"理性"。① 相反，当我们描述人工智能系统具有自主性时，我们通常的意思并不是它"自己"作出决策，而是它在没有人类进一步输入的情况下作出决策。

从这个角度理解，自主性的问题并不是人工智能系统固有的某种神秘特质。相反，这是一系列关于是否、如何以及用什么保障措施将人类的决策权移交给机器的问题。例如，算法决策直接引发了关于公共权力机构在多大程度上可以将其责任外包的问题。自主武器系统导致许多人认为某些决策根本不应该被外包。在自主（即"自动驾驶"）汽车的情况下，优化交通似乎是人工智能可以比人类驾驶员更有效地、最终可能更安全地移动人员和货物的一个领域。

当然，我们还没有达到那个程度。在伊莱恩·赫茨伯格在坦佩市去世近一年后，亚利桑那州亚瓦派县的检察官谢拉·波尔克（Sheila Polk）得出结论，没有证据显示优步负有刑事责任。然而，她同时建议对备用驾驶员瓦斯克斯女士进行进一步调查，瓦斯克斯女士在2020年9月被指控犯有过失杀人罪。沃尔沃XC90本身以及其车载计算机系统已经修复，并且可以推测其仍在路上行驶。

---

① 参见第5章第5.2节对安卓谬误的讨论。

第 3 章
不 透 明 性

埃里克·卢米斯（Eric Loomis）在美国威斯康星州拉克罗斯市（La Crosse）因涉嫌与一起驾车枪击事件有关而被捕时，年仅31岁。2013年2月一个星期一的凌晨2点后不久，一栋房子遭到短管猎枪的两轮射击。尽管没有人受伤，但警察很快就在离案发现场两公里外发现了卢米斯的道奇汽车。一场短暂的汽车追逐战在卢米斯开车撞进雪堆后结束；卢米斯和他的一名乘客改为步行，但他最终被捕并被控以危险驾驶和持有枪支罪。卢米斯否认参与枪击事件，但对逃避警察和驾驶盗窃车辆的轻罪指控认罪。

以上两罪都是卢米斯屡教不改的犯罪行为。卢米斯还是一名登记在册的性侵罪犯，此前因性侵犯罪被定罪，并因非法买卖处方药物而被监外执行。尽管如此，他的律师仍试图为他争取减轻处罚，强调他在寄养家庭度过的童年以及遭受虐待的经历；现在，卢米斯有了一个刚出生的儿子，并正在接受文身师培训。在判决之前，巡回法庭命令使用"替代性制裁犯罪矫正管理剖析软件"(COMPAS)对卢米斯进行风险评估。① 根据被告人的犯罪档案和面谈收集的信息,COMPAS 会生成 1 到 10 的分数,表示被告人再次犯罪的可能性。

伊奎文特(Equivant)公司②开发了 COMPAS 评分程序。虽然评分结果是公开的,但是生成评分的专有算法却是伊奎文特公司的商业机密。无论是卢米斯还是他的律师都无法查看或质疑这些数字是如何得出的,主审法官斯科特·霍恩(Scott Horne)在作出六年监禁判决辩护时引用了卢米斯的 COMPAS 评估分数,指出:"通过 COMPAS 评估,你被认定为对社区构成高风险的个体。"法官随后排除了判处卢米斯缓刑的可能性,"鉴于本次犯罪的严重性以及你的犯罪历史、监外执行的历史以及所使用的风险评估工具,你重新犯罪的风险极高。"③

不透明性是法律决策的对立面。对这些决策的问责通常要求决策者为决策或行为提供令人信服的理由。司法判决尤其重视推理。④ 在普通法传统中,只有"判决的法律依据"(ratio decidendi)才对下级法院具有约束力。向上级法院提起上诉要寻找法律或其在理由中披露的事实应用中的错误。未给出理由本身可能成为上诉的独立理由。⑤ 埃里克·卢米斯的量刑判决似乎违反了这些原则。一审法官依赖 COMPAS 的做法受到学者和民间社会的

---

① COMPAS 的英文全文是 Correctional Offender Management Profiling for Alternative Sanctions。
② 该公司的前身是 Northpointe, Inc。
③ *State v. Loomis*,881 NW 2d 749,755(Wis,2016)。
④ Herbert Wechsler,'Toward Neutral Principles of Constitutional Law'(1959)73 *Harvard Law Review* 1,19-20。
⑤ 当然,这也有例外。例如,陪审团不需要为其司法裁决提供理由说明。参见 Mathilde Cohen,'When Judges Have Reasons Not to Give Reasons: A Comparative Law Approach'(2015)72 *Washington & Lee Law Review* 483。

批评，并成为一项几乎进入美国最高法院的上诉的核心问题。

理解人工智能系统的问题并非新兴挑战。在《黑箱社会：控制金钱和信息的数据法则》一书中，弗兰克·帕斯奎尔（Frank Pasquale）将现代世界算法的作用与柏拉图的"洞穴"隐喻进行了比较，将普通大众视为被困其中的囚徒，只能看到"火焰背后投射出的闪烁影子"；囚徒们无法理解那些创造影像的人的行为，更不用说他们的意图了。① 更朴素地说，有人认为计算机模拟使人类从认识的中心地位上被排挤出去。在人类历史的大部分时间里，知识的拓展意味着人类知识和理解的拓展。超越我们能力的计算方法的出现，引起了保罗·汉弗莱斯（Paul Humphreys）所称的"人类中心主义困境"。② 与人工智能系统中自主性所带来的挑战不同，这些系统日益增加的不透明度不是对人类作为法律行为者核心地位的挑战，而更多是对我们理解和评估行动的能力的挑战，这对有意义的监管至关重要。

在此，"不透明性"（opacity）是指难以理解或解释的性质。就如在COMPAS案例中一样，这可能是因为某些技术具有专有性。为了保护投资，系统内部运作的详细知识可能仅限于拥有它的人。还有一种不透明性形式出现在需要专业技能才能理解的复杂系统中。这些系统随着时间的推移不断发展，不同的利益相关者不断加入，但原则上是可以解释的。

"专有性"（proprietary）或"复杂性"（complex）这两种不透明性形式都不会给法律带来新问题。知识产权法早已认识到保

---

① Frank Pasquale, *The Black Box Society: The Secret Algorithms That Control Money and Information*（Harvard UP 2015）190.
② Paul Humphreys, 'The Philosophical Novelty of Computer Simulation Methods'（2009）169 *Synthese* 615，617.

护人类智慧创造的无形成果及基于合理使用的例外。① 为应对复杂问题，政府和法官经常求助于专家。② 然而，天然不透明的系统则不一样。一些深度学习方法因为算法设计原因而天然具有不透明性，因为它们依赖于通过复杂的机器学习程序进行决策，而不是遵循透明的"决策树"模式作出决策。③

以本书前言中提到的一个例子为例，谷歌的阿尔法狗（AlphaGo）程序员无法解释该程序如何为古老的围棋游戏制定战略，从而在 2016 年击败了人类围棋大师李世石。李世石后来表示，在他们的第一局比赛中，该程序采取了一个没有人类棋手会采用的行动，而这个行动后来被证明为其胜利奠定了基础。④

这种基于成果的合法性——优化目标证明了不确定手段的正当性——在某些领域是适当的。例如，医学科学的进步基于具有严格统计分析的临床试验的成功或失败。如果净效应是积极的，那么一个手术或药物如何实现这些积极成果可能尚不明确，并且

---

① Amanda Levendowski, 'How Copyright Law Can Fix Artificial Intelligence's Implicit Bias Problem' (2018) 93 *Washington Law Review* 579. 关于人工智能创造的产品的知识产权问题，参见本书第 5 章第 5.2.2 节。

② See, eg, Carol AG Jones, *Expert Witnesses: Science, Medicine, and the Practice of Law* (Clarendon Press 1994).

③ 关于机器学习的介绍，请参见本书前言的脚注 2。另参见 Jenna Burrell, 'How the Machine "Thinks": Understanding Opacity in Machine Learning Algorithms' (2016) 3 (1) *Big Data & Society*. 这里使用的"决策树"是指事先指定的一组应当全程适用的静态参数，与通过机器学习开发的"决策树"模式不同。

④ 'Google's AI Beats World Go Champion in First of Five Matches', *BBC News* (9 March 2016). 随后版本的 AlphaGo Zero 只学习了围棋的基本规则，在三天内就掌握了这个古老的游戏。在与击败人类大师李世石的旧版本对战中，新版本以 100 比 0 击败了旧版本。参见 David Silver, *et al*, 'Mastering the Game of Go Without Human Knowledge' (2017) 550 *Nature* 354.

不会阻止它进入市场。① 尽管患者的自主权意味着重要决策由受影响最大的个体作出，但对不良反应的容忍已内置到该过程中，患者在接受治疗时会被告知可能出现的负面和积极结果的风险。② 与此不同，法律决策通常被认为不适合进行统计建模。尽管某些决策可能用证明责任来表示，如概率平衡、排除合理怀疑等，但这些决策应基于个案的个性化评估，而不是基于对大量案例中最可能结果的预测。

因为法律后果，越来越多的文献批评对算法决策的依赖，这种批评主要集中在不透明性方面，强调诸如偏见之类的特定问题，或者试图通过透明度寻求补救措施。然而，不透明性所带来的挑战不仅限于偏见，而且并非所有问题都可以通过呼吁透明度或"可解释性"来解决。本章通过对美国、欧盟以及中国较少研究的创新举措的分析，构建一套由专有、复杂和天然不透明性构成的挑战的分类体系。首先，"黑箱"决策可能导致劣质决策。问责和监督不仅仅是惩罚不良行为的工具，它们还鼓励良好行为。而排除这种可能性会减少发现不良行为的机会，也会减少决策受到有意义审查从而得到改进的机会。其次，不透明的决策实践可能为不可接受的决策提供掩护，如通过不透明的决策掩盖或实质性歧视。举例来说，即使统计模型表明特定种族的人应该被判

---

① Alex John London and Jonathan Kimmelman, 'Why Clinical Translation Cannot Succeed Without Failure' (2015) 4 *eLife* e12844. 特别是对精神疾病的研究，充满了对疾病根本原因和治愈机制的未知不确定性。另参见 Anne Harrington, *Mind Fixers: Psychiatry's Troubled Search for the Biology of Mental Illness* (Norton 2019)。

② 当然，患者会基于他们的病情、病史等获得个性化评估。但是，基于大范围人群进行研究还是通行做法。参见 Omer Gottesman, *et al*, 'Guidelines for Reinforcement Learning in Healthcare' (2019) 25 *Nature Medicine* 16。

更长的监禁期限，法官也不能接受这样的预测，人工智能系统也不应接受。最后，某些决策的合法性取决于决策过程的透明度，而不仅仅是决策本身。司法裁决是最好的例子，但不是唯一的例子。

显然，这种结构呼应了前一章关于自主性的具体挑战：结果质量的问题通过功利主义视角来处理；避免不可接受的决策反映了道义上的关切；而依赖适当的权威和程序则是为了赋予合法性——在这种情况下，合法性的基础不仅在于行为者的身份，还在于推理本身的公开性。

通常认为，通过透明度可以解决这些问题的部分或全部。① 然而，尽管专有不透明性可以通过法院命令处理，复杂的不透明性可以通过求助于专家解决，但天然不透明的系统可能需要新型的"解释"形式，或者接受某些机器生成的决策无法解释的事实。换句话说，某些决策根本不应由机器作出。

3.1 劣质决策

技术可能为了保护投资而变得不透明，同时也能够阻止审查。此类审查可能揭示商业秘密，也可能暴露无能。在最恶劣的情况下，不透明性可为故意操纵结果或阻挠调查提供掩护。例如，大众汽车编写了一个代码，在监管机构测试时进行误导，让人误以为车辆排放低于正常使用。② 优步也设计了一个应用程序版本，通过识别用户行为来判断他们是否为监管机构工作人员，

---

① 参见本书第6章。
② EPA，California Notify Volkswagen of Clean Air Act Violations/Carmaker Allegedly Used Software that Circumvents Emissions Testing for Certain Air Pollutants（US Environmental Protection Agency，18 September 2015）.

以限制他们收集证据的能力。①

　　一个更普遍的问题是，即使是善意的晦涩难懂也可能阻止对数据质量的质疑。在某些情况下，更大的透明度可能揭示使用了多少数据，从而引发隐私方面的担忧。在其他情况下，数据的不完整性可能暴露出来，引发关于过程可靠性或结果可信度的质疑。② 这种"输入垃圾，输出垃圾"的现象可以追溯到第一台计算机。英国通才查尔斯·巴比奇（Charles Babbage）被认为最早提出了数字计算机的设计思想，他在1864年提出了这个问题。他在回忆录中提到，曾有两次被议会成员问及，错误的数据输入差分引擎是否仍可能得出正确的答案。"我无法正确理解这种问题背后的混乱思维，"他评论到。③

　　人类的自满和自动化偏见使得这些问题不再是理论上的问题。随着人类在自动化流程中的参与——概念上"在"或"超过"循环④——被降低到最机械化的程度，接受默认建议的倾向就会增加。⑤ 这可以与前一章讨论的自动驾驶汽车所带来的危险相类比，即在这种情况下，人类"驾驶员"可以放开方向盘，但

---

　　① Leslie Hook，'Uber Used Fake App to Confuse Regulators and Rivals'，*Financial Times* (4 March 2017).
　　② Sandra Wachter and Brent Mittelstadt，'A Right to Reasonable Inferences: Re-thinking Data Protection Law in the Age of Big Data and AI' (2019) *Columbia Business Law Review* 494.
　　③ Charles Babbage，*Passages from the Life of a Philosopher* (Longman 1864) 67.
　　④ 参见本书第2章第2.3节。
　　⑤ Steven PR Rose and Hilary Rose，'"Do not Adjust Your Mind, There Is a Fault in Reality"—Ideology in Neurobiology' (1973) 2 *Cognition* 479, 498-99. 关于锚定效应在判决决定中的更大影响，参见 Birte Enough and Thomas Mussweiler，'Sentencing Under Uncertainty: Anchoring Effects in the Courtroom' (2001) 31 *Journal of Applied Social Psychology* 1535.

需要随时准备好重新掌握控制权。① 这是自满的一个例子。而偏见的产生，则是因为大多数人倾向于相信自动化系统在分析能力上更加优于他们自己。②

与此相关的一个问题是，这类系统也可能为人类代理人提供掩护。例如，加拿大对律师和法官进行的一项调查发现，许多人认为像 COMPAS 这样的软件比主观判断更优秀：尽管风险评估工具并不被认为是对未来行为的特别可靠预测工具，但它们仍然受到青睐，因为使用它们可以将律师和法官本人因其决定的后果而受到指责的风险降到最低。③

解决自满情绪和自动化偏见的问题远远超出了本书所关注的监管挑战。就目前而言，我们只需注意到，它们不应成为逃避狭义上的责任的依据，即相关主体有义务对某项决定作出说明（即使是在事后），或对为了避免作出该决定所造成的伤害承担责任。

像许多技术监管领域一样，欧盟根据其《通用数据保护条例》（GDPR）提供了相对较强的保护措施，明确规定不受自动化处理④的权利不能通过"象征性"的人类参与来规避。对自动化流程的例行接受是不够的；有意义的监督需要具有权威和能力的人来审查决策，包括获取"所有相关数据"权限。⑤

---

① 参见本书第 2 章第 2.1 节。

② Raja Parasuraman and Dietrich Manzey, 'Complacency and Bias in Human Use of Automation: An Attentional Integration' (2010) 52 *Human Factors* 381, 392.

③ Kelly Hannah-Moffat, 'The Uncertainties of Risk Assessment: Partiality, Transparency, and Just Decisions' (2015) 27 *Federal Sentencing Reporter* 244.

④ 参见本书第 2 章第 2.3.2 节。

⑤ Guidelines on Automated Individual Decision-Making and Profiling for the Purposes of Regulation 2016/679 (Article 29 Data Protection Working Party, 17/EN WP251rev.01, 3 October 2017) 20-21.

不透明导致劣质决策的观念在软件开发中由来已久。结合对专有不透明的抵制，这一认识是开放源码运动的核心所在。① 完全开放源码并不是在所有情况下都是适合或可能的，但不应该仅仅为了防止外部审查而限制开放的想法似乎是没有争议的。随着系统变得越来越复杂，输出越来越不容易得到客观评估，这些问题也变得更具有挑战性。

3.2 不可接受的决策

自动化决策的好处之一是，它可以减少人类决策的任意性。对于大量类似的问题，经过适当编程的计算机将提供可预测的、前后一致的答案。人类作出的许多评估决策是基于无意识的群体偏见和直觉反应，而算法则遵循为它们设定的参数。② 然而，自动化决策的优劣取决于所给予的数据和所提出的问题。实际上，算法可能实质性地强化现有的不平等现象——正如我们将看到的，特定决策程序没有人类有意识的偏见，实际上可能对通过反歧视法来纠正这些不平等的尝试产生不良影响。

一个突出的例子是筛选决策。许多行业现在使用人工智能系统简化重复性流程，如审查求职申请、评估信用度、设定保险费、检测欺诈等。这些系统通常依赖于两个独立的算法：筛选算法本身可以从求职申请池中选择候选人或对其进行评估打分，同

---

① Sheen S Levine and Michael J Prietula, 'Open Collaboration for Innovation: Principles and Performance' (2014) 25 *Organization Science* 1287.

② Sharad Goel, *et al*, 'Combatting Police Discrimination in the Age of Big Data' (2017) 20 *New Criminal Law Review* 181. 这在被委托授权和分散决策的系统中特别有用。参见 Katherine J Strandburg, 'Rulemaking and Inscrutable Automated Decision Tools' (2019) 119 *Columbia Law Review* 1851, 1857。

时也可以基于训练算法,利用数据改进筛选算法。

如果使用得当,筛选过程会更高效、一致地对同类情况进行处理。这在二元决策中最为有效,如判断一封电子邮件是否为垃圾邮件或者一个交易是否存在欺诈。使用预先定义的类别(如垃圾邮件、欺诈),给出客观答案——"垃圾邮件"或"欺诈",该答案在大多数评估该决策的人中是可验证的。误报和漏报可标记给训练算法,该算法再反馈给筛选算法,并逐步减少这些错误。

当涉及更有争议的类别,如公平性,或者当算法被用于预测特定个体的未来行为,如他们在某个工作中的表现如何,或者他们是否会再犯罪时,问题就会出现。在某些情况下,结果可能是荒谬的。对一种简历筛选算法的审查发现,在特定公司工作表现的两个最重要因素是被命名为"Jared"和曾在高中参加过曲棍球比赛。① 在其他情况下,依赖算法可能反映或强化歧视性做法。

3.2.1 偏见的产生

偏见至少可以通过两种方式被"习得"。如果公然的偏见影响了用于训练算法的数据,那么这种偏见可能被复制。但是,如果算法被用于基于样本人口进行推断,那么由于训练数据本身、变量选择和加权比重,或者输出结果的解释方式,可能暴露出无意的偏见。② 不同的学者将这种现象与美国公民权利判例中的

---

① Dave Gershgorn,'Robot Indemnity: Companies Are on the Hook if Their Hiring Algorithms Are Biased', *Quartz* (22 October 2018).
② Selena Silva and Martin Kenney, Algorithms, Platforms, and Ethnic Bias: An Integrative Essay (University of California, Berkeley, BRIE Working Paper 2018-3, 2018).

"差别待遇"、故意行为与"差别影响"之间的区别进行比较。① 以亚马逊的简历筛选算法为例,该算法是利用前后十年的历史数据进行训练的,但当程序员发现它"学会"歧视性地对待女性的申请后,不得不将这个算法关闭。②

无意偏见的例子包括一些面部识别软件,这些软件的训练使用了浅色皮肤,因而在识别深色皮肤面孔方面效果较差。③ 当然,使用非代表性数据的问题不仅仅存在于人工智能系统中。一项心理学研究的元分析发现,绝大多数已发表的研究依赖于西方大学生的参与,然后将他们视为全人类的代表。④ 在变量的选择和加权权重方面也可能产生不同的问题。例如,一个表面上中立的指标,如员工的生产力,如果不考虑女性比男性更可能休产假的事实,可能对女性产生不利影响。⑤

或许最大的风险来自对输出结果的解释,这使我们回到诸如COMPAS等风险评估工具的讨论。ProPublica 公司的一份被广泛引用的报告得出结论:COMPAS 在近 2/3 的案件中正确预测了累犯的可能性,但其误报和漏报都对非洲裔美国人产生了偏

---

① *Ricci v. DeStefano*, 557 US 557 (2009). See, eg, Solon Barocas and Andrew D Selbst, 'Big Data's Disparate Impact' (2016) 104 *California Law Review* 671, 694-712.

② Ignacio N Cofone, 'Algorithmic Discrimination Is an Information Problem' (2019) 70 *Hastings Law Journal* 1389, 1397-98.

③ Karl Manheim and Lyric Kaplan, 'Artificial Intelligence: Risks to Privacy and Democracy' (2019) 21 *Yale Journal of Law & Technology* 106, 159.

④ Joseph Henrich, Steven J Heine, and Ara Norenzayan, 'The Weirdest People in the World?' (2010) 33 *Behavioral and Brain Sciences* 61 (标题指的是被调查对象完全来自西方,受过良好教育,生活在工业化、富裕和民主社会)。

⑤ Cf Rafael Lalive, *et al*, 'Parental Leave and Mothers' Careers: The Relative Importance of Job Protection and Cash Benefits' (2014) 81 *Review of Economic Studies* 219.

见。在没有再次犯罪的人中，非洲裔美国人被贴上"高风险"标签的可能性几乎是白人的两倍；而在确实继续犯罪的人中，白人被评定为"低风险"的可能性几乎是非洲裔美国人的两倍。① 但是，这份报告也因过于简化风险评估、故意挑选评估结果和忽略现实中非洲裔美国人更高的监禁率而受到批评。② 同时，该报告还因未承认数据驱动的风险评估已多次被证明优于易受偏见影响的专业人类判断而受到质疑。③

这些争论融入了一部丰富的文献，该文献既捍卫也批评了美国自 20 世纪 70 年代以来的标准化决策：侧重于预防未来犯罪，并与普遍存在的大规模监禁问题以及特别针对非洲裔美国男性的监禁问题密切相关。像 COMPAS 这样的专有且不透明的工具的出现加剧了对这些模型的担忧，其直接原因是自满和自动化偏见，但根本问题是最古老的逻辑谬误之一："与此故因此"（*Cum hoc ergo propter hoc*）。换句话说，就是统计学入门教材中所表述的：关联非因果。

风险评估最初采用了回归模型。统计学中的回归是一种工具，它可以确定一组对特定结果有预测作用的变量。模型检验与选择能够确定最佳权重，以便最佳地预测评估结果。④ 例如，

---

① Julia Angwin, *et al*, 'Machine Bias: There's Software Used Across the Country to Predict Future Criminals. And It's Biased Against Blacks', *ProPublica* (23 May 2016).

② Anthony W Flores, Kristin Bechtel, and Christopher T Lowenkamp, 'False Positives, False Negatives, and False Analyses: A Rejoinder to "Machine Bias: There's Software Used Across the Country to Predict Future Criminals. And It's Biased Against Blacks"' (2016) 80 (2) *Federal Probation* 38.

③ Alexandra Chouldechova, 'Fair Prediction with Disparate Impact: A Study of Bias in Recidivism Prediction Instruments' (2017) 5 *Big Data* 153.

④ Andrew Gelman and Jennifer Hill, *Data Analysis Using Regression and Multilevel/Hierarchical Models* (CUP 2007).

COMPAS的"暴力再犯风险评分"是通过一个方程计算出来的，该方程将暴力史和违法纪录与年龄、首次被捕年龄和教育程度进行权衡并设定比重。正如该公司的手册所指出的，这与汽车保险公司估计客户发生事故风险的方式相似。① 然而，随着人工智能系统变得更加复杂并在影响个人权利和义务的决策中发挥更大作用，算法的不透明性以及由此引发的批评预示着未来的挑战将层出不穷。

人类监督下的机器学习技术体现了回归模型的许多问题，因为机器学习的目标是进行预测。尽管一些研究表明，机器学习比传统统计方法更准确，但这是以牺牲透明度为代价的。② 不透明性成为一个问题，因为这些技术的黑箱特性既模糊了决策过程，同时也在某些用户心中至少制造了更高级别和可靠性的幻觉。

该领域的学者们仍在争论，在改进风险评估模型的准确性时，社会、经济和心理因素需要考虑到何种程度。③ 一个更为根本的挑战，则首先质疑使用这些模型的目的。

像COMPAS这样的风险评估系统，是使用历史数据来预测未来的行为模式。对此有两个基本的反对意见：第一，惩罚通常由国家对过去已经犯下的罪行实施，而不是对未来可能犯下的罪

---

① A Practitioner's Guide to COMPAS Core (Northpointe, 2015) 29.
② Grant Duwe and KiDeuk Kim, 'Sacrificing Accuracy for Transparency in Recidivism Risk Assessment: The Impact of Classification Method on Predictive Performance' (2016) 1 *Corrections* 155.
③ See, eg, Kelly Hannah-Moffat, 'Sacrosanct or Flawed: Risk, Accountability and Gender-responsive Penal Politics' (2011) 22 *Current Issues in Criminal Justice* 193; Seth J Prins and Adam Reich, 'Can We Avoid Reductionism in Risk Reduction?' (2018) 22 *Theoretical Criminology* 258. 例如，心理健康往往被排除在外，以便风险评估模型可以更加关注可测量和变化显著的协变量。

行实施。尽管在选择可能的刑罚范围或考虑提前释放时，会适当地考虑当事人再犯的可能性，但在法律秩序良好的国家，真正的预防性拘留是极为少见的。① 第二，将汇总的一般统计数据套用于个体，正是我们一直批评的"刻板印象"。② 一个人来自犯罪率较高的社区，虽然可能让他或她更有可能犯罪，但这不能成为预先对他或她进行惩罚的依据。③

我们可以从警方使用个人身份识别数据的情况中找到有趣的类比。如果国家强制机关依赖于从过去被捕或被定罪的人那里收集的指纹和DNA样本，就会显著增加将来使用这些身份识别数据、针对特定群体的可能性，进而使歧视性做法根深蒂固。④ 随着面部识别技术的出现，关于它是否以及如何应该用于日常执法引发了广泛的争论。有限的用于识别目的的使用可能更为大众所接受，但依赖于犯罪嫌疑人的身份照片将复现指纹和DNA所面临的问题。为此，一个有争议的改进建议是，警方不得访问任何个人的生物识别数据，或者必须结合所有人的数据建立犯罪预防模型。⑤

---

① Hallie Ludsin, *Preventive Detention and the Democratic State* (CUP 2016).

② Oscar H Gandy, Jr, 'Engaging Rational Discrimination: Exploring Reasons for Placing Regulatory Constraints on Decision Support Systems' (2010) 12 *Ethics and Information Technology* 29, 33-34.

③ 还有一种方法是，寻求不是预测未来行为而是塑造未来行为的方法。因果推断就是这样一种方法，其目标不是将像埃里克·卢米斯这样的罪犯归类为高风险群体中，而是通过个性化评估和实验来最小化他们重新犯罪的风险。参见 Guido W Imbens and Donald B Rubin, *Causal Inference for Statistics, Social, and Biomedical Sciences: An Introduction* (CUP 2015).

④ Simon Chesterman, *One Nation Under Surveillance: A New Social Contract to Defend Freedom Without Sacrificing Liberty* (OUP 2011) 257-58.

⑤ Barry Friedman and Andrew Guthrie Ferguson, 'Here's a Way Forward on Facial Recognition', *New York Times* (31 October 2019).

3.2.2 偏见的消除

关于算法偏见问题的另一种解决方法是使它们在特定因素上"去偏见化"。这利用了算法相对于人类的优势之一：它们的决策过程可以成为实验的对象。比如，一个雇主在决定雇佣男性而非女性时，不太可能承认这一特定决策受到偏见的影响（实际上可能是无意识的偏见）。但对于算法，却可以通过调整参数来重复计算，以检查在不同情景下是否会得出不同的结果。① 然而，只有在仅有审计员或外部测试人员可以接触到算法本身的情况下（即在算法是透明的情况下），算法才能被改进优化。②

在前面讨论的案例里，埃里克·卢米斯在对量刑决定的上诉中提出的理由之一便是，COMPAS 在考虑犯罪者再犯风险时将性别因素纳入了考量。他承认，一般而言，男性的再犯率和暴力犯罪率是高于女性的，但他认为，将这一统计证据应用于他个人的案件，是侵犯了他的正当程序权利。法院援引了关于这个问题的一些文献并得出结论称，COMPAS 纳入性别因素"提高了准确性，最终使包括被告在内的司法系统受益"。法院认为，无论如何，卢米斯并未能证明性别构成法院对其量刑的一个因素。此外，正如法院之前指出的，算法的专有性质意味着关于性别是否被纳入考虑仍存在一定的不确定性。③

---

① Jon Kleinberg, *et al*,'Discrimination in the Age of Algorithms'(2018) 10 *Journal of Legal Analysis* 113. See also Amit Datta, Michael Carl Tschantz, and Anupam Datta,'Automated Experiments on Ad Privacy Settings: A Tale of Opacity, Choice, and Discrimination'(2015)(1)*Proceedings on Privacy Enhancing Technologies* 92.
② 参见本书第 6 章第 6.2.2（b）节。
③ *State v. Loomis*, 881 NW 2d 765-67 (Wis, 2016).

3.3 不合法决策

因此,不透明性可能导致劣质决策或掩盖不可接受的决策。这些问题需要减轻或纠正。然而,在第三类决策过程中,不透明性成为问题,因为此类决策过程本身的透明度可能与结果的有效性或适当性同样重要。

公共行为者的理性决策通常被认为是现代自由主义观念的基础。① 许多批评算法决策的文献在很大程度上集中关注决策的质量,包括由于数据不完整或损坏、缺乏监督相关系统的能力或受行业监管俘获而导致的劣质决策的可能性。② 此外,一些文献还批评强调这些决策的歧视性影响或不被允许的偏见。③

这些论点重述了本章前面部分讨论的问题。在此,我们关注的是两类决策,其中不透明性本身(而不是它可能掩盖的事物)会损害合法性。第一类是公共行为者的决策,其权威与可能被不透明性破坏的民主过程相联系。第二类是法院的裁决,其对法治的要求依赖于为广大社会所理解的公正理由:既要伸张正义,也要被认为伸张了正义。

---

① See, eg, John Rawls, *Political Liberalism* (Columbia UP 1996); Jeremy Waldron, 'Theoretical Foundations of Liberalism' (1987) 37 (147) *The Philosophical Quarterly* 127.

② Cf John Finch, Susi Geiger, and Emma Reid, 'Captured by Technology? How Material Agency Sustains Interaction Between Regulators and Industry Actors' (2017) 46 *Research Policy* 160. 另参见本书第8章第8.1.2节。

③ Philipp Hacker and Bilyana Petkova, 'Reining in the Big Promise of Big Data: Transparency, Inequality, and New Regulatory Frontiers' (2017) 15 *Northwestern Journal of Technology and Intellectual Property* 1, 7-9.

3.3.1 公共决策

美国社会学家爱德华·希尔斯（Edward Shils）在麦卡锡听证会后不久于20世纪50年代撰文，① 认为自由民主取决于保护个人隐私，并剥夺政府的隐私。事实上，随后的几十年见证了相反的情况发生：个人隐私消失，而政府变得越来越神秘。虽然决策不透明并不等同于保密性，但它具有类似的负面效果：两者都削弱了对决策者的问责可能性。事实上，决策不透明性比保密性更糟糕，因为就保密性而言，至少某些政府部门可以获取部分机密活动的详细信息，即使这些信息没有公之于众。实际上，在多个案例中，公共机构甚至将使用不透明算法本身作为机密。

这种不透明性既适用于微观，也适用于宏观层面。在微观层面上，算法的开发涉及许多既有政治性又有技术性的决策。参数的微调可能包括支持某一利益集团而损害另一利益集团的决定，或者影响公共资源分配的决定。② 对于误报和漏报的处理决定了谁承担错误的风险，许多实例表明，政府实际上将这种风险转嫁给了最弱势的公民，涉及福利津贴、缓刑决定和寄养抚养等领域。③

在美国，依据《宪法》第十四修正案规定的正当程序保护，一

---

① Edward A Shils, *The Torment of Secrecy: The Background and Consequences of American Security Policies* (Heinemann 1956) 21-25.
② Brent Daniel Mittelstadt, et al, 'The Ethics of Algorithms: Mapping the Debate' (2016) 3 (2) *Big Data & Society*.
③ See, eg, Jason Parkin, 'Adaptable Due Process' (2012) 160 *University of Pennsylvania Law Review* 1309, 1357-58 (welfare benefits); Robert Brauneis and Ellen P Goodman, 'Algorithmic Transparency for the Smart City' (2018) 20 *Yale Journal of Law & Technology* 103, 120 (probation decisions); Virginia Eubanks, *Automating Inequality: How High-Tech Tools Profile, Police, and Punish the Poor* (St Martin's 2017) 144-55 (foster care).

些诉讼成功地挑战了与停止福利和解雇公立学校教师有关的不透明政府决定。① 欧盟的保护措施更为严格，但这些措施通常与防止"自动处理"的保障措施相挂钩，而不是与不透明决策本身相关。②

欧盟 1995 年《数据保护指令》赋予个人获取有关其个人数据是否以及如何被处理的信息的权利，包括获得"了解自动处理所涉及的算法逻辑"的权利。③ 该规定适用于公共和私营部门的决策，但似乎至今尚未引起重大争议或诉讼。2016 年通过的《通用数据保护条例》（GDPR）扩展了这一权利，包括"与自动处理所涉及的算法逻辑以及此类自动处理的重要性和预期后果的有意义的信息"的访问权。④

GDPR 扩展的新规定，与公众对许多算法过程不透明性的关注日益增长相吻合。这是否相当于信息主体的"解释权"（right to explanation）将在本书第 6 章中进一步讨论。⑤ 这里特别值得

---

① Sarah Valentine, 'Impoverished Algorithms: Misguided Governments, Flawed Technologies, and Social Control' (2019) 46 *Fordham Urban Law Journal* 364, 413-19.

② European Ethical Charter on the Use of Artificial Intelligence in Judicial Systems and Their Environment (European Commission for the Efficiency of Justice (CEPEJ), 4 December 2018). 参见本书第 2 章第 2.3 节。Cf the separate 'right to good administration' recognized under EU law: Damian Chalmers, Gareth Davies, and Giorgio Monti, *European Union Law: Text and Materials* (4th edn, CUP 2019) 377-79.

③ Directive 95/46/EC of the European Parliament and of the Council of 24 October 1995 on the protection of individuals with regard to the processing of personal data and on the free movement of such data [欧盟《数据保护指令》第 12 (a) 条].

④ General Data Protection Regulation 2016/679 (GDPR) 2016 (EU), art 15 (1) (h).

⑤ 参见本书第 6 章第 6.3.1 节。

讨论的是"有意义"（meaningful）一词的含义。① 在这个问题上，欧盟负责这一主题的工作小组似乎采取了一种较为狭义的解释，主张该条款是要求为信息主体提供"关于处理的预期后果的信息，而不是对特定决策的解释"。② 考虑到复杂性带来的困难，提供信息的人按规定需要提供"简单的方法，以告诉信息主体其作出自动决策时背后的理由或所依赖的标准"，这不需要包括对"所使用的算法的复杂解释"或者算法本身的披露。③

另一个制约因素是解释权（如果存在的话）受限于个人数据不受自动处理权的限制。也就是说，GDPR限制了自主决策过程（包括那些不透明的过程），但并不直接适用于人类受到可能本身不透明的算法支持的决策过程。④ GDPR还允许必要时在合同、法律授权或基于主体"明示同意"的情况下进行自动处理。⑤ 这些权利的最终限制以例外形式出现。一个附录指出，访问权不应对"他人的权利或自由产生不利影响，包括商业秘密或知识产权，特别是保护软件的版权"⑥。此外，尽管GDPR适用于公共和

---

① Michael Veale and Lilian Edwards, 'Clarity, Surprises, and Further Questions in the Article 29 Working Party Draft Guidance on Automated Decision-Making and Profiling' (2018) 34 *Computer Law & Security Review* 398, 399-400.

② Guidelines on Automated Individual Decision-Making and Profiling for the Purposes of Regulation 2016/679 (Article 29 Data Protection Working Party, 17/EN WP251rev.01, 3 October 2017) 27 (emphasis in original).

③ Ibid., 25.

④ Lilian Edwards and Michael Veale, 'Enslaving the Algorithm: From a "Right to an Explanation" to a "Right to Better Decisions"?' (2018) 16 (3) *IEEE Security & Privacy* 46, 47. Guidelines on Automated Individual Decision-Making and Profiling for the Purposes of Regulation 2016/679 (Article 29 Data Protection Working Party, 17/EN WP251rev.01, 3 October 2017) 20-21.

⑤ GDPR, art 22 (2).

⑥ Ibid., recital 63.

私营部门的决策,但它明确排除了为预防、调查和起诉刑事犯罪而进行的数据处理。①

实际上,传统行政法或许是一种更有效的补救路径。例如,如果决策者不被允许将决策委托给第三方,他/她也不应该将其委托给人工智能系统;如果决策者被赋予自由裁量权,那么这种自由裁量权不应被非法限制。尽管决策者并不负有对所有决策给出理由的一般义务,但在法律规定或涉及司法、类司法性质的情况下,决策者往往负有给出理由的义务。如果使用人工智能系统使得决策者无法给出理由,司法审查可能认定该决策是不合理的,或者基于其无法证明是否考虑了关键因素以及未考虑非关键因素而认定其决策是可指摘的。②

然而,一个残留问题是不透明性的"自相矛盾":质疑决策的努力受到可能构成诉讼基础的不透明性的阻碍——人们不知道他们不知道什么。无论如何,如果是依赖于公民个体主张透明性,那就只有最有动力的人才会这样不辞辛苦。那么,解释权可能最终会像数据保护法中的同意原则一样,成为理论合法性的纸面基础,但在实践中不受平等者之间任何有意义的协议的约束。③

3.3.2 法院

试图限制公共机构不透明决策的努力在其有效性上受到诸多

---

① GDPR,art 2 (2) (d).

② Jennifer Cobbe, 'Administrative Law and the Machines of Government: Judicial Review of Automated Public-Sector Decision-Making' (2019) 39 *Legal Studies* 636, 650-51. Cf Danielle Keats Citron, 'Technological Due Process' (2008) 85 *Washington University Law Review* 1249.

③ Simon Chesterman, 'Introduction' in Simon Chesterman (ed), *Data Protection Law in Singapore: Privacy and Sovereignty in an Interconnected World* (2nd edn, Academy Publishing 2018) at 2-3.

限制，部分原因是许多公共决策的默认机制是，仅在被询问时相关机构才会给出理由。法院及其他司法机构则与此不同，出于程序正义要求，司法机构通常必须提供决策理由。

这并不是说法院从不依赖于黑箱决策。陪审团就是最突出的例子。在使用陪审团的法域，陪审员在民事和刑事案件中作出裁决时通常无须提供理由。然而，陪审团应该在法官的指导下进行操作，如果法官认为没有"合理"的陪审团会作出类似的决定，则其有权无视陪审团的决定。①

随着刑事司法系统对技术的依赖日益增加，这些问题将进一步加剧。从预测性警务模型到审判中使用的法医软件程序，受商业秘密保护的算法现已被应用于刑事诉讼的各个阶段。② 一个应对方法是在刑事审判中废除商业秘密特权，从根本上迫使相关公司披露其得出结论的过程。③ 另一个方法是，有些法庭已经完全排除那些透明度受到怀疑的证据的使用。④ 鉴于法官在算法使用、评估方面所受到的内外压力，以及他们在评估这些工具方面相对缺乏经验，这些措施的有效性尚不明确。

关于西方法院未来的一个愿景，可能可以从中国法律体系对技术的广泛应用中看出。中国对包括社会信用体系在内的事项进行自动监控，这已经有了大量的报道。但较少有人注意到的是，

---

① Cf Jason Iuliano, 'Jury Voting Paradoxes' (2014) 113 *Michigan Law Review* 405.

② Rashida Richardson, Jason M Schultz, and Kate Crawford, 'Dirty Data, Bad Predictions: How Civil Rights Violations Impact Police Data, Predictive Policing Systems, and Justice' (2019) 94 *New York University Law Review* 192.

③ Rebecca Wexler, 'Life, Liberty, and Trade Secrets: Intellectual Property in the Criminal Justice System' (2018) 70 *Stanford Law Review* 1343.

④ *People v. Fortin*, 218 Cal Rptr 3d 867 (California Court of Appeals, 2017).

算法现在是支持中国法律体系的方式，而对于管理这些问题的适当检查和平衡的不确定性则导致一些制衡措施则略显仓促。例如，2019年法国（再次成为对算法说"不"的非典型国家）通过了一项特别法，明确禁止公开对特定法官如何裁决案件的分析数据，违犯者可被判入狱监禁。据报道，这项法律的出台，是因为排除了另外一种替代方案，即公布判决时根本不提及法官姓名。①

在其他地方，法官们也在继续摸索。实际上，人们很难对算法在法庭中的使用提出异议。正如埃里克·卢米斯所经历的。卢米斯以其正当程序权利受到侵犯为由，对巡回法庭的判决提出上诉，却未能成功。威斯康星州最高法院承认被告人有权根据准确信息被量刑，但被告人有机会核实COMPAS计算分数时所给的答案就足够满足程序正义的要求了。至于分数本身是如何得出的，霍恩法官也正如卢米斯那样无法知晓，巡回法庭也并未将其作为判决的唯一依据。②

威斯康星州最高法院最终维持了这一判决，认为巡回法院的COMPAS分数是具有其他独立因素支持的，并且COMPAS分数并未"决定性地"影响法院对被告人的量刑。然而，该最高法院进一步表示了对此类软件使用的保留意见，要求今后使用时必须附有关于软件专有性质和准确性局限的"书面说明"。③ 首席大法官罗根萨克（Roggensack）还发表了一项赞同意见，澄清法院在量刑时可以考虑COMPAS这样的工具，但不能依赖它们。另一位法官则认为应该进一步强调，在量刑决定中应包括解释其局限

---

① Loi no 2019-222 du 23 mars 2019 de programmation 2018-2022 et de réforme pour la justice 2019（France），art 33；'France Bans Judge Analytics, 5 Years In Prison For Rule Breakers'，*Artificial Lawyer*（4 June 2019）.

② *State v. Loomis*，881 NW 2d 760-61（Wis，2016）.

③ Ibid.，753-64.

性的记录，作为"巡回法院在量刑时行使自由裁量权的长期基本要求"的一部分。① 美国最高法院拒绝受理该案的上诉。②

3.4　不透明性带来的问题

两个多世纪以前，杰里米·边沁（Jeremy Bentham）写道："'公开'是正义的灵魂……它使审判者在审判时也受到审判。"③ 司法裁决是一个明确需要限制使用不透明人工智能系统的领域的典型场景，但即使在司法场景，我们也看到了"算法渗透"。正如本章所展示的，计算方法已经在广泛的决策过程中提高了效率和优化了结果，虽然代价不菲。在某些情况下，这种利弊取舍是值得的。当算法输出的结果是合法的情况下，即使算法本身具有一定的不透明性，这也是可以被容忍的。然而，在选择使用具有不透明性的算法系统时，人们应当对其缺陷是知情的，并且选择行为是自主的，即这种选择应当充分考虑不透明性所带来的风险。

对这种不透明性的监管反应一直不一致，这在许多新技术中往往如此。④ 欧洲限制自动处理的努力显然更加重视有害的社会后果，而在中国看来这种后果并没有那么严重。美国预测性量刑的实践已充分说明，要限制一项在实际上已经很普遍的技术尤为困难。

---

① *State v. Loomis*，881 NW 2d 775（Wis，2016）.

② Certiorari denied，582 US（26 June 2017）（No 16-6387）.

③ Jeremy Bentham，'Draught for the Organization of Judicial Establishments (1790)' in John Bowring（ed），*The Works of Jeremy Bentham*（William Tait 1843）vol. 4，285 at 316.

④ 参见本书第 7 章第 7.2 节。

通常认为，不透明性的补救措施是透明度。然而，本章认为，不透明性问题应从三个不同的方面来分析：这类决策可能是劣质的，它们可能掩盖了不允许的偏见，或者它们仅仅因为不透明性就可能是非法的。每一方面的问题都需要不同的补救措施。

通过更严格的测试和验证可以改进劣质决策。成功决策的衡量标准在于这些决策的质量，是从功利主义角度进行成本效益分析来衡量的。相比之下，更清晰地了解算法如何以及为何被使用，可以极大地避免偏见。算法的目标不应该仅仅是优化决策，而应该适当地权衡社会和文化规范，并通过严格的审查确保这些社会与文化规范没有被侵蚀。① 就这一语境而言，成功决策的内涵更为复杂，因为反歧视的法律规范很少提供诸如关于允许算法控制致命武器的提案相媲美的明确界限。②

就第三个方面来说，对算法决策进行解释是程序合法性的要求，尤其适用于公共权力机关在涉及个人权利和义务的决策的情况。在某些情况下，无法解释决策是如何作出的，就相当于将决策本身不恰当地委托给了第三方。在这里，决策成功与否最直接地取决于是否完善人工智能系统的透明性和可解释性，以便对那些人类决策者进行监督和追责。

在埃里克·卢米斯上诉案中，代表威斯康星州政府的助理总检察长实际上质疑了这一信条的重要性。她认为："我们不知道

---

① 有学者据此进一步认为，这些可以服务于促进社会进步的目的——"算法肯定行动"。参见 Anupam Chander, 'The Racist Algorithm?' (2017) 115 *Michigan Law Review* 1023，1039-45。

② 参见本书第 2 章第 2.2 节。

法官的想法；这也是一个黑盒子。"① 至于卢米斯先生本人，他在 2019 年 8 月服满六年刑期，从杰克逊惩教所（Jackson Correctional Institution）获释。至少根据 COMPAS 的评估，他很有可能再次入狱。

---

① Jason Tashea, 'Risk-Assessment Algorithms Challenged in Bail, Sentencing and Parole Decisions', *American Bar Association Journal* (1 March 2017) (quoting Christine Remington).

PART TWO
第Ⅱ部分

监管人工智能的工具

第 4 章

法 律 责 任

　　法莱兹（Falaise）是法国诺曼底地区一个约有八千人口的小市镇，以征服者威廉的出生地而闻名。在这位最著名的英格兰第一位诺曼国王确立自己地位的三个世纪后，法莱兹成为一场骇人听闻的谋杀案的审判地。

　　琼内特·雪·毛克斯（Jonnet le Maux）三个月大的儿子在死后被残忍地肢解，成千上万的人前来观看"杀手"为其罪行受到制裁。审判过程很简短，"杀手"被判绞刑，但在行刑前，作为"杀手"的母猪的头和腿部已被刀割得七零八落。观众中有贵族和淑女、猎人和农民、老人和小孩，这一幕被记录在圣三一教堂穹顶的壁画上："囚犯"身穿不合身的新衣服在骑马的武装人员陪伴下出现，刽子手戴着一双新手套，以免因即将开始的可怕的任务而承担罪责，这是对报复原则的一种相当字面的应用——"以眼还眼、以牙还牙"（lex talionis）。[①]

　　19世纪，一场过于热情的粉刷使这幅壁画消失不见。但是，

[①] Hampton L Carson, 'The Trial of Animals and Insects: A Little Known Chapter of Mediæval Jurisprudence' (1917) 56 *Proceedings of the American Philosophical Society* 410.

刽子手保留了与此次行刑相关的收据，日期为 1386 年 1 月 9 日，内容为：手套十索尔，并额外支付十索尔作为他"绞死一头三岁左右的母猪"的报酬以及在法莱兹的法庭上行刑后拖曳的劳苦。①

在中世纪欧洲，对动物（尤其是猪）进行审判以追究其犯罪责任是相当普遍的现象。现代法庭的传统在这一时期仍在不断发展，但有时这些传统也适用于动物：配备律师、证人，甚至偶尔会有无罪的裁决。人们在家养动物和野生动物之间进行了必要的区分。虽然猪或牛可能被传唤到法庭，但对于昆虫或害虫来说，这是不现实的。法国律师巴塞洛缪·德·查塞纽（Barthélemy de Chasseneuz）因在 1508 年为奥图的老鼠辩护而成名，他为老鼠未能出庭找了一个借口：老鼠要面临漫长而艰难的旅程，而且由于猫这种致命敌人的普遍存在，这个旅程变得更加危险。②

我们可能把这些做法当作迷信加以轻视，但其中所体现的拟人化表明了审判的基本功能：对过错追究责任，否则罪恶将不会受到惩罚。

由第一部分的讨论可知，规范人工智能系统的一个重大挑战是其速度、自主性和不透明性可能导致超出现有公共控制体系范畴的不良损害。本部分将探讨应对这些损害的可用工具。从最高层次的一般性概括来看，针对第一部分中提出的问题的解决方案可以分为三大类。第一，许多活动可以通过运用现有或修改后的规范并追究传统法律主体责任来进行监管。例如，对自动驾驶汽车造成的民事损害承担责任挑战了侵权法的界限；某些活动（如

---

① EP Evans, *The Criminal Prosecution and Capital Punishment of Animals* (EP Dutton 1906) 335.

② Esther Cohen, 'Law, Folklore, and Animal Lore' (1986) 110 *Past & Present* 6, 14.

高频交易）可能需要放慢速度。但是，其底层原则是正确的。第二，人工智能系统的自主性增强最终将使其行为无法归因于传统法律主体，应赋予它们某种独立的法律地位。第三，要追究某个人或机器本身的责任，就要特别规定透明度或"可解释性"，以使相关的监管制度有效。

本章及接下来的两章将考虑这些命题及其局限性。然而，理解如何进行监管可能不如理解为什么进行监管重要。正如法莱兹母猪杀人案审判故事所示，对正义的渴望根深蒂固。与古希腊人对未受惩罚的谋杀行为会释放复仇女神的恐惧类似，中世纪的教会认为，一只杀人的动物可能传播恶魔附身。对人工智能系统造成伤害却可能免受惩罚的担忧，充斥在许多反乌托邦文学作品中，并引发了关于如何防止这种现象的诸多学术辩论。然而，从本书第一部分的讨论中可以看出，这些模糊的担忧可以通过三个独立的视角更清晰地审视，这三个视角为本章提供了进一步分析的结构框架。

首先，它从分配责任的实际问题入手，即以合理管理风险的方式分配责任。自动驾驶汽车是最显著但远非唯一需要以这种方式进行监管的人工智能系统的例子。这种功利主义视角适应现有的归因规则，并考虑了将产品责任应用于自主行为者的新途径。当人工智能系统从智能设备转向众多在线服务时，这种方法的局限性将变得明显，其有效性将取决于保险在将不可避免的风险分摊给受益者方面发挥的作用。其次，我们转向共同的道德要求下需要人类行为者负责的情况。战争中的指挥责任和更普遍的不可委托职责是道德原则要求确定的人应该为某些类型的伤害负责的情境，即使他们没有亲自参与决策或行动本身。最后，有些公共职能根本不应该外包，因为它们的合法性要求它们不仅仅是可归因于人类，而且实际上是由人类执行的。这些本质上属于政府职能的工作可能受到人工智能系统的启发，但决不能由它们来执行。

这种三分法——实用性、道德性、合法性，与本书第 2 章中讨论的不同自主水平大致相对应，即人在循环之中、人在循环之上、人在循环之外。① 然而，这里并不表示自主性不断升级，而是表示在不同行为领域允许的代表性限制以及其对风险管理、职责不得委托和应保持为政府固有职能的影响。

4.1 风险管控

与人工智能系统相关的风险管理在很大程度上是由开发和维护这些系统的关键行为者进行的。行业以及政府和政府间组织可以制定硬性或软性的规范来设定行为标准。② 但是，出现问题时该怎么办？本节将探讨对于过失行为或在产品责任制度下可能采取的措施，并讨论保险在其中可以发挥的作用及其应有的地位。

4.1.1 过失行为

正如在本书第 2 章关于自动驾驶汽车的讨论中所提到的，民事责任的基本规则可以涵盖许多由人工智能系统引起的潜在损害。③ 在普通法传统中，过失侵权中使用的概念，如注意义务、违约和因果关系等，都是为了适应新的情况而设计的，判例法也随着科学进步和新技术的发展而不断发展。④ 当无法将有害行为

---

① 参见本书第 2 章第 2.3 节。
② 参见本书第 7 章。
③ 参见本书第 2 章第 2.1.1 节。
④ Jonathan Morgan, 'Torts and Technology' in Roger Brownsword, Eloise Scotford, and Karen Yeung (eds), *The Oxford Handbook of Law, Regulation, and Technology* (OUP 2017) 522.

归咎于可识别的人，或者当损害与行为人之间关系过于疏远，不能说该人对受害方负有注意义务时，问题就会出现。违反这一义务涉及一系列独立的问题，包括随着技术的进步是否应该将标准提高到超出"理性人"的预期。在因果关系方面，在某些情况下，人工智能系统可能将错误行为的后果放大到无法预见的程度，或者可能构成它们自己的干预行为。

就负有责任的人而言，假设的过失诉讼可能针对人工智能系统的所有者、操作者或制造商。然而，随着这些系统变得越来越复杂和普及，识别这样的人可能存在实际困难。一些专业机构建议，对于超过一定复杂度的人工智能系统建立统一的注册登记制度，"以便可以找到谁应承担法律责任"。[1] 这种方法对于具有实体存在的机器人可能是有效的，但随着人工智能系统转向在线，并且具备改变自身和创建新系统的能力，对其法律责任追溯到传统的自然人或法人将变得更加困难。[2]

即使有可能确定所有者、运营者或制造商，由于人工智能系统日益增长的自主性，确立法律责任也会变得日益复杂。因此，一些学者转向研究"代理"概念。根据该概念，当代理人在其实际或明示权限范围内行事时，委托人可能需要承担其行为的责任。[3] 尽管这种类比直观上具有吸引力，但它似乎是基于计算机

---

[1] Ethically Aligned Design: A Vision for Prioritizing Human Well-being with Autonomous and Intelligent Systems (IEEE, 2019) 30. Cf Report of the Committee on Legal Affairs with Recommendations to the Commission on Civil Law Rules on Robotics (European Parliament, A8-0005/2017, 2017) 20.

[2] 参见本书第 8 章第 8.2.2（b）节。

[3] Ugo Pagallo, *The Laws of Robots: Crimes, Contracts, and Torts* (Springer 2013) 37-43; David C Vladeck, 'Machines Without Principals: Liability Rules and Artificial Intelligence' (2014) 89 *Washington Law Review* 117. See generally Roderick Munday, *Agency: Law and Principles* (3rd edn, OUP 2016).

科学家和律师对"代理人"一词含义的混淆。对前者而言，软件代理是计算机程序的一个子集。虽然其精确定义还存在争议，但其通常强调具有一定程度的独立行动能力。① 在当今的术语中，许多软件代理被称为"机器人"。相比之下，在法律上，"代理"是通过与委托人的关系来定义的，代理人作为自然人或法人的基本法律能力是被假定的。② 因此，除非人工智能系统获得某种形式的人格，否则它们无法在法律意义上充当代理人。

乌戈·帕加洛（Ugo Pagallo）等人认为，这种保守立场未能在使用人工智能系统的人以及与他们交易的各方之间适当地分配风险。这一观点还认为，建立一个更广泛的代理关系将能更好地反映人工智能系统在处理我们事务中的作用，同时保留追究责任可能性，又不至于让用户因其"机器人的决策而破产"。通过类比罗马法下奴隶的有限权利，巧妙地解决人工智能系统法律人格的难题。③

然而，在人工智能系统的速度、自主性和不透明性等问题变得棘手的地方，代理关系就不再有用了。一般意义上，委托人不对超出其实际或明示权限的代理行为承担责任；类似地，在英国法下的替代责任的多样语境中，雇主对员工雇佣过程之外的行为

---

① See, eg, Hyacinth S Nwana, 'Software Agents: An Overview' (1996) 21 *Knowledge Engineering Review* 205; Stan Franklin and Arthur C Graesser, 'Is It an Agent, or Just a Program?: A Taxonomy for Autonomous Agents' in JP Müller, MJ Wooldridge, and NR Jennings (eds), *Intelligent Agents* Ⅲ: *Agent Theories, Architectures, and Languages* (Springer 1997) 21.

② Restatement (Third) of Agency (American Law Institute, 2006), §1.01. "电子代理人"之类的术语加剧了这种混淆，"电子代理人"是指获得用户授权可以签署合同的特定程序。参见 Uniform Electronic Transactions Act 1999 (US), s 2 (6)。这些合同可能具有法律约束力，但这些特定程序只是工具，而不是作为法律上的"代理人"。

③ Ugo Pagallo, *The Laws of Robots: Crimes, Contracts, and Torts* (Springer 2013) 102-03。另参见本书第 5 章第 5.2.1 节。

不承担责任。① 在人工智能系统的情况下，最为困难的责任问题将出现在它们不再仅仅作为工具或器具、超出用户的控制或指示的情境。在这种情况下，代理关系对于解决假定人工智能系统本身存在基本责任这一问题，是没有什么用处的。②

支持该基本责任的论点将在下一章中加以讨论。这个问题的更简单的说明集中在这些系统的复杂性上，以及当人工智能系统无法按预期执行时，期待用户对此承担责任是否合理。

以英国为例，驾驶员要对其车辆的适用性负责，除非问题是潜在的、无法通过合理注意义务发现的。③ 而随着汽车变得越来越复杂，期望驾驶员防范潜在缺陷变得越来越不现实。英国法律委员会2018年在关于自动驾驶汽车的咨询文件中指出，目前保险公司支付的索赔中，已经很难区分驾驶员过失和车辆缺陷。对于复杂的自动驾驶汽车，由于驾驶员不大可能了解到系统缺陷，或者根本没有"驾驶员"，这种区别则可能变得更加明显。④

因此，人工智能系统从用户应承担的义务和他/她可以合理

---

① *Hilton v. Thomas Burton（Rhodes）Ltd.*［1961］1 WLR 705, 709。需要注意的是，足以建立替代责任的雇佣关系可能包括代理人，但不必然是代理人。参见 Peter Watts and FMB Reynolds, *Bowstead and Reynolds on Agency*（21st edn, Sweet & Maxwell 2018），para 8-176ff。

② 反对使用代理关系的另一个观点是，将人工智能系统定为人类代理是人为地降低了人工智能的能力标准。参见 Liability for Artificial Intelligence and Other Emerging Digital Technologies（EU Expert Group on Liability and New Technologies, 2019）25。

③ Road Traffic Act 1988（UK），s 50A。1970年的一个判例裁定，除非缺陷是"无法合理发现"的，否则卡车刹车失灵并不构成辩护理由。参见 *Henderson v. Henry E Jenkins & Sons*［1970］AC 282；Robert M Merkin and Jeremy Stuart-Smith, *The Law of Motor Insurance*（Sweet & Maxwell 2004）201。

④ Automated Vehicles: A Joint Preliminary Consultation Paper（Law Commission, Consultation Paper No. 240; Scottish Law Commission, Discussion Paper No. 166, 2018），para 6.12。

预期的注意标准两个方面挑战了传统的过失观念。关于因果关系，人工智能系统作出决策的过程也可能与人类的偏好相悖，进而挑战已经形成的预判或惯例。正如在象棋等游戏中表现出的，出其不意是非常有价值的。① 然而，在侵权责任的认定上，这却引发了一个问题，即自主系统行为本身是否构成避免责任的主动干预行为。②

4.1.2 严格责任

为避免不确定性并防范无法赔偿的损失，一些学者主张对某些人工智能系统的使用实行严格责任。③ 相关争论的核心是，如果一个人为了自己的利益进行某种活动，而这种活动本身对他人具有固有风险，那么当风险发生时，这个人应承担责任。

在英国传统中，这是对赖兰兹诉弗莱彻案（Rylands v. Fletcher）确立的规则的应用。该案裁定，如果土地所有者的财产的"非自然使用"损害了邻居的财产，即使他没有疏忽行为，也应对此承担赔偿责任。④ 在该案中，财产的"非自然使用"是一个导致邻居的矿井被淹没的水库。与人工智能系统更为相似的类比可能是对由动物造成的损害采用类似规则。在已知属于"危险物种"的动物的情况下，饲养者被推定知道它具有造成伤害的

---

① Nate Silver, *The Signal and the Noise: Why so Many Predictions Fail—But Some Don't* (Penguin 2012) 287-88.

② Matthew U Scherer, 'Regulating Artificial Intelligence Systems: Risks, Challenges, Competencies, and Strategies' (2016) 29 *Harvard Journal of Law & Technology* 353，363-66.

③ See, eg, Adam Rosenberg, 'Strict Liability: Imagining a Legal Framework for Autonomous Vehicles' (2017) 20 *Tulane Journal of Technology and Intellectual Property* 205; Hannah YeeFen Lim, *Autonomous Vehicles and the Law: Technology, Algorithms, and Ethics* (Edward Elgar 2018) 105.

④ *Rylands v. Fletcher*, (1866) LR 1 Exch 265.

倾向，并将在无须证明饲养者存在过错的情况下对其造成的损害承担责任。对于其他动物，必须证明饲养者知道这个特定的动物是危险的。这些关于动物的普通法规则现已由立法覆盖，① 但英国法院一直回避采用"超危险活动"的严格责任的一般原则。②

1907 年，美国一起汽车事故案例考虑了当时尚属新技术的汽车是否应被视为危险动物的问题。该案涉及一个儿童的死亡，他在街上玩耍时被一辆由汽车主人的儿子的朋友驾驶的汽车撞死。司机本人被判过失杀人罪并入狱，但提交给佐治亚州上诉法院的问题是，民事责任是否也可以归咎于汽车的所有者。上诉法院基于代理关系驳回了这一起诉，因为车主和驾驶员之间的联系过于薄弱。另一种观点则认为，车主应承担严格责任，因为汽车应与"凶猛动物"归为一类，其所有者应该承担类似的严格责任。但是，法院最终没有采纳这一观点，部分原因是他们自己在这一领域的有限经验：

> 我们应该担心的不是汽车的凶猛，而是驾驶汽车的人的凶猛。在人类介入之前，汽车通常是无害的。由于本州法官的薪酬水平原因，他们中很少有人拥有过这些机器，但他们中的一些人偶尔乘坐过，从而了解了一些关于它们的知识。我们发现，有时这些机器不仅缺乏凶猛性，而且表现出不愿移动的倾向，以至于人类的智慧也难以让它们移动起来。它们不应与凶猛的狗、恶性的公牛、恶劣的骡子等相提并论。③

---

① Animals Act 1971 (UK).
② Christian Witting, *Street on Torts* (15th edn, OUP 2018) 453.
③ *Lewis v. Amorous*, 59 SE 338, 340 (Court of Appeals of Georgia, 1907).

据此，法院认为，在州政府"颁布对这种新型交通方式有益的法规"之前，责任的分配将根据普通法来确定；在本案中，侵权责任将由粗心大意的（人类）驾驶员承担。

一个受到严格责任制约的技术实例是航空。美国法学会于1939年在《侵权法第一次重述》中指出，"在当前发展阶段，航空是极度危险的"。① 因此，即使操作员尽了最大的努力，他或她仍需对飞机本身或从飞机上掉下的物品造成的损害承担责任。② 随着时间的推移，航空旅行变得越来越普遍，严格责任也随着行业标准的发展日益受到质疑，并最终被完全抛弃。

尽管严格责任的某些方面适用于下文将要讨论的产品责任，但基于技术内在危险的原因，将严格责任普遍适用于人工智能系统的用户，则是根本性的错误。通常情况下，大多数人工智能系统的目的是提高安全性和效率。③ 人工智能的某些应用，如致命的自主武器，或者被赋予造成伤害能力的机器人，会引发危险的结果。在此，我们可以将其有限地类比为饲养高度危险的动物。④ 除了这些特殊的具体案例或类似于存储和运输危险物质的情况，

---

① *Restatement of the Law*, *First*, *Torts* (American Law Institute 1939), §520.

② 在英国和许多其他法域，当时的立法制定了类似的规定。参见 'Liability for Aircraft Damage to Ground Occupiers-A Study of Current Trends in Tort Law' (1955) 31 *Indiana Law Journal* 63。

③ 事实上，随着机器变得更加安全，有论者认为，实施严格责任可能会阻碍进一步的创新；即使人工智能系统的表现超过了假设的"合理人"，严格责任也要求用户和供应商承担责任。参见 Ryan Abbott, 'The Reasonable Computer: Disrupting the Paradigm of Tort Liability' (2018) 86 *George Washington Law Review* 1。

④ See, eg, Sam N Lehman-Wilzig, 'Frankenstein Unbound: Towards a Legal Definition of Artificial Intelligence' (1981) 13 *Futures* 442, 448; Sophia H Duffy and Jamie Patrick Hopkins, 'Sit, Stay, Drive: The Future of Autonomous Car Liability' (2013) 16 *SMU Science and Technology Law Review* 453, 468-73.

严格责任的适用范围是极其有限的。此外，正如前文所强调的，人工智能系统的日渐增加的复杂性，使得将责任归咎于用户而非制造商变得更不合适。

4.1.3 产品责任

将责任归咎于人工智能系统的制造商与 20 世纪消费者保护的根本性转变相一致，即从传统的"购者留心（货物出门概不退换）"[*caveat emptor* (let the buyer beware)]观念转向制造商的严格责任。加州最高法院法官在 1944 年的一份判决书附属意见中写道："公共政策要求将责任确定在一个平衡点，以最有效地减少市场上存在的缺陷产品对生命和健康的危害。"[①]二十年后，同一法官在另外一个案件中将这一精神正式写进多数意见中，将其正式提升为具有法律约束力的普通法判例。[②] 随着后续案例的发展，制造商和零售商现在可能因产品存在制造或设计缺陷、未能警告用户非明显危险而承担责任。在认定具有设计缺陷时，受害人需要证明制造商本可以采用"合理的替代设计"，以降低或避免可预见的伤害风险。[③] 除了美国之外，英国、欧盟、中国等法域都先后采纳了针对缺陷产品的严格责任制度。

产品责任法已经适用于许多人工智能系统。例如，大多数法域的产品责任已经涵盖自动驾驶汽车。[④] 对于人工智能系统和其他设备，产品责任的优势在于可以明确确定负责任方，即"生产者"，通常是指制造商，但还包括进口商、分销商和零部件制造

---

① *Escola v. Coca-Cola Bottling Co.*, 24 Cal 2d 453, 462 (1944) (Traynor J).
② *Greenman v. Yuba Power Products*, 59 Cal 2d 57, 62 (1963) (Traynor J).
③ Restatement (Third) of Torts: Product Liability (American Law Institute, 1998), §2.
④ 无过错责任险除外，参见本书第 4 章第 4.1.4 节。

商。即使无法确定其他责任方,通常仍可以起诉产品的供应商。①

当然,在人工智能泛滥的情况下,恶意的设备或操作系统可能无法追溯到供应商。对此,可能的补救原则是"市场份额责任"。这一原则系美国独有,曾用于解决一起原告因使用无法与特定制药公司联系的非处方药而受害的案例。同样,加州的一家法院借鉴一篇福特汉姆法学院学生撰写的文章,提出了一个富有创意的解决方案。②该法院认为,如果原告针对一个可替代产品的大部分市场份额的生产者提起诉讼,并且该产品已经造成伤害,那么证明他们没有造成伤害的举证责任就转移到该生产者身上,否则他们将按照市场份额承担责任。③

可以尝试采用类似的方法来处理人工智能系统的"制造商",但还是有些障碍。尽管该原则得到美国最高法院的支持,④但适用此原则的案件背景却是非常特殊的:一种由少数制药公司以完全相同的方式制造的单一药物,多年后损害了一类患者,这些患者不能因为未能将责任指向特定的行为者而受到指责。即使在美国,尽管学者们不时呼吁,法院也拒绝将该原则扩展到其他药物或产品责任。⑤更广泛的批评是,该原则实际上是一个自由主义州的法院试图弥补美国严重不足的社会保障的一种尝试。虽然这一政策目标极为高尚,最好还是通过下一小节讨论的各种保险方

---

① See, eg, EU Product Liability Directive, art 3 (3).
② Naomi Sheiner, 'DES and a Proposed Theory of Enterprise Liability' (1978) 46 *Fordham Law Review* 963.
③ *Sindell v. Abbott Laboratories*, 607 P 2d 924 (Cal., 1980).
④ *Rexall Drug Co v. Tigue*, 493 US 944 (1989).
⑤ Logan L Page, 'Write This Down: A Model Market-Share Liability Statute' (2019) 68 *Duke Law Journal* 1469。将人工智能系统与多个制造商生产的相同药物之间的类比,会比较牵强。

案来实现。

　　假设可以确定一个或多个生产商,适用产品责任规则的第二个障碍是人工智能系统是否真正属于"产品"的问题。诸如自动驾驶汽车或家用清洁机器人,显然是产品。但是,许多人工智能系统更接近服务。① 欧盟《产品责任指令》(Product Liability Directive)将"产品"定义为"所有可移动的物",包括电力;② 英国立法中的"产品"涵盖"任何货物或电力"。③ 美国《侵权法重述》将"产品"定义为"通过商业形式分销的,用于使用或消费的有形个人财产",也包括房地产和电力,但明确排除了服务。④ 令人惊讶的是,目前尚不清楚软件是否应被认定为产品。⑤ 早在1991年,美国加州的一起判例在附带说明中表明应该将软件认定为产品;⑥ 在美国《统一商法典》下,通过大规模市场销售的软件被认定为商品,而为特定客户专门开发的软件则被视为服务。在英国和欧盟,软件的性质仍然是一个"悬而未决的问题"。⑦

　　如果适用产品责任规则,只需证明产品存在缺陷并且导致损害即可,消费者无须证明产品缺陷的原因。例如,撞上墙的自动

---

　　① Jacob Turner, *Robot Rules: Regulating Artificial Intelligence* (Palgrave Macmillan 2019) 95-98.

　　② EU Product Liability Directive, art 2.

　　③ Consumer Protection Act, s 1 (2).

　　④ Restatement (Third) of Torts: Product Liability (American Law Institute, 1998), §19. See David W Lannetti, 'Toward a Revised Definition of "Product" Under the Restatement (Third) of Torts: Products Liability' (2000) 35 *Tort & Insurance Law Journal* 845.

　　⑤ Nicholas J McBride and Roderick Bagshaw, *Tort Law* (6th edn, Pearson 2018) 364.

　　⑥ *Winter v. GP Putnam's Sons*, 938 F 2d 1033, 1035 (9th Cir, 1991).

　　⑦ White Paper on Artificial Intelligence [European Commission, COM (2020) 65 final, 19 February 2020] 14.

驾驶汽车显然是有缺陷的。对于诸如医疗技术等更复杂的产品，决策不透明性将使确定实际存在的缺陷以及缺陷与损害的因果关系变得更加困难。① 即使确定了产品缺陷，"合理替代设计"标准在尖端技术案例中也很难发挥作用。② 对于更先进的人工智能系统，特别是具有自我修改能力的系统，生产商还可能以产品在流通时不存在缺陷、当时的科学知识不足以发现缺陷等作为免责抗辩理由。③

从理论上讲，产品责任规则应该鼓励拥有信息优势的开发商在设计产品时充分考虑产品安全性，同时通过定价和保险来分担风险。然而，在像人工智能这样的新兴行业中，高速度、自主性以及通用人工智能潜在危险等不确定性使得准确计算伤害概率（由于不透明性）和损害的量度变得极为复杂。④ 多年前，瑞安·卡洛（Ryan Calo）曾警告称，这种不确定性将限制创新，因此应该给予人工智能开发商一定的免责空间。⑤ 尽管没有法定免责，人工智能最近十来年却依旧获得了迅猛的发展，这在一定程度上证伪了卡洛的警告。尽管如此，他关于应该有强制保险的相关主

---

① Xavier Frank, 'Is Watson for Oncology per se Unreasonably Dangerous? Making A Case for How to Prove Products Liability Based on a Flawed Artificial Intelligence Design' (2019) 45 *American Journal of Law & Medicine* 273。欧盟已提出要求人工智能系统记录其活动，并在记录失败时举证责任倒置。另参见 A different argument against using agency is that holding AI systems to the standard of human agents would be an artificially *low* benchmark：Liability for Artificial Intelligence and Other Emerging Digital Technologies (EU Expert Group on Liability and New Technologies, 2019) 47-48。

② Mark A Geistfeld, 'The Regulatory Sweet Spot for Autonomous Vehicles' (2018) 53 *Wake Forest Law Review* 101, 124-25.

③ EU Product Liability Directive, art 7.

④ 参见本书第 5 章第 5.3 节。

⑤ M Ryan Calo, 'Open Robotics' (2011) 70 *Maryland Law Review* 603, 601-09.

张还是合理的,可以说是管理超出传统的损失分配制度之列的人工智能系统风险的最佳途径。

4.1.4 保险

长期以来,保险在侵权法的责任分配问题中一直都被认为是无关紧要的。① 尽管这种说法在教义上是逻辑准确的,但实践中,保险的设计显然会影响是否提出索赔的决定,包括保险公司通过代位求偿权获得向责任人索赔。② 尤其是强制保险,对涉及机动车辆事故的法律产生了重大影响。荷兰是一个特殊的例子,该国立法规定,在几乎所有的机动车辆与自行车碰撞事故中,驾驶员都要承担严格责任。这样的立法规定,与驾驶机动车必须投保而骑自行车者则不必保险的体系有关。③

自动驾驶汽车展示了保险如何应对至少某些人工智能系统相关的风险。如果制造商声称的自动驾驶汽车在安全方面的好处是真实的,④ 那么由于交通事故造成的伤害的成本将会降低。然而,在中期内,随着驾驶员将汽车控制权交给人工智能系统,与对制造商提出的索赔相比,对驾驶员提出的索赔比例将会下降。这些费用将从驾驶员支付的保险费转移到制造商的产品责任保险上,然后通过提高车辆价格再回到驾驶员身上。⑤ 在这一过渡期间,产品责任规定可能出现的空缺应通过法律规定,将责任转向制造

---

① See, eg, *Capital and Counties Plc v. Hampshire CC* [1997] 1 QB 1004, 1044.

② See generally Rob Merkin and Jenny Steele, *Insurance and the Law of Obligations* (OUP 2013).

③ Wegenverkeerswet [Road Traffic Act] 1994 (Netherlands), art 185.

④ 参见本书第2章第2.1节。

⑤ Daniel A Crane, Kyle D Logue, and Bryce C Pilz, 'A Survey of Legal Issues Arising from the Deployment of Autonomous and Connected Vehicles' (2017) 23 *Michigan Telecommunications and Technology Law Review* 191, 256-59.

商并附加强制保险来弥补。①

　　保险在汽车工业诞生之日起就发挥着这样的作用。例如，在英国，自1930年起，任何使用机动车辆的人都需要购买强制性的第三者保险。② 如今，基本的汽车保险在大多数主要法域已成为强制性要求，包括美国几乎所有的州。在德国和日本，传统的车主的严格责任与强制保险制度相辅相成，尽管关于责任是否应转移到车辆制造商的争议仍在持续。③ 2003年，中国也引入了强制保险制度，尽管第三方保险覆盖范围有限。④

　　在绝大多数情况下，保险责任由驾驶员或驾驶员的雇主承担。英国《2018年自动驾驶和电动汽车法案》（Automated and Electric Vehicles Act 2018）将这一保险要求扩展到自动驾驶汽车，由自动驾驶汽车本身故障导致的事故受害者（包括"驾驶员"）将得到赔偿；没有保险是一种刑事犯罪，车主要为此承担法律责任。⑤ 该法案的目的是确保驾驶员和车辆责任在同一保单下得到保障，防止"延误或妨碍赔偿"的纠纷。⑥ 展望未来，

---

① Cf Kenneth S Abraham and Robert L Rabin, 'Automated Vehicles and Manufacturer Responsibility for Accidents: A New Legal Regime for a New Era' (2019) 105 *Virginia Law Review* 127.

② Road Traffic Act 1930 (UK), s 35.

③ Frank Henkel, *et al*, Autonomous Vehicles: The Legal Landscape of DSRC in Germany (Norton Rose Fulbright, July 2017); Gen Goto, Autonomous Vehicles, Ride-share Services, and Civil Liability: A Japanese Perspective (Asian Law Institute, June 2019).

④ 《中华人民共和国道路交通安全法》（2003年）；Xu Xian and Fan Chiang-Ku, 'Autonomous Vehicles, Risk Perceptions and Insurance Demand: An Individual Survey in China' (2019) 124 (C) Transportation Research Part A: Policy and Practice 549.

⑤ Automated and Electric Vehicles Act 2018 (UK), s 2.

⑥ Automated Vehicles: A Joint Preliminary Consultation Paper (Law Commission, Consultation Paper No 240; Scottish Law Commission, Discussion Paper No 166, 2018), para 6.17.

自动驾驶汽车的广泛使用，将促使要求为汽车而非驾驶员投保的法律成为行业标准。① 另一种方案，则是已经在以色列、瑞典、美国十几个州以及澳大利亚、加拿大部分地区实行的无过错责任制度。②

但是，通过保险分配风险这种方法，是否可以扩展到自动驾驶汽车之外的人工智能应用领域呢？市场有可能以无形之手解决许多情况。当产品责任规则将特定风险转嫁到制造商身上时，他们会为潜在的诉讼投保。这种风险分担机制将适用于越来越多的机器人和智能设备，包括备受瞩目的"物联网"。但是，当某些人工智能系统不被认定为法律意义上的"产品"，或者生产商以合同的形式约定不承担基本责任时，便会出现市场失灵问题。特别是在那些参与者背景多样化和潜在损害增加的行业，法定强制保险或类似于机动车无过错责任制度则尤为必要。

一个极端的例子是新西兰：无论有无过错，法律都为所有事故提供无过错赔偿。这一制度设计的优点是，损害赔偿是基于受害程度而非过错大小来计算的。例如，无论某个幼童是被自动驾驶汽车、无人机还是有故障的算法伤害，都无关紧要。新西兰事故赔偿委员会的资金来源于对工资和汽油征收的特殊税费以及其他一般性的税收。③ 然而，这一制度的最大局限在于，它仅适用于人身伤害，而排除了财产损失和其他纯经济损失。

---

① Cf Mark A Geistfeld, 'A Roadmap for Autonomous Vehicles: State Tort Liability, Automobile Insurance, and Federal Safety Regulation' (2017) 105 *California Law Review* 1611.

② See, eg, Maurice Schellekens, 'No-Fault Compensation Schemes for Self-Driving Vehicles' (2018) 10 *Law, Innovation and Technology* 314.

③ Trish O'Sullivan and Kate Tokeley, 'Consumer Product Failure Causing Personal Injury Under the No-Fault Accident Compensation Scheme in New Zealand—a Let-off for Manufacturers?' (2018) 41 *Journal of Consumer Policy* 211.

长期以来，人们一直认可新西兰在这一领域的特殊做法，其他国家采用类似制度却面临各种政治障碍。随着人工智能系统在社会中发挥越来越大的作用，其他国家也可能学习新西兰的实践，至少在因人工智能系统导致的伤害或者其他超出传统责任制度范围的伤害赔偿方面，可以借鉴新西兰事故赔偿委员会制度，通过向受益于人工智能的行业征收税收或特别费用来筹集资金。①

在短期内，强制性税费制度将受限于特定行业，尤其是那些潜在个人伤害概率较高的领域。在交通领域，除了自动驾驶汽车，在快递和监控方面的应用越来越广泛的无人机也应该纳入一般机动车辆赔偿制度之中。② 医疗设备是另外一个明显的候选行业，范围可包括从诊断工具到机器人手术。③

随着人工智能系统在日常生活的其他方面发挥更大的作用，产品和服务之间的区别将变得更加棘手。尽管人们的想象普遍倾向于拥有一个类人机器人与血肉之躯的人类同频互动的世界，但诸如智能助手等虚拟服务将可能产生更大的影响。④ 服务提供者的强制保险可以填补这一潜在的空白。或者，可能需要为最后救

---

① Jacob Turner, *Robot Rules: Regulating Artificial Intelligence* (Palgrave Macmillan 2019) 103.

② Bryan Casey, 'Robot Ipsa Loquitur' (2019) 108 *Georgetown Law Journal* 225, 249.

③ Jonathan H Chen and Steven M Asch, 'Machine Learning and Prediction in Medicine—Beyond the Peak of Inflated Expectations' (2017) 376 (26) *New England Journal of Medicine* 2507; Jianxing He, *et al*, 'The Practical Implementation of Artificial Intelligence Technologies in Medicine' (2019) 25 *Nature Medicine* 30.

④ Cf Robert D Lang and Lenore E Benessere, 'Alexa, Siri, Bixby, Google's Assistant, and Cortana Testifying in Court: Novel Use of Emerging Technology in Litigation' (2018) 35 (7) *Computer and Internet Lawyer* 16.

济的索赔提供保险,以涵盖无法识别或未投保的技术。①

这种方法中的保险远非与责任问题无关,反而会成为塑造行为的重要手段。作为一种监管工具,保险经常被忽视,但它实际上具有两个独立的功能:赔偿损失和分配风险。在新兴技术领域,由于风险的不确定性,很难正确为保单定价。定价过高会抑制创新;定价过低,或强制性地将保单推向消费者,则会导致生产者不承担错误的成本,从而产生道德风险。同时,随着时间的推移,越来越多的数据将被收集起来,风险会在将来变得更易量化。②

保险还可以通过不提供保险产品、服务或确立使保险失效的行为,起到威慑某些行为的作用。以私营军事和安全公司为例,承保人拒绝承保某些与战争相关的活动,有时比禁止这些行为的规范对行为产生的影响更大。

因此,通过向那些最有能力最小化危害的人施加成本和向那些最有可能遭受损失的人提供赔偿,保险有助于管理与新技术相关的风险。其目标是功利主义的。然而,在某些情况下,保险可能达不到充分、有效的结果,因为责任归属不仅仅是关于风险管理。

4.2 不可委托职责

侵权法,特别是通过法经济学分析来看,旨在减少事故造成

---

① European Parliament Resolution with Recommendations to the Commission on Civil Law Rules on Robotics [2015/2103 (INL)] (European Parliament, 16 February 2017), para 59; A different argument against using agency is that holding AI systems to the standard of human agents would be an artificially *low* benchmark: Liability for Artificial Intelligence and Other Emerging Digital Technologies (EU Expert Group on Liability and New Technologies, 2019) 62.

② Mark Chinen, *Law and Autonomous Machines: The Co-Evolution of Legal Responsibility and Technology* (Edward Elgar 2019) 118-20.

的损害、降低避免事故的成本。它还可以被理解为体现了一种纠正性正义：补偿自己造成的不当损失的义务。刑法也可以通过类似的视角来分析，但往往被认为更具有义务论的特点：即使刑法不是一种有效的威慑手段，某些行为的道德谴责也要求社会作出回应。①

通过调整责任模型和保险制度以适应新的挑战，可以实现对某些人工智能系统（最突出的是自动驾驶汽车）风险的管理。然而，仅仅管理风险是不够的。在某些情况下，即使确定责任从经济效益分析角度是"非高效"的，也还是有必要确定具体的责任分配。下文将从两个方面展开讨论：普通法中的不可委托职责和国际人道法中的指挥责任。

4.2.1 普通法中的不可委托职责

侵权法的很大一部分使命是纠正错误，将损害的成本从无辜的原告转至有过错的被告。其普通法起源可追溯到早期的诸如蓄意伤害和威胁、侵权、过失等形式的司法诉讼，这些诉讼被认为是纠正个人权利侵害的重要手段。然而，这并非侵权法的唯一功能。现在普遍认可的观点是，侵权法还具有引导人们行为的调控功能。本章前面的讨论，主要关注的是侵权法及法定代理关系如何基于过错分配损失，包括在哪些情况下放弃过错原则以便更有效地将损失分散到特定利益群体中。后面的讨论将重点关注侵权法的调控功能，特别是在侵权法规定的不可委托职责的情势下，责任人不仅要承担注意义务，还要采取具体的注意措施。②

这种不可委托职责有时会与代理责任相混淆。然而，后者是一种次要的责任形式，被代理人因他人的侵权行为而承担责任。

---

① 参见本书第 5 章第 5.1.2（b）节。
② Christian Witting, 'Breach of the Non-Delegable Duty: Defending Limited Strict Liability in Tort' (2006) 29 *UNSW Law Journal* 33, 34-35.

相比之下，不可委托职责是一种主要的责任形式，要求义务人在特定活动中"确保"采取合理的谨慎。这在人工智能系统的背景下很重要，因为责任并不取决于首先找到雇员或代理人犯有过错，这引发了与代理相似的人工智能人格问题。①

正如普通法中有时出现的情况，不可委托职责是原则演绎发展起来的，并在学者和法官之间引起了一定程度的混淆。② 2014年，英国最高法院试图将不可委托职责归纳为两大类。第一类涉及从事本质上危险活动的独立承包商，并回顾了早先关于严格责任的讨论。第二类涉及法律因被告与受害方的关系而对其施加特殊义务的情况，包括对特定人群采取积极措施以免其受到伤害的义务。这种义务是"根据与被告的关系而确定的"。③ 例如，医院对患者治疗方面的责任，学校对学生人身安全的责任。这可能扩展到其他存在高风险和需要承担相应高度责任的情况。④

将这些原则应用于人工智能系统，可以避免前面提到的一些问题，包括归责问题和过错证明问题。⑤ 本质上危险活动包括部署具有攻击能力的人工智能系统，如安保无人机。医院与患者之间的特殊关系涵盖医疗技术的使用。在学校，虽然机器人教师尚未成为现实，但使用技术手段确保校园安全和维护学校纪律却早

---

① 参见本书第 4 章第 4.1.1 节。
② John Murphy, 'The Liability Bases of Common Law Non-Delegable Duties: A Reply to Christian Witting' (2007) 30 *UNSW Law Journal* 86; Simon Deakin, 'Organisational Torts: Vicarious Liability Versus Non-Delegable Duty' (2018) *Cambridge Law Journal* 15.
③ *Woodland v. Essex County Council* [2014] AC 547, paras. 6-7.
④ Simon Deakin and Zoe Adams, *Markesinis and Deakin's Tort Law* (8th edn, OUP 2019) 572.
⑤ Cf Kumaralingam Amirthalingam, 'The Non-Delegable Duty: Some Clarifications, Some Questions' (2017) 29 *Singapore Academy of Law Journal* 500, 516-17.

就很常见了。①

如前所述，这其中的一些领域非常适合强制保险制度。然而，不可委托职责的重要性不仅仅在于损失的分配，而且旨在使义务人首先思考如何防止损失。② 随着人工智能系统的使用变得更加普遍，这种不可委托职责将更广泛地出现，类似于20世纪产品责任和占有者责任的扩展。

4.2.2 国际人道法中的指挥责任

普通法中的不可委托职责确立了一种道义和法律责任，但主要关注的是如何分配损害成本。尽管各法域可能存在惩罚性赔偿，但重点仍然在于赔偿。相比之下，刑法则更强调道义问题，定罪的门槛也更高：犯罪行为必须比单纯的疏忽更有过错；证明的标准是排除合理怀疑，而非概率平衡。③

正如本书第2章所讨论的，刑事责任并非解决人工智能系统行为失范的正确途径。例如，随着车辆自主性的提高，机动车辆的违章行为将被视为需要纠正的错误，而不是应受惩罚的罪行。如果"驾驶员"对车辆或控制其行为的代码几乎没有控制权，对他或她进行惩罚是不合适的。④ 一些法域设置产品责任规则，对在市场上推出不"安全"产品者补充施加刑事制裁。⑤ 如果产品被认为

---

① Echo Xie, 'Artificial Intelligence Is Watching China's Students but How Well Can It Really See?', *South China Morning Post* (16 September 2019).

② 通过这种方式引导责任，鼓励提前规划，包括通过事先的合同约定在制造商和组件供应商之间分担未来的责任成本。

③ Matthew Dyson, *Comparing Tort and Crime: Learning from Across and Within Legal Systems* (CUP 2015) 457.

④ 参见本书第2章第2.1.2节、第5章第5.1.2 (b) 节。

⑤ See, eg, Directive 2001/95/EC of the European Parliament and of the Council of 3 December 2001 on General Product Safety 2001 (EU); General Product Safety Regulations 2005 (UK); 15 USC § 2070.

是危险的,或者制造商未尽职尽责确保其安全,这种制裁是恰当的。

这里的关注点是,传统法律主体是否可以为具有某种自主性或不透明度的人工智能系统的行为承担责任,而这些特性在其他情况下可能使该法律主体无可指责。关于这个问题的辩论往往集中在一小部分不太可能进入公开市场但又出于道义而非实践原因被归责的人工智能系统:自主武器系统。

关于致命自主武器系统可能实际上比人类"更安全"的观点误解了人们的担忧。虽然国际人道法的起源可以追溯到减少苦难的愿望,① 但在作战决策中要求有实体人类参与实乃出于道义考虑而非基于功利主义原则。在国际层面上,联合国法外处决、即决处决或任意处决问题特别报告员在 2013 年关于致命自主机器人的报告中写道,国际人道法的基本概念"比例原则"涉及"独特的人类判断"。② 根据武装冲突法,比例原则的标准是在特定情况下合格的军事指挥官会采取什么行动。虽然有时有人提出这样的判断对计算机来说过于复杂,但复杂性是反对将决策交给机器的较弱论点之一。有意义的人类控制的更强论点不是人类会作出更好的决策,而是人类可以被追究责任。③ 联合国政府专家组能够达成一致的少数事项之一是一个"指导原则",即必须保留人类对决定使用武器系统的责任,"因为责任不能转移到机器上"。④

---

① Simon Chesterman, *Civilians in War* (Lynne Rienner 2001).
② Report of the Special Rapporteur on Extrajudicial, Summary, or Arbitrary Executions, Christof Heyns, UN Doc A/HRC/23/47 (2013), para 72.
③ 参见本书第 2 章第 2.2.2 节。
④ Report of the 2019 Session of the Group of Governmental Experts on Emerging Technologies in the Area of Lethal Autonomous Weapons Systems, UN Doc CCW/GGE.1/2019/3 (2019), Annex Ⅳ. 另一个问题是,在国际法中,一个国家在多大程度上应当为自主武器系统的错误行为承担责任。参见本书第 8 章第 8.2.1 (b) 节。

将该原则应用于现行法律并非简单的任务，这使得一些人得出这样的结论，即单凭这一点就足以完全禁止自主武器。抛开这些武器本身是否非法的问题，如果给定的自主系统被赋予非法的目标参数，或者在一个有平民但没有能力区分平民和战斗人员的区域部署，那么这种系统的使用将受到现行法律的约束。在这两种情况下，部署系统的操作员可能被追究责任。[1]

当操作员未对目标进行编程，而是有权否决它们时，问题变得更加复杂，这是一个"人工干预"的场景。考虑到需要迅速作出决策并且没有其他信息来源，未能制止机器可能不满足成立战争罪所需的主观成分。[2]

展望未来，在自主性和不透明性增加的情况下，国际人道法如何处理因无法归因于非法指令、硬件或软件缺陷而杀害平民的人工智能系统？一些人认为这个问题永远不应该出现，因为使用行为不可预测的武器本身就从根本上违反了战争法。[3] 另一些人愿意接受一定程度的失败率，指出法律并不要求在战斗中部署的士兵完美无缺，并容忍设备故障。例如，由于疲劳而犯错误的士兵或偏离航线的导弹可能都不足以认定个人对战争罪负有责任。[4]

---

[1] Carrie McDougall, 'Autonomous Weapon Systems and Accountability: Putting The Cart Before the Horse' (2019) 20 *Melbourne Journal of International Law* 58, 69. See also Neha Jain, 'Autonomous Weapons Systems: New Frameworks for Individual Responsibility' in Nehal Bhuta, et al (eds), *Autonomous Weapons Systems: Law, Ethics, Policy* (CUP 2016) 303 at 308-10.

[2] Amos N Guiora, 'Accountability and Decision Making in Autonomous Warfare: Who is Responsible?' (2017) *Utah Law Review* 393, 397.

[3] See, eg, Charles J Dunlap, Jr., 'Accountability and Autonomous Weapons: Much Ado About Nothing' (2016) 30 *Temple International & Comparative Law Journal* 63, 71.

[4] Ian S Henderson, Patrick Keane, and Josh Liddy, 'Remote and Autonomous Warfare Systems: Precautions in Attack and Individual Accountability' in Jens David Ohlin (ed), *Research Handbook on Remote Warfare* (Edward Elgar 2017) 335 at 361-63.

将此扩展到真正的自主武器发生故障的情况是合适的,类似于火箭发射失败。但完全可以预见的是,人工智能系统可能被赋予进行目标选择的权力,并以无法完全解释的原因违反国际规则。[①] 而容忍这一行为就像容忍训练不足或纪律松弛的士兵的非法行为一样。

通过应用指挥责任原则可以解决潜在的问责不足问题。例如,根据《国际刑事法院罗马规约》(Rome Statute of the International Criminal Court),军事指挥官可能因其"有效指挥和控制"下的部队犯下的罪行而承担刑事责任。在这种情况下,其罪行是因为未能正确行使控制权而导致的,指挥官知道或本应知道这些罪行,并且未能采取其所能采取的一切必要和合理措施来防止或制止这些罪行。[②] 不具军衔的平民作为上级也可能承担责任,尽管门槛较高,他们要"知道或者故意忽视清楚表明"下属正在犯罪或即将犯罪的信息。[③]

将这一原则应用于自主武器系统时,可能引发两类反对意见:一种是形式上的,另一种是实质上的。形式上的反对意见是,指挥责任假定指挥官与下属之间存在等级关系。类似于前面关于代理关系和雇主责任的讨论,如果指挥责任要求的下属是一个独立实施犯罪的法律主体,那么将该原则应用于人工智能系统将是另一类错误。[④] 二战后这一原则的早期应用确实将其视为一

---

① Joshua Hughes, 'The Law of Armed Conflict Issues Created by Programming Automatic Target Recognition Systems Using Deep Learning Methods' [2019] Yearbook of International Humanitarian Law 99.

② Statute of the International Criminal Court (Rome Statute), UN Doc A/Conf. 183/9 (1998), art 28 (a).

③ Ibid., art 28 (b).

④ See, eg, Rebecca Crootof, 'War Torts: Accountability for Autonomous Weapons' (2016) 164 University of Pennsylvania Law Review 1347, 1378-81.

种对上级指挥下的人犯罪的同谋责任，指挥责任也通常被认为是一种从犯责任形式。① 这种类比适用于指挥官对犯罪实际知情的情况，但对于未能防止这些犯罪的责任，法学家们感到非常为难。从犯责任的解释甚至难以与指挥官在事实发生后未能惩罚犯罪而承担刑事责任的事实相统一。② 一个可能更有道理的论点是，指挥官的责任不在于对下属犯罪的贡献，而在于对职责的过失。③ 正如前南斯拉夫国际刑事法庭上诉庭所强调的，"被告并未因其下属的罪行而受到指控，而是因其作为上级未履行控制权的职责"。④

实质上的反对意见是，即使将这一原则扩展到自主武器系统是适当的，在实践中也是行不通的。指挥官知道或应该知道任何犯罪的要求可能排除了他或她在假设人工智能系统会按照编程操作并遵守战争法的情况下部署人工智能系统的情况。⑤ 同样，对于一位战地指挥官来说，未能采取一切必要且合理的措施可能受到严格限制。士兵们预期与他们的指挥官建立直接的关系，而指挥官反过来有助于建立文化和团队精神。相比之下，自主武器系统很可能被视为一种成品工具，直接供给战地指挥官使用。

---

① Jack M Beard, 'Autonomous Weapons and Human Responsibilities' (2014) 45 *Georgetown Journal of International Law* 617, 657; Jens David Ohlin, 'The Combatant's Stance: Autonomous Weapons on the Battlefield' (2016) 92 *International Law Studies* 1, 28.

② Chantal Meloni, 'Command Responsibility: Mode of Liability for the Crimes of Subordinates or Separate Offence of the Superior?' (2007) 5 *Journal of International Criminal Justice* 618, 636-37; Antonio Cassese, Cassese's International Criminal Law (3rd edn, OUP 2013) 192.

③ Guénaël Mettraux, *The Law of Command Responsibility* (OUP 2009) 40.

④ *Prosecutor v. Krnojelac* (17 September 2003) Case No IT-97-25-A (ICTY Appeals Chamber), para 171.

⑤ Carrie McDougall, 'Autonomous Weapon Systems and Accountability: Putting The Cart Before the Horse' (2019) 20 *Melbourne Journal of International Law* 58, 77.

即使在传统战争中，适用指挥责任也存在困难，这从国际刑事法院第一个提出该论点的案件中就可以看出。2016 年，刚果领导人让-皮埃尔·贝姆巴（Jean-Pierre Bemba）因其指挥下的军队在邻近的中非共和国犯下战争罪和反人类罪被定罪。① 两年后，该判决被推翻，使得该原则的法律地位产生了一定程度的不确定性。② 上诉法院法官多数意见的核心是，部队是在另一个国家作战，这给贝姆巴作为一个远程指挥官采取措施来控制他们的行动带来了"困难"。③ 评估他是否采取了一切合理和必要的措施，需要"考虑当时在何种情况下他……可以采取的措施"。④

尽管贝姆巴案未涉及自主武器，但它提出了将指挥责任应用于现场指挥官可能面临的潜在障碍。另一种方法是关注致命自主武器系统确定行动参数的开发阶段。这可能导致对指挥责任的重新概念化，将注意力从使用武器的现场指挥官转移到负责采购和部署武器的指挥官或政治领导人身上。⑤ 这里的一个关键问题是，

---

① *Prosecutor v. Jean-Pierre Bemba Gombo* (21 March 2016) Case No. ICC-01/05-01/08 (International Criminal Court, Trial Chamber).

② See, eg, Trenton W Powell, 'Command Responsibility: How the International Criminal Court's Jean-Pierre Bemba Gombo Conviction Exposes the Uniform Code of Military Justice' (2017) 225 *Military Law Review* 837; Leila Nadya Sadat, 'Prosecutor v Jean-Pierre Bemba Gombo' (2019) 113 *American Journal of International Law* 353.

③ *Prosecutor v. Jean-Pierre Bemba Gombo* (8 June 2018) Case No. ICC-01/05-01/08 (International Criminal Court, Appeals Chamber), para 171。这种对指挥责任的隐含限制是有争议的。实际上，即便是形成多数意见的附和意见也对"地理上的偏远"本身作为一个单独因素表示怀疑。Ibid., Concurring Separate Opinion of Judge Eboe-Osuji, para 258.

④ Ibid., para 168.

⑤ Geoffrey S Corn, 'Autonomous Weapons Systems: Managing the Inevitability of "Taking the Man out of the Loop"' in Nehal Bhuta, et al (eds), *Autonomous Weapons Systems: Law, Ethics, Policy* (CUP 2016) 209 at 232.

离涉嫌犯罪越远,确立责任就越困难。例如,关注自主武器系统的开发意味着大部分行为甚至可能不在武装冲突的背景下发生——这是战争罪起诉的要求。① 此外,确定责任的心理要素可能是不可能的。②

除了制定专门规定来管理自主武器系统使用的可能性外,解决潜在问责差距的一个短期方法是建立专门的指挥结构,类似于监督陆地、空中和海上部队的独立指挥链。人工智能系统的指挥结构需要拥有足够的资源和技能,以承担这些系统行动的责任;未来,在没有这样的结构的情况下部署它们本身可能被视为违反战争法。③

4.2.3 责任的终结

法律很少惩罚真正的不作为或未能实施的行为。众所周知,或者说臭名昭著的是,普通法并不强制要求一个人去救助一个溺水的陌生人,也不要求阻止一个自己没有参与的犯罪。而自主行动的人工智能系统的出现将挑战这些传统普通法的责任边界。

本节已经展示了传统法律主体可以被迫承担更高责任的两种方式:一种是通过不可委托的注意义务来保护弱势群体,另一种是通过军事行动背景下的指挥责任保护受害者。展望未来,责任

---

① Tim McFarland and Tim McCormack,'Mind the Gap: Can Developers of Autonomous Weapons Systems be Liable for War Crimes?'(2014) 90 *International Studies* 361, 372-74.

② Tetyana Krupiy,'Regulating a Game Changer: Using a Distributed Approach to Develop an Accountability Framework for Lethal Autonomous Weapon Systems'(2018) 50 *Georgetown Journal of International Law* 45.

③ Peter Margulies,'Making Autonomous Weapons Accountable: Command Responsibility for Computer-Guided Lethal Force in Armed Conflicts' in Jens David Ohlin (ed), *Research Handbook on Remote Warfare* (Edward Elgar 2017) 405 at 433.

分配将不仅是有效管理风险的手段,而且极有可能转换、升格为一种道德底线。如何实现有效的责任分配将取决于每个法域的具体情况。缺乏有效的责任分配机制,有可能导致主权国家作为兜底责任承担者,为具有国际危害性的不法行为负责,这将是本书第 8 章要探讨的主题。

4.3 政府固有职能和外包的局限性

在某些情况下,仅仅知道一个人要为某个决策负责——责任终止于某个地方,可能仍然不够。对于某些决策,有必要让人类"参与其中",积极参与这些决策。

在本书第 2 章中,我们从算法决策和不受自动处理的权利的角度考察了欧洲的实践。① 同样,在本书第 3 章中,我们强调了由于人工智能系统的不透明性,应该避免在某些公共决策中依赖人工智能系统的场景,如量刑裁定。② 本节的重点是,更广泛地研究是否存在一些决策类别,对于这些决策,人类不仅能够承担决策义务,而且应该为决策结果负责。直观而言,许多涉及公共权力行使的场景都是这样的,尽管它并不总是被清晰地表述出来。迄今为止,许多讨论都是被动的,比如在特定领域抵制算法决策的泛化,赋予个人质疑特定人工智能自动决策的权力。随着人工智能系统变得更加普遍,我们有必要主动地应对问题:确定不应该将哪些功能委托给这些系统。③

---

① 参见本书第 2 章第 2.3.2 节。
② 参见本书第 3 章第 3.3 节。
③ Cf Dillon Reisman, et al, Algorithmic Impact Assessments: A Practical Framework for Public Agency Accountability (AI Now, April 2018).

一个有用的类比是政府对第三方外包的限制。如果某些公共权力不能委托给第三方，那么它们也不应该被委托给高速决策、自主决策和不透明决策的人工智能机器。这种限制的正当性包括两个层面：其一，如果将某些功能从政府组织中剥离出来，从法律意义上可能很难进行监管。其二，有些功能与公共利益关系密切，需要由符合政治程序产生的政府机构进行监督。[①]

在这个领域，美国的情况并不典型，关于政府决策市场化的争论与欧洲的论述形成鲜明对比。在欧洲，关于公共决策的讨论通常关注的问题是将政府职能转移给私人主体的正当性。而在美国，囿于国内的法律和政治环境，公共决策讨论的首要关注点却是政府职能本身的公共属性的正当性。[②] 因此，美国对"固有政府职能"的理解并非作为一个需要保护的领域出现，而是作为推动私有化更普遍趋势的一个例外。1998年，美国国会通过的一项法案将其定义为"与公共利益密切相关，因此需要由联邦政府雇员执行的职能"。[③] 美国政府问责办公室（Government Accountability Office）在2002年的一份报告中指出，关于如何应用这一宽泛的定义存在一些不确定性，但是"很明显，政府工作人员需要执行某些战斗、司法、执法、监管和政策制定职能"。[④] 2011

[①] Simon Chesterman and Angelina Fisher, 'Conclusion: Private Security, Public Order' in Simon Chesterman and Angelina Fisher (eds), *Private Security, Public Order: The Outsourcing of Public Services and Its Limits* (OUP 2009) 222 at 225-26.

[②] Government Contractors: Are Service Contractors Performing Inherently Governmental Functions? [US General Accounting Office (GAO), GAO/GGD-92-11, 18 November 1991] 2.

[③] Federal Activities Inventory Reform (FAIR) Act 1998 (US), s 5.

[④] Commercial Activities Panel: Improving the Sourcing Decisions of the Federal Government [US General Accounting Office (GAO), GAO-02-847T, 27 September 2002] 21.

年，美国政府管理和预算办公室（Office of Management and Budget）的一封政策信函详细说明，政府职能包括在行使政府权力或代表政府作出价值判断时行使自由裁量权。①

在美国之外，"公共职能"这个概念并不常见。英国没有类似内涵外延的概念，尽管会偶尔使用"公共职能"这个术语。例如，2013年英国国防部关于采购的白皮书中出现了"公共职能"这个术语。② 欧盟出于安全和产业方面的综合考虑，没有对这一领域进行监管，③ 尽管一些成员国对公共部门将服务外包给私人企业有宪法上的限制。④ 在中国，多年来这个问题可能是无关紧要的，因为外包的概念与共产党"为人民服务"的宗旨是不契合的。当然，中国也出现了公权力由市场主体有限行使的探索，特别是那些"适合高科技解决方案"的领域，⑤ 比如司法系统对于

---

① Policy Letter 11-01, Performance of Inherently Governmental and Critical Functions (Office of Federal Procurement Policy, 12 September 2011). Cf Thomas J Laubacher, 'Simplifying Inherently Governmental Functions: Creating a Principled Approach from Its Ad Hoc Beginnings' (2017) 46 *Public Contract Law Journal* 791, 822; Fiona O'Carroll, 'Inherently Governmental: A Legal Argument for Ending Private Federal Prisons and Detention Centers' (2017) 67 *Emory Law Journal* 293.

② Better Defence Acquisition: Improving How We Procure and Support Defence Equipment (HMSO, Cm 8626, 2013), para 38. See William T Kirkwood, 'Inherently Governmental Functions, Organizational Conflicts of Interest, and the Outsourcing of the United Kingdom's MOD Defense Acquisition Function: Lessons Learned from the US Experience' (2015) 44 *Public Contract Law Journal* 443.

③ Martin Trybus, 'The New EU Defence Procurement Regime' in Christopher Bovis (ed), *Research Handbook on EU Public Procurement Law* (Edward Elgar 2016) 523 at 524.

④ Christopher H Bovis, *EU Public Procurement Law* (Edward Elgar 2007) 43。对个人数据转移的限制也将阻碍某些外包行为。

⑤ Zhang Mengzhong and Sun Jian, 'Outsourcing in Municipal Governments: Experiences from the United States and China' (2012) 35 *Public Performance & Management Review* 696, 715.

人工智能的利用,已经处于世界的最前沿。①

国际人道主义法再次提供了一个有趣的对比。例如,《日内瓦公约》要求战俘营"置于关押国正规军队中负责任的军官的直接领导下"②。同样,关押平民的拘留场所也应置于"负责任的军官的领导下,该军官须来自关押国的正规军队或常规文官管理机构"③。

然而,这些规定在直接应用于人工智能及其在公共部门中的作用方面存在难以言说的问题。在其他方面,政府对人工职能系统软件的依赖通常不会被视为是"外包"行为。但是,如果政府对人工职能系统软件的依赖程度过高,相当于代表政府行使自由裁量权或进行价值判断时,那么适用于受委托的第三方的限制同样适用于人工智能系统。

正如美国的经验所示,准确界定什么是"本质上属于政府的"和"非政府的"职能的边界极为复杂。④ 例如,每年,美国卫生与公众服务部(Department of Health and Human Services)都要努力在保持一致性和效率的前提下,处理数以千计的采购合同。因此,2019年,该部门利用过去的工作说明和联邦指导方针训练了一个递归神经网络系统,以"帮助采购人员作出决策"。

---

① 参见本书第3章第3.3.2节、第9章引言。
② Convention Relative to the Treatment of Prisoners of War (Third Geneva Convention), done at Geneva, 12 August 1949, art 39.
③ Convention Relative to the Protection of Civilian Persons in Time of War (Fourth Geneva Convention), done at Geneva, 12 August 1949, art 99.
④ Cf John R Luckey, Valerie Bailey Grasso, and Kate M Manuel, Inherently Governmental Functions and Department of Defense Operations: Background, Issues, and Options for Congress (Congressional Research Service, 2009) 54.

即使在概念验证阶段，该系统也能够基本保证 86% 的正确率。①尽管这是一个令人印象深刻的自然语言处理示例，但确定什么是或不是"本质上属于政府的"职能的责任，本身至少应该是一项本质上属于政府的任务。

4.4 法律责任的局限性

距离美国第三巡回上诉法院认定"机器人不能被起诉，但它们可以造成毁灭性损害"已经过去了三十多年。②那个案例涉及一台棒球投球机，其缺陷使其"比一个不稳定的投手更为难以控制"。正如本章所展示的，过失和产品责任等法律规则可以解决许多由这类机器造成的损害。

但是，还是很多不适用的情况。即使在确定责任的主要动机是分散风险和弥补损失的情况下，人工智能系统的高速性、自主性和不透明性也会导致问责的落空。自动驾驶汽车的例子，说明可以通过强制保险填补归责制度的漏洞，这种方法应该扩展到人工智能系统的其他领域。但是，风险和损失并非潜在危害的唯一衡量标准。在某些情况下，政治伦理与合法性要求政府公职人员亲自履行公共职责，而不是将其委托给第三方，无论是由金属和硅组成的机器人，还是血肉之躯的自然人。在另外一些情况下，追究特定主体的责任是出于道义考量：某些关系，比如医院与病人之间，学校与学生之间，需要更高水平的关怀；而那些关于生

---

① Troy K Schneider, 'Can AI Decide if Work Is "Inherently Governmental?"', *Federal Computer Week* (16 September 2019).

② *United States v. Athlone Industries, Inc.*, 746 F 2d 977, 979 (3d Cir, 1984).

死的决定，还需要由人类灵魂去权衡。

托马斯·阿奎那（Thomas Aquinas）似乎理解了这一点。早在法莱兹母猪杀人案审判的一百年前，他就在《神学大全》（Summa Theologica）中写道，动物因其天性而无法为其行为感到愧疚，因此惩罚它们毫无意义。他还进一步指出，这些动物的天性正是上帝意志的体现。因此，人类诅咒它们不仅毫无意义，甚至还可能是亵渎神明。①

然而，阿奎那终究是少数派，动物审判在欧洲持续了长达半个世纪。这反映了教会法庭的历史角色，也反映了法律和习俗之间的相互影响。到18世纪中叶，这类动物审判变得罕见且非正式，并被认为是历史遗留下来的乡村司法的一种形式。

然而，正如我们将看到的，对于那些原本不应被惩罚的罪行，人们想要找到某个人来负责的愿望仍然存在。尽管在本章中已经提到了多种可能性，但未来仍会出现无法归咎于自然人或者法人的伤害案例，保险对于损失的补偿也不一定是充分的。例如，一名儿童被无法确定身份的无人机击中身亡，或被致命的自主武器误杀。在这样的案例中，任何赔偿都不足以弥补损失；人们对正义的渴望需要得到尊重。而拟人化的裁判与惩罚也可能是一种必要，至少会有来自社区的悲痛的公众要求惩罚不义，如将机器人装扮成人类模样，像对待法莱兹母猪杀人案中的母猪一样将其悬挂在公共广场上示众。

---

① Thomas Aquinas, *Summa Theologica* (Fathers of the English Dominican Province tr, first published 1265-1274, Benziger Brothers 1911), Second Part of the Second Part, Question 76.

… 第 5 章

法 律 人 格

2021年,英格兰银行完成从纸币向塑料币的过渡,发行了一张新的 50 英镑塑料币。在公众选拔过程中,将近 25 万人提名了新塑料币的钞票人物;最终的决定于 2019 年 7 月宣布,艾伦·图灵(Alan Turing)成为新塑料币的形象。图灵因在第二次世界大战期间破译密码而成为英雄。他还是计算机科学学科的奠基者,并为我们现在所称的"人工智能"奠定了基础。然而,他最著名的贡献或许是以他的名字命名的关于何时真正实现"智能"的测试。

图灵以 20 世纪 50 年代流行的一种室内游戏为模型。一男一女坐在另一个房间里,为问题提供书面答案;其他参与者需要猜测哪个答案是由谁提供的。图灵提出,可以用计算机进行类似的"模仿游戏"。当一台机器能够使人们相信它是人时,我们或许可以说它是智能的。①

这一思想在 20 世纪 60 年代早期取得了一些成功,如伊丽莎(Eliza)等程序。用户被告知伊丽莎是一名通过在计算机中输入

---

① AM Turing, 'Computing Machinery and Intelligence', (1950) 59 *Mind* 433.

文字进行沟通的心理治疗师。实际上，"她"是一个使用简单列表处理语言的算法。只要用户输入一个被识别的短语，它就会被重新构建成一个问题。所以，在用户输入"I'm depressed"（我沮丧）之后，伊丽莎就会回答："Why do you say that you are depressed?"（你为什么说你沮丧？）如果它没有识别出短语，程序将提供一些通用的内容，如"Can you elaborate on that?"（你能详细说明一下吗？）即使在被告知其工作原理后，仍有一些用户坚称伊丽莎"理解"了他们。①

撇开这种室内游戏不谈，计算机为何要具备"智能"呢？几十年来，图灵测试更多地与人工智能是否可能实现的问题密切相关，而非与体现这些特质的实体的法律地位有关。然而，自劳伦斯·索伦（Lawrence Solum）1992年的开创性文章以来，人们在讨论人工智能的法律人格时经常提到图灵测试。②尽管在技术层面上，图灵测试不再被视为衡量现代人工智能的重要指标，但其作为一种惯用方法的持久性揭示了关于人工智能人格的争论中经常被忽视的紧张关系。

随着人工智能系统变得更加复杂并在社会中发挥更大作用，至少有两个明显的原因可能导致它们在法律上被认定为"人"。

---

① Richard S Wallace,'The Anatomy of ALICE' in Robert Epstein, Gary Roberts, and Grace Beber（eds）, *Parsing the Turing Test: Philosophical and Methodological Issues in the Quest for the Thinking Computer*,（Springer 2009）181 at 184-85.

② Lawrence B Solum,'Legal Personhood for Artificial Intelligences'（1992）70 *North Carolina Law Review* 1231, 1235-37。索伦（Solum）本人将最早提出这种可能性的功劳归于克里斯托弗·斯通（Christopher Stone），后者在二十年前的一个脚注中提出了这个观点。参见 Christopher D Stone,'Should Trees Have Standing? Towards Legal Rights for Natural Objects'（1972）45 *Southern California Law Review* 450, 456 n26。

一个原因是，当事情出错时，需要有人来承担责任。这被认为是弥补由其速度、自主性和不透明性所产生的潜在问责空白的解决方案。然而，承认其法律人格的第二个原因是确保在事情顺利进行时有人可以受到奖励。例如，越来越多的文献研究由人工智能系统创造的知识产权归属问题。

这些讨论中的紧张关系在于，授予人工智能系统法律人格地位是基于工具性原因还是固有性原因。争论通常以工具性术语来构建，将其与最常见的人造法人——公司进行比较。然而，在许多争论中，或者在它们的说明和实例中，都隐含着这样一个观点：当人工智能系统接近与人类无法区分的地步，即通过图灵测试时，它们应当享有与自然人相当的地位。

一直以来，这些论点都是纯粹的推测。2017年，沙特阿拉伯授予类人机器人索菲亚（Sophia）[1]"公民身份"，一个具有七岁男孩形象的在线系统被授予日本东京的"居留权"。[2]这些都是噱头，索菲亚实际上是一个带有面孔的聊天机器人。[3]然而，同一年，欧洲议会通过了一项决议，呼吁其委员会从长远出发考虑为机器人创造一种特定的法律地位，使得至少最先进的自主机器人能够被确定为具有电子人格的地位，负责弥补其可能造成的任何损害，并可能在机器人作出自主决策或以其他方式独立与第三方

---

[1] Olivia Cuthbert, 'Saudi Arabia Becomes First Country to Grant Citizenship to a Robot', *Arab News* (26 October 2017).

[2] Anthony Cuthbertson, 'Artificial Intelligence "Boy" Shibuya Mirai Becomes World's First AI Bot to Be Granted Residency', *Newsweek* (6 November 2017).

[3] Dave Gershgorn, 'Inside the Mechanical Brain of the World's First Robot Citizen', *Quartz* (12 November 2017).

我们，机器人？
人工智能监管及其法律局限

互动的情况下应用电子人格。①

本章首先讨论最紧迫的问题，即某种形式的法律人格是否会填补责任空白或给法律制度带来其他优势。基于公司和其他法律拟制人的历史，似乎毫无疑问，大多数法律制度可以赋予人工智能系统某种法律人格；更有趣的问题是，它们是否应该拥有某种法律人格，以及这种人格可能具有什么内涵。

随后，本章转向人工智能系统与自然人的类比。机器永远不可能成为自然人，这一点似乎是不言而喻的。然而，几个世纪以来，奴隶和妇女也未被认定为完整的人类。如果将图灵测试推向逻辑的终点，《银翼杀手》的结论是，与人类无法区分的人工智能系统有朝一日可能要求同样的法律地位。尽管目前关于"机器人权利"的争论仅局限于边缘领域，但许多赞成人工智能系统拥有其创造的知识产权的观点中都隐含着这种可能性。

更为重要的是，人工智能系统可以与人类平起平坐的想法提出了赋予其法律人格的第三个理由。因为一旦实现了平等，就没有理由认为人工智能的进一步演化会止步于此。虽然通用人工智能目前仍是科幻想法，但它引发了人们的思考：如果人类智能被人工智能超越，法律是否能塑造或约束人工智能的行为？当然，如果真的到了这种地步，问题可能不是我们是否承认通用人工智能的权利，而是通用人工智能是否承认我们人类的权利。

---

① European Parliament Resolution with Recommendations to the Commission on Civil Law Rules on Robotics［2015/2103（INL）］（European Parliament, 16 February 2017），para 59（f）.

5.1 可踢之躯？

法律人格是任何法律体系的基础。谁可以作出法律行为，谁可以成为权利和义务的主体，这些问题几乎是其他所有问题的前提条件。然而，对这些基础的仔细审查揭示了令人惊讶的不确定性和分歧。尽管如此，正如约翰·杜威（John Dewey）在1926年指出的那样，"法院和立法者在涉及人格性质的特殊问题的裁决时，没有达成一致的意见，有时甚至没有任何概念或理论"，也会继续进行他们的工作。他接着说，的确，求助于理论"不止一次地妨碍了对特定权利或义务问题的裁决，而不是促进了这些问题的解决"。[①]

在实践中，绝大多数法律体系承认两种形式的法律人：自然人和法人。自然人因为是人类的基本事实而被承认。[②] 相比之下，法人是非人类实体，由法律赋予其某些权利和义务。公司和其他形式的商业组织是最常见的法人，但法人还有许多其他可能的形式，如宗教、政府和政府间实体也可以在国家和国际层面作为法人行事。

值得注意的是，这些都是人类行为的集合体，尽管有一些例子表明，确实存在被授予法人人格的非人类实体。除了在前言中

---

① John Dewey, 'The Historic Background of Corporate Legal Personality' (1926) 35 *Yale Law Journal* 655, 660.

② 当然，这假定了对"人类"以及"出生"和"死亡"等术语的含义有一个共识。参见 Ngaire Naffine, 'Who Are Law's Persons? From Cheshire Cats to Responsible Subjects' (2003) 66 *Modern Law Review* 346.

提到的例子之外，还包括印度的寺庙①、新西兰的一条河流②以及厄瓜多尔的整个生态系统③。毫无疑问，一个国家可以为人工智能系统这样的新实体赋予某种法人人格；④ 如果发生这种情况，其他国家也可能给予承认。⑤

5.1.1 法律人格理论

正如前面讨论过的那样，学者和法律改革机构已经提议赋予人工智能系统某种法律人格，以帮助解决法律责任问题，如在自动驾驶汽车的案例中，自动驾驶系统实体的行为可能不受"驾驶员"的控制，制造商或所有者也无法预测其行为。⑥ 少数学者进一步认为，需要制定程序来审判机器人罪犯，并为通过重新编程或在极端情况下进行销毁的"惩罚"做好准备。⑦

这些论点表明了对于法人人格的工具主义方法，但学者对最常见的法人主体——公司的地位提供了不同的解释，这有助于回答是否应将该地位扩展至人工智能系统的问题。

集合论，有时也被称为"契约论"或"象征论"，认为公司是一种法律创设的工具，可使自然人将自己组织成一个团体，并

---

① See, eg, *Shiromani Gurdwara Prabandhak Committee*, *Amritsar v. Shri Somnath Dass* AIR 2000 SC 1421 (Supreme Court of India).

② Te Awa Tupua (Whanganui River Claims Settlement) Act 2017 (New Zealand), s 14 (1). 这是在将 Te Urewera 国家公园指定为"一个法律实体，拥有一个法人的所有权利、权力、职责和责任"之后的事情。参见 Te Urewera Act 2014 (New Zealand), s 11 (1)。

③ Constitution of the Republic of Ecuador 2008 (Ecuador), art 10.

④ John Dewey, 'The Historic Background of Corporate Legal Personality' (1926) 35 *Yale Law Journal* 655, 660.

⑤ 参见 *Bumper Development Corp. v. Commissioner of Police for the Metropolis* [1991] 1 WLR 1362 (判决承认了印度庙宇在英国法律下的法人地位)。

⑥ 参见本书第 2 章第 2.1.2 节。

⑦ 参见本书第 5 章第 5.1.2（b）节。

在与其他方的法律关系中体现这种组织。团体成员可以与其他方建立限制责任等方面的单独合同关系，而公司形式使他们能够以较低的成本集体实现这一目标。① 这一理论受到诸多批评，它对人工智能系统的适用性最低。②

虚构论和特许论对公司法人人格的解释有着不同的起源，但归根结底是相同的：公司之所以具有法人人格，是因为法律体系选择赋予它们这种身份。正如美国最高法院在1819年指出的，公司是"一个人造的、无形的、抽象的存在，仅在法律上存在"。③ 法人人格是为了实现政策目标（如鼓励创业），或是为法律体系的连贯性和稳定性做贡献（如通过某些实体的永久性）。在通过特许或立法明确授予法人人格时，目的性方面曾经更为明显；在20世纪，这只是形式化的。④ 这些实证主义的解释与立法和司法实践中承认法人人格的做法最为一致，可以包括将其扩展至人工智能系统。

相反，现实主义理论认为，公司既不是虚构的，也不仅仅是象征性的，而是在法律体系赋予法人人格之前就客观存在的实体。尽管它们拥有成员，但它们独立行事，其行为可能不可归因

---

① Ronald Coase, 'The Nature of the Firm' (1937) 4 *Economica* 386. Cf Victor Morawetz, *A Treatise on the Law of Private Corporations* (Little, Brown 1886) 2（"一个不言而喻的事实是，公司实际上并不是一个与其组成部分不同的个体或事物。'公司'这个词只是公司成员的集体名称。"）.

② Nadia Banteka, 'Artificially Intelligent Persons' (2020) 58 *Houston Law Review* (*forthcoming*).

③ *Trustees of Dartmouth Coll. v. Woodward*, 17 US 518, 636 (1819).

④ See, eg, Christine E Amsler, Robin L Bartlett, and Craig J Bolton, 'Thoughts of Some British Economists on Early Limited Liability and Corporate Legislation' (1981) 13 *History of Political Economy* 774; Giuseppe Dari-Mattiacci, *et al*, 'The Emergence of the Corporate Form' (2017) 33 *Journal of Law, Economics, and Organization* 193.

于这些成员。在极端的情况下，有人认为公司不仅是法律上的人，还是道义上的人。[1] 这一理论更受理论家和社会学家的青睐，而立法者和法官则不然，但它呼应了本章引言中强调的紧张关系：法律人格不仅是被赋予的，而且是应得的。然而，在实践中，作为法律主体的实际承认仍然取决于国家的赋予。[2]

结论是，杜威一个世纪前的观点是正确的："'人'的含义取决于法律的规定。"[3] 然而，尽管是否具有法律人格是二元选择问题，但法律人格的具体内涵却是丰富多彩的。我们暂且将人工智能系统应该在法理上被赋予法律人格的问题搁置起来，如果立法者最后决定赋予人工智能系统特定的法律人格，那就也应该认可人工智能需要承担法定义务，享受法定权利。

5.1.2 法律人格的内容

法律人格随之带来权利和义务，但在一个法律制度内的所有人不一定都有相同的权利和义务。即使在自然人中，争取妇女、少数族裔和其他弱势群体平等权利的斗争也反映了这一事实。

例如，可以只授予权利而不承担义务。这种赋予自然法人法律地位的方法在理论上是可能的，当它首次于1972年[4]被提倡时就是如此，在实践中也是如此，如厄瓜多尔《宪法》[5]。这种"人

---

[1] Peter French, 'The Corporation as a Moral Person' (1979) 16 *American Philosophical Quarterly* 207.

[2] Katsuhito Iwai, 'Persons, Things and Corporations: The Corporate Personality Controversy and Comparative Corporate Governance' (1999) 47 *American Journal of Comparative Law* 583; Susan Mary Watson, 'The Corporate Legal Person' (2019) 19 *Journal of Corporate Law Studies* 137.

[3] John Dewey, 'The Historic Background of Corporate Legal Personality' (1926) 35 *Yale Law Journal* 655.

[4] Christopher D Stone, 'Should Trees Have Standing? Towards Legal Rights for Natural Objects' (1972) 45 *Southern California Law Review* 450, 456 n26.

[5] Constitution of the Republic of Ecuador, arts 71-74.

格"可以说只是为了避免立场问题的手段：使人类个体能够代表非人类权利持有者行事，而不是要求它以自己的身份建立立场。①无论如何，这与考虑人工智能系统的人格地位的原因并不相符。

另一方面，人工智能法律人格可能只伴随义务。表面上看，这似乎很有吸引力，但只要这些义务旨在解决前几章描述的问责空白，就会引发一些明显的问题。例如，民事责任通常导致损害赔偿，而这只有在侵权者拥有财产的情况下才能支付。② 这些支付可能来自一个中央基金，尽管这更类似于本书第 4 章讨论的强制保险制度。③"人格"将仅仅是形式。

对公司而言，法人资格意味着具有起诉和被起诉、签订合同、承担债务、拥有财产以及被定罪的能力。在权利方面，公司是否享有与自然人相当的宪法保护程度是一个持续争论的问题。尽管美国已经给予公司实体许多保护，但在免于自我归罪等方面，仍然有所限制。④ 总的来说，法人享有的权利要少于自然人。（在国际法中，国家享有完全的法人资格，而国际组织可能具有不同程度的法人资格。⑤）

---

① Christopher Rodgers, 'A New Approach to Protecting Ecosystems' (2017) 19 *Environmental Law Review* 266. 与此不同，新西兰设立了专职受托人，以代表被赋予人格特征的环境要素场景。

② Cf Liability for Artificial Intelligence and Other Emerging Digital Technologies (EU Expert Group on Liability and New Technologies, 2019) 38.

③ 参见本书第 4 章第 4.1.4 节。

④ Scott A Trainor, 'A Comparative Analysis of a Corporation's Right Against Self-Incrimination' (1994) 18 *Fordham International Law Journal* 2139. Cf *Citizens United v. Federal Election Commission*, 558 US 310 (US Supreme Court, 2010).

⑤ Simon Chesterman, 'Does ASEAN Exist? The Association of Southeast Asian Nations as an International Legal Person' (2008) XII *Singapore Year Book of International Law* 199.

(a) 私法

对于人工智能系统来说,具有法人资格的主要吸引力之一是可以被起诉,正如欧洲议会所承认的。① 当然,这假设了存在可以而且应该填补的有实质性的问责制度空白。到目前为止,本书大部分内容都认为这些空白往往被夸大了。对于这种补救方法的另一个担忧是,即使它确实起到了填补空白的作用,赋予人工智能系统法人资格也会将现行法律下的责任从现有法人转移出去。实际上,这将激发将风险转移给"电子法人",以保护自然法人和传统法人免受风险的动机。② 公司也存在这个问题,它们可以保护投资者免受超出其投资固定金额的责任——事实上,这通常是采用公司制度的首要目的。重新分配风险的合理性在于它鼓励投资和创业。③ 典型的保障措施包括要求有限责任实体的名称包含其性质(如有限公司,Ltd.;有限责任公司,LLC),以及可能穿透公司面纱以防止滥用法人形式。④ 在人工智能系统的情况下,也可以制定类似的揭示面纱机制——尽管如果一个人操纵人工智能系统以保护自己免担责任,这种能力可能表明相关的人工智能系统不值得拥有独立的法人身份。⑤

---

① Paul Humphreys,'The Philosophical Novelty of Computer Simulation Methods'(2009) 169 *Synthese* 615,617.

② Joanna J Bryson, Mihailis E Diamantis, and Thomas D Grant,'Of, for, and by the People: The Legal Lacuna of Synthetic Persons'(2017) 25 *Artificial Intelligence and Law* 273,287.

③ Frank H Easterbrook and Daniel R Fischel,'Limited Liability and the Corporation'(1985) 52 *University of Chicago Law Review* 89.

④ David Millon,'Piercing the Corporate Veil, Financial Responsibility, and the Limits of Limited Liability'(2007) 56 *Emory Law Journal* 1305.

⑤ Jacob Turner, *Robot Rules: Regulating Artificial Intelligence* (Palgrave Macmillan 2019) 193.

合同订立有时被认为是授予人工智能系统法人资格的原因之一。① 然而，利用电子代理达成具有约束力的协议并非新鲜事物。在第 1 章所讨论的高频交易现象中，算法代表传统主体与其他算法达成协议。尽管人工智能系统的自主性可能挑战现有学说的适用性——特别是在出现问题（如错误）的情况下，但第 2 章已经阐明，这仍然可以在不诉诸新的法律主体的情况下解决。②

承担债务和拥有财产是可以被起诉和订立合同的必要条件。③ 人工智能系统积累财富的可能性引发了关于它们是否或如何被征税的问题。有人提议对机器人征税，作为解决因自动化而导致的税基减少和工人失业的一种手段。④ 比尔·盖茨等人认为，机器人（或拥有它们的公司）应当纳税。⑤ 行业代表们认为，这将对竞争力产生负面影响，因此到目前为止还没有实施。⑥ 另一种方法是不着眼于机器，而是关注滥用市场地位的公司，可能的方法

---

① See, eg, Samir Chopra and Laurence F White, *A Legal Theory for Autonomous Artificial Agents* (University of Michigan Press 2011) 160.

② 参见本书第 2 章第 2.3.1 节。

③ 一些学者认为，这是公司独立法人地位的最重要功能。参见 Henry Hansmann and Reinier Kraakman, 'The Essential Role of Organizational Law' (2000) 110 *Yale Law Journal* 387. Cf Hans Tjio, 'Lifting the Veil on Piercing the Veil' [2014] *Lloyd's Maritime and Commercial Law Quarterly* 19. 缺乏拥有财产能力的人工智能系统仍然可以受到某些形式的法律程序的约束，如禁令，并且可以通过其"劳动"来抵销债务。

④ Brett A King, Tyler Hammond, and Jake Harrington, 'Disruptive Technology: Economic Consequences of Artificial Intelligence and the Robotics Revolution' (2017) 12 (2) *Journal of Strategic Innovation and Sustainability* 53.

⑤ Kevin J Delaney, 'The Robot that Takes Your Job Should Pay Taxes, says Bill Gates', *Quartz* (18 February 2017).

⑥ Lawrence Summers, 'Robots Are Wealth Creators and Taxing Them Is Illogical', *Financial Times* (6 March 2017).

包括更积极地对利润进行征税或要求分散股份所有权。① 无论如何，对人工智能系统的征税就像赋予其承担债务和拥有财产的能力一样，是授予其法人资格的附随而非理由。②（关于人工智能系统是否拥有其创造物的问题将在下一节中考虑。）

除了拥有财产外，人工智能系统还可能被要求管理财产。例如，2014 年，中国香港的一家风险投资公司宣布任命一款名为"维塔尔"（Vital）的计算机程序为其董事会成员。③ 与沙特阿拉伯授予类人机器人索菲亚公民身份一样，这更多的是一种形式而非实质。根据中国香港法律，该程序并未被任命负责任何职位；在几年后的一次采访中，该公司的管理合伙人承认，公司只是将维塔尔视为具有观察员身份的董事会成员。④ 在大多数公司法制度下，人类董事可以将部分责任委托给人工智能系统，但他们不会被免除对组织的最终管理责任。⑤ 大多数法域要求这些董事是自然人，尽管在某些法域，法人（通常是另一家公司）可以在董事会任职。⑥ 肖恩·拜恩（Shawn Bayern）进一步指出，美国商

---

① 'Why Taxing Robots Is Not a Good Idea', *Economist* (25 February 2017).

② Cf Luciano Floridi, 'Robots, Jobs, Taxes, and Responsibilities' (2017) 30 *Philosophy & Technology* 1.

③ Rob Wile, 'A Venture Capital Firm Just Named an Algorithm to Its Board of Directors', *Business Insider* (13 May 2014).

④ Nicky Burridge, 'AI Takes Its Place in the Boardroom', *Nikkei Asian Review* (25 May 2017).

⑤ Florian Möslein, 'Robots in the Boardroom: Artificial Intelligence and Corporate Law' in Woodrow Barfield and Ugo Pagallo (eds), *Research Handbook on the Law of Artificial Intelligence* (Edward Elgar 2018) 649 at 658-60.

⑥ See, eg, Personen-und Gesellschaftsrecht (PGR) 1926 (Liechtenstein), art. 344; Companies Ordinance 2014 (HK), s 457。这种情况在英国法律中一直持续到 2015 年。参见 Small Business, Enterprise and Employment Act 2015 (UK), s 87。

业实体法中的漏洞可以用来创建没有任何人类成员的有限责任公司。① 这需要对该法进行有些曲折的解释——自然人创建公司，将人工智能系统添加为成员，然后辞职②——但这表明了未来可能对法律人格进行调整的方式。

（b）刑法

法律人格的最后一个特质是最直观且值得详细阐述的：接受惩罚的能力。

如果赋予人工智能系统与公司相当的法律人格，也就没有必要再去争论它是否可以根据刑法被起诉。只要确立了犯罪的客观和主观要件，③ 就可以对这样的实体处以罚款或没收其财产；暂停或撤销相关经营许可。在一些法域，可以对法人下达清算令；如果无法对其进行资格清算，足以使实体破产的巨额罚款可能产生相同的效果。在极端情况下，甚至可以想象一个"机器人罪犯"被物理性销毁。但这是否可取，是否有效？

刑罚的最常见原因包括惩戒、剥夺犯罪能力、威慑和矫正。④

---

① Shawn Bayern, 'Of Bitcoins, Independently Wealthy Software, and the Zero-Member LLC' (2014) 108 *Northwestern University Law Review* 1485, 1495-500.

② Shawn Bayern, 'The Implications of Modern Business-Entity Law for the Regulation of Autonomous Systems' (2015) 19 *Stanford Technology Law Review* 93, 101.

③ 对于公司而言，确认主、客观要件虽然困难却并非不可克服。尽管公司缺乏自由意志或道德责任，但它们仍能被判定违反刑事法律。这一事实也批驳了反对人工智能系统刑事责任的论点。参见 VS Khanna, 'Corporate Criminal Liability: What Purpose Does It Serve?' (1996) 109 *Harvard Law Review* 1477, 1513; Samuel W Buell, 'Criminally Bad Management' in Jennifer Arlen (ed), *Research Handbook on Corporate Crime and Financial Misdealing* (Edward Elgar 2018) 59.

④ 有人可能会争辩说，刑法的象征性作用并不都需要实际的惩罚——在实践中不执行法律并不罕见。然而，这通常依赖于明确或隐含的决定不去调查或起诉特定的犯罪，而不是接受某一类行为者根本不能被惩罚。

惩戒是最古老的刑罚原因，将受害者的复仇欲望转化为向社会展示错误行为必然导致后果的行动。① 对这些后果的校准在"以眼还眼，以牙还牙"的法则中体现得最为直接。正如本书第 4 章所述的法莱兹母猪被审判、绞死以恢复社区秩序一样，对公司法人或者电子"人"处以相应的罚款带来的示范效应，可能比犯罪行为未受惩罚更可取。②

刑罚制度还可以用来剥夺犯罪分子的作案能力，从物理上阻止他们再次犯罪。这可以通过不同形式的监禁来实现，但也可能包括流放、截肢、阉割和执行死刑。对于公司，这可能包括撤销营业执照或强制清算令。③ 在这里，可以直接类比对待危险动物和机械的做法，尽管采取如安乐死恶犬或报废有缺陷的车辆等措施属于行政处罚而非刑事惩罚，且不依赖于"有罪"的裁定。④ 在某些法域，儿童和精神病患者可能被认为无法犯罪，但如果被判定对自己或社区构成危险，他们仍可能被国家强制机关拘留。⑤ 这些个体不会失去他们的法律人格；在人工智能系统的情况下，不需要赋予它们法律人格，就可以对其实施类似于限制行动的措施，如召回产品或撤销许可。

威慑是近现代的刑罚理由，它以犯罪者的理性为理论预设。

---

① 谴责有时也被视为惩罚的独立理由。参见 Bill Wringe, *An Expressive Theory of Punishment* (Palgrave Macmillan 2016).

② Christina Mulligan, 'Revenge Against Robots' (2018) 69 *South Carolina Law Review* 579; Ying Hu, 'Robot Criminals' (2019) 52 *University of Michigan Journal of Law Reform* 487, 503-07.

③ W Robert Thomas, 'Incapacitating Criminal Corporations' (2019) 72 *Vanderbilt Law Review* 905.

④ See, eg, Deborah Legge and Simon Brooman, *Law Relating to Animals* (Cavendish Publishing 2000).

⑤ Arlie Loughnan, *Manifest Madness: Mental Incapacity in the Criminal Law* (OUP 2012).

通过设定惩罚措施，以威慑对行为施加成本，旨在使这一成本超过任何潜在利益。将犯罪行为归结为经济分析的能力似乎特别适用于公司和人工智能系统。然而，对公司法人而言，激励措施实际上是针对可能通过公司谋取个人和公司利益的人类管理者。①就人工智能系统而言，只有当其编程寻求经济利益最大化，而不考虑潜在的刑法本身时，罚款的威慑效应才会影响行为。②

最后一种刑罚的理由是矫正。与剥夺犯罪能力和威慑一样，它具有前瞻性，旨在降低重新犯罪率。然而，与剥夺犯罪能力不同的是，它旨在影响是否犯罪的决定，而非犯罪能力本身；③与威慑不同的是，这种影响力旨在从内在而非外在发挥作用。④对于自然人犯罪而言，矫正在理论上比在实践中得到了更多的认可；在美国，矫正在20世纪70年代失宠。⑤然而，在公司方面，影响较为明确的杠杆作用导致试验性地采用狭义的惩罚措施，旨在鼓励良好行为，同时也阻止不良行为。⑥这种方法似乎非常适合人工智能系统，因为人工智能系统违反刑法的行为可被视为需要调试的错误，而非应受惩罚的罪行。⑦实际上，关于这一主题

---

① Assaf Hamdani and Alon Klement，'Corporate Crime and Deterrence'(2008) 61 *Stanford Law Review* 271.

② 参见本书第9章第9.3.1节。

③ Jeremy Bentham，'Panopticon Versus New South Wales' in John Bowring (ed)，*The Works of Jeremy Bentham* (William Tait 1843) vol. 4，173 at 174.

④ See Tony Ward and Shadd Maruna，*Rehabilitation* (Routledge 2007).

⑤ See，eg，Albert W Alschuler，'The Changing Purposes of Criminal Punishment: A Retrospective on the Past Century and Some Thoughts About the Next'(2003) 70 *University of Chicago Law Review* 1，9. Cf Francis T Cullen and Karen E Gilbert，*Reaffirming Rehabilitation* (2nd edn，Anderson 2013).

⑥ Mihailis E Diamantis，'Clockwork Corporations: A Character Theory of Corporate Punishment' (2018) 103 *Iowa Law Review* 507.

⑦ 参见本书第9章第9.3.2节。

的论著已经直接将矫正的教育方面类比为机器学习。① 然而，要确保机器学习产生不违反刑法的输出结果，无须赋予其法律人格地位，也无须动用国家的强制力。

5.1.3 无灵魂可诅咒

虽然支持公司承担责任的论点通常是出于工具性的考虑，但令人惊讶的是，新兴的关于"机器人罪犯"的文献却滑向拟人化。这个术语本身暗示着一种特殊的愿望，即与具有不同自主程度的家用电器或云端操作的无实体人工智能系统相比，类人人工智能系统应遵循更高的标准。② 这种区别没有原则上的理由，但它说明了人工智能系统法律人格论证中的紧张关系，这些论证混合了工具性和固有性的理由。

有趣的是，关于公司法律人格的争论主要集中在与人相异的问题上。这一点被第一任瑟洛男爵（First Baron Thurlow）形象地描述为"无可诅咒之灵魂，无可踢之躯体"。③ 尽管没有灵魂，但公司法人资格并未受到阻碍，也没有原则上的障碍阻止人工智能系统被类似地对待。然而，公司法人资格不同于人工智能法人资格，因为公司是由人组成的，通过人类来运作，而人工智能系统是由人类创造的。④

---

① Gabriel Hallevy, *Liability for Crimes Involving Artificial Intelligence Systems*（Springer 2015）210-11.

② Cf Jack M Balkin, 'The Three Laws of Robotics in the Age of Big Data'（2017）78 *Ohio State Law Journal* 1217，1219.

③ Mervyn A King, *Public Policy and the Corporation*（Chapman and Hall 1977）1. See, eg, John C Coffee, Jr, '"No Soul to Damn; No Body to Kick": An Unscandalized Inquiry into the Problem of Corporate Punishment'（1981）79 *Michigan Law Review* 386.

④ SM Solaiman, 'Legal Personality of Robots, Corporations, Idols and Chimpanzees: A Quest for Legitimacy'（2017）25 *Artificial Intelligence and Law* 155，174.

因此，工具主义原因可能证明将法人资格授予人工智能系统是合理的，但这并不是必需的。特别是，工具主义隐含的人工智能系统拟人论回避了其他问题。例如，当某个人工智能系统具有多种功能或者是分布式系统时，界定其法律人格的内容将极其困难。法律上或许可以创建类似于公司的独立法人主体——每辆自动驾驶汽车、智能医疗设备、简历筛选算法等都可以拥有独立的法律人格。如果真的存在责任空白，那么这种法律形式可能填补它们。然而，这种安排的主要受益者将是生产商和用户，他们将因此免于现行法律下的部分或全部责任。① 而更好的方法是，在最开始就防止这些空白出现。

5.2 我思故我在？

然而，工具主义并非法律体系承认人工智能系统法律人格的唯一原因。对于自然人而言，无须通过图灵测试：仅出生这一事实就能使其被赋予法律上的人格地位。②

然而，并非一直如此。在人类历史的大量时间中，奴隶像财产一样被买卖；③ 土著人被比作在土地上游荡的动物，从而为剥夺他们的土地寻求理由；④ 在长达几个世纪的英国法律中，妇女的地位就是布莱克斯通总结的那样："丈夫和妻子是一个人，丈

---

① 参见本书第 4 章。

② 参见联合国 1948 年《世界人权宣言》第 1 条；《公民权利和政治权利国际公约》（1976 年 3 月 23 日实施）第 6 (1) 条。

③ See Jean Allain (ed), *The Legal Understanding of Slavery: From the Historical to the Contemporary* (OUP 2013).

④ Simon Chesterman, ' "Skeletal Legal Principles": The Concept of Law in Australian Land Rights Jurisprudence' (1998) 40 *Journal of Legal Pluralism and Unofficial Law* 61.

夫就是那个人。"① 即使在今天，自然人也只有在成年、精神健全且未被监禁的情况下才能享有完全的权利和义务。

如前所述，许多赞成人工智能系统应具有法律人格的论点都有一个隐含或明确的假设，即人工智能系统正以一种让它们在法律面前获得与人类相当认可的方式逼近人类特质。这些论点在分析和影响方面都受到了批评。在分析方面，尼尔·理查兹（Neil Richards）和威廉·斯马特（William Smart）将人工智能系统拟人化的倾向称为"类人机器人谬误"。② 一次又一次的实验表明，人们更容易根据机器人的类人外观、自然语言交流或仅仅是被赋予一个名字的事实，将诸如道德感之类的人类特质归于机器人。③ 关于人工智能接近人类特质的更严肃的论证通常未能检查关于这些特质如何在我们人类自身中表现的假设。④

从影响的角度来看，2017年欧洲议会的决议促使来自整个欧洲大陆的数百名人工智能专家在一封公开信中警告，从"伦理和法律角度"来看，赋予人工智能系统法律人格是不合适的。有趣的是，这些警告本身可能因假定基于自然人模型的法律地位必然

---

① Lee Holcombe, *Wives and Property: Reform of the Married Women's Property Law in Nineteenth-Century England* (Martin Robertson 1983) 18.

② Neil M Richards and William D Smart, 'How Should the Law Think About Robots?' in Ryan Calo, A Michael Froomkin, and Ian Kerr (eds), *Robot Law* (Edward Elgar 2016) 3 at 18-21.

③ Cf Luisa Damiano and Paul Dumouchel, 'Anthropomorphism in Human-Robot Co-evolution' (2018) 9 *Frontiers in Psychology* 468.

④ See, eg, Elisabeth Hildt, 'Artificial Intelligence: Does Consciousness Matter?' (2019) 10 (1535) *Frontiers in Psychology*, 1-3; Gunter Meissner, 'Artifcial Intelligence: Consciousness and Conscience' (2020) 35 *AI & Society* 225, 231. 关于约翰·塞尔（John Searle）著名的"中文房间"（Chinese room）理论，参见 John R Searle, 'Minds, Brains, and Programs' (1980) 3 *Behavioral and Brain Sciences* 417, 417-24。

会带来欧盟法律下保证的所有"人类"权利而触犯类人机器人谬误。① 其他专家坦率地承认，否认人工智能系统法律人格的唯一依据是一种物种主义——因为我们这些立法者是人类，所以会优先考虑人类福祉而不是机器人福祉。② 如果人工智能系统变得如此复杂，以至于这是我们最有力的辩护理由，问题可能不在于它们的法律地位，而在于我们自己。③

尽管如此，本节还是认真对待了某些人工智能系统可能因其固有特质而具有法律人格的观点。不过，这些特质如何表现的技术方面的细节，以及它们所模仿的人类特质的详细解析，都超出了本书的范围。④ 相反，我们将重点关注自然人的人格地位以及可能如何扩展。首先要检查的问题是，过去是如何处理这个问题的，如赋予长期以来被视为低于白人男性的自然人以参政权和授权。最近，活动家和学者们基于非人类动物（如黑猩猩）的固有特质，敦促进一步扩展它们的某些权利。然后，转向如今倡导人工智能系统以固有原因而非工具性原因而争取有意义的权利的最有力表述：它们应该能够拥有自己创造的东西。

5.2.1 自然人格的扩展

正如马丁·路德·金（Martin Luther King）博士说过的一

---

① Open Letter to the European Commission: Artificial Intelligence and Robotics (April 2018), para 2 (b). Cf Jacob Turner, *Robot Rules: Regulating Artificial Intelligence* (Palgrave Macmillan 2019) 189-90.

② Cf Peter Singer,'Speciesism and Moral Status'(2009) 40 *Metaphilosophy* 567.

③ 参见本书第 5 章第 5.3 节。

④ See, eg, Jean-Marc Fellous and Michael A Arbib, *Who Needs Emotions? The Brain Meets the Robot* (OUP 2005); Wendell Wallach and Colin Allen, *Moral Machines: Teaching Robots Right from Wrong* (OUP 2009).

句名言:"道德宇宙的弧线漫长,但它朝着正义的方向弯曲。"在1776年美国起草《独立宣言》时,"所有人"(原文如此)生而平等的观念显然是不成立的。十年后,法国《人权宣言》同样宣称所有人拥有自然而不可剥夺的权利,而这一宣言也被杰里米·边沁斥为"踩在高跷上的胡说八道"。① 如卢梭在《社会契约论》的开篇所言,人或许是生来自由,但却无处不在枷锁之中。②

然而,在接下来的几个世纪,这些崇高理想逐渐实现,权利观念得到广泛传播。到20世纪中叶,《世界人权宣言》已然宣称所有人类"生来自由,在尊严和权利上一律平等",尽管彼时全球仍有1/3的人口生活在联合国划分的非自治领土上。随后,去殖民化运动、废除种族隔离、妇女解放和其他权利运动风起云涌。今天,虽然权利的具体边界仍然众说纷纭,但没有哪个国家会宣称成年公民在法律面前不具备平等人格。③

有趣的是,一些支持赋予人工智能系统法律人格的观点并非建立在自然人人格的进步主义叙事上,而是建立在奴隶制的黑暗历史上。例如,安德鲁·卡茨(Andrew Katz)和乌戈·帕加洛发现了人工智能系统与古罗马法中的"家庭财产制度"(peculium)下的奴隶有类似之处,即奴隶虽然缺乏法律人格,但却能发

---

① Jeremy Bentham, 'Anarchical Fallacies' in John Bowring (ed), *The Works of Jeremy Bentham* (William Tait 1843) vol 2, 489 at 501.

② Jean-Jacques Rousseau, *The Social Contract* (GDH Cole tr, first published 1762, JM Dent 1923) 49.

③ 关于叛教者以及残疾人等特殊例外情况,参见 Paul M Taylor, *A Commentary on the International Covenant on Civil and Political Rights* (CUP 2020) 449-54. 关于无脑畸形婴儿,参见 Visa AJ Kurki, *A Theory of Legal Personhood* (OUP 2019) 9.

挥超过作为其主人的仆从角色的作用。①（2017 年，法国成立了一个名为"Peculium"的数字银行，可能是为那些从未学过拉丁文的投资者设立的。）作为对法律人格富有创意的解释的例子，卡茨等对古罗马法中的奴隶的法律属性的解读很有新意，虽然它依据的是工具性理由，而非奴隶本身固有的属性。正如帕加洛指出的，家庭财产制实际上是一种"初级形态的有限责任公司"（proto-limited liability company）。② 当下的法律体系没有禁止创建类似的人工智能系统的人格结构，至于是否应该这样做，依赖于与奴隶制相关的早已废弃的古罗马法律或许不是最具有说服力的。③

另一种方法是考虑法律体系如何对待动物。④ 在大多数情况下，它们被视为可以买卖的财产，但同时也应该受到"人道"的对待。⑤ 在第 4 章中已经讨论了动物主人对由动物造成损害的责任问题，⑥

---

① Andrew Katz,'Intelligent Agents and Internet Commerce in Ancient Rome'(2008) 20 *Society for Computers and Law* 35; Ugo Pagallo, *The Laws of Robots*: *Crimes*, *Contracts*, *and Torts* (Springer 2013) 103-06. See also Hutan Ashrafian,'Artificial Intelligence and Robot Responsibilities: Innovating Beyond Rights'(2015) 21 *Science and Engineering Ethics* 317, 325; Sergio Nasarre-Aznar,'Ownership at Stake (Once Again): Housing, Digital Contents, Animals, and Robots'(2018) 10 *Journal of Property*, *Planning*, *and Environmental Law* 69, 78; Eduard Fosch-Villaronga, *Robots*, *Healthcare*, *and the Law*: *Regulating Automation in Personal Care* (Routledge 2019) 152.

② Ugo Pagallo, *The Laws of Robots*: *Crimes*, *Contracts*, *and Torts* (Springer 2013) 104.

③ Mark Chinen, *Law and Autonomous Machines*: *The Co-Evolution of Legal Responsibility and Technology* (Edward Elgar 2019) 19.

④ See, eg, Visa AJ Kurki and Tomasz Pietrzykowski (eds), *Legal Personhood*: *Animals*, *Artificial Intelligence and the Unborn* (Springer 2017); Saskia Stucki,'Towards a Theory of Legal Animal Rights: Simple and Fundamental Rights'(2020) 40 *Oxford Journal of Legal Studies* 533.

⑤ Cf Katie Sykes,'Human Drama, Animal Trials: What the Medieval Animal Trials Can Teach Us About Justice for Animals'(2011) 17 *Animal Law* 273.

⑥ 参见本书第 4 章第 4.1.2 节。

这一章节的重点则在于，这些动物是否可能在法律上具有独立的人格地位。

赋予非人类动物一定程度的人格地位的多种努力一直收效甚微。例如，2013 年，美国动物权益保护组织"非人权利项目"（Nonhuman Rights Project）代表四只被圈养的黑猩猩提起诉讼，主张这些动物展现出高级认知能力、自主性和自我意识。纽约州上诉法院虽然拒绝授予这些动物人身保护令，但是并未质疑黑猩猩的认知能力等事宜，而是认为，人格权等法律权利的扩展传统上与社会契约形式的法律义务负担挂钩。法院认为，"众所周知，这些黑猩猩并未承担任何法律义务，那么它们就无法享有自由权等人格权利"。① 法院的这个依据，其实是比较牵强的。因为许多缺乏民事行为能力或责任能力的人，比如婴儿、植物人，在法律上仍被视为"人"。② 在另外一个类似的案例中，该观点以同义反复的逻辑驳回了对非人类动物人格地位的诉求，主张"这些缺乏民事行为能力或责任能力的人仍然是自然人，是人类社会的成员"③。虽然上诉请求被拒绝，但其中一位法官尤金·费伊（Eugene Fahey）发表了一份赞同意见，就这类诉讼的未来发展表达了推测性观点。费伊认为，对动物人格地位这个问题的探讨意义深远且影响广泛："最终，我们将无法回避这个问题。虽然人们对黑猩猩是不是'人'有不同意见，但毫无疑问的是，黑猩猩也绝非一般的'物'。"④

---

① *People ex rel Nonhuman Rights Project*, *Inc. v. Lavery*, 998 NYS 2d 248（App Div, 2014）.

② Randall S Abate, *Climate Change and the Voiceless: Protecting Future Generations, Wildlife, and Natural Resources*（CUP 2019）101-02.

③ *Nonhuman Rights Project*, *Inc. ex rel Tommy v. Lavery*, 54 NYS 3d 392, 396（App Div, 2017）.

④ *Nonhuman Rights Project*, *Inc. ex rel Tommy v. Lavery*, 100 NE 3d 846, 848（NY, 2018）.

加布里埃尔·哈列维（Gabriel Hallevy）则认为，在考虑情感性而非理性时，动物比人工智能系统更接近人类，但这并未导致它们在法律上被赋予人格地位。相反，人工智能系统的理性为其提供了人格地位的依据。① 在构建犯罪心智要素方面，这可能是正确的。但是，虐待黑猩猩可能构成犯罪，却不存在虐待计算机的犯罪。这也表明了法律在评价黑猩猩与计算机这两种实体时存在重要的差异。无论人工智能系统的内部处理有多么复杂，保护那些能够引起人类情感反应的具体化人工智能系统可能是一个更有力的论点。在未来的某个时段，法律也需要改革，采用类似于反动物虐待法的形式保护这种"社交机器人"的权益。届时，这些法律变革的法理依据，很可能是受到社会习俗的指导，而不是一致的生物学或技术标准。②

大多数法律体系都默认法律人格仅限于人类拥有，这一观点已经根深蒂固，以至于甚至没有被明确地提出。同时，连我们最近的进化近亲（指动物，尤其是类人猿）都没有被赋予类似的权利，这对于那些主张基于人工智能系统固有特质赋予其法律人格的人来说并不是一个好的预兆。③

5.2.2 奖励创造力

考虑是否应将人工智能系统视为人的另一个独特原因，关注

---

① Gabriel Hallevy, *Liability for Crimes Involving Artificial Intelligence Systems* (Springer 2015) 28.

② Kate Darling, 'Extending Legal Protection to Social Robots: The Effects of Anthropomorphism, Empathy, and Violent Behavior Towards Robotic Objects' in Ryan Calo, A Michael Froomkin, and Ian Kerr (eds), *Robot Law* (Edward Elgar 2016) 213 at 226-29. 进一步的讨论参见本书第 7 章第 7.3.2 节。

③ Cf Visa AJ Kurki, *A Theory of Legal Personhood* (OUP 2019) 176-78（讨论了人工智能系统是否可以被认为是"终极有价值的"，因而有资格获得人格权）。

的不是它们是什么，而是它们能做什么。本书第 1 章展示了人工智能系统的速度如何影响知识产权的侵权行为，① 这里我们将讨论其对知识产权的创作产生的影响。这通常被解构为个人或公司是否可以主张对人工智能系统完成的工作的所有权问题。然而，在这类讨论中，隐含或明示的理解是，如果这项工作是由人类完成的，那么他或她本人就会拥有所有权。

实际上，关于机器辅助创作是否可以获得著作权保护的讨论历史悠久。② 例如，早期的照片没有受到保护，因为通过照相机的镜头捕捉光线并不被视为真正的作者创作。③ 在奥斯卡·王尔德（Oscar Wilde）的一幅标志性照片最终通过美国最高法院确认之前，机械制作的作品并未被承认著作权。④ 今天的问题有所不同：不是摄影师是否可以"拥有"被机器被动捕捉的图像，而是谁可能拥有由一个机器主动创作的新作品。诸如文字处理器这样的计算机程序，并不拥有在其上输入的文本，正如钢笔不拥有用它所写的文字。但是，人工智能系统现在可以撰写新闻报道、创作歌曲、绘制图片——这些活动创造了价值，但它们能否并且应

---

① 参见本书第 1 章第 1.1 节。

② James Grimmelmann, 'There's No Such Thing as a Computer-Authored Work—and It's a Good Thing, Too' (2016) 39 *Columbia Journal of Law & the Arts* 403.

③ Madeleine de Cock Buning, 'Artificial Intelligence and the Creative Industry: New Challenges for the EU Paradigm for Art and Technology by Autonomous Creation' in Woodrow Barfield and Ugo Pagallo (eds), *Research Handbook on the Law of Artificial Intelligence* (Edward Elgar 2018) 511 at 524.

④ *Burrow-Giles Lithographic Co. v. Sarony*, 111 US 53 (1884). Arguments continued, however, with Germany withholding full copyright of photographs until 1965. Axel Nordemann, 'Germany' in Ysolde Gendreau, Axel Nordemann, and Rainer Oesch (eds), *Copyright and Photographs: An International Survey* (Kluwer 1999) 135.

该受到著作权法的保护？

在大多数法域，答案是否定的。

例如，美国版权局表示，立法保护的"原创性作者作品"①仅限于"由人类创作"的作品。它不会注册"由机器或仅仅通过机械过程随机或自动产生，而没有来自人类作者的任何创造性输入或干预的作品"②。关键词是"任何"，并引发了人类参与程度需要多少才能主张作者身份的问题。③

以世界上最著名的自拍照——黑猩猩的自拍照为例。大卫·斯莱特（David Slater）前往印度尼西亚为这些濒临灭绝的黑猩猩拍照，但它们太紧张，不让他靠近拍摄。于是，他架设了一台相机，让它们自己拍照。④ 在这些照片获得大量关注后，动物权益活动人士认为，黑猩猩比相机的拥有者更有权被视为照片的作者。斯莱特最终赢得了这场纷争，反映了现行法律的偏好。⑤ 作为纠纷和解的一部分，斯莱特同意将来自这些照片版税收入的25％捐赠给黑猩猩保护组织。随着计算机越来越独立于人类程序员之外生成更多内容，人类将越来越难以获得功劳。这将不仅仅是类似于训练一只黑猩猩如何按下按钮拍照，而是更像老师试图将其学生的作品据为己有。

回到人工智能系统本身是否应该拥有所有权的规范问题，著

---

① 17 USC §102 (a).

② *Compendium of US Copyright Office Practices* (3rd edn, US Copyright Office 2019), §313.2.

③ See Daniel J Gervais, 'The Machine as Author' (2020) 105 *Iowa Law Review* 2053.

④ Chris Cheesman, 'Photographer Goes Ape over Monkey Selfie: Who Owns the Copyright?', *Amateur Photographer* (7 August 2014).

⑤ *Naruto v. Slater*, 888 F 3d 418 (9th Cir, 2018). 法院裁定，纳鲁托根据美国版权法没有起诉的资格，并且对斯莱特发布的照片没有索赔权。

作权背后的政策通常被认为是激励创新。长期以来，人们一直认为这对计算机来说是不必要的或不合适的。帕梅拉·塞缪尔森（Pamela Samuelson）在1986年写道："只需要电力（或其他动力来源），就可以让这些机器投入生产。"① 但是，图灵测试提供了一种不同的要求：越是设计类似于人类特征的人工智能机器人，这种激励就可能变得越发重要。

一直以来，中国法都遵循人工智能产生的作品不享有著作权保护的正统观点。② 然而，2019年12月，中国的一家地方法院裁定，未经许可，不得复制由算法生成的文章。这篇文章是腾讯发表的一篇财经报道，注明是由腾讯开发的新闻写作程序Dreamwriter"自动编写"的。上海盈讯科技公司未经许可复制了这篇文章，遭到腾讯起诉。鉴于被告已撤下相关报道文章，法院判决被告支付人民币1500元（约216美元）用于弥补原告"经济损失"和支持其"权益保护"。③

中国的判例反映了承认著作权的一个独特因素，即保护创作过程中的前期投资。这种观点认为，如果没有法律保护，相关的投资终将枯竭，最后导致创意作品的供应减少。④ 这种对著作权

---

① Pamela Samuelson, 'Allocating Ownership Rights in Computer-Generated Works' (1986) 47 *University of Pittsburgh Law Review* 1185, 1199.

② *Beijing Feilin Law Firm v. Baidu Corporation* (*No. 239*) (25 April 2019) (Beijing Internet Court); Chen Ming, 'Beijing Internet Court Denies Copyright to Works Created Solely by Artificial Intelligence' (2019) 14 *Journal of Intellectual Property Law & Practice* 593.

③ 深圳市腾讯计算机系统有限公司诉上海盈讯科技有限公司案（深圳市南山区人民法院）。另参见 Zhang Yangfei, 'Court Rules AI-Written Article Has Copyright', *China Daily* (9 January 2020).

④ Kal Raustiala and Christopher Jon Sprigman, 'The Second Digital Disruption: Streaming and the Dawn of Datadriven Creativity' (2019) 94 *New York University Law Review* 1555, 1603-04.

的处理方式与普通法中关于在雇佣过程中创作的作品的保护原则基本一致,在美国这被称为"雇佣作品",根据这一原则,尽管实际的"作者"是其他人,但公司雇主或委托作品的个人拥有著作权。① 然而,在更注重人类作者道德权利的民法体系中可能不存在这种情况。②

实际上,1988年英国通过的法律确实为"计算机生成"的作品提供了著作权保护,其"作者"被视为承担了"创作作品所必需的安排"的人。③ 新西兰④、印度⑤、爱尔兰⑥和中国香港地区⑦也采用了类似的立法。尽管关于谁实施了"必需的安排"可能产生争议,但被认可的法律主体或根本无人拥有著作权仍然是可能的结果。⑧

2020年4月,欧洲议会发布了一份草案报告,认为人工智能系统生成的作品可以被视为"等同于"智慧作品,进而受到著作权保护。然而,该报告反对赋予人工智能系统本身以任何形式的法律人格,而是建议所有权归"合法准备和发布作品的人,前提

---

① Cf *Asia Pacific Publishing Pte Ltd. v. Pioneers & Leaders (Publishers) Pte Ltd.* [2011] 4 SLR 381, 398-402 (Singapore Court of Appeal)(区分了署名权和所有权)。

② Daryl Lim, 'AI & IP: Innovation & Creativity in an Age of Accelerated Change' (2018) 52 *Akron Law Review* 813, 843-46.

③ Copyright, Designs and Patents Act 1988 (UK), s 9 (3)。"计算机生成"的定义见于该法第178条,意为该作品是"在没有人类作者的情况下由计算机生成的"。

④ Copyright Act 1994 (NZ), s 5 (2) (a).

⑤ Copyright Amendment Act 1994 (India), s 2.

⑥ Copyright and Related Rights Act 2000 (Ireland), s 21 (f).

⑦ Copyright Ordinance 1997 (HK), s 11 (3).

⑧ See, eg, *Nova Productions v Mazooma Games* [2007] EWCA Civ 219; Abbe Brown, et al, *Contemporary Intellectual Property: Law and Policy* (5th edn, OUP 2019) 100-01.

是技术设计者没有明确保留以这种方式使用作品的权利"。① 这种与智慧作品的"等同性"观点非常有趣,这里的法理依据是在承认作品时基于"创造性结果"而非创造过程的认知转变。②

因此,人工智能系统当前还无法独立拥有著作权。当然,也不需要通过拥有著作权,以承认这些人工智能系统的创造性。然而,赋予"计算机生成"的作品有限权利,明显反映了对其他人拥有权利的保留。一般来说,这类作品的保护期较短,被视为"作者"的人无法主张道德权利,比如要求确认作品的作者身份。③ 世界知识产权组织(WIPO)的一份报告认识到这一困境,指出排除这些作品将以牺牲为消费者提供最大数量的创作作品为代价,倾向于将"人类创造力的尊严置于机器创造力之上"。WIPO认为,一个折中的方法是缩短保护期和进行其他限制。④

5.2.3 保护发明人

在著作权法中,争论的焦点是谁拥有人工智能系统创作的作品;在专利法中,问题是这些作品是否能成为法律上的客体。

---

① Stéphane Séjourné, Draft Report on Intellectual Property Rights for the Development of Artificial Intelligence Technologies (European Parliament, Committee on Legal Affairs, 2020/2015 (INI), 24 April 2020), paras 9-10.

② Ibid., Explanatory Statement.

③ Copyright, Designs and Patents Act, s 12 (7)(对此类作品的保护仅限于50年,而不是作者去世后的70年), s 79(精神权利的例外规定)。

④ Revised Issues Paper on Intellectual Property Policy and Artificial Intelligence (World Intellectual Property Organisation, WIPO/IP/AI/2/GE/20/1 REV, 21 May 2020), para 23. See also Marcus du Sautoy, *The Creativity Code: Art and Innovation in the Age of AI* (Harvard UP 2019) 102; Ryan Abbott, *The Reasonable Robot: Artificial Intelligence and the Law* (CUP 2020) 71-91.

大多数法域的专利法明定或推定"发明人"必须是人类。2019年,斯蒂芬·塞勒(Stephen Thaler)决定挑战这些法律规定,向英国、欧盟和美国分别提交了一项将人工智能系统"统一感知的自主引导设备"(Device for the Autonomous Bootstrapping of Unified Sentience,DABUS)列为"发明人"的专利申请。① 英国知识产权局(British Intellectual Property Office)愿意接受DABUS创造了这些发明,但相关法规要求发明人必须是自然人,而不是机器。② 欧洲专利局(European Patent Office,EPO)采取了更迂回的方式得出类似的裁定,以将机器列为发明人不满足"形式要件"为由拒绝了塞勒的申请,这些形式要件包括载明"发明人的姓氏、名字和详细地址"。③ 欧洲专利局指出,姓名不仅仅是用来识别一个人的,它还使他们能够行使权利,并成为他们法律人格的一部分。相比之下,DABUS等人工智能系统作为"物",没有姓、名可以让它们行使相应的(人格)权利。④

塞勒在美国的申请也遭到拒绝,部分原因是相关法规反复提

---

① 这些专利涉及的是"食品容器"和"吸引增强注意力的设备和方法"。

② Patents Act 1977 (UK), ss 7, 13. See *Whether the Requirements of Section 7 and 13 Concerning the Naming of Inventor and the Right to Apply for a Patent Have Been Satisfied in Respect of GB1816909.4 and GB1818161.0* (BL O/741/19) (4 December 2019) (UK Intellectual Property Office), paras 14-20。法庭接着指出,塞勒无法从DABUS获得所有权,"因为发明者本身不能持有财产"(第23段)。这一认定也被随后的高等法院判决维持。参见 *Thaler v. The Comptroller-General of Patents, Designs And Trade Marks* [2020] EWHC 2412 (Pat).

③ European Patent Convention, done at Munich, 5 October 1973, in force 7 October 1977, art 81, rule 19 (1).

④ *Grounds for the EPO Decision on Application EP 18 275 163* (27 January 2020) (European Patent Office), para 22.

到发明人使用"特定于自然人的代词",如"他自己"和"她自己"。美国专利商标局(Patent and Trademark Office,USPTO)援引了一些案例,认为"构思"——"发明者身份的试金石"——是一种在"发明人的头脑中"发生的"心智行为"。这些案例得出的结论是,这种意义上的"发明人"仅限于自然人,而不包括公司法人。据此,美国专利商标局裁定,将人工智能系统列为"发明人"的申请是不完整的,但它谨慎地避免对是"谁"或"什么"实际上创造了有关发明作出任何判断。①

欧美国家的这些决定与世界其他法域的案例和专利局的做法是一致的。迄今为止,尚无一个专利局将人工智能系统认定为专利的发明人。与著作权法类似,专利制度的一个目的是通过授予有限期的垄断权,以换取公开披露来鼓励创新。正如DABUS的创造者所承认的,人工智能系统不会因为专利保护的前景而有创新动力。任何动力都将在其编程中找到:它必须被指示去创新。②

至于一个人类"发明人"是否能因此类人工智能系统所做的工作获得认可,目前还没有雇佣作品原则的对等解释。要成为发明人,人类必须确实构思了这个发明。③ 当然,联合发明是可能的,贡献不需要相同,但在没有自然人做出重要的概念性贡献的

---

① *In re Application No*: *16/524*, *350* (*Decision on Petition*)(22 April 2020)(US Patent and Trademark Office).
② *UK IPO Decision on GB1816909.4 and GB1818161.0* (n 122),para 28.
③ *Manual of Patent Examining Procedure*(*MPEP*)(9th edn, US Patent and Trademark Office 2017),§2137.01.

情况下，根据现行法律，人工智能系统的发明无法获得专利保护。①

在这些最新发展中，令人感兴趣的方面之一是得出这些结论背后的法律逻辑。与著作权的情况一样，几乎没有人怀疑人工智能系统能够创造出可以媲美人类的可以获得专利的创新。英国知识产权局明确认可 DABUS 已经做到这一点；② 美国专利商标局小心翼翼地避免得出这样的结论；欧洲专利局则坚持认为，由于人工智能系统本身没有法律人格，"人工智能系统或机器人不能拥有专属于发明人的权利"。③ 相对而言，欧洲专利局的裁定最为直接。但是，上述三个监管机构的裁定都依赖于法律形式主义：相关法规中的语言明定或推定相关权利仅限于自然人。美国专利商标局甚至查阅了《韦氏大学词典》，得出"'whoever'（任何人）的使用暗示着'自然人'的结论"。④

法律裁定经常要应对实质正义和程序正当性之间的辩论。诉讼时效规定旨在为法律关系提供确定性；衡平法院的出现是为了使这种确定性与正义性协调、融合。但是，著作权法和专利法继续将人类创造力置于机器创造力之上，最终可能要借助前文提到

---

① Jeremy A Cubert and Richard GA Bone, 'The Law of Intellectual Property Created by Artificial Intelligence' in Woodrow Barfield and Ugo Pagallo (eds), *Research Handbook on the Law of Artificial Intelligence* (Edward Elgar 2018) 411 at 418. 有一个牵强的论点认为，解释的空间可能在于美国法律将"发明者"定义为"发明或发现"发明标的的人（35 USC § 101）。另参见 Ryan Abbott, 'I Think, Therefore I Invent: Creative Computers and the Future of Patent Law' (2016) 57 *Boston College Law Review* 1079, 1098。

② *UK IPO Decision on GB1816909.4 and GB1818161.0* (n 122), para 15.

③ *Grounds for the EPO Decision on Application EP 18 275 163* (n 124), para 27.

④ *In re Application No: 16/524, 350* (n 125) 4.

的黑猩猩自拍照著作权纠纷中体现的人类中心主义来进行合理化辩护。① 然而，在为维护法律现状的合理化辩护时，有时需要将所使用的法律语言与保持财产关系合理地位的旧有法律形式相呼应：人工智能系统不能拥有专利权，本质上是因为法律规定只有自然人才能享有专利。而这个逻辑和财产关系的逻辑是一样的，即只有自然人才能拥有财产。例如，在否决诸如 DABUS 这样的人工智能系统可以拥有或转让专利权时，欧洲专利局驳回了将机器人类比为雇员："与其说机器是被雇佣"，欧洲专利局得出结论，"不如说它们被拥有"。②

目前，这样的说法是准确的。但是，如果通用人工智能的支持者的预测是正确的，当这些人工智能系统在将来出现某种形式的自我意识时，那么，将人工智能系统仅仅视为工具或财产的法律观念可能变得不再适用。相比之下，将人工智能系统的法律地位与奴隶制度中对奴隶施加的限制进行类比可能更为合适。

5.3 管控超级智能

如果人工智能系统可能达到与人类智能相匹敌的水平，那么它们的进化也会继续，最后超过人类智能。长期以来，人工智能被描绘为具有超越人类智慧和能力的潜力，这一直是科幻小说中一个经久不衰的主题。③ 虽然目前而言，大多数专业研究学者还不认为通用型人工智能会在不久的将来出现，但科幻作品有着预

---

① 参见本书第 9 章引言。
② *Grounds for the EPO Decision on Application EP 18 275 163*（n 124），para 31.
③ See，eg，Harry Harrison，*War with the Robots*（Grafton 1962）；Philip K Dick，*Do Androids Dream of Electric Sheep?*（Doubleday 1968）；Arthur C Clarke，*2001: A Space Odyssey*（Hutchinson 1968）.

示现实世界科学创新的丰富历史。① 尼克·博斯特罗姆（Nick Bostrom）将"超级智能"（superintelligence）定义为：在几乎所有相关领域都大大超越人类认知表现的人工智力。② 此类超级智能，将大概率在未来一个世纪内出现。③

与超级智能发展相关的风险将很难量化。④ 尽管一个恶意的超级智能试图消灭或奴役人类是最为戏剧性的情景，但更可信的情景包括价值观不一致，比如超级智能所追求的目标与人类的目标发生冲突，或者超级智能具有自我保护的欲望，而可能阻止人类损害其正常运作的能力。一系列新兴的文献研究了超级智能可能具有哪些最终目标和工具目标，⑤ 尽管这一领域长期以来不为传统主流学界所待见。⑥ 例如，维萨·库尔基（Visa Kurki）近期

---

① Philipp Jordan, *et al*, 'Exploring the Referral and Usage of Science Fiction in HCI Literature' (2018) *arXiv* 1803.08395v2.

② Nick Bostrom, *Superintelligence：Paths, Dangers, Strategies* （OUP 2014）22. 关于超级智能的早期猜想通常追溯到 Irving John Good, 'Speculations Concerning the First Ultraintelligent Machine' in FL Alt and M Rubinoff （eds）, *Advances in Computers* （Academic 1965）vol 6, 31. 图灵本人在1951年的一次演讲中提出了这一可能性，参见 AM Turing, 'Intelligent Machinery, A Heretical Theory' （1996）4 *Philosophia Mathematica* 256, 259-60；他又将这一想法归功于更早的一个来源：塞缪尔·巴特勒1872年出版的科幻小说《埃里翁》。

③ See, eg, Oren Etzioni, 'No, the Experts Don't Think Superintelligent AI is a Threat to Humanity', *MIT Technology Review* （20 September 2016）。作者引用了对美国人工智能协会（AAAI）80位院士的调查，询问他们何时能实现博斯特罗姆定义的超级智能。没有人认为能在未来10年内实现；7.5％的人认为能在未来10—25年内实现；67.5％的人认为需要25年以上；25％的人认为永远不会实现。

④ Patrick Bradley, 'Risk Management Standards and the Active Management of Malicious Intent in Artificial Superintelligence' （2019）35 *AI & Society* 319；Alexey Turchin and David Denkenberger, 'Classification of Global Catastrophic Risks Connected with Artificial Intelligence' （2020）35 *AI & Society* 147.

⑤ See, eg, Olle Häggström, 'Challenges to the Omohundro-Bostrom Framework for AI Motivations' （2019）21 *Foresight* 153.

⑥ See David J Chalmers, 'The Singularity：A Philosophical Analysis' （2010）17（9-10）*Journal of Consciousness Studies* 7.

关于法律人格的专著中，单辟一章专门讨论人工智能的人格问题，最后得出结论："当然，如果某些人工智能最终变得有感知力，本章讨论的许多问题将需要重新考虑。"①

面对众多的未知因素，有两种缓解风险的基本应对策略。第一种是确保任何这样的实体都受到严格的控制，不论是通过限制其与世界互动的能力，还是通过"紧急制动开关"②等制约方式。然而，假设系统具有某种目的，那么实现这一策略的最佳途径很可能是让它继续运行。在一个经典的思想实验中，一个超级智能系统被告知制造回形针，它却可能开始摧毁世界，努力把一切都变成回形针。如果人类试图通过"紧急制动开关"将它关闭，但它却在所能找到的一切计算机系统上自我复制，因为关闭会干扰它的任务：制造更多回形针。③

认为没有真正的超级智能会做出如此愚蠢的事情的观点依赖于常识和拟人化，而这两者都不应被认为是其代码的一部分。此外，真正的超级智能将具有预测和避免人类干预的能力，或欺骗我们不进行干预。④ 完全有可能的是，专注于控制这样一个实体的努力可能导致它们试图阻止的灾难。⑤

因此，许多作者优先考虑第二种策略，即确保任何超级智能

---

① Visa AJ Kurki, *A Theory of Legal Personhood* (OUP 2019) 189.

② Nick Bostrom, *Superintelligence: Paths, Dangers, Strategies* (OUP 2014) 127-44.

③ Nick Bostrom, 'Ethical Issues in Advanced Artificial Intelligence' in Iva Smit and George E Lasker (eds), *Cognitive, Emotive and Ethical Aspects of Decision Making in Humans and in Artificial Intelligence* (International Institute for Advanced Studies in Systems Research 2003) vol. 2, 12.

④ John Danaher, 'Why AI Doomsayers Are Like Sceptical Theists and Why It Matters' (2015) 25 *Mind and Machines* 231.

⑤ Wolfhart Totschnig, 'The Problem of Superintelligence: Political, Not Technological' (2019) 34 *AI & Society* 907.

与我们自己的价值观保持一致——强调的不是它能做什么,而是它可能想做什么。这个问题也吸引了科幻作家的兴趣,尤其是艾萨克·阿西莫夫(Isaac Asimov),他的机器人三定律将在本书第7章中进行探讨。在这里,较为狭义的关注点是,在短期内赋予人工智能系统法律人格,是否可以作为防范未来出现超级智能风险的手段。

这实际上是赋予人工智能系统法律人格的另一个工具性原因。当然,我们没有理由认为将人工智能系统纳入人类社会结构并善待它们会必然导致它们在成为主导力量时回报我们。① 然而,在假定通用人工智能具有理性的前提下,有多位作者提出了类似于让人工智能系统适应人类行为的方法。② 例如,为避免机器只是被告知"制造回形针"的"巫师学徒问题",它的目标可以与人类的喜好和经验相联系。③ 这可能通过在它们实现超级智能之

---

① Jacob Turner,*Robot Rules*:*Regulating Artificial Intelligence*(Palgrave Macmillan 2019)164.

② Ray Kurzweil,*The Singularity Is Near*:*When Humans Transcend Biology*(Viking 2005)424;Nate Soares and Benya Fallenstein,'Agent Foundations for Aligning Machine Intelligence with Human Interests:A Technical Research Agenda' in Victor Callaghan,*et al*(eds),*The Technological Singularity*:*Managing the Journey*(Springer 2017)103 at 117-20.

③ "巫师学徒问题"(sorcerer's apprentice problem)源自一个德国民间故事,后来被改编成迪士尼电影《巫师学徒》。这个故事讲的是,一个年轻的学徒使用魔法来让一把扫帚帮助自己打水,但因学徒无法停止扫帚导致水源泛滥,无法控制局面。在计算机科学和人工智能领域,该词汇被用来描述一种情况,即计算机程序或人工智能系统接受一个指令,但无法正确理解和控制该指令的后果,导致系统出现意料之外的行为,无法停止或控制。上文中提到一个人工智能系统被告知制造回形针的例子。如果人工智能系统仅仅按照指定目标行动,而没有能力理解人类的意愿和经验,就可能出现类似于巫师学徒问题的情况。为了避免这种问题,可以将人类的偏好和经验嵌入人工智能系统的代码中,使其目标与人类的价值观和体验相一致,以确保人工智能系统的行为符合人类的期望并能够受到控制。——译者注

前将这些价值观嵌入这些系统的代码中来实现。因此，目标将不仅仅表达为纯粹的优化，如制造回形针的数量，而是诸如最大化实现人类偏好之类的模糊目标，① 或者灌输一种伦理框架和反思平衡，以匹配人类道德本身的进步发展。②

对于律师来说，这听起来很像是将这些人工智能新实体纳入法律体系。③ 如果法律体系的一个功能是对其主体进行道德教育，以这种方式收录人工智能新实体可能有助于实现一种反思平衡，从而鼓励最终的超级智能接受与我们相容的价值观。

目前，这更像是一个思想实验，而不是一个政策方案。如果出现通向超级智能的现实途径，这将成为一个更紧迫的现实问题。④ 虽然不能保证这种方法会有效，但我们可以从这样一个事实中获得一些小小的安慰，即在大多数法域认可的法人类别以及它们享有的权利方面，随着时间的推移，它们往往会扩大而非收缩。那些剥夺法律承认与保护的制度是最不可取的。抛开末日情景不谈，将我们人类和我们的硅基兄弟姐妹定位为平等主体，可能有助于加强一种规范体系的建立，使我们的利益保持一致或至

---

① Stuart J Russell, *Human Compatible: Artificial Intelligence and the Problem of Control* (Viking 2019). 根据博斯特罗姆的意见，超级智能的目标可以被表述为"实现我们本来会希望人工智能在我们深思熟虑后实现的目标"。参见 Nick Bostrom, *Superintelligence: Paths, Dangers, Strategies* (OUP 2014) 141.

② Eliezer Yudkowsky, 'Complex Value Systems in Friendly AI' in Jürgen Schmidhuber, Kristinn R Thórisson, and Moshe Looks (eds), *Artificial General Intelligence* (Springer 2011) 388.

③ Cf Steve Omohundro, 'Autonomous Technology and the Greater Human Good' (2014) 26 *Journal of Experimental & Theoretical Artificial Intelligence* 303, 308.

④ 如果这条路径是通过增强人类而不是纯粹的人工智能实体实现的，那么这些人类很可能仍然是法律的主体。

少不对立,以应对我们可能被人工智能超越的情况。①

反之,如同纽约笼子里的黑猩猩,人类最大的希望可能是被当作平等的伙伴,而不仅仅是作为权利客体的物。

5.4 法律人格的局限性

1991 年,纽约慈善家休·洛布纳(Hugh Loebner)设立了一个特别奖项,以鼓励对图灵测试进行更有挑战的实践。首批获奖者之一设计了专门的程序,故意生成只有疏忽大意的人类才会产生的拼写错误,欺骗性地获得了特别奖。② 尽管图灵测试仍是一个标志性基准,但它已经不再是当前人工智能研究的最佳衡量标准了。正如一本在该领域具有权威性的教科书所指出的,当莱特兄弟停止模仿鸟类、开始研究空气动力学时,飞行的探索反而取得了最后的成功。③ 如今,航空工程师并不把他们领域的目标定义为制造出飞得像鸽子一样、达到以假乱真愚弄其他鸽子那种程度的机器。

同样地,大多数赞成赋予人工智能独立法律人格的论点之所以不受欢迎,是因为它们不是过于简单,便是过于复杂。其一,有些论点过于简单,因为人工智能系统的性质和特点存在模糊的

---

① See also Steven Livingston and Mathias Risse,'The Future Impact of Artificial Intelligence on Humans and Human Rights'(2019) 33 *Ethics and International Affairs* 141; James Dawes,'Speculative Human Rights:Artificial Intelligence and the Future of the Human'(2020) 42 *Human Rights Quarterly* 573.

② 'Artificial Stupidity', *The Economist* (1 August 1992).

③ Stuart J Russell and Peter Norvig, *Artificial Intelligence:A Modern Approach* (3rd edn,Prentice Hall 2010) 3.

边界，目前尚没有明确的可以用于此类认可的有意义的范畴；如果需要在某些特定情况下进行认可，可以利用现有的法律形式来解决。其二，有些论点过于复杂，因为其中许多是对类人机器人谬误的变体，基于对未来人工智能系统发展的假设，认为人工智能系统拥有法律人格不仅是有用的，而且也是其应得的。然而，在可预见的未来，更好的解决方案是依靠现有的法律规范，将责任归于用户、所有者或制造商，而不是直接归于人工智能系统本身。例如，自动驾驶汽车正在采用这种方法，从为驾驶员投保转向为车辆投保。①

这种情况可能发生改变。可以想象，有一天会出现具有与人类道德价值相当的人工合成生命体。如果不能认识到这种价值，我们可能被认为是一种"自闭物种"，无法理解其他类型生命体的思维，②或者仅仅是对那些与我们不同的人存有偏见。如图灵在1951年假设的那样，如果发生这种情况，"一旦机器思维方法开始，就很可能很快超越我们微弱的能力"③。

图灵本人从未亲眼见过计算机尝试他的测试。1952年，他因同性恋行为被起诉，选择化学阉割以避免入狱。两年后，他在41岁时结束了自己的生命，通过吃下掺有氰化物的苹果自杀。2013年，英国女王签署了正式赦免令，随后宣布图灵将成为新50英镑纸币的人物。④

---

① 参见本书第4章第4.1.4节。
② See, eg, Samir Chopra and Laurence F White, *A Legal Theory for Autonomous Artificial Agents* (University of Michigan Press 2011) 191.
③ AM Turing, Intelligent Machinery, a Heretical Theory (lecture given to the '51 Society' at Manchester) (Turing Digital Archive, AMT/B/4, 1951) 6.
④ See generally Dermot Turing, *Prof Alan Turing Decoded: A Biography* (History Press 2015).

然而，对图灵更恰当的致敬可能是伊恩·麦克尤恩（Ian McEwan）的小说《像我一样的机器》（Machines Like Me）。① 这部小说设想了一个图灵没有离世并因为他的贡献而被封为爵士的平行时空。这部小说认真地探讨了真正的人工智能的前景，以一个忧郁的人工合成的亚当的形象出现，他通过创作成千上万首"俳句"（haikus）来向名为"米兰达"（Miranda）的人类表达爱意。然而，拥有自主意识对于机器人来说却是一个负担：它们努力在世界中找到自己的位置，但却困于单纯的机器意识，无法调和人类固有的美德与恶习之间的矛盾。

作者还为图灵提供了一个重新思考图灵测试的机会。小说里，70岁的图灵谈到他年轻时的自己时说："在那些日子里，我对'人'是什么有着高度机械化的观点。身体是一台机器，一台非凡的机器，而我对心灵的看法主要是从智力的角度，它最好是通过对国际象棋或数学的参考来建模。"②

当然，现实情况是，国际象棋并不能代表生活。生活是一个开放的系统；它也是混乱的，不可预测的。在小说中，人工智能

---

① 在小说中，亚当展示出高度智能和情感，它具有对世界和人类的思考能力，并通过创作俳句来表达自己的情感和观点。然而，亚当的意识也成为它的负担。它质疑自己的存在和人类的道德价值，发现自己无法完全融入人类社会和人类的行为模式中。机器人的纯粹性使得它们无法调和人类的美德和恶习。它们缺乏人类的情感和经验，无法真正理解和体验人类的情感、欲望和动机。这导致了机器人与人类之间的隔阂和困惑。尽管亚当尝试通过创作俳句和表达情感来接近人类，但它仍然感到孤独和无法真正理解人类的复杂性。这种困扰和隔阂揭示了意识对机器而言的复杂性和困难。意识赋予机器人思考、感知和体验世界的能力，但也使它们面临理解人类行为和道德的挑战。机器人的纯粹性和无法调和人类美德和恶习的困境，进一步展现了人类和机器之间的差异和不可逾越的鸿沟。这本小说揭示了意识对机器而言的困扰和负担，以及它们努力寻找自身在世界中的位置的挣扎。它们纯粹无邪，无法理解人类的情感和行为，这进一步凸显了机器和人类之间的差异和隔阂。——译者注

② Ian McEwan, *Machines Like Me*（Vintage 2019）300.

机器人的首要任务是禁用可能关闭它们的开关。然而，大多数机器人最终还是自我毁灭了——就像现实中的图灵那样——它们无法调和自己与周围世界的不公正。在询问我们是否可以创造这样的智能机器之前，麦克尤恩提醒：我们或许应该先停下来，问一问我们是否应该这么创造智能机器人?!

第 6 章
透 明 原 则

2015年7月,一个名为"Impact Team"的黑客组织攻破了一家加拿大公司的网站,窃取了该公司的用户数据库和八年的交易记录。几周后,他们开始在网上公布了超过3000万客户的个人信息。数据泄露事件并非罕见,但此事涉事公司是阿什利·麦迪逊(Ashley Madison),其业务模式是在"生命短暂,享受婚外情"这一极具争议性的口号下安排婚外私情。此次被公开的详细信息不仅包括用户的姓名和计费信息,还包括用户的性取向和性幻想。

最初,这一泄露事件在一定程度上引发了大众的幸灾乐祸:一群通奸者得到了他们应得的惩罚。然而,当记者们试图翻阅泄露的数据,寻找名人八卦时,不同的新闻故事却浮出水面。一个以科幻和科技爆料为主的在线杂志通过深入挖掘,揭示了此次丑闻的重点可能是错误的。AshleyMadison.com上的绝大多数互动不是已婚男女之间,而是发生在以男性为主体的人类和谎称是女性的机器人之间。安娜莉·纽维茨(Annalee Newitz)在Gizmodo网站上写道:"这不是一群男人欺骗妻子的堕落乐园,而更像是一个科幻的未来,地球上的每一个女人都死了,一些像迪尔伯特(Dilbert)的工程师用设计糟糕的女性机器人替代了她们。"①

次月，受害者在马里兰州提起了一起极不寻常的集体诉讼。用户寻求赔偿的诉由不是平台怠于保护个人数据，而是平台涉嫌欺诈用户。具体而言，克里斯托弗·拉塞尔（Christopher Russell）代表自己和其他用户，指控该网站利用"人工智能'机器人'和伪造的档案诱导人类用户购买服务"。他要求被告对其违反消费者保护法的欺骗行为进行赔偿，以及返还其因不诚信行为获取的不当得利。② 拉塞尔（在加入网站时已与妻子分居）花了100美元购买积分在网站上与"女性"聊天，他要求的赔偿金超过500万美元。

1993年7月，《纽约客》（New Yorker）杂志发表一则后来成为互联网最早表情包之一的漫画：一只狗停下敲打台式电脑的动作，转向旁边坐着的另一只狗："在互联网上，"第一只狗解释道，"没有人知道你是一只狗。"匿名和化名问题长期以来一直困扰着网络行为的监管者。对许多人来说，主要的担忧是身份盗窃，像网络"钓鱼"这样的新词被创造出来，用来描述通过冒充窃取敏感数据的行为。如今，人工智能系统日益复杂，意味着许多在线流程（无论合法与否）都是通过机器人自动化处理的。

对于人类用户来说，了解他们是否在与另一个人互动被视为一项基本权利。③ 这是一个最基本的公开透明问题，争议不大。④

---

① Annalee Newitz，'Almost None of the Women in the Ashley Madison Database Ever Used the Site'，*Gizmodo*（26 August 2015）.

② *In re Ashley Madison Customer Data Security Breach Litigation*，148 FSupp 3d 1378，1380（2015）.

③ White Paper on Artificial Intelligence（European Commission，COM(2020) 65 final，19 February 2020）20.

④ 然而，如何在现实中保障这一权利却不是容易的事情。参见本章第6.4节以及第7章第7.4节。

这个基本问题与人工智能系统的日益不透明有关。正如本书第3章所论述的，这种不透明性给监管带来了独特的挑战。没有类似于人类决策中常有的审查和问责机制，人工智能系统的不透明性和自主性会导致无效率、不道德或者不合法的结果。

通常认为，针对这个问题的补救措施，是提高透明度或"可解释性"（explainability）。这是又一个新词，代表了一个可解释人工智能（XAI）的新兴研究领域；这也是欧盟《通用数据保护条例》（GDPR）中创造的一种新的"解释权"。然而，这些术语的使用经常是很模糊的，特别是在技术专家和法律专家之间，可能导致沟通和理解上的困难。

本章探讨了在人工智能系统背景下提高透明度的合理性和可能性，以及它在主要法域的实践经验。第一节阐述了透明性、可解释性及相关术语的含义：可以和应该提供什么信息，何时提供，向谁提供，以及产生哪些成本。第二节则转向如何将这些概念映射到计算机科学的进步和可解释人工智能领域，以及如何填补可能存在的差距。第三节考虑了监管机构的经验，尤其是欧盟，如何将某些形式的透明性（包括可能的解释权）付诸立法、司法、执法实践。

本章的关键发现是，这三种论述之间存在内生冲突，过分强调针对个案的事后解释，而忽视了本书第3章中论证的内生系统性问题。在某些情况下，随机的审查执法可能比不透明性本身更不可取，因为它给人一种透明性的错觉。虽然天然不透明的人工智能系统变得更为普遍，为单一决策生成"理由"仍然是可能的。但是，在没有系统性和主动的措施来确保真正的透明性（或弥补其缺失）的情况下，我们面临着一叶障目、不见泰山的风险。

6.1 一般理论

在第 3 章中,"不透明性"(opacity)被定义为难以理解或解释的特质。"透明性"(transparency)则与此相反。① 同样,提高透明度的目的在于应对不透明性带来的危险:提高透明度可以提高决策质量,阻止或披露不正当决策,进而增加决策的合法性和可信任度。② 关于那些专有和复杂的不透明性,现有的法律工具使监管机构和法院能够强制披露商业机密或引入专家证人。③ 本节讨论的重点是那些天然不透明的人工智能系统,不对这些系统本身进行根本性改变,将无法实现真正有意义的透明性。

正如乔治·博克斯(George Box)所警告的,"所有模型都是错误的,但有些却是有用的。"④ 这句格言强调了可解释性作为透明度替代方案所面临的核心挑战。在这个背景下,解释意味着对如何使用某些因素作出特定决策的描述。为了使可解释性发挥效果,解释必须清晰,并使相关人员能够了解特定输入对输出的

---

① See generally David Heald,'Varieties of Transparency' in Christopher Hood and David Heald (eds),*Transparency: The Key to Better Governance?* (OUP 2006) 25。作者 Heald 在其中对事件和过程的透明度、事后透明度与实时透明度、名义上的透明度与有效的透明度等进行了有益的区分。

② Cf Tal Z Zarsky,'Transparent Predictions'(2013) *University of Illinois Law Review* 1503.

③ "专有性"(proprietary)指的是某些技术或算法的所有权和知识产权受到保护,不对外公开或共享。这种专有性导致了不透明性,因为外部人员无法准确了解或解释该技术或算法的运作方式。"复杂性"(complexity)指的是技术或算法本身的复杂性,涉及多个层面、各种参数和交互关系。这种复杂性使得人们难以全面理解技术或算法的内部工作过程,因此也导致了不透明性。——译者注

④ George EP Box and Norman R Draper,*Empirical Model-Building and Response Surfaces* (Wiley 1987) 424.

影响程度。这包括使用了哪些变量，以及是否改变一个或多个变量会产生不同的决策结果；可解释性还应使人们能够比较不同的决策，同时揭示决策差异性或相似性的原因。①

这或许是一个合理的目标，但是使人工智能系统可理解的目标存在两个问题：第一，为了使其易于理解，必须简化原始系统。第二，它假设解释的目的是帮助人们理解单一的决策。正如我们在下文将具体阐述的，这些只是可解释性所能表达的一部分内容，可解释性和透明原则远不止只需实现这两个目标，它们应当具有更广泛的含义。

6.1.1 披露什么？

诸多学者提出了两种不同的进路，以帮助理解人工智能系统的不透明运作。② 第一种进路是早期关于算法问责的研究，要求实现广泛意义上的透明性，有时被称为"全局或以模型为中心的可解释性"，其目的是揭示人工智能系统的运作方式。在极端情况下，甚至要求公开人工智能系统的全部代码。这种进路，虽然在一定意义上实现了完全透明性，但如果人工智能系统的运作方式本质上是不透明的，那么这种透明性并不会有特别的用处。更有用的可能是公开说明模型背后意图的描述、使用的训练数据、

---

① Finale Doshi-Velez and Mason Kortz, Accountability of AI Under the Law: The Role of Explanation (Berkman Klein Center for Internet & Society, 2017) 2-3.

② See, eg, Christoph Molnar, *Interpretable Machine Learning* (Lulu 2019). Cf Riccardo Guidotti, *et al*, 'A Survey of Methods for Explaining Black Box Models' (2018) *arXiv* 1802.01933v3, 16（区分了四种可能的方法：解释模型、解释结果、内部检查黑匣子模型，以及提供"透明解决方案"）。

性能指标等关键信息。① 然而，随着人工智能系统变得日益复杂，即使对其算法作出描述并公开算法背后的运作逻辑，也会与算法的实际运作相去甚远。②

第二种进路则转向了基于实例的解释，也被称为"局部或以主体为中心的解释性"：理解影响特定决策的因素。其重点不在于模型如何运作，而在于特定的决策何以作出。③ 这一进路产生了不同形式的解释。比如，哪些因素对结果重要？某些因素的变化是否会导致不同的决策结果？④ 这突出了人工智能系统的一个优点，即它们能够在特定变量改变的同时重复同样的决策过程。⑤ 重要的是，生成这样的解释并不需要了解系统所作决策的具体细节。⑥

---

① Lilian Edwards and Michael Veale, 'Slave to the Algorithm? Why a "Right to an Explanation" Is Probably Not the Remedy You Are Looking For' (2017) 16 *Duke Law & Technology Review* 18, 55-56. See generally David Brin, *The Transparent Society：Will Technology Force Us to Choose Between Privacy and Freedom?* (Addison-Wesley 1998).

② 这段话的主要论点是，对于不透明的人工智能系统，理解其运作的方式有两种：全局或模型中心的可解释性。全局可解释性可能包括公开整个系统的代码，但对于天然不透明的系统来说，这可能不太有用。相反，更有用的是描述背后的意图、训练数据和性能指标等。然而，随着系统变得越来越复杂，其实际运作与描述之间的差距也变大。作者指出，这意味着系统的实际运作可能变得更加复杂和难以理解，而对系统的描述只能提供一定程度的解释和理解，但可能无法完全捕捉和呈现系统的所有细节和运作方式。因此，随着系统复杂性的增加，描述与实际运作之间的差距变得更加明显。——译者注

③ Brent Mittelstadt, Chris Russell, and Sandra Wachter, 'Explaining Explanations in AI' (2018) *arXiv* 1811.01439v1, 2.

④ 这有时也被称为"反事实的忠实性"。

⑤ 参见本书第 3 章第 3.2.2 节。

⑥ Finale Doshi-Velez and Mason Kortz, Accountability of AI Under the Law：The Role of Explanation (Berkman Klein Center for Internet & Society, 2017) 7.

从全局解释到局部解释的转变是由实际效用驱动的。只是大概模拟一个天然不透明的人工智能系统的全局模型对于理解系统如何运作或如何做出决策都没有帮助。更有针对性的解释至少会给予受影响的人更多的信息和改变行为以达到不同结果的可能性，如影响拒绝贷款决策的因素如果反映了更高的工资，结果是否会有所不同。然而，我们将看到，这些"局部"解释可能引发自身的问题。

6.1.2 何时披露？

第一个问题是何时应考虑透明度问题。在监管文献中，两种广泛的监督理论范式被通俗地称为"警察巡逻"和"火灾报警"。在"警察巡逻"范式中，对活动进行抽样调查，旨在发现和纠正问题行为，并通过这种监视来阻止它。在"火灾报警"范式中，建立了一个体系，使相关利益群体有权发出警报，从而启动应对机制。[①] 在人工智能系统的背景下，时间问题通常被分解为决策"之前"和"之后"。然而，这两个阶段都无法完全契合监督理论中的隐喻：天然不透明的系统可能无法通过事前抽样揭示问题；而依靠事后警报只有在用户知道自己受到了伤害时才会产生反应。此外，"之前"的阶段实际上可能有多个阶段：模型的设计，训练数据的选择，验证等。[②]

转向可解释性表明人们接受了一种观点，即如果要寻求问

---

① Mathew D McCubbins and Thomas Schwartz, 'Congressional Oversight Overlooked: Police Patrols Versus Fire Alarms' (1984) 28 *American Journal of Political Science* 165, 166-76.

② 因为机器学习算法本身会随时间变化，这就衍生出更多的复杂性。参见 Mike Ananny and Kate Crawford, 'Seeing Without Knowing: Limitations of the Transparency Ideal and Its Application to Algorithmic Accountability' (2018) 20 *New Media & Society* 973, 982; Machine Learning Workflow (Google Cloud, 2020)。

责,必须在事后进行解释。这意味着解释性在一定程度上承认了事后问责的必要性,但这引发了两个问题。其一,它对用户施加了重大负担,其中许多用户可能不知道不利的决策,或不愿意、无法挑战它们。其二,为了支持事后问责,某些行业可能采取措施,例如要求审计跟踪记录和类似于飞行数据记录器的故障问责机制。这些将在下一节中讨论。

第二个问题是它忽视了监管的价值。除了完全禁止某些形式的不透明决策的可能性外,算法影响评估可以用来估计自动化的潜在危害。对特定行业的算法进行定期审核也可以用来检测偏见,而无须等待受到侵害的个人出面。通过委托机构组织"巡逻"来实施这些措施将会很有帮助。这些措施也将在下文中讨论。①

6.1.3 向谁披露?

要解决不透明决策的问题,谁可以执行透明度要求或行使解释权也有两个不可回避的方面:

第一个方面是调用这些权力或权利的门槛。在透明原则要求的背景下,监管机构的监督角色可能使其能够要求获取关于人工智能系统如何运作的信息的权力。如果无法获取信息,监管机构可能禁止外包某些功能。在这种情况下,监管机构可能包括监督特定部门的实体,如消费者信贷监管机构,或者像警察这样的机构。它们也可能包括新的机构,如下一节中涉及的"算法调解员"。在某些情况下,只有那些受到决策不利影响的人才有权利通过起诉寻求人工智能系统行为的解释,而起诉资格的要求可能产生第 3 章中所指出的"第 22 条军规"悖论:只有那些受决策不利影响的人才有权提起诉讼,但在某些情况下,除非有人提起诉

---

① 参见本书第 6 章第 6.2.2 节、第 8 章第 8.3.4 节。

讼，否则没人会知道不利的影响。①

第二个方面涉及假定监管机构或用户具有的知识或专业技能。人们通常说，披露的信息必须是"可解释的"，如从能被人理解的意义上看。但是，真能被所有人理解吗？向计算机科学家解释机器学习过程跟向外行解释之间存在显著差异，而"可以为人类所理解"并没有一致的标准——尽管这正是可解释性的要点。② 在只有计算机科学家能理解他们同行的工作的程度上，让技术专家负责问责进一步增加了监管机构被俘获的风险。③

6.1.4 披露有哪些代价？

最后一个需要考虑的问题是，透明度并非毫无代价。正如本书第3章所讨论的，虽然对不透明的人工智能系统实行全面封禁是可能的，但却没有必要。同时，封禁将意味着我们错失人工智能带来的诸多好处。然而，要求人工智能系统充分"透明"也可能限制创新或者导致低效发展。因为如果企业担心商业机密会被披露给竞争对手，就可能不愿意公开这些信息，或者不愿意投入

---

① 参见本书第3章第3.3.1节。一种方法是借鉴数据保护法，将法律上的伤害视为事实上的伤害，以便具备诉讼资格。另参见 *Patel v. Facebook, Inc.*, 932 F 3d 1264 (9th Cir, 2019)。

② Cf Paul B de Laat, 'Algorithmic Decision-Making Based on Machine Learning from Big Data: Can Transparency Restore Accountability?' (2018) 31 *Philosophy & Technology* 525; Richard Tomsett, *et al*, 'Interpretable to Whom? A Role-based Model for Analyzing Interpretable Machine Learning Systems' (2018) *arXiv* 1806.07552; Danding Wang, *et al*, 'Designing Theory-Driven User-Centric Explainable AI' (2019) CHI '19: Proceedings of the 2019 CHI Conference on Human Factors in Computing Systems Paper No 601; Umang Bhatt, *et al*, 'Explainable Machine Learning in Deployment' (2020) 1909.06342v4 *arXiv*。

③ Leif Hancox-Li, 'Robustness in Machine Learning Explanations: Does It Matter?' (2020) *ACM Conference on Fairness, Accountability, and Transparency* (FAT*) 640。参见本书第8章第8.1.2节。

时间和资源开发复杂的算法。限制模型中变量的数量可以使得算法更简单易懂，从而增强了其可解释性和透明度。但是，由于模型在处理数据时不能捕捉更多的信息，其准确性就降低了。①

回应用户有关不透明性投诉，会增加运营成本。② 为所有自动化决策（正面和负面）搭配额外解释的提案，也将产生更多的运营成本。③ 另外，过度信息公开还可能产生其他额外的问题，比如意外泄露个人数据或者间接帮助意图规避、操控人工智能决策的用户。

当然，某些成本可以被视为是对完善人工智能系统合法性和正当性的必要投资，但我们需要平衡潜在的危害和减少这些危害措施带来的额外成本。然而，平衡这些不同的诉求是很难的，比如，消费者权益保护者更偏向于关注消费者的需求和利益，而相对忽视技术的迅速发展需要。

6.2 实践经验

提高人工智能系统的透明度或可解释性的实践，始于是否能

---

① See, eg, AI in the UK: Ready, Willing, and Able? (House of Lords Select Committee on Artificial Intelligence, HL Paper 100, 2018), para 99。持相反观点的学者则认为，复杂模型的更高准确性经常被夸大。参见 Cynthia Rudin, 'Stop Explaining Black Box Machine Learning Models for High Stakes Decisions and Use Interpretable Models Instead' (2019) 1 *Nature Machine Intelligence* 206。

通常情况下，人工智能模型的性能取决于其对输入数据的理解和模式识别能力。如果限制模型可以考虑的变量数量，那么模型对输入数据的表征能力可能受到限制，无法捕捉到更丰富和复杂的特征。而这可能导致模型在处理数据时丢失一些重要的信息，从而影响模型的准确性。——译者注

② See, eg, General Data Protection Regulation 2016/679（GDPR）2016（EU), art 12 (5)（允许对显然无理由或超过必要限度的信息请求收取费用）。

③ 参见本书第 6 章第 6.2.1 节。

够访问这些系统的内部运作。设计上的透明度或可解释性是假定可以访问人工智能系统内部运作，甚至愿意以牺牲功能性为代价，优先考虑透明性或可解释性。即便对于无法访问的黑箱，也并不必然意味着不可能实现可解释性。通过分析输入和输出的信息，我们可以推断某个人工智能模型的性能。事实证明，完全可以通过分析有限的信息，合理推断其他人工智能系统。①

6.2.1 提高透明度的方法

传统上，提高透明度是通过披露内部运作方式来实现的。除了完全公开源代码外，这种传统方式还包括披露系统组件（可分解性）②或训练算法（算法透明度）③。但是，随着对可模拟性的关注日渐增多，这种传统方式对天然不透明的人工智能系统的透明度效果极为有限：如何发展一种基于性能的机械理解，专注于分析人工智能系统在特定情况下能做到什么，而不是如何去做的。这种转变意味着，不需要访问人工智能系统内部运作的外源性方法④，可能比我们以前预想的更有效。实际上，诸如"教育型""替代型"以及其他"模型不可知"方法，近年来已经在促

---

① See, eg, Wojciech Samek, *et al*, 'Evaluating the Visualization of What a Deep Neural Network Has Learned' (2017) 28 (11) *IEEE Transactions on Neural Networks and Learning Systems* 2660.

② See, eg, Grégoire Montavon, *et al*, 'Explaining Nonlinear Classification Decisions with Deep Taylor Decomposition' (2017) 65 *Pattern Recognition* 211.

③ See, eg, Anupam Datta, Shayak Sen, and Yair Zick, 'Algorithmic Transparency via Quantitative Input Influence: Theory and Experiments with Learning Systems' (2016) *IEEE Symposium on Security and Privacy* (SP) 598. 相关的可检查性概念意味着能够检查人工智能系统中嵌入的逻辑和规则。

④ See, eg, Ashley Deeks, 'The Judicial Demand for Explainable Artificial Intelligence' (2019) 119 *Columbia Law Review* 1829, 1835.

进人工智能系统的透明度上取得了显著的进步。①

如前所述，这体现了从透明原则（全局可解释性）到可解释性（解释特定决策）的转变。遗憾的是，这两者常常被混为一谈。例如，电气和电子工程师协会（Institute of Electrical and Electronics Engineers，IEEE）关于人工智能道德准则设计的报告，将透明原则列为八个总原则之一，但将其界定为"特定决策的基础应始终可查"。② 类似地，"阿西洛马原则"（Asilomar Principles）也将透明限定为"故障透明"：如果人工智能系统造成损害，就需要解释。③

这种从透明性向可解释性的转变，部分是由如何便利用户（特别是不满意的用户）因素驱动的。可解释人工智能系统在实践中也更容易操作。人工智能系统设计可以在事后促进可解释性。一些遵循规则、决策树或线性模型的旧系统可以编写具有内置自动解释的程序。④ IEEE 认为，预测更先进的人工智能系统会

---

① Alejandro Barredo Arrieta，et al，'Explainable Artificial Intelligence (XAI)：Concepts, Taxonomies, Opportunities, and Challenges Toward Responsible AI' (2020) 58 *Information Fusion* 82, 82-84. 其中，较为知名的包括局部可解释模型不可知解释（Local Interpretable Model-Agnostic Explanations，LIME）及其变体。其他的还包括贝叶斯规则列表（Bayesian Rule Lists，BRL）和沙普利加性解释（Shapley Additive Explanations，SHAP）。

② Ethically Aligned Design：A Vision for Prioritizing Human Well-being with Autonomous and Intelligent Systems (IEEE, 2019) 27.

③ Asilomar AI Principles (Future of Life Institute, 6 January 2017).
"阿西洛马原则"，是指由人工智能（AI）研究者和专家在 2017 年在美国加州阿西洛马会议上共同制定的一系列原则。该会议旨在讨论 AI 的发展和应用，并探讨如何确保 AI 的安全和道德使用。该原则参考翻译及英文原文可查询（原文内容非常简短没有更多背景信息）：https://futureoflife.org/open-letter/ai-principles-chinese/。——译者注

④ Alberto Blanco-Justicia，et al，'Machine Learning Explainability via Microaggregation and Shallow Decision Trees' (2020) 194 *Knowledge-Based Systems* 105532, 1-2.

做什么有很大的难度，因此主张通过可追溯性来减轻潜在的风险。① 其他论者，则主要通过标准化记录模型性能特性和训练数据，以提高可解释性。②

这些主张都与透明原则不同。美国国防高级研究项目局（Defense Advanced Research Projects Agency，DARPA）在2017年的一份报告中指出，可解释人工智能系统的目标是使人类用户能够"理解、适当地信任并有效地管理新一代的人工智能合作伙伴"③。DARPA认为，理解和信任是非常重要的，对于个体用户而言，衡量解释效果的关注点主要集中在"用户满意度"等指标上。

其他研究试图衡量可解释人工智能（XAI），将其"好处"、对用户的有用性和满意度、改善用户心理模型的程度，以及解释对模型性能、受众信任和依赖的影响等归因为定量值。④ 其中一种更为突出的解释形式被称为"反事实"（counterfactual），意味着解释试图强调通过不同的输入变量可能达到的替代结果。⑤ 这

---

① Ethically Aligned Design: A Vision for Prioritizing Human Well-being with Autonomous and Intelligent Systems (IEEE, 2019) 137.
② 参见本书第6章第6.2.2（b）节。
③ David Gunning, Explainable Artificial Intelligence (XAI), Program Update (Defense Advanced Research Projects Agency (DARPA), DARPA/I2O, November 2017) 7.
④ Robert R Hoffman, et al, 'Metrics for Explainable AI: Challenges and Prospects' (2019) *arXiv* 1812.04608v2; Sina Mohseni, Niloofar Zarei, and Eric D Ragan, 'A Multidisciplinary Survey and Framework for Design and Evaluation of Explainable AI Systems' (2020) *arXiv* 1811.11839v4.
⑤ See, eg, Ramaravind Kommiya Mothilal, Amit Sharma, and Chenhao Tan, 'Explaining Machine Learning Classifiers Through Diverse Counterfactual Explanations' (2020) *ACM Conference on Fairness, Accountability, and Transparency* (FAT*) 607.

类似于美国信贷法所要求的"主要原因"解释，其目的是为用户提供可行的指导，如改变财务状况可能使他们得以获得贷款或更低的利率。① 这种进路的优点之一是，可以在无须人工干预和无须披露底层模型的情况下生成相应的解释。但其局限性在于，它最适用于二元结果，假设模型随时间保持稳定，并依赖于更改的值映射到现实世界的行动，而其他因素保持不变。②

这些都是重要的发展，但从监管的角度看，这些进路针对的是不同的受众和不同的法益。对偏离用户需求或期望的决策进行重点解释，只涵盖了人工智能系统所作决策的一小部分，其余的决策可能因为用户没有投诉和自动化偏见填补了空白而被接受。③ 然而，如果透明原则的目标是提高决策质量，防止或惩罚不可接受的决策，提高合法性，那么需要更多的监管方案。同时，技术解决方案必须与监管方案相结合，局部解释必须辅之以全局透明性。④

---

① 在美国信贷法中，"principal reason"指的是信贷决定的"主要原因"或"主要依据"。根据美国联邦法律中的条款，信贷机构需要向贷款申请人提供一个解释，说明为何他们的贷款申请被拒绝或获得不利的条款。这个解释必须包括明确的"principal reason"，即对决定做出的主要依据。"principal reason"解释通常是指涉及借款人信用历史、收入情况、债务负担、就业状况等因素的决策原因。通过提供这种解释，借款人可以更好地理解为何贷款决策做出，并有机会纠正或提供更多的证据来支持他们的申请。——译者注

② Solon Barocas, Andrew D Selbst, and Manish Raghavan, 'The Hidden Assumptions Behind Counterfactual Explanations and Principal Reasons' (2020) *ACM Conference on Fairness, Accountability, and Transparency* (FAT*) 80.

③ 参见本书第3章第3.1节。

④ 可解释人工智能领域发展迅速，本书在此无意完整展现计算机科学文献的内容。有关内容可参见年度ACM公平性、问责性和透明性会议信息，网址：https://facctconference.org。该会议最初被称为FAT，但在2020年被改为FAccT。与此相关的算法公平性领域也超出了本书的研究范围，可参见Pak-Hang Wong, 'Democratizing Algorithmic Fairness' (2020) 33 *Philosophy & Technology* 225。

6.2.2 提高透明度的工具

本节讨论的重点在于透明原则下的有发展前景的三种监管工具：算法影响评估、算法审计和人工智能监察机构。本书第8章将进一步讨论更广泛意义上的人工智能监管工具。

（a）算法影响评估

算法影响评估（algorithmic impact assessments）是数据（或隐私）保护影响评估的一种，这种评估基于环境影响评估。这种渊源主要出自两大方面：

第一，与环境影响的类比有助于将评估与现有政策和实践相连接：在承诺进行某个项目之前，研究其在敏感领域可能产生的后果。针对环境影响，对特定项目的成本与收益评估会得出相应的结论，即特定项目是否应该推进，或者应该采取何种保护措施以减轻污染、破坏野生动物等不良影响。这种环境评估机制至少可以追溯到1970年，彼时它首次被引入美国法律。[1]

第二，隐私影响评估则出现得相对较晚。新西兰1993年颁布了相关立法，[2] 紧随其后的是加拿大、澳大利亚和美国。[3] 欧盟在其1995年的《数据保护指令》中规定，成员国必须对某些活动对权利和自由的风险进行评估。[4] 但是，正式的数据保护影响

---

[1] National Environmental Policy Act 1970 (US). See generally Neil Craik, *The International Law of Environmental Impact Assessment: Process, Substance and Integration* (CUP 2008).

[2] Privacy Act 1993 (NZ), s 105.

[3] 例如，Electronic Government Act 2002 (US) 参照 Federal Privacy Act 1974 (US) 5 USC § 552a (r)，也要求公共机构更改记录系统时应允许评估对隐私权的影响。

[4] Directive 95/46/EC of the European Parliament and of the Council of 24 October 1995 on the protection of individuals with regard to the processing of personal data and on the free movement of such data（欧盟《数据保护指令》第20条）。

评估直到 2016 年《通用数据保护条例》(GDPR)才确立。GDPR 的这项要求，与其他有关自动处理的条款相结合，成为算法影响评估的基石性规定。这也是我们注意其渊源的原因之一。因为它仅限于"预期的处理操作对个人数据保护的影响"。① 如我们所见，不透明的人工智能系统可能产生的负面后果包括但绝对不限于对个人数据的影响。

理论上，算法影响评估应该帮助人们认识到哪些人工智能系统在影响他们的生活，以提高决策质量，同时借由专家和当事人审查自动化流程以确保更全面的问责制。② 与较狭义的解释权不同，算法影响评估的目的是确保在作出决定之前提供相关的文件。③ 理想的过程应该是特定主体公开其打算使用的每个人工智能系统的详细信息，并评估可能的危害，以及解决这些危害的方法，并且还应允许可能受影响的个人在规定时限内质疑已经被预估的伤害或者提出的响应。④

最佳的评估是在特定项目层面而非组织层面进行的，是事先而非事后进行的，采用广泛的方式考虑利益相关者的利益和考虑的规范，并专注于解决问题而不仅仅是突出问题。⑤ 然而，在实践中，数据保护影响评估的记录表明，它们更关注数据质量和安

---

① GDPR, art 35 (1)。另参见本书第 6 章第 6.3.1 节。

② Dillon Reisman, *et al*, Algorithmic Impact Assessments: A Practical Framework for Public Agency Accountability (AI Now, April 2018) 5.

③ Andrew D Selbst, 'Disparate Impact in Big Data Policing' (2017) 52 *Georgia Law Review* 109, 169-93.

④ Dillon Reisman *et al*, Algorithmic Impact Assessments: A Practical Framework for Public Agency Accountability (AI Now, April 2018) 9-10.

⑤ Margot E Kaminski and Gianclaudio Malgieri, 'Multi-layered Explanations from Algorithmic Impact Assessments in the GDPR' (2020) *ACM Conference on Fairness, Accountability, and Transparency* (FAT *) 68, 71.

全,而非更广泛的社会和法律影响。①

影响评估还有一个局限性:它们通常是自愿的,或者,如在 GDPR 的情况下,给予了相关主体极大的自由裁量权。② 对每个主体使用的所有人工智能系统都要求进行全面评估可能是不切实际的。然而,正如本书第 3 章中所论述的,这可以通过分级方式进行管理。通说认为,某些政府的固有职能不应被外包:设计恰当的影响评估可以帮助决定是否应部署不透明的人工智能系统,以及应采取何种保障措施。

(b) 算法审计

审计,特别是外部审计,常用于改善业务流程和防范不当行为。它们还旨在验证公开披露的信息(如财务报表)是否真实、公正地反映了公司财务状况。对于不透明的人工智能系统,审计可以用来确定算法是否按预设的方式运营,以及它是否容易出现不可接受的偏见。③ 审计日志提供了一个有用的记录,可以回顾查看训练数据的来源或模型对用户群体的总体影响,更重要的是,审计日志能够模拟新用户并系统地测试是否存在如本书第 3 章中讨论的那种偏见的结果。④

即便如此,确定哪些因素构成不可接受的偏见以及如何测试、验证这些偏见仍可能是具有挑战性的。较为简单的是那些已

---

① Alessandro Mantelero,'AI and Big Data: A Blueprint for a Human Rights, Social, and Ethical Impact Assessment'(2018)34 *Computer Law & Security Review* 754,761-62.

② 参见本书第 6 章第 6.3.1 节。

③ IEEE 软件开发标准将审计定义为"对软件产品和流程是否符合适用的法规、标准、指南、计划、规范和程序的独立评估"。参见 IEEE Standard for Software Reviews and Audits (IEEE, Standard 1028-2008, 2008)。

④ 参见本书第 3 章第 3.2 节。

经在反歧视法中规定的因素，比如性别、种族、年龄、宗教、残疾等。① 然而，如果没有这些法定基准，确定其他偏见的因素可能会很困难。机器学习过程通常是在使用前将数据分为训练数据和验证数据。虽然这似乎提供了筛查偏见因素的机会，但用来测试模型性能的数据可能与用来训练模型的数据具有相同的偏见。② 即使是出于善意的努力，如果无法考虑社会环境，使用算法来对抗偏见也会失败。例如，"公平"并不是技术系统的属性，而是该系统所在社会的属性。③

另一个困难是，算法审计通常将被审查的人工智能系统视为一个黑箱，这就限制了从不同的测试结果中推断原因的能力，以及验证更多的输入变化是否会导致不同（并可能带来问题）结果的能力。④ 一个更理想的方案是对开发过程的每个阶段都进行审计，特别是在模型开发的早期阶段，并与风险登记表的开发同时进行。⑤ 当然，这一方案可能与技术创新的文化相冲突，因为审

---

① See generally Tarunabh Khaitan, *A Theory of Discrimination Law* (OUP 2015); Nina Grgić-Hlača, *et al*, The Case for Process Fairness in Learning: Feature Selection for Fair Decision Making (Symposium on Machine Learning and the Law at the 29th Conference on Neural Information Processing Systems (NIPS), 2016).

② Karen Hao, 'This Is How AI Bias Really Happens—and Why It's so Hard to Fix', *MIT Technology Review* (4 February 2019).

③ Richard Berk, *Machine Learning Risk Assessments in Criminal Justice Settings* (Springer 2019) 115-30; Andrew D Selbst, *et al*, 'Fairness and Abstraction in Sociotechnical Systems' (2019) *ACM Conference on Fairness, Accountability, and Transparency* (FAT*) 59. Cf Ifeoma Ajunwa, 'The Paradox of Automation as Anti-Bias Intervention' (2020) 41 *Cardozo Law Review* 1671.

④ Cf Joshua A Kroll, *et al*, 'Accountable Algorithms' (2017) 165 *University of Pennsylvania Law Review* 633, 661.

⑤ See Fiona D Patterson and Kevin Neailey, 'A Risk Register Database System to Aid the Management of Project Risk' (2002) 20 *International Journal of Project Management* 365.

计必须是按部就班的、乏味的、缓慢的，但在早期阶段进行内部审计，并在整个过程中做好记录，可能是识别和防止某些不可接受的决策生成的唯一方案。①

最近的两个标准可能对创建这样的文件很有用。"模型卡"（model cards）包括有关模型的构建方式、在其发展过程中的预设以及不同族群的特定行为类型。②机器学习数据集的"数据表"（data sheets）以电子行业硬件文档的方式进行类比，并建议每个数据集都要有一个数据表，记录其动机、组成、收集过程、推荐用途等方面的信息。③

（c）人工智能监察机构

人工智能不透明性的根本问题在于，人们不知道自己不知道什么。大多数现有的问责制度，依赖于受害者对一个不透明的人工智能系统的开发者或所有者提起诉讼（前文已经阐述了胜诉可能面临的重重障碍）。④ 在人工智能系统正式应用之前的影响评估，以及在应用期间和之后的内、外部审计，将解决一些低劣、不可接受和不合法决策的问题。但在许多法域，拥有一个专门的监察机构，能够代表公众利益处理人工智能系统问题，调查不适用于现有诉由体系的投诉，将对现状起到改善作用。

对于算法或更广泛的人工智能监管，建立这样的监察机构或监察专员（ombudsperson），已经有不少学者进行了论证。如果

---

① Inioluwa Deborah Raji, *et al*, 'Closing the AI Accountability Gap: Defining an End-to-End Framework for Internal Algorithmic Auditing'（2020）2001.00973v1 *arXiv*.

② Margaret Mitchell, *et al*, 'Model Cards for Model Reporting'（2019）*ACM Conference on Fairness, Accountability, and Transparency*（FAT*）220.

③ Timnit Gebru, *et al*, 'Datasheets for Datasets'（2020）*arXiv* 1803.09010v7.

④ 参见本书第6章第6.1.3节。

创建,其职责将大大超越透明度或可解释性的问题,在这里提及,是因为相对灵活性可以使其对由于底层技术的不确定性而导致信息有限的情况,监管能够作出及时、相称的回应。我们将在第 8 章就此展开更全面的讨论。①

6.3 立法规定

正如人工智能监管的其他许多领域一样,在不透明和透明度监管问题上,技术迭代已经领先于法律变革。一些法域已经接受了这一点。例如,新加坡采用了一种技术性中立的非强制立法规范模式;即使采用这种模式制定的非约束性文件,也承认"完美的可解释性、透明性和公平性是不可能的"。② 已经通过强制性立法(或试图立法)的法域,正面临着抑制创新或无法遏制技术不良效应的困境。③ 欧盟的经验已经表明,他们还可能发现,为了解决这个问题的妥协性立法语言本身就带来了诸多不确定性。

6.3.1 欧盟法规定了解释权

在欧盟《通用数据保护条例》(GDPR) 2018 年 5 月 25 日生效的倒计时期间,一场奇怪而激烈的争论蔓延到那些通常更习惯于刊发沉闷的学术评论的专业期刊上。一方观点认为,经过四年谈判达成的 GDPR 已经在根本上改变了欧盟数据保护的透明度监

---

① 参见本书第 8 章第 8.3.4 节。
② Model Artificial Intelligence Governance Framework (2nd edn) (Personal Data Protection Commission, 2020) 15.
③ 参见本书第 7 章第 7.2 节。

管范式，创造了一项新的"解释权"。① 另一方反对的观点则认为，GDPR 被严重误读了，实际上并没有创设新的解释权。②

现在看来，当时论战的双方都过于简化了核心问题，很大部分原因是 GDPR 的序言说明和正文条款之间存在明显的脱节。GDPR 非约束性的序言第 71 条要求，针对"获得（通过）完全自动化处理得出的决策"，个人应有权获得充分的解释。③ 正文第 22 条规定了何种情势下处理个人数据是合规的（参见本书第 2 章）。④ 然而，在解释权方面，正文条款并未规定更详尽的配套措施。曾有一项立法建议，提议将"获得人类评估和已达成决策的解释"列入"适当措施"之中。⑤ 然而，这一表述在最后公布的 GDPR 中被删除了，这导致一些人得出"解释权"曾被考虑但已被 GDPR 放弃的结论。这一结论是不准确的，它忽略了 GDPR 正文第 15 条规定的一项权利，即用户有权要求解释是否存在自动化决策机制，以及"自动化决策涉及的逻辑原理、对用户的重要性和产生的预期后果"等信息的合理说明。⑥

该争论演变成关于一般意义上的"解释权"和特定意义上的

---

① Bryce Goodman and Seth Flaxman, 'European Union Regulations on Algorithmic Decision Making and a "Right to Explanation"' (2017) 38 (3) *AI Magazine* 50.

② Sandra Wachter, Brent Mittelstadt, and Luciano Floridi, 'Why a Right to Explanation of Automated Decision-Making Does Not Exist in the General Data Protection Regulation' (2017) 7 *International Data Privacy Law* 76.

③ GDPR, Recital 71.

④ 参见本书第 2 章第 2.3 节。

⑤ Report of the Committee on Civil Liberties, Justice and Home Affairs on the proposal for a regulation of the European Parliament and of the Council on the protection of individuals with regard to the processing of personal data and on the free movement of such data (General Data Protection Regulation) [European Parliament, COM (2012) 0011-C7-0025/2012-2012/0011 (COD), 2013] (emphasis added).

⑥ GDPR, art 15 (1) (h).

"信息解释权利"之间差异的语义争论，①但似乎已经由欧洲数据保护委员会解决。该委员会之前被称为"第29条工作小组"，其关于实施GDPR的指南规定，"有意义的信息"无须包括算法的复杂解释或完整算法的披露，但应该"足够全面，以便数据主体理解决策的原因"。②

然而，这些规定仍然存在显著的漏洞。相关规定仅适用于基于"完全自动化处理"的决策，这些决策产生法律或类似效果。③访问权也应以不"对他人的权利或自由产生不利影响，包括商业秘密或知识产权，特别是保护软件的著作权"的方式解释。④

GDPR还规定了"数据保护影响评估"（Data Protection Impact Assessment，DPIA），该评估可能与前面提议的算法影响评估有很多重叠。⑤GDPR第35条规定，组织评估拟议的系统，必须包括其与所述目的的必要性和比例性；评估还必须涵盖受影响个人的权利和自由所面临的风险以及解决这些风险的措施。

然而，这里仍然存在显著的局限性。首先，要求进行DPIA的门槛最初被认为是对自然人权利和自由存在"高风险"的情况，尽管这个门槛后来被定义为包括"对自然人进行个人方面系

---

① GDPR的德文文本使用了"aussagekräftige Informationen"一词，意思接近"有意义的信息"，而相应的法文"informations utiles"和荷兰文"nuttige informative"则可以直译为"有用的信息"。

② Guidelines on Automated Individual Decision-Making and Profiling for the Purposes of Regulation 2016/679（Article 29 Data Protection Working Party，17/EN WP251rev. 01，3 October 2017）25. Cf Profiling and Automated Decision-Making (Information Commissioner's Office, 2017) 15.

③ GDPR, art 22 (1).

④ Ibid., Recital 63.

⑤ 参见本书第6章第6.2.2（a）节。

统性和广泛性的评估",从而导致具有法律或类似效果的决策。①正如一群学者讽刺地指出的,证明不需要进行 DPIA 本身可能就需要进行 DPIA。② 其次,至少目前来说,另一个缺点是它侧重于个人数据保护。这一点很重要,但与不透明算法运作相关的问题远不止这些。最后,欧盟的 DPIA 仅规定了有限的协商——在内部与数据保护官员进行协商,仅"在不损害商业或公共利益或处理操作的安全的情况下"与数据主体本身进行协商。③ 早期关于强制性协商的提案被放弃了,因为人们认为这会给数据控制者带来不成比例的负担。同样,只有在组织自己的评估得出在没有采取缓解措施的情况下存在高风险的结论时,才需要与其法域内的相关数据保护机构进行协商。④ 此外,评估无须公开。

尽管有这些保留意见,GDPR 仍有可能产生影响。2019 年 1 月,谷歌被法国数据保护机构——国家信息与自由委员会(Commission Nationale de l'Informatique et des Libertés,CNIL)罚款 5000 万欧元。该次判罚是 GDPR 出台以来对科技公司实施的最高额度罚款。谷歌的违规行为包括未提供有关在其 Android 设备上提供定向广告所使用的个人数据的信息,使用户"无法充分理解此类处理对他们的特定后果"。⑤ 2020 年 6 月,谷歌对法国最高行政法院的上诉被驳回,法院认定相关信息未以足够清晰和明确

---

① GDPR, art 35 (1), (3).
② Bryan Casey, Ashkan Farhangi, and Roland Vogl, 'Rethinking Explainable Machines: The GDPR's "Right to Explanation" Debate and the Rise of Algorithmic Audits in Enterprise' (2019) 34 *Berkeley Technology Law Journal* 145, 176.
③ GDPR, art 35 (2), (9).
④ Ibid., art 36.
⑤ Deliberation of the Restricted Committee Pronouncing a Financial Sanction Against Google LLC (CNIL, SAN-2019-001, 21 January 2019), para 111.

的方式提供，无法有效地获得用户的同意。①

尽管此案涉及透明度问题，但影响理解的障碍与神经网络关系不大，更多的是与法律术语有关。关于谷歌如何使用个人数据的解释分散在多个文件中，这些文件含糊不清，难以获取，有时需要进行五到六次操作才能找到它们。这违反了 GDPR 关于以"清晰"和"可理解"的方式②提供有关收集和使用个人数据信息的义务，而不是质疑使用不透明的人工智能系统本身。尽管如此，该决定仍然值得注意，因为它是由代表近万名用户的两个非营利组织发起的。虽然没有指控具体的损害，但这被认为足以让法国国家信息与自由委员会开始进行调查，虽然这项调查只在网上进行。未来的集体诉讼有可能针对使用不透明算法的行为，尽管证明授权语言的不充分性要比证明收集到的个人数据如何被使用的不透明性要简单得多。

6.3.2 欧洲委员会《第 108 号公约》

欧洲委员会《关于在自动处理个人数据方面保护个人的公约》(《第 108 号公约》) 于 1981 年首次通过，并在 1985 年生效。除了 1999 年向欧盟开放的措施外，最重要的修正案是在 2018 年 (GDPR 生效前一周) 通过的，旨在解决人工智能系统带来的"新挑战"。③

---

① RGPD：le Conseil d'État rejette le recours dirigé contre la sanction de 50 millions d'euros infligée à Google par la CNIL [GDPR：The Council of State Rejects the Appeal Against the Sanction of 50 Million Euros Imposed on Google by the CNIL] (Conseil d'État，19 June 2020).
② GDPR，art 12 (1).
③ Protocol amending the Convention for the Protection of Individuals with regard to Automatic Processing of Personal Data (ETS No 108)，done at Elsinore，Denmark，17-18 May 2018.

除其他变化外，这些修正案引入了新的透明性义务，涉及数据控制者的身份以及数据处理的法律依据和目的。据此，用户有权"在要求下获得关于数据处理所依据的推理，并且此类处理结果是否适用于他或她"①。然而，正如解释性报告所表明的那样，2018年修正案假定数据控制者拥有这种信息，并应将其提供给数据主体。②因此，它在这里的适用范围有限。

6.3.3 法国的立法实践

2016年，法国通过了《数字共和国法》（Loi pour une République numérique）。这项主要适用于行政机关的法律，详细规定了要求获取有关算法决策信息的权利，包括算法的规则和主要特征。③ 随后的法令详细说明了该信息应包括算法的参数以及它们的权重，并且应以"可理解的形式"呈现。④ 这项最后的规定指向了"解释"或"透明度"作为解决不透明性的补救措施的一个关键限制。以一种对普通人可理解的方式提供信息，但又足够完整地对算法过程进行全面解释，而又不会过度侵犯商业秘密

---

① Convention for the Protection of Individuals with regard to Automatic Processing of Personal Data (Convention 108), done at Strasbourg, 29 January 1981, ETS No 108, in force 1 October 1985, art 9 (1) (c).

② Explanatory Report to the Protocol amending the Convention for the Protection of Individuals with regard to Automatic Processing of Personal Data (Council of Europe, 10 October 2018), para 77.

③ Loi no 2016-1321 du 7 octobre 2016 pour une République numérique 2016 (France), art 4.

④ Décret n° 2017-330 du 14 mars 2017 relatif aux droits des personnes faisant l'objet de décisions individuelles prises sur le fondement d'un traitement algorithmique 2017 (France), art 1. See also Lilian Edwards and Michael Veale, 'Enslaving the Algorithm: From a "Right to an Explanation" to a "Right to Better Decisions"?' (2018) 16 (3) IEEE *Security & Privacy* 46, 48-49.

或允许用户操纵系统。这是极其困难的。①

6.3.4 美国的立法实践

2019年4月，美国参议院和众议院提出了一项新的《算法问责法案》（Algorithmic Accountability Act）。该法案呼应了广泛报道的算法偏见，其新闻稿也援引了脸书（Facebook）因允许广告商基于种族、宗教和残疾状态进行歧视而被指控违反《公平住房法》。拟议中的法案要求对"高风险"的自动化决策系统进行影响评估，包括这些系统的"准确性、公平性、偏见、歧视、隐私和安全性"。但是，此项法案仅适用于年收入超过5000万美元或拥有超过100万客户数据的实体；它将不会设置私人诉讼权，也不会具有域外管辖权；执法工作将通过联邦贸易委员会（FTC）或州检察长进行。②

虽然不太可能成为法律，但该立法草案至少有两个值得关注的理由。其一，它将会是处理人工智能的通用性法律，而不是针对特定领域的专门立法。几十年来，特定领域专门立法模式已经破坏了美国隐私和数据保护法的体系性、一致性。③ 它对歧视的监管，将从基于一系列现有法律的零散性执法转变为基于单一法律的预防或缓解。其二，它的适用范围更适当地扩展覆盖了算法的开发和使用方式。拟议的影响评估包括系统本身以及其开发过程，包括算法设计和数据训练，尽管没有要求公开评估结果。与

---

① Sandra Wachter, Brent Mittelstadt, and Chris Russell, 'Counterfactual Explanations Without Opening the Black Box: Automated Decisions and the GDPR' (2018) 31 *Harvard Journal of Law & Technology* 841, 842-43.

② Algorithmic Accountability Act of 2019, S 1108, HR 2231, 116th Congress 2019 (US).

③ Simon Chesterman, *One Nation Under Surveillance: A New Social Contract to Defend Freedom Without Sacrificing Liberty* (OUP 2011) 244.

GDPR 不同的是，自动决策被定义为"作出决策或促进人类决策"的计算过程，避免了将保护措施局限于"完全基于自动处理"的决策的问题。①

其新闻稿中有这样一句话："算法不应该从我们的反歧视法中获得豁免"。这过分简化了解决算法偏见的监管挑战，算法不能是"法外之地"。但是，它们的不透明性确实使得发现或纠正歧视性行为更加困难。如果该立法或类似的立法获得通过，将会使这两方面的工作更加容易。

6.3.5 加拿大的立法实践

2020年4月，加拿大的《自动化决策指令》开始生效。该指令涵盖了大多数联邦行政决策，要求在部署"任何协助或取代人类决策者判断的技术"之前，必须进行算法影响评估。②算法影响评估遵循一个标准的形式，必须在相关技术正式投入使用之前完成。

算法影响评估覆盖范围的广度很重要。但特别值得注意的是，《自动化决策指令》根据潜在危害的程度，对透明度的要求设置了"滑动标尺"（sliding scale）。如果决策可能对个人或社区产生"很少或没有影响"，则不需要通知。对于具有"中度"影响的决策，必须在该项目或服务的网站上发布通俗易懂的说明。如果预计会产生"高"或"非常高"的影响，网站还必须包括对有关组件如何运作的描述、支持该决策的说明、任何审查或审计的结果以及对训练数据的描述（或链接到匿名化数据本身，如果可以公开获得）。另外，还有一项关于解释决策过程的规定。那些影响最小的决策，只需要在网站上提供一个"常见问题"部分

---

① GDPR, art 22 (1).
② Directive on Automated Decision-Making 2019 (Canada), Appendix A.

进行说明。中度影响的决策应根据要求提供"有意义的解释"。对于具有高影响和非常高影响的决策,如果拒绝提供某项利益或服务,则应在拒绝决定中包含解释性说明,这样可以帮助受影响的人理解为什么被拒绝,以增加透明度和可追溯性。①

尽管只限于公共部门,但加拿大的这项指令是迄今为止最具进步性的一项立法。政府机构此前已被敦促使用开源软件;该指令增加了一个前提,即加拿大政府所拥有的系统的自定义源代码也应该公布,但需要遵守诸如机密和其他数据的例外规定。现在对该指令的实施效果进行评估还为时过早,但一些人已经对其在移民决策中取代更正式、强制性的标准表示了担忧。②

6.3.6 其他法域的立法实践

其他法域也已经考虑在利用人工智能的同时保持或鼓励透明的方法,尽管大多数都还停留在与前面讨论的新加坡示范框架相类似的自愿原则领域。③例如,在澳大利亚,联邦政府于2019年11月发布了《人工智能伦理原则》,其中指出,人们应该能够"知道他们何时受到人工智能系统的重大影响,并能够了解人工智能系统何时与他们接触"④。一些政府已经效仿加拿大的做法,

---

① Directive on Automated Decision-Making 2019 (Canada), Appendix A, s 6.2.

② Fenwick McKelvey and Margaret MacDonald, 'Artificial Intelligence Policy Innovations at the Canadian Federal Government' (2019) 44 (2) *Canadian Journal of Communication* 43, 46.

③ Model Artificial Intelligence Governance Framework (2nd edn) (Personal Data Protection Commission, 2020) 15.

④ AI Ethics Principles (Department of Industry, Science, Energy and Resources, November 2019)。与此对比的是2019年澳大利亚联邦科学与工业研究组织(Commonwealth Scientific and Industrial Research Organisation, CSIRO)的讨论文件,该文件呼吁对透明度进行广义的解释:"当算法的使用影响到用户时,用户应有权获得有关该算法使用了哪些信息以作出相应的决策。"参见 D Dawson, *et al*, Artificial Intelligence: Australia's Ethics Framework (Data61 CSIRO, 2019) 6-7。

探索对公共部门流程进行更严格的限制。2020年7月，新西兰公布了其《算法宪章》（Algorithm Charter），根据该宪章，政府机构承诺"清楚地说明重大决策是如何由算法决定的"。草案中还包含了机构将说明"谁对自动化决策负责"的语句，但这一内容在最终文本中被删除了。[①]

2019年，中国国家新一代人工智能治理专业委员会发布《新一代人工智能治理原则——发展负责任的人工智能》（以下简称《人工智能治理原则》），旨在确保人工智能系统的安全、可控和可靠。《人工智能治理原则》规定了八项原则，与其他国家的类似框架有很多重叠，[②]但对透明性的重视并不高。《人工智能治理原则》提倡公平，消除歧视，但透明性和可解释性是"持续改进"的目标，同时"逐步实现"可审计性。[③]

6.4 透明原则的局限性

透明原则是一种手段，而非目的。在一定程度上，它的目的是避免或限制本书第3章所讨论的不透明性带来的低效的、不合理和不合法的决定的风险。透明性还能建立信任。缺乏信任通常被认为是普遍存在的问题，是人们采纳和接受新技术（特别是

---

① Algorithm Charter for Aotearoa New Zealand (Department of Internal Affairs, July 2020).
② 参见本书第7章引言。
③ 《新一代人工智能治理原则——发展负责任的人工智能》（2019年6月17日发布），第2段（"消除……歧视"），第5段（"人工智能系统应不断提升透明性，可解释性……逐步实现可审核"）。

人工智能）的主要障碍之一。① 本章讨论了从透明度到可解释性的监管重心转换，承认了人工智能系统的个体化使用问题，以及人工智能系统的天然不透明性带来的实际挑战。虽然针对人工智能系统个案的解释说明有助于纠正低劣的决策或者揭示不合理的决策，但这取决于受影响的用户知道自己受到伤害并有能力提起投诉。这种解释并不能解决人工智能决策的合法性问题，特别是那些应当事前解释说明而不是事后补充的决策。

即使抱着最好的意图和充足的资源，我们也需要认识到透明原则的局限性。实际上，对这些局限性的公开本身，可能是最重要的提高透明度的一种形式。② 但是，透明度并非灵丹妙药。有时它会产生干扰，有时它是不可取的。

作为一种干扰，虚幻的透明度可能比不透明更糟糕。虚幻的透明度，有时被称为"透明度谬论"，有两种表现形式。其一，就像一些政府通过把选民埋在非结构化的记录中来展示他们对"开放"的承诺一样，提供大量的数据或源代码可能只是形式上的透明。③ 其二，理论上的个体解释权如果未在实践中充分落实，那么它只会转移批评焦点，而无法提供真正的补救措施。即使理解了这一点，在缺乏利用信息实现系统性变革的可能性的情况

---

① See, eg, Robin C Feldman, Ehrik Aldana, and Kara Stein, 'Artificial Intelligence in the Health Care Space: How We Can Trust What We Cannot Know' (2019) 30 *Stanford Law & Policy Review* 399.

② Cf Karl de Fine Licht and Jenny de Fine Licht, 'Artificial Intelligence, Transparency, and Public Decision-Making: Why Explanations Are Key when Trying to Produce Perceived Legitimacy' (2020) 35 *AI & Society* 917.

③ 非结构化的记录在政府文件或数据存档中可能指的是缺乏明确结构和标准化的记录方式，使得这些记录不易被公民或研究人员理解和利用。这种情况下，政府可能通过提供大量非结构化的记录来淹没公民，使其难以获取有用的信息，从而掩盖事实或限制透明度。——译者注

下，它也无助于实现有意义的问责。正如用户理论上的同意长期以来为数据保护法提供了掩护一样，透明度的假象可能给那些试图追究人工智能系统责任的人带来虚假的安慰。

在某些情势下，公开透明原则是不可取的。旨在维护安全、防止欺诈或其他不法行为的系统，应保持足够的不透明性以实现其职能。① 披露某些算法的细节，如安检站对哪些人会进行更彻底的筛查，可能揭示算法偏见，但也会使操纵算法成为可能。② 另外，如果基础数据集被公开，构成某些决策基础的个人信息将被曝光。即使没有公开数据集，针对特定算法模型的解释也可以被利用来揭示潜在的训练数据。③ 在个人数据保护法中出现许多与透明度相关的条文，正是这个原因。

对透明度和可解释性的另一种批评是，我们有时要求它们做得太多。对人工智能系统透明度的呼吁往往是源于对人类决策的质疑性假设。例如，将算法处理与传统决策进行对比，在传统决策中，人类决策者在被询问时只受限于他们作出解释的意愿和能力，以及提问者理解它的能力，"原则上"可以阐明他们的决策理由。④ "原则上"，在这里异常关键。众所周知，人类实际的决策过程与直觉、预感、个人印象以及事后推理密不可分。⑤ 当我们

---

① Jenna Burrell, 'How the Machine "Thinks": Understanding Opacity in Machine Learning Algorithms' (2016) 3 (1) *Big Data & Society*, 4.

② Anupam Chander, 'The Racist Algorithm?' (2017) 115 *Michigan Law Review* 1023, 1034.

③ Reza Shokri, Martin Strobel, and Yair Zick, 'On the Privacy Risks of Model Explanations' (2020) *arXiv* 1907.00164v5.

④ Brent Daniel Mittelstadt, et al, 'The Ethics of Algorithms: Mapping the Debate' (2016) 3 (2) *Big Data & Society*, 7.

⑤ John Zerilli, et al, 'Transparency in Algorithmic and Human Decision-Making: Is There a Double Standard?' (2019) 32 *Philosophy & Technology* 661, 665-68.

要求人类决策者给出理由时，我们并没有要求他们进行功能性核磁共振成像，以了解实际达成决策的物理认知过程。

语言在解释决策时并不总是有帮助。当考虑解释不同现象时，我们从"理由"（reasons）而非"原因"（causes）的角度思考有自由意志的人类行为。① 当解释人类决策时，提出特定选择的"原因"会显得奇怪。尽管我们可能说新鞋子是我们以别扭方式行走的"原因"，但我们不会说它们的折扣价格"导致"我们购买它们。在物理世界中，情况恰恰相反：我们通常不会谈论火灾发生的"理由"，除非是作为解释"原因"的前提说明。② "理由"这一语言表达，假定了行为者具有一定程度的主观性和理智性，而"原因"这一语言表达则不然。③ 那么，在计算机的情况下，对"理由"的要求表明了另一种拟人化。从计算机做 X（如关闭或起火）的"原因"，我们推导出计算机做 Y（如拒绝给我贷款、建议我观看特定电影等）的"理由"。

人们追求人工智能系统的透明度，目的并非为了透明度本身，而是出于与追求人类决策中透明度类似的目的。然而，实现人工智能系统透明度的方法是不同的。有时这是有益的，比如我们可以通过进行多次模拟测试偏见，而不必担心人工智能系统会变得具有防御性并掩饰事实。有时这是充满挑战的。一个有用的

---

① "reasons"（理由）通常指与人类行为相关的动机、意图或理由，与主观的、理性的决策过程相关，反映了人类的意愿、动机和思考方式。"causes"（原因）则更强调事件或行为的物理或因果关系，通常与客观的、物理的因果关系相关，更注重描述某个事件或结果是由于特定的原因而发生。也可以将它们分别理解为：主观的因果关系、客观的因果关系。——译者注

② 例如，"The reason that the fire started was because…"（火灾开始的理由是因为……），这句英文的开头部分"The reason that"（理由）便是多余的。

③ Tim Miller, 'Explanation in Artificial Intelligence: Insights from the Social Sciences' (2019) 267 *Artificial Intelligence* 1, 16.

类比是，不仅仅是要解释为什么发生了 X，还要解释为什么是 X 而不是 Y。人工智能系统具有选择性，因为它们会优先考虑相关性和背景因素，而不是完整性。人类决策的解释不是纯粹的统计概率，而是强调影响决策的因素，并以适合有关主体各自的世界观的方式来表达。这点对人工智能系统来说极为困难。

此类透明性问题，对于某些特定的决策，特别是在决策结果的合法性与决策者的身份息息相关的公共决策场景下尤为重要。① 许多警告不透明的人工智能系统决定人类命运的论调描绘了一个没有解释的反乌托邦世界，弗朗茨·卡夫卡的《审判》便是其典型代表。② 在这部作品中，一个被称为"约瑟夫·K"的男子被未知的代理人因未知的罪行逮捕并起诉；试图理解或摆脱他荒谬的困境都是徒劳的。这个隐喻十分引人入胜，但它是有缺陷的。因为《审判》的力量并不在于对无助的约瑟夫·K隐瞒了一些隐藏的解释，而在于他的困境根本没有逻辑。

增强人工智能系统在决策或辅助决策中的作用，在很多情况下会将结果优化；被拒绝服务或受到这些决策负面影响的个人有权获得解释。但是，要避免低效的、不合理或不合法的决策，需要的不仅仅是这些。决策前的影响评估，决策过程中的审计，以及决策之后的说明解释，都将增强决策的科学性，同时也能够增加公众对这些决策的信任。

人工智能系统参与决策这一事项需要透明公开。目前，这在大多数情况下是一个简单的有或没有（人工智能系统参与决策）

---

① 参见本书第 3 章第 3.3 节。
② See, eg, Andrew Selbst and Solon Barocas, 'The Intuitive Appeal of Explainable Machines' (2018) 87 *Fordham Law Review* 1085, 1118; Daniel J Solove, 'Privacy and Power: Computer Databases and Metaphors for Information Privacy' (2001) 53 *Stanford Law Review* 1393, 1419-23.

的问题。然而，人工智能辅助决策将越来越多地融合人类和机器。一些聊天机器人，从开始的自动（人类不介入）处理基本咨询，然后提供由人审核的建议性响应（人类参与），再升级到直接与人类接触（人类完全参与），以处理不寻常或更复杂的人、机互动。① 虽然"完全基于自动处理"的决策正在增多，但"机器辅助"的决策更可能呈几何基数暴增。就像自动驾驶汽车中的乘客需要清楚地知道是谁在握着方向盘一样，与人工智能系统互动的人类应该知道他们在与谁打交道或与什么在打交道。

这种需求是双向的。为了防止过度使用或恶意攻击，许多网站现在采用挑战测试，如验证码。这起初是一种反向图灵测试，计算机需要证明用户是人类而不是另一台计算机。②

在前述阿什利·麦迪逊公司数据泄露事件一年后，其母公司将公司名称从"Avid Life"改为"Ruby Life"，并聘任了新的总经理，而公司本身也采用了新的口号："寻找你的时刻"。公司的标志，也从结婚戒指和一个女人把手指放在嘴唇上变成红宝石，寓意"多面性"并能关联到更广泛用户群体。据报道，除了用户提起的集体诉讼之外，美国联邦贸易委员会也正在调查该公司使用机器人与付费男性用户聊天的行为。

然而，不到十二个月，"享受婚外情"这个词汇又回到了公

---

① See, eg, Pavel Kucherbaev, Alessandro Bozzon, and Geert-Jan Houben, 'Human-Aided Bots' (2018) 22 (6) *IEEE Internet Computing* 36.

② 验证码的英文"captcha"是一个人为创造的首字母缩写，英文全称是"completely automated public Turing test to tell computers and humans apart"。参见 Luis von Ahn, *et al*, 'CAPTCHA: Using Hard AI Problems for Security' in Eli Biham (ed), *Advances in Cryptology-EUROCRYPT 2003* (Springer 2003) 294; Henry S Baird, Allison L Coates, and Richard J Fateman, 'PessimalPrint: A Reverse Turing Test' (2003) 5 *International Journal on Document Analysis and Recognition* 158.

司的视线，公司重新把重心放在婚外情上。在接受《纽约邮报》采访时，该公司的公关部副总裁表示，2015年夏天的事件让公司业务得到了"前所未有的媒体报道"。尽管是负面报道，但是用户数量却增加了一半以上，达到5000多万人。他还坚称，公司已经不再使用机器人，因为新注册用户中男性和女性的数量几乎相等，这使得使用机器人假冒女性用户成为不必要。"虽然我们每月的新增会员并未得到第三方的验证"，他承认，"但我们相信这些数据。"① 该公司后来进一步采取行动，聘请了安永会计师事务所进行了一次极不寻常的审计。除了验证新用户注册信息，此次审计还确认了"机器人程序"已被停用。②

最终，美国联邦贸易委员会（FTC）对阿什利·麦迪逊公司的调查以及用户针对该公司的集体诉讼，也都达成和解。③ 美国联邦贸易委员会对该公司处以160万美元的罚款，并要求其建立全面的数据安全方案。集体诉讼方面，该公司将1120万美元存入专用账户。因为许多用户使用虚假的电子邮件地址注册，所以该公司购买了定向横幅广告，以扩大潜在索赔人的范围。42名未公开姓名的原告寻求以化名参加诉讼和和解，"以减少对他们及他们的家人可能带来的潜在灾难性后果"。法院对这些原告表示同情，但拒绝了他们的请求，认为他们对尴尬的焦虑并没有超过公众对透明度的关注。④

---

① Richard Morgan, 'Ashley Madison Is Back—and Claims Surprising User Numbers', *New York Post* (21 May 2017).

② Ruby Life, Inc.: Report on Customer Statistics for the Calendar Year 2017 (Ernst & Young LLP, 2018) 1.

③ 'Operators of AshleyMadison.com Settle FTC, State Data Breach Charges' (2017) 34 (3) *Computer and Internet Lawyer* 27.

④ *In re Ashley Madison Customer Data Security Breach Litigation* MDL No 2669 (Eastern District of Missouri, Eastern Division, 6 April 2016).

PART THREE
第Ⅲ部分

可能性

第 7 章
新　规　则

20 世纪 40 年代，科幻小说作家艾萨克·阿西莫夫（Isaac Asimov）想象，未来机器人会成为日常生活的一个组成部分。作者曾经回想创作时的想象，多数机器人可以划分为两种类别。一种是作为威胁存在的机器人，科技创新发展到机器人可以对抗其创造者，如同玛丽·雪莱（Mary Shelley）1818 年小说《弗兰肯斯坦》所描述的那样，但相关共鸣至少可以追溯至普罗米修斯这个希腊神话，而普罗米修斯也正是《弗兰肯斯坦》这本小说副标题所包含的内容。另一种不太常见的故事是机器人作为悲情角色存在，即可爱的机器人被其残忍的人类主人像奴隶那样对待；这是有关危险性的寓言，讲述的不是人类创造的机器人带来的危险，而是人类本身所造成的危险。①

阿西莫夫的贡献是创造了第三种机器人，即作为工程师所建造的工业产品而存在的机器人。在阿西莫夫的想象世界里，安全装置以机器人三定律形式植入道德中立的机器人。其中，第一定律是机器人不能伤害人类，也不能通过不作为放任人类伤害自

---

① Isaac Asimov，*The Complete Robot*（Doubleday 1982）9-10。关于文学作品中的机器人启示录，参见本书第 5 章第 5.3 节。另参见本书结论中关于《罗萨姆的万能机器人》的讨论。

己。第二定律是机器人必须遵守人类给出的指令，除非该指令违反第一定律。第三定律是机器人必须保护自己，除非这与第一定律或第二定律相冲突。①

这三大定律是关于规范新科技的文献的一个基本内容，但与图灵测试一样，三大定律更像是文化的象征，而不是严肃的科学建议。② 不过，三大定律的假设前提是需要解决具有人类智能水平的实体化机器人所带来的问题，即本书第 5 章所讨论的类人机器人谬误的例子。③ 三大定律同时也受到批评，批评的理由是三大定律将义务施加于技术本身，而没能施加于创造技术的人。④ 此处值得注意的是，三大定律不是国家执行命令意义上的"法律"，而是植入虚构作品中的正电子大脑的编码：限制机器人可以做什么，而不是明确规定机器人应该做什么。⑤

更重要的是，就当前目的而言，那些认为伦理原则可以减少到几十个词语或可以以人工智能系统解读的方式进行编码的观点，误解了伦理和法律的本质区别。⑥ 然而，据报道，韩国在 2007 年曾考虑将伦理原则作为拟议《机器人伦理宪章》的基础。⑦ 自世纪之交以来，特别是 2004 年于意大利圣雷莫（Sanremo）举

---

① Isaac Asimov, 'Runaround', *Astounding Science Fiction* (March 1942).

② See, eg, Susan Leigh Anderson, 'Asimov's "Three Laws of Robotics" and Machine Metaethics' (2008) 22 *AI & Society* 477。关于图灵测试，参见本书第 5 章引言部分。

③ 参见本书第 5 章第 5.2 节。

④ Jack M Balkin, 'The Three Laws of Robotics in the Age of Big Data' (2017) 78 *Ohio State Law Journal* 1217.

⑤ 关于限制假想的超级智能（如通过"终止开关"）的局限性的讨论，参见本书第 5 章第 5.3 节。

⑥ 参见本书第 9 章第 9.1 节。

⑦ 'South Korea Creates Ethical Code for Righteous Robots', *New Scientist* (8 March 2007). See Intelligent Robots Development and Distribution Promotion Act 2008 (Republic of Korea).

办的第一届机器人伦理研讨会唤起加速推进机器人伦理规范编撰以来,韩国相关做法是机器人或人工智能规范编撰方面的诸多尝试之一。欧洲机器人研究网络(European Robotics Research Network)于 2006 年制定了"机器人伦理路线图",而第一套多学科视角下的机器人原则则于 2010 年在两个英国研究委员会举办的"机器人务虚会"上得以通过。①

2016 年以来,人工智能方面的指南、框架和原则激增。其中一些指南、框架和原则产生于会议或行业协会,特别是 2016 年人工智能伙伴关系组织制定的《人工智能合作信条》、② 2017 年生命未来研究所制定的《阿西洛马人工智能原则》、③ 2019 年北京智源人工智能研究院制定的《人工智能北京共识》、④ 2009 年电气和电子工程师协会制定的《符合伦理的设计》。⑤ 其他的指南、框架和原则则由个别公司自行起草,包括微软发布的《负责任的人工智能原则》、⑥ 国际商业机器公司(IBM)发布的《信任与透明度原则》、⑦ 谷歌发布的《人工智能原则》,⑧ 这些均发布于 2018 上半年。

政府在制定人工智能法律方面行动迟缓。⑨ 然而,不乏个别

---

① Principles of Robotics (Engineering and Physical Sciences Research Council and Arts and Humanities Research Council, 2010).
② Tenets (Partnership on AI, 28 September 2016).
③ Asilomar AI Principles (Future of Life Institute, 6 January 2017).
④ 北京智源人工智能研究院:《人工智能北京共识》(2019 年 5 月 25 日)。
⑤ Ethically Aligned Design: A Vision for Prioritizing Human Well-Being with Autonomous and Intelligent Systems (IEEE, 2019).
⑥ The Future Computed: Artificial Intelligence and Its Role in Society (Microsoft, 17 January 2018) 57.
⑦ IBM's Principles for Trust and Transparency (IBM, 30 May 2018).
⑧ Artificial Intelligence at Google: Our Principles (Google, 7 June 2018).
⑨ 针对具体行业的回应包括解决高频交易(参见本书第 1 章第 1.2 节)、自动驾驶汽车(参见本书第 2 章第 2.1 节)和算法透明度(参见本书第 6 章第 6.3 节)的措施。

国家就人工智能制定了软规范，包括新加坡 2019 年发布的《人工智能监管框架示范》、①澳大利亚 2019 年发布的《人工智能道德原则》②、中国 2019 年发布的《人工智能治理原则》、③新西兰 2020 年发布的《算法宪章》。④在政府间组织层面，除了经济合作与发展组织（OECD）2019 年发布的《人工智能委员会建议》，⑤七国集团 2018 年通过了《沙勒沃伊人工智能未来的共同愿景》，⑥欧盟 2019 年发布了《可信赖人工智能的道德准则》，⑦甚至教皇也已表示支持 2020 年《人工智能伦理罗马倡议》中的一系列原则。⑧

令人惊叹的是，上述文件在人工智能监管规范方面存在重叠共识。⑨尽管这些文件的语言表述和强调重点有所不同，但自

---

① A Proposed Model Artificial Intelligence Governance Framework (Personal Data Protection Commission, 2019).

② AI Ethics Principles (Department of Industry, Science, Energy and Resources, November 2019).

③ 中国国家新一代人工智能治理专业委员会：《新一代人工智能治理原则——发展负责任的人工智能》（2019 年 6 月 17 日）。

④ Algorithm Charter for Aotearoa New Zealand (Department of Internal Affairs, July 2020).

⑤ OECD, Recommendation of the Council on Artificial Intelligence (OECD/LEGAL/0449, 22 May 2019).

⑥ Charlevoix Common Vision for the Future of Artificial Intelligence (G7, 9 June 2018).

⑦ Ethics Guidelines for Trustworthy AI (European Commission High-Level Expert Group on Artificial Intelligence, 8 April 2019).

⑧ Rome Call for AI Ethics (Pontificia Accademia per la Vita, 28 February 2020).

⑨ Cf Anna Jobin, Marcello Ienca, and Effy Vayena, 'The Global Landscape of AI Ethics Guidelines' (2019) 1 *Nature Machine Intelligence* 389; Jessica Fjeld, *et al*, Principled Artificial Intelligence: Mapping Consensus in Ethical and Rights-Based Approaches to Principles for AI (Berkman Klein Center for Internet & Society, 2020); Thilo Hagendorff, 'The Ethics of AI Ethics: An Evaluation of Guidelines' (2020) 30 *Minds & Machines* 99.

2018年以来的几乎所有文件均围绕下述六个主题展开：

（1）人类控制：人工智能应当增强而不是降低人类潜能，同时，人工智能应处于人类控制之下。

（2）透明度：人工智能系统应当具有可理解性，人工智能决策应当能够被解释。

（3）安全：人工智能系统应当按照人类预期运行，同时具有抵御黑客入侵的能力。

（4）问责制：尽管通常没有与人工智能问责制相关的定义，但负责任的人工智能对其造成的损害应当提供可以采取的补救措施。

（5）非歧视：人工智能系统应当具有包容性和"公正性"，避免存在不允许的偏见。

（6）隐私：鉴于人工智能依赖于对个人数据等数据的访问，隐私或个人数据保护通常被强调为需要保护的特定权利。

其他概念包括开发和部署人工智能系统的人员需要承担专业责任，以及人工智能需要提升人类价值或"行善"。① 这些主题相当于呼吁人们应普遍支持人工智能伦理，特别是支持人类控制原则。一些文件呼吁人工智能应当可持续发展、公平分配人工智能所带来的利益，② 尽管这些文件更恰当地阐释了应如何部署人工智能，但不适合解决人工智能应当或不应当做哪些事情。

前述列明的六个原则貌似并无争议。然而，尽管花费大量的时间和精力来召开研讨会并起草各种文件，但令人奇怪的是，实

---

① See, eg, Floridi. Luciano, et al, 'AI4People—An Ethical Framework for a Good AI Society: Opportunities, Risks, Principles, and Recommendations' (2018) 28 *Minds and Machines* 689, 696-97.

② See, eg, Ethics Guidelines for Trustworthy AI (European Commission High-Level Expert Group On Artificial Intelligence, 8 April 2019).

践中鲜少依照这些原则所指明的内容实施或探讨如何实施这些原则。人们有时会明确承认并提及这种情况，给出的理由是起草的各种文件旨在用于未知科技并解决尚未预见的问题。①

另外一个问题是：上述原则中的每个原则是否实际上均是必要的。遵守问责制、非歧视和隐私方面的要求，实质上等于要求人工智能系统的发明者或使用者遵守多数法域已经存在的法律。正如本书第一部分所讨论的，这些法律足以规制人工智能在多数情况下所引发的损害。例如，安全要求与第 4 章所阐述的产品责任问题相类似，② 同时安全要求还涉及采取合理的网络安全预防措施。③ 透明度本身不是一项伦理原则，而是理解并评估相关行为所必需的前提条件。④ 然而，透明度与人类控制可共同构成开发人工智能系统的潜在约束，超越现有法律规定。

本章讨论的重点并不是哪些新规则在监管人工智能方面是必需的，即本章不重点讨论人工智能规则的数量扩张。⑤ 相反，本章试图回答三个问题：（1）为什么人工智能监管是必需的；（2）何时应当改变监管结构（包括规则）；（3）应当如何实施人工智能的监管措施。希望对这些问题的阐释将揭示人工智能监管所必需的新规则，以及采用何种程序来保持规则的先进性。本书第

---

① See, eg, Model Artificial Intelligence Governance Framework (2nd edn) (Personal Data Protection Commission, 2020) 10. See also the compendium of use cases developed under the framework.

② 参见本书第 4 章第 4.1.3 节。

③ See, eg, Draft Report with Recommendations to the Commission on a Civil liability regime for Artificial Intelligence [EU Parliament Committee on Legal Affairs, 2020/2014 (INL), 27 April 2020], art 8 (2) (b).

④ Matteo Turilli and Luciano Floridi, 'The Ethics of Information Transparency' (2009) 11 *Ethics and Information Technology* 105. 另参见本书第 6 章。

⑤ Cf Jacob Turner, *Robot Rules: Regulating Artificial Intelligence* (Palgrave Macmillan 2019).

8 章将阐述应当由谁来监管人工智能。

7.1 为什么（不）监管？

理论上，政府监管的目的是解决市场失灵问题或是为了支持社会政策或其他政策。实践中，与产业和政治利益的关联可能导致政客以不那么符合原则的方式作为或不作为。① 尽管大型科技公司与政府之间的关系有据可查，② 但本节将假设监管机构具有诚信，进而勾勒其作出决策选择的考量因素。（监管俘获及其相关问题将在第 8 章讨论。③）

就人工智能系统而言，监管的市场合理性包括解决技术生产者和消费者之间的信息失衡，以及保护第三方免受人工智能部署所引发的外部损害。这大致对应前几章所讨论的实践中需要对人工智能进行监管的缘由，即监管目的是确保风险的适当分配和责任归属。例如，就自动驾驶汽车而言，我们已经看到责任从驾驶员转移到制造商的趋势，制造商可能有义务购买足够险级的保险。④ 这为其他一些人工智能系统引起伤害的民事责任提供了一个模型，尤其是为更普遍的运输（包括无人机）和医疗设备等人

---

① Robert Baldwin, Martin Cave, and Martin Lodge, *Understanding Regulation: Theory, Strategy, and Practice* (2nd edn, Oxford University Press 2011) 15-24.

② See, eg, Carlotta Alfonsi, 'Taming Tech Giants Requires Fixing the Revolving Door' (2019) 19 *Kennedy School Review* 166; Tony Romm, 'Tech Giants Led by Amazon, Facebook, and Google Spent Nearly Half a Billion on Lobbying over the Past Decade, New Data Shows', *Washington Post* (22 January 2020).

③ 参见本书第 8 章第 8.1.2 节。

④ 参见本书第 2 章第 2.1.1 节。

工智能系统提供了民事责任模型。①

然而，监管目的并不仅仅是为市场运行提供便利，它还可以捍卫权利或促进社会政策，但在某些情况下可能课加额外成本。②这些正当理由反映了限制人工智能的伦理依据。例如，就偏见而言，基于种族或性别的歧视是被禁止的，即使在某些其他方面是"有效"的情况下也是如此。③ 同样，基于功利主义很难得出禁止人工智能系统在武装冲突中作出杀戮决定是站得住脚的，这可能不符合功利主义所追求的更好结果；这些人工智能系统可能最终比人类更遵守武装冲突法。前述"禁止"源于这样一个决定，即伦理要求人们对其选择负责。正如第 4 章所论证的，"不可委托职责"可能适用于保护弱势个体的情况，这比潜在利益最优化更重要。例如，"不可委托职责"适用于医院和患者、学校和学生之间。④

不同的考量要素可能限制将某些职能外包给人工智能系统，尤其是某些公共决策，其正当性取决于决策过程和达到结果的效率。即使人们认为人工智能系统可以作出比政客和法官更好的决策，也依然应该由承担相应职务的公职人员来执行那些影响个体权利和义务的固有政府职能，以便可以通过政治或宪法机制追究他们的责任。⑤

监管人工智能的另一个原因更本质上是出于程序考量。正如第 6 章所讨论的，透明度是有效监管的前提。尽管不是灵丹妙药且会带来额外成本，但最低透明度要求和解释决策的能力要求可

---

① 参见本书第 4 章第 4.1.3 节、第 4.1.4 节。
② See Tony Prosser, 'Regulation and Social Solidarity' (2006) 33 *Journal of Law and Society* 364.
③ 参见本书第 4 章第 4.2 节。
④ 参见本书第 4 章第 4.2 节。
⑤ 参见本书第 4 章第 4.3 节。

以使监管和问责成为可能。

尽管如此，如果监管会限制创新、施加额外负担或扭曲市场，政府也可能有不监管某一特定行业的充分理由。① 尽管人工智能监管在许多法域采取与数据保护法一致的手段，但不同政治团体仍以不同方式权衡前述考量要素。例如，美国在很大程度上遵循以市场为基础的监管手段，在 50 个州进行相对宽松的行业监管和试验。美国在数据保护领域也是如此，并没有通用的联邦数据保护法，但儿童隐私或金融机构等特定利益主体或行业受到法律管制。就人工智能而言，在 2016 年奥巴马政府即将结束时，美国国家科学与技术委员会（US National Science and Technology Council）反对对人工智能研究或实践进行广泛监管。在监管所带来的结果是增加合规成本或减缓创新的情况下，美国国家科学与技术委员会则主张在不损害安全性或市场公平的前提下放宽监管措施。②

欧盟《通用数据保护条例》在颁布六个月后得以确定最终文本，该条例涵盖数据保护及我们所观察到的数据自动处理方面的广泛新权力。③ 欧盟采取以人权优先为特点的监管手段，自二战后将隐私作为一项权利纳入人权范畴，④ 构成 1995 年《数据保护

---

① See generally Mehmet Ugur (ed), *Governance, Regulation, and Innovation: Theory and Evidence from Firms and Nations* (Edward Elgar 2013).
② Preparing for the Future of Artificial Intelligence (National Science and Technology Council, October 2016) 17. Cf Remarks of FCC Chairman Ajit Pai at FCC Forum on Artificial Intelligence and Machine Learning (Federal Communications Commission, 30 November 2018)（描述了"监管谦抑"的必要性）。
③ 参见本书第 2 章第 2.3.2 节。
④ [European] Convention for the Protection of Human Rights and Fundamental Freedoms, done at Rome, 4 November 1950, 213 UNTS 222, in force 3 September 1953, art 8.

指令》及现在的《通用数据保护条例》的基石。人权也是欧盟对于人工智能考量的最重要主题，①尽管偶尔有人抱怨这会降低欧洲大陆的竞争力。②

中国提供了另外一种监管模式，政府在其中扮演更有力的监管角色，对于市场或人权方面的关切较少。与数据保护一样，保护主权是监管的主要驱动力。在数据保护方面，通过数据本地化要求来表达主权，借此确保中国政府当局可以访问个人数据。③ 对于人工智能而言，中国政府 2006 年将其确立为重要发展目标，④ 2016 年将其确立为国家优先发展领域。⑤ 2017 年，中国国务院发布《新一代人工智能发展规划》，肯定了市场的作用，设定 2025 年目标为人工智能基础理论实现重大突破，应用程序达到"世界领先"水平，"初步确立人工智能法律和法规"。⑥

尽管对中国缺乏监管的看法容易让人产生怀疑，有人认为中国对个人数据的宽松监管手段给其人工智能产业带来了极大优

---

① White Paper on Artificial Intelligence ［European Commission，COM (2020) 65 final，19 February 2020］10. 另参见欧盟委员会 2021 年 4 月 21 日公布的监管条例草案。

② See，eg，Ulf Pehrsson，'Europe's Obsession with Privacy Rights Hinders Growth'，*Politico* (17 June 2016).

③ Anupam Chander and Uyên P Lê，'Data Nationalism' (2015) 64 *Emory Law Journal* 677；John Selby，'Data Localization Laws：Trade Barriers or Legitimate Responses to Cybersecurity Risks，or Both?' (2017) 25 *International Journal of Law and Information Technology* 213. 关于中国立场的微妙但准官方的辩护，参见 Jinhe Liu，'China's Data Localization' (2020) 13 *Chinese Journal of Communication* 84。

④ 中华人民共和国国务院《国家中长期科学和技术发展规划纲要（2006—2020年）》（国务院公报 2006 年第 9 号）。

⑤ 《中华人民共和国国民经济和社会发展第十三个五年规划纲要》。

⑥ 《国务院关于印发新一代人工智能发展规划的通知》（国发〔2017〕35 号，2017 年 7 月 8 日）。

势①，但对于新兴科技的未来监管规划而言，真正的深层问题不是是否监管，而是何时监管。

7.2 何时监管

戴维·科林格里奇（David Collingridge）于1980年在英国伯明翰的阿斯顿大学撰文指出，任何控制新技术的努力都面临着双重困境。在技术控制可行的早期阶段，人们对技术造成的有害社会后果知之甚少，不足以减缓技术发展。然而，当那些后果显现时，技术控制已变得代价高昂且缓慢。②

气候紧急情况提供了一个示例，即当今所称的"科林格里奇困境"。在汽车广泛使用之前，英国皇家委员会1906年研究了新机器在英国道路上行驶的潜在风险，其中最主要的潜在风险是汽车后面扬起的灰尘。③ 如今，交通运输产生的二氧化碳排放量约占所有与能源相关的二氧化碳排放量的1/4，而且其持续增长可能超过所有其他缓解措施。④ 尽管2020年暴发的新冠病毒感染疫情对排放产生了明显影响，但减少这些排放的监管工作仍面临经

---

① Huw Roberts, et al, 'The Chinese Approach to Artificial Intelligence: An Analysis of Policy, Ethics, and Regulation' (2021) 36 *AI & Society* 59.

② David Collingridge, *The Social Control of Technology* (Frances Pinter 1980) 19.

③ Royal Commission on Motor Cars (Cd 3080-1, 1906).

④ CO2 Emissions from Fuel Combustion: Overview (International Energy Agency, 2020); Ralph Sims, et al, 'Transport' in O Edenhofer, et al (eds), *Mitigation of Climate Change. Contribution of Working Group III to the Fifth Assessment Report of the Intergovernmental Panel on Climate Change* (Cambridge University Press 2014) at 403.

济和政治障碍。①

　　许多解决技术创新的努力都聚焦于困境的首个要点：预测和避免损害。本章开头部分探讨了解决困境的诸多原则方法。除了会议和研讨会，还成立了科研机构来评估人工智能风险，对通用人工智能发出了一些世界末日般的警告。② 如果通用人工智能真的对人类生存造成威胁，那么它可能能够证明禁止研究是合理的，从而像限制生化武器那样禁止研究人工智能。③ 然而，世界上没有哪个主要法域禁止研究人工智能，这或者因为人工智能所带来的威胁貌似并未迫近，或者因为担心此等禁止只会将人工智能研究推向别处。例如，美国 2001 年限制干细胞研究，其主要后果是该领域的美国研究人员落后于国际同行。④ 另一个挑战是，如果监管针对的是近期威胁，那么技术创新的步伐将导致监管者陷入无休止的追赶游戏。技术可以呈现指数级别的变化，而社会、经济和法律体系往往是逐渐改变。⑤ 基于这些原因，本章开

---

　　① See，eg，Yong-Hong Liu，*et al*，'Reduction Measures for Air Pollutants and Greenhouse Gas in the Transportation Sector：A Cost-Benefit Analysis'（2019）207 *Journal of Cleaner Production* 1023.
　　② 参见本书第 5 章第 5.3 节。
　　③ 《禁止细菌（生物）和毒素武器的发展、生产及储存以及销毁这类武器的公约》和《关于禁止发展、生产、储存和使用化学武器及销毁此种武器的公约》［Convention on the Prohibition of the Development，Production and Stockpiling of Bacteriological (Biological) and Toxin Weapons and on Their Destruction，done at Washington，London，and Moscow，10 April 1972，in force 26 March 1975；Convention on the Prohibition of the Development，Production，Stockpiling，and Use of Chemical Weapons and on Their Destruction，done at Paris，13 January 1993，in force 29 April 1997］．另参见本书第 8 章第 8.1.1 节中讨论的对重组 DNA 的自我限制。
　　④ Varnee Murugan，'Embryonic Stem Cell Research：A Decade of Debate from Bush to Obama'（2009）82 *Yale Journal of Biology and Medicine* 101.
　　⑤ Larry Downes，*The Laws of Disruption：Harnessing the New Forces That Govern Life and Business in the Digital Age*（Basic Books 2009）2.

头所讨论的原则旨在具有未来性和技术中立性。这样处理的好处是适用范围足够广泛，能够适应不断演变的情势，尽管存在原则的模糊性使其无法在具体案件中提供有意义指导的风险。

科林格里奇认为，与其试着预测风险，不如为解决困境的第二个层面奠定基础：确保技术决策灵活或可逆。① 第二个层面的困境解决并非易事，如同一些人戏称的那样，面临着马已经逃跑之后关闭门的"谷仓门"问题。正如本书开头所描述的，监管控制措施缺位导致监视资本主义（surveillance capitalism）兴起，社交媒体和零工经济即为例证。②

本节考虑有关监管时机的两种方法，即预防原则和巧妙的不作为，这有望解决或减轻科林格里奇困境。

7.2.1 预防原则

谨慎是对不确定性的自然反应。根据预防原则，如果一项活动的后果可能很严重，但存在科学不确定性，则应采取预防措施，或者根本不开展该活动。③ 该原则在许多国家国内环境法中具有重要地位，并在大多数有关该主题的国际文件中发挥了重要作用。例如，1992年《里约宣言》指出，"遇有严重或不可逆的损害时，缺乏充分的科学确定性不应成为推迟采取经济、有效的措施以

---

① David Collingridge, *The Social Control of Technology* (Frances Pinter 1980) 23-43.

② Shoshana Zuboff, *The Age of Surveillance Capitalism: The Fight for a Human Future at the New Frontier of Power* (Public Affairs 2019); Jeremias Prassl, *Humans as a Service: The Promise and Perils of Work in the Gig Economy* (Oxford University Press 2018); Pedro Domingos, *The Master Algorithm: How the Quest for the Ultimate Learning Machine Will Remake Our World* (Basic Books 2015) 286.

③ Terje Aven, 'On Different Types of Uncertainties in the Context of the Precautionary Principle' (2011) 31 *Risk Analysis* 1515.

防止环境退化的理由"。① 在执行过程中，该原则等同于举证责任倒置：那些主张行为具有安全性的人，必须证明情况确实如此。②

批评家认为，预防原则含糊、不连贯，或两者兼有。对预防原则的弱解释等同于老生常谈，因为很少有人会主张采取预防措施需要具有科学确定性；对该原则的强解释则是自我矛盾的，因为预防措施本身可能产生不利后果。③ 卡斯·桑斯坦（Cass Sunstein）谴责其为"欧洲化"，详细描述了这一原则以可预见的非理性方式在审议式民主中发挥作用，尤其是高估损失和公众舆论对风险的反应。也就是说，在风险成为现实之前或可以量化之前，至少存在一些风险需采取预防措施来加以应对，这一观点已被广泛接受。④

在人工智能领域，人们惯常采取预防原则的领域为自动驾驶⑤、致命性自主武器⑥、司法系统处理个人数据的算法使用⑦、

---

① 1992年《里约环境与发展宣言》原则十五。
② Ginevra Le Moli, Parthan S Vishvanathan, and Anjali Aeri, 'Whither the Proof? The Progressive Reversal of the Burden of Proof in Environmental Cases before International Courts and Tribunals' (2017) 8 *Journal of International Dispute Settlement* 644.
③ Thomas Boyer-Kassem, 'Is the Precautionary Principle Really Incoherent?' (2017) 37 *Risk Analysis* 2026.
④ 桑斯坦本人接受了反灾难原则的观点。参见 Cass Sunstein, *Laws of Fear: Beyond the Precautionary Principle* (Cambridge University Press 2005) 109-15。
⑤ Bryant Walker Smith, 'Regulation and the Risk of Inaction' in Markus Maurer, et al (eds), *Autonomous Driving: Technical, Legal and Social Aspects* (Springer 2016) 571 at 572.
⑥ Nehal Bhuta and Stavros-Evdokimos Pantazopoulos, 'Autonomy and Uncertainty: Increasingly Autonomous Weapons Systems and the International Legal Regulation of Risk' in Nehal Bhuta, et al (eds), *Autonomous Weapons Systems: Law, Ethics, Policy* (Cambridge University Press 2016) 284 at 290-94.
⑦ European Ethical Charter on the Use of Artificial Intelligence in Judicial Systems and Their Environment [European Commission for the Efficiency of Justice (CEPEJ), 4 December 2018] 56.

通用人工智能攻击人类创造者的可能性①。然而，仅有最后一个领域援引预防原则是适当的，因为该领域的相关风险性质及其可能性存在真正的不确定性。例如，尽管自动驾驶故障的精确概率可能是未知的，但自动驾驶造成的损害本身是已知的，并且能够与人类驾驶员所造成的威胁进行平衡。② 关于致命性自主武器，反对者明确反对采取成本效益分析方法，支持在涉及人类生命的决策方面画定鲜明的道德底线；尽管人们一直在争论人类控制的适当程度，但"风险"本身并不是问题。③ 同样，将公共部门决策外包给机器的谨慎性，并不是或至少不仅仅是建立在可能产生的后果的不确定性之上。相反，它与这样一种观点有关，即这种决定应该由人类在政治问责体系内作出。④

然而，如前所述，尽管通用人工智能存在风险，但尚不存在限制该领域纯学理研究或应用研究的协同努力。更有希望实现的是聚焦科林格里奇困境的第二个层面：在人工智能中引入终止开关之类的措施要求，或努力协调任何未来超智能价值与我们人类价值相一致。这些可以视为人类优先原则的应用。如果通往通用人工智能的路径变得更为清晰，这些原则应成为强制要求。⑤

7.2.2 巧妙的不作为

对不确定性的另一种回应是不作为。为了避免先发制人的规

---

① Matthijs M Maas, 'Regulating for "Normal AI Accidents": Operational Lessons for the Responsible Governance of Artificial Intelligence Deployment' (2018) Proceedings of 2018 AAAI/ACM Conference on AI, Ethics, and Society (AIES '18) 223.
② 参见本书第 2 章第 2.1 节。
③ 参见本书第 2 章第 2.2 节。
④ 参见本书第 4 章第 4.3 节。
⑤ 参见本书第 5 章第 5.3 节。

则制定扭曲市场或通过司法裁判推迟其演进发展，避免采取作为措施可能是适当的。有时用于描述这种情况的术语被称为"巧妙的不作为"（masterly inactivity）。① 该种不作为起源于 19 世纪英国对阿富汗的政策，表明在不合适的替代措施面前应保持警惕性克制。② （值得注意的是，英国在阿富汗的介入以耻辱的失败告终。）

在人工智能领域，许多政府采取的"巧妙的不作为"等同于"观望"。然而，被动地允许事件发生与积极监视并与新兴市场及其参与者互动是有差别的。本章开头所描述的政府参与并使得原则得以产生就是一个例子，政府鼓励行业协会制定标准和研究治理的可能性也是一个例子。

不作为也可以是推诿责任的行为。即使政府选择不监管，也会产生具有法律后果的决策，其中最显著的是普通法传统下行使法律制定职能的法官。正如我们所看到的，这些决策已经在从计算机程序之间的合同③到判决中使用算法④以及由人工智能创造的知识产权所有权归属⑤等领域影响相关规范。如果由于具体案件向法庭提出的方式变幻莫测而将法律推向无益的方向，那么这可能是有问题的。同时，正如英国下议院科学和技术委员会（British House of Commons Science and Technology Committee）所警告的那样，法官裁决限于事件发生后应用法律原则，即"失

---

① Dominika Nestarcova, Report on Tech. Law Fest 2018 (Centre for Banking & Finance Law, National University of Singapore Faculty of Law, CBFL-Rep-1804, February 2018) 5 (quoting Singaporean Minister Vivian Balakrishnan).

② Major-General John Adye, 'England, Russia, and Afghanistan', *The Times* (18 October 1878); Kaushik Roy, *War and Society in Afghanistan: From the Mughals to the Americans, 1500-2013* (Oxford University Press 2015) 69.

③ 参见本书第 2 章第 2.3.1 节。

④ 参见本书第 3 章第 3.3.2 节。

⑤ 参见本书第 5 章第 5.2.2 节。

控事件已经发生"。①

巧妙的不作为不是一种策略。然而，适当地使用"巧妙的不作为"可以为积极作为争取时间。

7.3 如何监管

正如本书前言部分所强调的，"监管"是个有争议的概念，涵盖的内容不仅仅限于"规则"。② 一个著名文献区分了监管的三种模型，这有助于考虑哪种监管是有用的。第一，监管可以指某一套特定指示，这些指示对于致力于实现监管目的的机构具有约束力。第二，监管可以广泛地指代国家的影响，包括财政和其他激励措施。第三，更广义的监管有时涵盖所有形式的社会或经济影响，包括市场影响力。③ "智慧监管"（smart regulation）理论已经表明，监管职能不仅可以由国家机关承担，也可以由专业委

---

① Robotics and Artificial Intelligence, Fifth Report of Session 2016-17 (House of Commons Science and Technology Committee, HC 145, 2016), para 54 (quoting a submission from the Law Society).

② Barry M Mitnick, *The Political Economy of Regulation: Creating, Designing, and Removing Regulatory Forms* (Columbia University Press 1980); Anthony Ogus, *Regulation: Legal Form and Economic Theory* (Hart 2004); Robert Baldwin, Martin Cave, and Martin Lodge (eds), *The Oxford Handbook of Regulation* (Oxford University Press 2010); Tony Prosser, *The Regulatory Enterprise: Government, Regulation, and Legitimacy* (Oxford University Press 2010) 1-6; Philip Selznick, 'Focusing Organizational Research on Regulation' in Roger Noll (ed), *Regulatory Policy and the Social Sciences* (University of California Press 1985) 363; John Austin, *The Province of Jurisprudence Determined* (first published 1832, Cambridge University Press 1995) 18-37; Robert Baldwin, Martin Cave, and Martin Lodge, *Understanding Regulation: Theory, Strategy, and Practice* (2nd edn, Oxford University Press 2011) 3.

③ Robert Baldwin, Martin Cave, and Martin Lodge, *Understanding Regulation: Theory, Strategy, and Practice* (first published 1999, 2nd edn, OUP 2011) 3.

员会、标准制定机构和宣传团体执行。在多数情况下，多样化工具和一系列监管主体共同发挥的作用优于仅仅局限于单个监管主体所发挥的作用。① 不同的监管模型可能相互影响。例如，某个行业由于担心自我监管失败会陷入更具胁迫性监管的国家之手，则可能投资于自我监管。

监管不仅限于限制或禁止不良行为；它也可能促成积极行为或为其提供便利，即采取"绿灯"监管而不是"红灯"监管。② "响应式监管"（responsive regulation）主张建立更具有合作性的关系，鼓励受监管方遵守法律目标，而不仅仅是严格遵守规则。③ 其他监管手段更强调效率：尽管对未来风险的确认、选择和优先排序具有不确定性以及涉及规范和政治选择，以风险为基础和以问题为中心的监管技术仍试图优先考虑最重要的问题。④

监管机构的可用工具可以分为三类：传统的规则制定、法院或法庭的裁决以及非正式指导，最后一类工具包括标准、解释指南以及有关监管活动的公共和私人交流。蒂姆·吴（Tim Wu）批判性地建议，正在经历快速变化行业的监管机构应该考虑通过发出"威胁"将第三种和前两种监管工具结合起来，即在可能的

---

① Neil Gunningham and Peter Grabosky, *Smart Regulation: Designing Environmental Policy* (Clarendon Press 1998). Cf Michael Guihot, Anne F Matthew, and Nicolas P Suzor, 'Nudging Robots: Innovative Solutions to Regulate Artificial Intelligence' (2017) 20 *Vanderbilt Journal of Entertainment & Technology Law* 385.

② Carol Harlow and Richard Rawlings, *Law and Administration* (3rd edn, Cambridge University Press 2009) 1-48.

③ Ibid.

④ Robert Baldwin and Julia Black, 'Driving Priorities in Risk-Based Regulation: What's the Problem?' (2016) 43 *Journal of Law and Society* 565. See generally Malcolm K Sparrow, *The Regulatory Craft: Controlling Risks, Solving Problems, and Managing Compliance* (Brookings Institution 2000).

法制化和执法阴影下非正式地提出合规要求。①

人工智能监管的诸多讨论都在重复可用的选项，即"滑动标尺"（sliding scale）、"金字塔"（pyramid）、"工具箱"（toolbox）等，但这些应用要么过于笼统，要么过于具体。不证自明的是，不宜采取一种监管手段来处理人工智能影响的所有活动。同样，为每一种活动都制定法律也是不切实际的。然而，使用先前所开发的分析工具来区分人工智能涉及的三类问题可以在一定程度上明晰监管方向：管理某些风险，禁止另一些风险，确保遵守适当程序来处理第三种情况。

7.3.1　管理风险

正如第 4 章所讨论的，民事责任为风险责任分配提供了基础，特别是为那些基于成本效益分析领域的责任分配提供了基础。民事责任可以适用于人工智能在私营部门的大部分或绝大部分活动，具体包括从交通到医疗设备、从智能家居应用到"认知增加和植入"（cognitive enhancements and implants）行业和领域。此处的问题不是新规则，而是如何将现有规则应用于快速、自主且具有不同程度不透明运作的技术。为确保人们可以识别人工智能系统②且有害行为可以归因于适当的所有者、运营者或生产者，最低透明度要求可能是必需的。③ 强制保险能够更有效地分散这些风险。④ 但是，基本原则仍应合理可靠。

对于适合进行成本效益分析但潜在风险难以确定的情况，监

---

① Tim Wu, 'Agency Threats' (2011) 60 *Duke Law Journal* 1841. Cf Nathan Cortez, 'Regulating Disruptive Innovation' (2014) 29 *Berkeley Technology Law Journal* 175.
② 参见本书第 8 章第 8.2.2（b）节。
③ 参见本书第 4 章第 4.1.1 节。
④ 参见本书第 4 章第 4.1.4 节。

管"沙盒"(sandboxes)允许在受控环境中测试新技术。尽管一些法域已将此应用于具体技术,如为自动驾驶汽车指定区域,①但该方法特别适用于在线运行的人工智能系统。沙盒起源于计算机科学,虚拟沙盒可以使软件以限制潜在损害的方式运行,以防出现错误或漏洞。尽管不能像瑞安·卡洛所主张的那样完全免除损害,②但沙盒为创新产品试验免于立即引发所有的规范性监管后果提供了"安全空间",这对于机器人研究是至关重要的。③该技术最常用于金融科技领域,这使企业家们能够与真实客户一起测试产品,减少监管限制,降低执法行动带来的风险,以及获得监管机构的持续指导。④该技术2016年由英国率先尝试实践,伦敦金融科技领域因此获得先发优势而备受赞誉,此后全球其他法域也予以效仿。⑤

7.3.2 红线

然而,在某些情况中,需要明确允许事项与禁止事项的边界。这些红线在某些情况中不仅仅是将现有规则应用于人工智能,而是与维持人类控制的伦理原则相关联,一个显而易见的备

---

① See, eg, Road Traffic (Autonomous Motor Vehicles) Rules 2017 (Singapore), rule 9.
② 参见本书第4章第4.1.3节。
③ Regulatory Sandbox [Financial Conduct Authority (UK), November 2015] 1.
④ Dirk A Zetzsche, *et al*, 'Regulating a Revolution: From Regulatory Sandboxes to Smart Regulation' (2017) 23 *Fordham Journal of Corporate & Financial Law* 31, 45; Mark Fenwick, Wulf A Kaal, and Erik PM Vermeulen, 'Regulation Tomorrow: What Happens When Technology Is Faster than the Law?' (2017) 6 *American University Business Law Review* 561, 591-93.
⑤ Hillary J Allen, 'Regulatory Sandboxes', (2019) 87 *George Washington Law Review* 579, 580. See, eg, Federal Law No 123-FZ 2020 (Russia).

选原则是禁止人工智能作出使用致命武力的决定。①

然而，即使是这个看似明确的禁令，经仔细分析也会变得模糊不清。如果机器能够作出使用致命武力决定之前的每一个选择——扫描环境、识别和选择目标、提出攻击角度，最终使用致命武力的决定可能是人为的。那么，正如第 3 章所讨论的，自动化偏见使得默认选择在这种情况下更容易被接受。② 这个观点并不是反对禁令，而是为了确保不仅至少有人类"参与"或"掌握"人工智能作出决定，而且知道其将承担相应的责任。③ 这就是人类控制原则和问责制之间的关联：并不是人类处于控制地位而机器将被追责，而是即使行为是机器作出的，人类（和其他法人）将继续对其行为负责。

另一个需要新规则的领域涉及人类与人工智能系统的互动。该领域的空白并不是缺少保护我们免受机器人侵害的法律，而是缺少保护机器人免受我们侵害的法律。温和的例子包括新加坡 2017 年年初颁布的法律，将干扰自动驾驶试验定为犯罪行为。④ 人们更恰当地认为这些是此类技术相关的风险管理的扩展。⑤ 那些保护人类伦理并使人类针对机器人犯罪免受惩罚的法律，是更有问题的。正如第 5 章所讨论的，目前虐待黑猩猩构成犯罪，但折磨电脑不构成犯罪。随着"社交机器人"在老年护理乃至卖淫

---

① 参见本书第 2 章第 2.2 节。
② 参见本书第 3 章第 3.1 节。
③ 参见本书第 4 章第 4.2.2 节。
④ Road Traffic (Amendment) Act 2017 (Singapore)。从 2018 年开始，新加坡交通警察发布的基本驾驶指南增加了一个页面，描述了与试验中的自动驾驶汽车的互动。参见 *Basic Theory of Driving* (10th Edition) (Singapore Traffic Police，2018) 76。
⑤ 要求用户更新安全关键软件的法律也是如此。参见 Automated and Electric Vehicles Act 2018 (UK), s 4 (1) (b)。

等行业中越来越普及，可能有必要规定可以创造什么以及如何使用这些创造物的法律。

例如，2014年，罗纳尔·阿金（Ronald Arkin）提议使用儿童性机器人来"治疗"恋童癖患者，就像海洛因成瘾者使用美沙酮那样，这引起争议。① 尽管不同法域对模拟色情制品的处理方式不同，② 但许多国家现在通过对现有法律的创造性解释或通过新法律禁止制造和使用这些设备，如美国《遏制现实剥削性性爱电子娈童机器人法》。③

随着类人机器人越来越普及，在社会中扮演越来越主动的角色，保护这些机器人将不仅仅是为了降低故障风险，更是因为伤害它们本身即被视为错误行为。最贴切的类比是禁止虐待动物法。④ 这可以说是类人机器人谬误的另一个表现：购买类人机器人并将其点燃比删除其操作系统会造成更多的痛苦。然而，随着人工智能系统认知疼痛和理解其不复存在的能力的不断发展，算法可能改变。⑤

---

① Kashmir Hill, 'Are Child Sex-Robots Inevitable?', *Forbes* (14 July 2014) (quoting Georgia Institute of Technology Professor Ronald Arkin).

② See, eg, Nicola Henry and Anastasia Powell, 'Sexual Violence in the Digital Age: The Scope and Limits of Criminal Law' (2016) 25 *Social & Legal Studies* 397. 一般来说，有关不法行为（虐待儿童或暴力行为）的图像是被禁止的，但问题在于模拟本身是否属于不法行为。例如，美国最高法院推翻了1996年《儿童色情制品预防法》的规定，该法将这种"不记录犯罪、不制造受害者"的"言论"定为犯罪。参见 *Ashcroft v. Free Speech Coalition*, 535 US 234 (2002)。

③ Curbing Realistic Exploitative Electronic Pedophilic Robots (CREEPER) Act 2017 (US). See generally John Danaher, 'Regulating Child Sex Robots: Restriction or Experimentation?' (2019) 27 *Medical Law Review* 553.

④ 参见本书第5章第5.2.1节。

⑤ See, eg, Hutan Ashrafian, 'Can Artificial Intelligences Suffer from Mental Illness? A Philosophical Matter to Consider' (2017) 23 *Science and Engineering Ethics* 403; Muh Anshar and Mary-Anne Williams, 'Simplified Pain Matrix Method for Artificial Pain Activation Embedded into Robot Framework' (2021) 13 *International Journal of Social Robotics* 187-95.

这提出了一个问题，即是否应就可能产生自我意识或第 5 章所讨论的超级智能方面的人工智能研究画定红线。① 尽管很多专家认为应对通用人工智能的前景保持警惕，但没有人号召停止该领域研究，也没有政府如此行事。② 如前所述，试图遏制或阻碍通用人工智能带来人们想避免的威胁，可能难以实现。"预防原则"可能因为缺乏此等性能而停止发挥作用。通用人工智能还没有远远超出我们目前的能力范围，如果现在执行预防原则，则是一种过度的反应。

无论在何种情况下，一个法域的禁令可能无法约束其他法域。缺乏国际条约以及执行该条约的机构，禁令将无法发挥效用。第 8 章将探讨制定此类条约以及设立条约执行机构的前景。③

7.3.3　程序合法

限制外包给人工智能的决策范围是有必要也有可能制定新规则的领域。

正如第 4 章所讨论的，其中一个办法是限制人工智能承担政府固有的职能。偶尔有人呼吁禁止政府使用算法，这通常是为了回应公共部门决策实际或被臆想的失败，如澳大利亚④和荷兰⑤声称使用自动程序辨识利益欺诈、英国声称新冠病毒感染疫情导致

---

① 参见本书第 5 章第 5.3 节。

② See, eg, Research Priorities for Robust and Beneficial Artificial Intelligence: An Open Letter (Future of Life Institute, 2015).

③ 参见本书第 8 章第 8.2.2 节。

④ Matthew Doran, 'Robodebt Legal Warning Came on Same Day Scheme Was Suspended by Federal Government', ABC News (*Australia*) (6 February 2020) (讨论澳大利亚政府的在线合规干预措施，俗称"Robodebt")。

⑤ 'Government's Fraud Algorithm SyRI Breaks Human Rights, Privacy Law', *DutchNews.nl* (5 February 2020) (讨论荷兰政府基于算法的欺诈检测系统 SyRI)。

大学招生问题的丑闻。①

其他法域已禁止诸如人脸识别等特定应用程序。美国旧金山2019年因为禁止警察和其他机构使用人脸识别而登上头条，美国多个城市和加州效仿发布此等禁止，但美国联邦层面没有如此行事。正如在数据保护领域，美国迄今一直反对广泛立法，欧洲对此则适用《通用数据保护条例》，并提出整个欧洲大陆禁止或暂停使用人脸识别。② 中国对人脸识别的限制要少得多，尽管中国政府承认需要对人脸识别提供更多指导，并且在该领域已发生至少一起（不成功的）诉讼。③

完全禁止算法是没有必要的，最重要的是，任何定义均可能含有算术或其他基本计数功能，但这些功能并没有独立性。更重要的是，它误判问题。回到第2章和第3章所讨论的自主性和不透明性，问题不在于机器作出决策，而在于人们放弃对这些决策追责。公共部门行使政府固有职能所作出的决策具有合法性，不是因为这些决策是正确的，而是因为可以通过政治或其他程序对公共部门施行问责制。

这些顾虑触发了本章开头所讨论的两个原则：人类控制和透明度。对公共部门人工智能进行监管的一种更现实、更可推广的方法是，在公共部门决策中升级人类控制和透明度方面的规定。

---

① Adam Satariano，'British Grading Debacle Shows Pitfalls of Automating Government'，*New York Times*（20 August 2020）. 另参见本书第2章第2.3.2节及第3章第3.3节。

② 'US and Europe Clash over Facial Recognition Law'，*Biometric Technology Today*（February 2020）1. 另参见欧盟委员会2021年4月21日公布的监管条例草案。

③ Seungha Lee，Coming into Focus：China's Facial Recognition Regulations（Center for Strategic and International Studies，4 May 2020）.

我们已经在加拿大关于行政决策透明度的规定中看到这一点。①新西兰在《算法宪章》中采用了类似方法。经 24 个政府部门签署，《算法宪章》根据算法对"人民福祉"影响的可能性和严重性作出了选择性至强制性的矩阵式规定。除其他条款外，《算法宪章》的强制性应用要求"人类监管"，该"人类监管"包含公共询问联络点、对决策提出上诉的途径以及"明确阐释人类在带有算法决策中所发挥的作用"。《算法宪章》还包含透明度条款，这些条款不仅包含可解释性概念的透明度规定，还要求就算法作出简明英文文件编制说明，以及发布有关数据收集、保护和存储的信息的要求。②

这些都是重要的步骤，但还不够。对于此类公共部门决策，这不仅是《算法宪章》所述的在获取算法能力与维护公民信任、信心之间取得"适当平衡"的问题。更基本的承诺是确保存在挑战这些决策的手段：在违反法律的情况下，不仅在法律层面而且在政治层面，识别处于公众信任岗位的人类决策者，通过民主程序追究其作为或不作为责任。

7.4 规则前景

如果阿西莫夫三定律能够避免或解决机器智能的所有伦理困境，他的文学生涯将是短暂的。事实上，其故事重点是一个机器人，该机器人因第二定律和第三定律之间的矛盾而瘫痪，只有人

---

① 参见本书第 6 章第 6.3.5 节。
② See Algorithm Charter for Aotearoa New Zealand (Department of Internal Affairs，July 2020).

类将自己置于危险之中以援引第一定律才能解决瘫痪问题。①

当被迫两害相权取其轻时，不伤害人类的一揽子规则显然是不够的。阿西莫夫本人后来添加了一条"第零个定律"，规定机器人的最高职责是对整个人类负责。在阿西莫夫的最后一部小说中，有人问机器人如何确定对整个人类有害的事物。机器人回答道："先生，精确而言，理论上，第零个定律是问题的答案。实际上，我们永远不能作出决策。"②

人们往往夸大对处理人工智能的新规则的需求。例如，瑞安·阿博特（Ryan Abbott）在新书中提出，监管变革的指导原则是确立人工智能的法律中立，即法律不应对人类行为和人工智能行为作出任何歧视。③尽管这一规则提出得极具挑战性，但其完整意义很快就被抛弃了：人们不寻求人工智能系统具有个性，也不寻求将人工智能（标题中的"理性机器人"）标准适用于人类行为。相反，阿博特的观点可以浓缩为对人工智能活动的不同领域进行个案审查，借此决定特定领域是否需要改变。④

这是一个足够明智的方法，但是，为了确保本章开头所引用的人类控制和透明度这两个"原则"得以实现，需要制定一些通用的新规则。人类控制要求限制可以开发的人工智能系统类别。尽管人类控制原则可以在致命性自主武器等伦理案件中作出最明确的决策，但预防原则提供了一个思考此类风险的方法。公共部

---

① 机器人一开始试图遵从一个措辞含糊的命令，而这个命令将导致它自身的毁灭，最终因为不可解释的原因，机器人陷入了一种"平衡"（引自英国剧作家 Gilbert 和作曲家 Sullivan）状态，直到拯救人类生命的需要使其重获自由。参见 Isaac Asimov, 'Runaround', *Astounding Science Fiction*（March 1942）。

② Isaac Asimov, *Foundation and Earth*（Doubleday 1986），ch 21.

③ Ryan Abbott, *The Reasonable Robot: Artificial Intelligence and the Law*（Cambridge University Press 2020）2-4.

④ Ibid. 136-43.

门需要接受更微妙的限制，这并不是要限制人工智能系统的行为，而是限制公职人员将决策外包给人工智能的能力范围。在透明度问题上，公职人员的问责制也要求限制不透明程序的使用。除此之外，第 6 章所讨论的措施，即影响评估、审计、人工智能监察员的措施，应当减轻某些危害并应有助于确保其他危害可归咎于能够被追究责任的法人。①

随着人工智能变得越来越复杂和普遍，一个关键问题将是用户是否应意识到他们正在与人工智能系统还是人类进行互动。正如第 6 章所指出的，这将被视为一项基本权利。奥伦·埃齐奥尼（Oren Etzioni）和弗兰克·帕斯奎尔等人认为，要求人工智能系统披露它们不是人类的信息应该是更新版的阿西莫夫定律中的一项；② 托比·沃尔什（Toby Walsh）对此表示同意，但他认为这应成为自主系统识别自身的一个积极义务，这个积极义务的设定类似于 19 世纪的红旗法：为警示即将到来的危险，红旗法要求人应走在机动车前面。③

商业压力已经阻碍信息披露，因为当人工智能系统的性质不为人知或至少未公开披露时，它们与人类的互动会更有效。④ 然

---

① 其他规则可能包括要求放慢某项功能的运行速度，如第 1 章讨论的高频交易。还有一些规则可能利用人工智能的优势，如保存详细记录的能力，这有助于了解伤害的原因。例如，可以要求自动驾驶汽车保留有关其功能的信息，类似于现代飞机使用的飞行数据记录器。另参见本书第 8 章第 8.2.2（b）节和第 9 章第 9.3.2 节。

② Oren Etzioni, 'How to Regulate Artificial Intelligence', *New York Times* (1 September 2017); Frank Pasquale, *New Laws of Robotics: Defending Human Expertise in the Age of AI* (Belknap Press 2020).

③ Toby Walsh, *Android Dreams: The Past, Present, and Future of Artificial Intelligence* (Hurst 2017) 111. See also Jacob Turner, *Robot Rules: Regulating Artificial Intelligence* (Palgrave Macmillan 2019) 320-24.

④ Alex Engler, *The Case for AI Transparency Requirements* (Brookings Institution, 22 January 2020).

而，更大的挑战可能是实践问题，因为许多面向消费者的人工智能系统，如聊天机器人，在不同程度的人类参与下运作。虽然人类呼叫中心可以清楚地区分授权级别，将电话询问从人工智能中介转移到人类经理，但聊天机器人可能在移交询问中的复杂或异常问题给人类主管的同时，仍在执行不间断的"对话"，从而模糊了这些界限。①

这再次凸显了人工智能监管的核心挑战，与其说缺乏规则，不如说是规则在特定情况下的适用性及其应用存在不确定性。问题将不是阿西莫夫的工业产品寻找它们在宇宙中的伦理路径，而是分布式系统在跨越法域边界"环路"（loop）内外的情况下与人类一起运行。这将要求以新方式思考人工智能监管，尤其是要有新的机构来执行监管。

---

① Natalie Petouhoff, 'What Is a Chatbot and How Is It Changing Customer Experience?', *Salesforce Blog*（3 March 2020）。另参见本书第 6 章第 6.4 节。

第 8 章

新 机 构

大约在阿西莫夫发表有关机器人三定律的短篇小说的同时，世界上第一个核反应堆正在美国芝加哥大学的一个足球场的看台下建造。人们曾经对人口稠密的城市中心启动连锁反应存在一些不安，但领导该实验的意大利物理学家恩里科·费米（Enrico Fermi）计算出这样做是安全的。在最初的成功运行中，芝加哥第一座核反应堆运行了四分钟，产生了不到一瓦的功率，大约可以照亮一个小圣诞树装饰品。该反应堆是核能发展的重要一步，也是曼哈顿计划所取得的最早的技术成就之一。这是美国在第二次世界大战期间发起的倡议，最终造成 1945 年投至日本广岛、长崎的原子弹。[①]

参与其中的科学家知道他们的工作既有创造的潜力，也有破坏的潜力。虽然原子弹的威力和战争的紧急情况意味着保密是一种"不受欢迎的必要"，但费米本人认为，阻止基础知识传播就

---

① Richard Rhodes, *The Making of the Atomic Bomb* (Simon & Schuster 1986).

像希望地球停止围绕太阳旋转。① 问题在于如何确保其在发电和医药等和平用途中的有益使用不会导致威胁人类生存的武器扩散。

战争结束后，联合国大会于1946年1月通过了有关原子能问题的首个决议。该决议设立了一个委员会，委员会负责建议如何消除核武器，同时使所有国家都能从和平利用核能中受益。② 五个月后，美国、英国和加拿大提议成立一个新的国际组织，由该国际组织独家控制核能所涉及的所有方面，从核原料的拥有至核电站的运营。对西方的动机心存疑虑的苏联拒绝了该计划，这造成的裂痕后来被视为引发并导致冷战的发生。③

七年后，美国总统德怀特·艾森豪威尔（Dwight Eisenhower）向联合国提出了一种替代想法。如果早先计划是乌托邦式的，那么艾森豪威尔的"和平利用原子能"演讲则是不同方式的理想主义：与其将材料和专业知识集中在一个超国家机构中，不如将它们广泛传播，鼓励各国将其用于和平目的，作为交换，各国应承诺放弃研究原子弹。④ 出于以下三个原因，维护核安全的努力历史与人工智能监管具有相关性。

---

① Enrico Fermi, 'Atomic Energy for Power' in AV Hill (ed), *Science and Civilization: The Future of Atomic Energy* (McGraw-Hill 1946) 93 at 103; Enrico Fermi, 'Fermi's Own Story', *Chicago Sun-Times* (23 November 1952).

② Establishment of a Commission to Deal with the Problems Raised by the Discovery of Atomic Energy, UN Doc A/RES/1 (I) (1946).

③ Larry G Gerber, 'The Baruch Plan and the Origins of the Cold War' (1982) 6 (4) *Diplomatic History* 69, 70.

④ Address by Mr. Dwight D Eisenhower, President of the United States of America, to the 470th Plenary Meeting of the United Nations General Assembly (Atoms for Peace) (United Nations, 8 December 1953); Robert L Brown, *Nuclear Authority: The IAEA and the Absolute Weapon* (Georgetown University Press 2015) 41-50。到1953年，俄罗斯和英国也都成功进行了自己的核武器试验。

第一，作为一个具有巨大潜力的技术和破坏力的例子，核技术在多数情况下已得到积极使用。目前，虽然人们并不青睐核能，但核能确是少数几个现实的碳氢化合物的替代能源选择之一；人们在医药和农业领域更愿接受并使用核能。在冷战的黑暗时期，观察家们预料到了这一点，但如果他们得知1945年以后核武器未在武装冲突中使用，并且到世纪之交只有少数几个国家拥有核武器，他们一定会感到惊讶。①

第二，国际体制为全球层面的人工智能监管提供了一个可能的模式。在艾森豪威尔发表演讲的四年后，国际原子能机构（IAEA）得以成立，其核心是一个宏伟的交易，即核技术可以按照其仅用于有益用途的保障机制来分配，以确保这些是其唯一的应用目的。这种权衡提高了当时的超级大国之间、有核国家和无核国家之间的信任水平。人工智能的等效武器化，无论是狭义上的自主武器系统的发展，还是广义上的可能威胁人类的通用人工智能或超级智能，如今已超过大多数国家的能力范围。至少对于武器系统而言，这种技术差距不会持续太久。② 正如各国决定不发展核武器并确立不扩散制度，因此拥有核武器的国家数量很少一样，对于人工智能危险应用程序的限制将需要依赖各国抉择及其执法保障。

第三，可以相比较的是，就像费米和他的同事一样，深入参与人工智能研究的科学家一直最强烈地呼吁国际监管。第7章中讨论的各种指南、框架和原则主要是由科学家推动的，而国家往

---

① 存在一种极端观点，参见 Kenneth Waltz, The Spread of Nuclear Weapons: More May Be Better (International Institute for Strategic Studies, Adelphi Papers, Number 171, 1981)。

② See, eg, Elsa B Kania, 'AI Weapons' in China's Military Innovation (Brookings Institution, April 2020)。

往倾向于跟随而不是领导人工智能监管。然而，正如核不扩散制度所表明的那样，良好的规范是必要的，但不足以实现有效监管。

本章探讨了监管制度的可能性安排，包括完全自由的市场到国际组织的全球控制。介于两者之间的是或多或少的正式行业协会和部门协会，以及国家和国际层面的公共机构。与其将其作为菜单列出，不如再次使用第 2 章中的视角：关注监管需求，而不是供给来源。与人工智能相关的风险管理可以且应当在很大程度上取决于行业标准，如人工智能领域的最佳实践和互操作协议等的演进速度将继续快于法律制定的速度。本章第 1 节讨论如何在机制机构方面支持这种演进，而不是阻碍演进。

然而，并不是所有风险均应得到管理。为了禁止某些活动，有必要画定红线。最明显的是，武器化或不可控的人工智能活动应当予以禁止，但应禁止的活动并不限于此。① 同时，仅仅依靠行业自我约束并不能维持此类禁止。另外，如果要持续并有效地执行这些红线，则需在全球协作与合作层面采取一些措施。此处，将人工智能监管与核武器相类比是最贴切的。本章第 2 节假定以国际原子能机构为模型，提议设立国际人工智能机构来实现前述目标。

本章第 3 节回归到国家的合法行为。尽管欧盟在建立超国家规范方面走得最远，但公共权力外包限制意味着需要依靠各成员国来执行这些超国家规范。事实上，大多数监管人工智能的规范亦是如此。尽管行业标准将影响实践以及国际条约可以限制行业标准，但国家仍是必不可少的参与者，国家能够使用命令和控制

---

① 参见本书第 7 章第 7.3.2 节的讨论，有必要立法保护"社交机器人"免受伤害。

方法，并在必要时挥舞"监管之锤"。①

正如 20 世纪 50 年代核生命周期的完全国际化是不现实的，但让这一领域不受约束地发展也是不可想象的一样，此处的目的是基于现有机构，特别是以国家为基础，同时构建激励措施和协调机制。通过这种方式，应当可以解决实用性、伦理性和合法性问题，理想的情况是不发生任何炸弹爆炸。

8.1 行业标准

技术企业家的自由主义倾向根深蒂固。多年来，比尔·盖茨一直吹嘘微软在华盛顿特区甚至没有办公室，他不想从政府那里得到任何东西，只想政府别管微软。盖茨代表了硅谷更广泛的文化：大多数人认为他们的工作不值得监管，然而，很多人认为他们在道德层面优越于那些试图强加监管的政府。②

在 20 世纪头十年，这种情况开始发生改变。有三个因素似乎已经发挥作用。第一，专家们越来越意识到，无节制的创新可能带来的潜在损害确实会造成不小的灾难性损害风险。正如费米及其同事看到核能的危险一样，世界上一些领先的技术倡导者开

---

① Margot E Kaminski, 'Binary Governance: Lessons from the GDPR's Approach to Algorithmic Accountability' (2019) 92 *Southern California Law Review* 1529, 1564. 在国际公法中，这被称为"辅助性原则"。参见 Andreas Follesdal, 'The Principle of Subsidiarity as a Constitutional Principle in International Law' (2013) 2 *Global Constitutionalism* 37.

② See, eg, Emanuel Moss and Jacob Metcalf, 'The Ethical Dilemma at the Heart of Big Tech Companies', *Harvard Business Review* (14 November 2019). Cf David Broockman, Greg F Ferenstein, and Neil Malhotra, 'Predispositions and the Political Behavior of American Economic Elites: Evidence from Technology Entrepreneurs' (2019) 63 *American Journal of Political Science* 212.

始警告人工智能技术的潜在危险。除了公开警告和签署关于有必要确保人工智能对人类有益的公开信外，埃隆·马斯克（Elon Musk）等人还向这项事业捐赠了数千万美元。①

第二，剑桥分析公司丑闻是一个转折点，消费者对科技公司的信任度在丑闻发生后受到侵蚀。该公司的数据收集始于2014年，这些数据最显著的用途是影响2016年美国总统大选，但是相关报道一直是匿名的，直至2018年3月一名举报人公开表明此事。②脸书的股价在接下来的一周下跌了近1/4，市值损失超过1300亿美元。2018年年初，微软、谷歌和国际商业机械公司（IBM）均发布了相关人工智能原则。③

第三个原因与上述第二个原因相关，即公司和研究人员正确地预测到消费者的不信任将导致政府采取行动。尽管欧盟《通用数据保护条例》已经制定了相当长的时间，同时其他法域正在考虑对个人数据或通用技术采取额外监管措施，但消费者的不信任是《通用数据保护条例》生效的一个诱因。④

关于组织机构承担法律合规之外的义务方面的争论，并不是技术行业所特有的。随着对气候变化和经济不平等影响的更大担忧，人们越来越认识到企业除了赚钱之外还有其他责任。⑤例如，

---

① Research Priorities for Robust and Beneficial Artificial Intelligence: An Open Letter (Future of Life Institute, 2015)。另请参见本书前言中引用的警告。

② Matthew Rosenberg, Nicholas Confessore, and Carole Cadwalladr, 'How Trump Consultants Exploited the Facebook Data of Millions', *New York Times* (17 March 2018).

③ 参见本书第7章引言。同年5月，脸书宣布成立自己的人工智能伦理团队。

④ 这些举措还与对科技公司的税务策略和反竞争行为的批评有关。

⑤ Cf Simon Chesterman, 'The Turn to Ethics: Disinvestment from Multinational Corporations for Human Rights Violations—The Case of Norway's Sovereign Wealth Fund' (2008) 23 *American University International Law Review* 577.

2019年8月，美国商业圆桌会议发表了一封关于企业目的的公开信。公开信表示，其成员致力于为股东、员工、供应商、客户和社区等所有利益相关者提供价值。① 文字平淡无奇，在大大小小的公司年度报告和招股说明书中都能找到这样的表述。但是，从苹果公司至沃尔玛公司的181位首席执行官签署了公开信，表示相关内容应采纳为政策，这在经济界引起了小小的轰动。尤其需要指出的是，这是对米尔顿·弗里德曼（Milton Friedman）所倡导的观点的公开否定，弗里德曼认为首席执行官的主要责任是实现股东利润最大化，其理由是企业的业务就是经商。②

由于受到篇幅限制，本章节不可能妥善阐释企业社会责任或全球商业活动与人权方面的争论。③ 此处将聚焦两个问题：行业在建立行业安全标准中的作用是什么？这种方法的局限性是什么？

8.1.1 共同语言、最佳实践

研究人员最常引用的自治示例是1975年关于重组脱氧核糖核酸（DNA）的阿西洛马会议（Asilomar Conference）。考虑到这项新技术（也称"基因切割"）所伴随的不确定风险，美国科

---

① Business Roundtable Redefines the Purpose of a Corporation to Promote 'An Economy That Serves All Americans' (Business Roundtable, 19 August 2019).

② Milton Friedman, 'The Social Responsibility of Business Is to Increase Its Profits', *New York Times* (13 September 1970). See Claudine Gartenberg and George Serafeim, '181 Top CEOs Have Realized Companies Need a Purpose Beyond Profit', *Harvard Business Review* (20 August 2019).

③ See generally Abagail McWilliams, et al (eds), *The Oxford Handbook of Corporate Social Responsibility: Psychological and Organizational Perspectives* (Oxford University Press 2019); John Gerard Ruggie, Guiding Principles on Business and Human Rights: Implementing the United Nations 'Protect, Respect and Remedy' Framework, UN Doc A/HRC/17/31 (2011).

学家最初曾呼吁停止相关研究。阿西洛马会议聚集了全球一百多名生物学家，这些专家制定了未来研究指南。该指南强调，在实验设计中"遏制"（containment）是一个基本考量因素，遏制水平应尽可能与预估风险相匹配。那些无法保证"遏制"的高风险实验，将被"延迟"进行，本质上就是禁止此类实验。[1] 该指南很快在许多国家被认可为法律或成为资金申请需遵守的要求，实验很快又重新开始。

四十二年后，生命未来研究所在相同地点起草《阿西洛马人工智能原则》（Asilomar AI Principles）并非巧合。《阿西洛马人工智能原则》对风险的处置手段是加强与预期影响相匹配的控制措施、有效禁止无指导或不可遏制的人工智能发展。[2] 然而，人们对于1975年阿西洛马会议的缅怀，高估了这样一次聚会在今天所能产生的影响。参加1975年阿西洛马会议的生物学家几乎都在公共机构工作，而且相信人们会遵守有关暂停DNA部分实验的要求将会受到尊重；那时候在一次活动中聚集全球领先的大多数研究人员也是可能的。[3] 人工智能领域的差异性和竞争性使得任何规范都难以监控，更别提管制了。[4] 此外，《阿西洛马人工智能原则》目前不过是数十份文件中的一个，虽确实受到关注，但很难说是权威性的。[5]

---

[1] Paul Berg, *et al*, 'Summary Statement of the Asilomar Conference on Recombinant DNA Molecules' (1975) 72 *Proceedings of the National Academy of Sciences* 1981.

[2] Asilomar AI Principles (Future of Life Institute, 6 January 2017).

[3] Paul Berg, 'Asilomar 1975: DNA Modification Secured' (2008) 455 *Nature* 290.

[4] 'After Asilomar' (2015) 526 Nature 293. 例如，2001年美国对干细胞研究的限制只是将研究转向了别处。参见本书第7章第7.2节。

[5] 参见本书第7章引言。

尽管如此，生命未来研究所等机构显然可以在人工智能规制中发挥一定的作用。至少而言，就术语达成一致可以确保人工智能开发者和监管者能够互相对话。正如我们在第 2 章所看到的，描述"自主"交通工具的行业标准遵守了美国汽车工程师协会（SAE）所确立的级别标准。① 同样，电气和电子工程师协会（IEEE）阐释了符合伦理的人工智能系统设计原则，旨在为自动和智能系统提供标准和参照点。②

实际上，私有主体所确立的秩序主导了数十年来互联网的诸多方面。尽管起源于美国军方，互联网名称与数字地址分配机构（Internet Corporation for Assigned Names and Numbers，ICANN）自 1998 年以来一直管理着互联网领域，该机构是由全球代表性多元利益主体构成的非营利机构，成立于美国加州。③ 这种安排是可取的，因为它避免了与一国利益过于紧密捆绑的问题，也避免了被一群国家的最低共同点所拖累的问题。④ 更为普遍的是，国际标准化组织（International Organization for Standardization，ISO）等机构制定的技术标准和组织标准已成为事实

---

① 参见本书第 2 章第 2.1 节。

② Ethically Aligned Design: A Vision for Prioritizing HumanWell-Being with Autonomous and Intelligent Systems (IEEE, 2019).

③ Jeanette Hofmann, Christian-Katzenbach, and Kirsten Gollatz, 'Between Coordination and Regulation: Finding the Governance in Internet Governance' (2017) 19 *New Media & Society* 1406.

④ Hans Klein, 'ICANN and Internet Governance: Leveraging Technical Coordination to Realize Global Public Policy' (2002) 18 *The Information Society* 193; Manuel Becker, 'When Public Principals Give Up Control over Private Agents: The New Independence of ICANN in Internet Governance' (2019) 13 *Regulation & Governance* 561. Cf Jonathan GS Koppell, 'Pathologies of Accountability: ICANN and the Challenge of "Multiple Accountabilities Disorder"' (2005) 65 *Public Administration Review* 94.

上的规范,尽管这些机构在传统的国内法或国际法结构之外运作。① 这些标准可能适合新兴行业或实践,此外,这些标准有助于在侵权诉讼的责任认定中确定什么是"合理"行为。②

8.1.2 不当激励、监管俘获

标准是必要的,但仅有标准还不够。如果运作得当,鼓励科学家之间进行结构化和非结构化对话,可以帮助他们就规范达成共识并识别危险行为,就像阿西洛马重组 DNA 方面限制的情况一样。非正式互动可能暴露异常行为,如俄罗斯和南非的非正式互动暴露了生物武器计划,学术"八卦"有助于追踪第二次世界大战期间纳粹在原子弹方面的尝试。③ 然而,即使可以就适用于人工智能的规范达成一致,但当今参与人工智能研究和开发的参与者数量过多且过于多样化,对全行业的集体行动不能寄予太大的希望。许多领域已明显地显露一种更可能的情形,即监管领域和不受监管领域存在分裂。④ 这就是我们今天在互联网上所看到的暗网形式。⑤

另外,对行为自我监管的依赖可能导致组织机构将监管更多地视为沟通问题而不是合规问题。就像"漂绿"(greenwashing)

---

① See Nico Krisch and Benedict Kingsbury,'Global Governance and Global Administrative Law in the International Legal Order'(2006) 17 *European Journal of International Law* 1.

② 参见本书第 4 章第 4.1.1 节。

③ Jeffery T Richelson, *Spying on the Bomb: American Nuclear Intelligence from Nazi Germany to Iran and North Korea*(Norton 2006)35.

④ Stephen M Maurer, *Self-Governance in Science: Community-Based Strategies for Managing Dangerous Knowledge*(Cambridge University Press 2017)215-17.

⑤ Robert W Gehl, *Weaving the Dark Web: Legitimacy on Freenet, Tor, and I2P*(MIT Press 2018).

的出现一样，公司可以表达其环境价值观，而不必承诺遵守具体标准，① 科技公司的伦理委员会有时可能成为营销工具，而不是管理工具。例如，谷歌于2019年3月成立了先进技术外部咨询委员会，但不到两周后，该委员会因内部批评和负面宣传而关闭。

即使人们普遍认可并认真对待标准，与行业的紧密联系也会增加监管俘获风险。这种现象是指负责监督的人员更加了解被监管团体的目标和问题，从而无法独立或有效地履行职责。② 监管俘获问题并非仅仅存在于行业监管者之间，也可能存在于政府官员、法官和其他主体之间。通过将监管机构的独立性制度化并加强信息流动，可以帮助防范监管俘获。③ 此外，多层次治理可以减轻复杂性带来的困难以及何时监管新兴技术的科林格里奇困境。④ 特别是就人工智能而言，跨部门和跨国界互联意味着多层次治理中的一个层级需要全球性治理。

8.2　全球红线

正如第1章所讨论的，人工智能监管所面临的一个关键结构

---

① Ho Cheung Brian Lee, Jose M Cruz, and Ramesh Shankar, 'Corporate Social Responsibility (CSR) Issues in Supply Chain Competition: Should Greenwashing Be Regulated?' (2018) 49 *Decision Sciences* 1088.

② Michael E Levine and Jennifer L Forrence, 'Regulatory Capture, Public Interest, and the Public Agenda: Toward a Synthesis' (1990) 6 (Special Issue) *Journal of Law, Economics, and Organization* 167; Jean-Jacques Laffont and Jean Tirole, 'The Politics of Government Decision-Making: A Theory of Regulatory Capture' (1991) 106 *Quarterly Journal of Economics* 1089.

③ Ernesto Dal Bó, 'Regulatory Capture: A Review' (2006) 22 *Oxford Review of Economic Policy* 203.

④ 参见本书第7章第7.2节。

性挑战是距离的消失。① 一个法域的法律可能无法在另一个法域得到执行；防止或遏制全球范围内异常行为的努力的力度取决于其中最薄弱的环节。这并不新鲜，它影响各种形式的跨境损害。人们在全球层面解决这些不足的意愿一直不一致，因为国际法的性质导致难以达成一致同意，同时国际法缺乏强有力的执行机构导致其难以获得有效执行。尽管国际组织可以促进标准的制定，但国际组织无法对人工智能进行全面的全球监管，这是不现实的，也是不可取的。因此，人工智能监管的重点应当是确立共同红线，即画定违反基本规范或构成重大跨境威胁活动的红线，制度安排应仅限于这些目的。

8.2.1　结构性挑战

人工智能系统不仅是国际组织需要管理的问题，它们也可能破坏这些国际组织本身。在某种程度上，这是因为一些人工智能系统代表着权力从国家手中转移。间接而言，这是正确的，因为人工智能系统能使公民在没有传统公共机构中介的情况下获取信息并参与交易。然而，举一个极端但绝非虚幻的例子，通过传播"虚假新闻"以及操纵选举，人工智能系统会破坏人们对制度或程序的信心，从而可能直接对国家造成威胁。②

从历史上看，国际组织在应对技术创新方面一直效率低下。如果国内监管滞后，那么国际监管也会滞后。③主权平等和达成共

---

①　参见本书第 1 章第 1.1 节。

②　Eyal Benvenisti, 'Upholding Democracy amid the Challenges of New Technology: What Role for the Law of Global Governance?' (2018) 29 *European Journal of International Law* 9.

③　Rosemary Rayfuse, 'Public International Law and the Regulation of E-merging Technologies' in Roger Brownsword, Eloise Scotford, and Karen Yeung (eds), *The Oxford Handbook of Law, Regulation, and Technology* (Oxford University Press 2017) 500.

识的需要，鼓励国际社会就规范采取最低程度的普遍共识方法，这需要数年或数十年的时间进行谈判。此外，可以理解的是，联合国等论坛的普遍会员制使得各国对共享敏感信息持谨慎态度。①

国际法方面取得一定成功的两个相关领域是禁止特定武器和促进全球互联互通。从 1868 年关于爆炸性子弹的《圣彼得堡宣言》到最近禁止地雷和核武器方面的尝试，国际人道法一直致力于减轻冲突中的人类痛苦。正如第 2 章所讨论的，国际人道法已经延伸到致命性自主武器系统引起的担忧。② 国际组织也支持全球化。最古老的此类机构之一是国际电信联盟（ITU），该联盟成立于 1865 年，当时名为"国际电报联盟"，于 1934 年采用现名。尽管国际电信联盟作为联合国专门机构而成立，但该机构就监管互联网内容需要其发挥更大作用的提议，引起了多方利益主体的警惕，这些利益主体担心国际电信联盟将限制网上信息的自由流动。③

在提供其他公共产品方面，国际记录仍然参差不齐。消灭天花是世界卫生组织（WHO）的伟大成就之一，但它花了近两百年的时间。虽然 18 世纪末即已研制出天花疫苗，但直到经过十多年的全球联合行动后，这种疾病才于 1980 年被宣布根除。④ 正如 2020 年暴发新冠病毒感染疫情所证明的，当国家利益相冲突

---

① Simon Chesterman, 'Does the UN Have Intelligence?', (2006) 48 (3) *Survival* 149.

② 参见本书第 2 章第 2.2 节。

③ Cf Ramses A Wessel, 'Regulating Technological Innovation through Informal International Law: The Exercise of International Public Authority by Transnational Actors' in Michiel A Heldeweg and Evisa Kica (eds), *Regulating Technological Innovation* (Palgrave Macmillan 2011) 77; Ingo Take, 'Regulating the Internet Infrastructure: A Comparative Appraisal of the Legitimacy of ICANN, ITU, and the WSIS' (2012) 6 *Regulation & Governance* 499.

④ DA Henderson, *Smallpox: The Death of a Disease* (Prometheus 2009).

时，协调全球应对危机仍然极其困难。① 当目标范围狭小且具有共同性时，采取全球行动是最容易的。② 例如，在环境领域，与解决全球气候变化所面临的巨大障碍相比，保护臭氧层免受氯氟烃破坏更容易获得成功。③

尽管存在政治意愿且应受监管的行为相对清晰，但如果不能就可适用的规范达成一致，则无法在国际法层面将违法行为归因于国家或其他主体，或者对于违法行为的惩治后果不充分，国际法则无法发挥效用。

(a) 规范

在规范问题层面，除非国家明确同意禁止某项行动，否则国际法通常无法禁止国家采取行动。④ "禁止"可以通过条约义务或习惯国际法的形式来实现，习惯国际法通过以各国接受为法律的一般实践来证明。⑤ 例如，正如我们在第2章所看到的，适用于致命性自主武器的制度在很大程度上是依赖条约来实现的。⑥ 对于第3章所讨论的禁止歧视而言，也有赖于国际法确立的人权规范。⑦

习惯国际法确实规范了跨境损害：各国有义务确保其管辖和控制范围内的活动不会对国家控制范围之外的其他国家或地区造

---

① Peter G Danchin, *et al*, 'The Pandemic Paradox in International Law' (2020) 114 *American Journal of International Law* 598.

② Eyal Benvenisti, 'The WHO-Destined to Fail? Political Cooperation and the Covid-19 Pandemic' (2020) 114 *American Journal of International Law* 588, 592.

③ Chris Peloso, 'Crafting an International Climate Change Protocol: Applying the Lessons Learned from the Success of the Montreal Protocol and the Ozone Depletion Problem' (2010) 25 *Journal of Land Use & Environmental Law* 305.

④ *Case of the SS 'Lotus' (France v. Turkey) (Merits) (1927 1927) PCIJ Series A*, No 10 (Permanent Court of International Justice).

⑤ *Statute of the International Court of Justice*, 1945, art 38 (1).

⑥ 参见本书第2章第2.2.1节。

⑦ 参见本书第3章第3.2节。

成损害。① 在有限的情况下，这已经通过条约扩展为严格责任。② 1972 年《空间物体所造成损害的责任公约》提供了一个有趣的模式，根据该模式，国家"绝对有责任"就其领土所发射的空间物体对地球表面所造成的损害进行赔偿。③ 然而，在大多数情况下，根据活动的性质、当时的科学知识以及相关国家能力，只需要尽到应有的注意义务就足够了。④ 只要满足这一点，国家即不对非故意行为或意外行为负责，包括不对流氓行为者的恶意行为负责。⑤ 在这种情况下，国家的义务仅限于通知可能受影响的国家，尽管就灾难性风险而言，这可能不足以避免威胁。⑥

那么，如果没有条约，人工智能系统跨境威胁所涉及的义务

---

① *Legality of the Threat or Use of Nuclear Weapons* (*Advisory Opinion*) [1996] ICJ Rep 226 (International Court of Justice), para 29. Cf *Corfu Channel* (*United Kingdom v. Albania*) (*Merits*) [1949] ICJ Rep 4, 22 (每个国家都有义务"不允许在知情的情况下将其领土用于违反其他国家权利的行为")。

② 参见本书第 4 章第 4.1.2 节.

③ Convention on International Liability for Damage Caused by Space Objects, done at London, Moscow, and Washington, 29 March 1972, in force 1 September 1972, art Ⅱ。这可能与公海上较为有限的责任制度形成对比，在公海上，海盗或其他敌对活动可免除国家的责任。参见 Joel A Dennerley, 'State Liability for Space Object Collisions: The Proper Interpretation of "Fault" for the Purposes of International Space Law' (2018) 29 *European Journal of International Law* 281; Trevor Kehrer, 'Closing the Liability Loophole: The Liability Convention and the Future of Conflict in Space' (2019) 20 *Chicago Journal of International Law* 178. Cf Vienna Convention on Civil Liability for Nuclear Damage, done at Vienna, 21 May 1963, in force 12 November 1977。

④ *Pulp Mills on the River Uruguay* (*Argentina v. Uruguay*) (*Judgment*) [2010] ICJ Rep 14, para 197; *Responsibilities and Obligations of States with Respect to Activities in the Area* (*Advisory Opinion*) [2011] ITLOS Reports 10, paras 117-20.

⑤ Patricia Birnie, Alan Boyle, and Catherine Redgwell, *International Law and the Environment* (3rd edn, Oxford University Press 2009) 147-50.

⑥ International Law Commission, Prevention of Transboundary Harm from Hazardous Activities (Articles), UN Doc A/RES/62/68, Annex (2007), art 17; Grant Wilson, 'Minimizing Global Catastrophic and Existential Risks from Emerging Technologies through International Law' (2013) 31 *Virginia Environmental Law Journal* 307, 342.

则为防止损害发生的谨慎义务和损害发生情况下的通知义务，其中的跨境威胁包括污染河流、通用人工智能夺取军事资产等。

重点强调的是，这些义务由国家承担。诸如在人权领域，国家义务可能是尊重权利并确保这些权利得到保护，有时需要国家通过立法或采取行政行为来避免直接侵犯有关权利。① 某些国际法律义务则直接由个人承担，尤其是第 4 章所讨论的国际刑事法律制度，② 但国际法首先管理的是国家之间的关系，很少未经同意就触及国家内部关系。③ 那么，一个关键问题是，是否可以将违法行为或未能阻止违法行为归因于某个国家。

(b) 归因

国际法委员会（ILC）花了半个世纪的时间来研究这个主题，最终制定了《国家对国际不法行为的责任条款草案》，这些条款现在被认为反映了国际惯例。④ 这些条款之所以能够完成，只是因为国际法委员会巧妙搁置了什么是国际不法行为等主要问题，转而关注技术性更强、政治性更少的次级问题，即责任归属和后果问题。

总体而言，国家对行使政府职权的"个人或主体"的行为负责。⑤"政府职权"这个短语并没有相关定义，因为它取决于"特

---

① 这包括本书第 3 章中讨论的一些被禁止的歧视。比照参见 Paolo G Carozza, 'Subsidiarity as a Structural Principle of International Human Rights Law' (2003) 97 *American Journal of International Law* 38。

② 参见本书第 4 章第 4.2.2 节。

③ 最突出的例子是根据《联合国宪章》第七章对于威胁和平的对象采取强制行动。大体上可参考 Simon Chesterman, *Just War or Just Peace? Humanitarian Intervention and International Law* (Oxford University Press 2001)。

④ James Crawford, *The International Law Commission's Articles on State Responsibility: Introduction, Text and Commentaries* (Cambridge University Press 2002)。

⑤ International Law Commission, Responsibility of States for Internationally Wrongful Acts (Articles on State Responsibility), UN Doc A/56/83, Annex (2001), art 5。国际法委员会的评注明确指出，"实体"不限于法人。

定的社会、历史和传统",但该短语与第 4 章所讨论的"政府固有职能"存在明显重合。① 国家责任涵盖了涉及行使"独立自主或行使权力的个人或实体"的情况,即使该主体在以该身份采取行动时"超越授权或违反指示"。②

国家责任将涵盖政府机构和分包商所使用的人工智能系统,即使该人工智能系统随后超越拟定的议定书。尽管国家可能承担防止跨界损害的具体条约承诺或习惯义务,但私人个体或公司的行为不会被直接追责。③ 未能履行条约承诺或习惯义务的,至少应归因于国家。

可能出现的情况是,很难将行为归因于一个特定国家或实际上的任何行为人。这是网络犯罪中广为人知的实践挑战,而不是规范挑战。④ 然而,这指向了全球所需的潜在"红线":在全球范围内要求确保人工智能系统行为可追踪到至少在一个国家存在的实体。⑤

(c) 后果

然而,国际法所面临的最大障碍是合规方面的执行困难。与

---

① 参见本书第 4 章第 4.3 节。

② International Law Commission, Responsibility of States for Internationally Wrongful Acts (Articles on State Responsibility), UN Doc A/56/83, Annex (2001), art 7; International Law Commission, Draft Articles on Responsibility of States for Internationally Wrongful Acts, with Commentaries, UN Doc A/56/10 (2001) 43.《国家对国际不法行为的责任条款草案》第 8 条单独规定,如果"个人或群体"实际上是在该国的指导或控制下行事,则该国也应对其行为负责。必要的"控制"水平尚不清楚,但无论如何,这似乎不太适用于真正自主的人工智能系统。

③ 参见本书第 8 章第 8.2.1 (a) 节。

④ See, eg, Peter Margulies, 'Sovereignty and Cyber Attacks: Technology's Challenge to the Law of State Responsibility' (2013) 14 *Melbourne Journal of International Law* 496; Florian J Egloff, 'Public Attribution of Cyber Intrusions' (2021) 6 *Journal of Cybersecurity* 1.

⑤ 参见本书第 8 章第 8.2.2 (b) 节。

国内法律制度相比，这是对国际法律制度的常规批评，人们时常指责国际法根本不是真正意义的"法律"。① 在很大程度上，这些争论由于缺乏有力的国际法理论支持而毫无结果，而接受国际法合法性的实践广泛存在。② 这些争论没能考虑规范体制的结构性差异：国际法假定名义上主权平等或准主权实体之间存在的是横向结构，而国内法假定主权之下的主体之间是纵向等级结构。③

国际法的这个弱点是其特点，而不是缺陷。法律越严格，遵守者就越少；机构越强大，成员越少。尽管如此，当集体行动问题显现时，管理不当的期望会导致沮丧，例如，就气候变化或流行病而言，国际协调与合作委托给缺乏权力的机构来实施。④

8.2.2 国际人工智能机构？

尽管存在上述警告，人工智能的有效监管需要规范与制度在全球层面运行。许多学者和政策制定者已认识到这一点，最常见的建议是多利益相关者模式。例如，雅各布·特纳（Jacob Turner）提议设立一个与互联网名称与数字地址分配机构（ICANN，维护和支持全球互联网的关键基础设施）类似的机构。⑤ 其详尽

---

① See, eg, HLA Hart, *The Concept of Law* (3rd edn, Clarendon Press 2012) 213-37.

② Louis Henkin, *How Nations Behave: Law and Foreign Policy* (2nd edn, Columbia University Press 1979).

③ See Simon Chesterman, 'An International Rule of Law?' (2008) 56 *American Journal of Comparative Law* 331.

④ Sam Johnston, 'The Practice of UN Treaty-Making Concerning Science' in Simon Chesterman, David M Malone, and Santiago Villalpando (eds), *The Oxford Handbook of United Nations Treaties* (Oxford University Press 2019) 321 at 328-31.

⑤ Jacob Turner, *Robot Rules: Regulating Artificial Intelligence* (Palgrave Macmillan 2019) 240-42. See also Jeanette Hofmann, Christian Katzenbach, and Kirsten Gollatz, 'Between Coordination and Regulation: Finding the Governance in Internet Governance' (2017) 19 *New Media & Society* 1406.

的治理模式包括来自公共部门、私营部门和技术专家的代表。鉴于其主题和人员与人工智能产业的重叠，这种治理模式的直观吸引力是可以理解的。然而，ICANN 的实际功能仅限于协调域名系统并解决相关争议。① 尽管这很重要，但对于全球规制机构来说，人工智能监管的需求超越技术协调。

依照 30 年前设立的政府间气候变化专门委员会（Intergovernmental Panel on Climate Change，IPCC）模式，加拿大和法国于 2018 年 12 月宣布设立国际人工智能小组（International Panel on AI）。② 该小组后来更名为"人工智能全球合作伙伴组织"（Global Partnership on AI），秘书处设在巴黎的经合组织。③ 与气候变化相类比，人们承认人工智能给全球带来了类似的集体行动问题。然而，与经合组织的关联及其对人权的强调，与其说是出于有效管理的担忧，不如说是出于排除中国的愿望。实际上，美国曾因其对商业的潜在影响而拒绝加入，但后来改变了立场，理由是需要检查中国对人工智能的处置方法。④ 专家们将参加主题工作组，包括负责任的人工智能、数据治理、未来工作、创新与商业化——都是有价值的目标追求，但会增加分裂互联网以及对人工智能的一种与全球响应相对立的方式发展的风险。

上述及其他示例认识到采取行动的必要性，但也对国家之间寻求共识的实际性和可取性持谨慎态度。例如，从理论上讲，可

---

① Bylaws for Internet Corporation for Assigned Names and Numbers (ICANN, 1 October 2016) s 1.1.

② France and Canada Create New Expert International Panel on Artificial Intelligence (Gouvernement, 7 December 2018).

③ Joint Statement from Founding Members of the Global Partnership on Artificial Intelligence (US State Department, 15 June 2020).

④ Max Chafkin, 'US Will Join G-7 AI Pact, Citing Threat from China', *Bloomberg* (28 May 2020).

以委托联合国或国际电信联盟承担这样的职责。它们可能是制定规范的有益场所,但如果让它们承担运营角色则可能激起人们的反对,就会像当初提议让国际电信联盟接任互联网名称与数字地址分配机构(ICANN)来管理互联网那样遭到反对。①

国际机构建设是一项妥协工程。② 从提议设立较不正式的机构开始,为更详尽的可能发展奠定基础,在寻找相同之处时反映现实挑战。③ 然而,这些不够雄心壮志或更具有政治性的提议,缺少规范性"牙齿"以及对普遍主义的渴望,即不具备解决全球挑战所需的深度和广度。

在这方面,国际原子能机构提供了一个更好的模式作为示例,它直接面对监管的不足,限制核武器扩散,同时公开接受其面临的政治局势:允许无核国家加入并获得技术支持,同时向有核国家保证其军事优势不会丧失(至少在未来某个不特定时刻不会丧失)。

---

① Cf Ramses A Wessel, 'Regulating Technological Innovation Through Informal International Law: The Exercise of International Public Authority by Transnational Actors' in Michiel A Heldeweg and Evisa Kica (eds), *Regulating Technological Innovation* (Palgrave Macmillan 2011) 77; Ingo Take, 'Regulating the Internet Infrastructure: A Comparative Appraisal of the Legitimacy of ICANN, ITU, and the WSIS' (2012) 6 *Regulation & Governance* 499. 2020 年 5 月,联合国秘书长编写了一份关于数字合作的报告,指出目前的主要不足在于缺乏包容性、协调和能力建设。参见 Report of the Secretary-General on the Road Map for Digital Cooperation, UN Doc A/74/821 (2020), para 56。

② Timothy LH McCormack and Gerry J Simpson, 'A New International Criminal Law Regime?' (1995) 42 *Netherlands International Law Review* 177.

③ See, eg, Olivia J Erdélyi and Judy Goldsmith, 'Regulating Artificial Intelligence: Proposal for a Global Solution' (2018) AAAI/ACM Conference on AI, Ethics, and Society (AIES'18) 95; Jiabao Wang, et al, 'Artificial Intelligence and International Norms' in Donghan Jin (ed), *Reconstructing Our Orders: Artificial Intelligence and Human Society* (Springer 2018) 195.

第 8 章　新机构

正如前文所指出的，国际原子能机构创设于人们对核能的潜在应用过于乐观之时，同时担心核能武器化而受到影响。国际原子能机构所阐明的目标是"加速和扩大原子能对全世界和平、健康及繁荣的贡献"，同时确保核能不会被进一步用于任何军事目的。① 第一个目标是通过技术转让来实现，尽管电费"太便宜而无法计量"的梦想从未实现，但核能在医药和农业方面取得的成就多于在发电领域所取得的成就。② 第二个目标是最终签署《不扩散核武器条约》。该条约正式确立了有核国家和无核国家的两级体系，国际原子能机构的任务是核实无核国家不将核原料转用于武器项目。③ 核大国则承诺就裁军问题"进行善意谈判"④，但纵观国际原子能机构历史，不得不承认国际原子能机构与冷战期间的核军备竞赛"本质上无关"。⑤

至少在最初阶段，国际原子能机构在更广泛的标准制定方面发挥的只是一个附带角色。国际原子能机构章程规定，该机构可以制定"保护健康和尽量减少生命、财产危险的安全标准"。⑥ 尽管这些标准不具有约束力，但各国实际上依赖这些标准来制定并

---

① Statute of the International Atomic Energy Agency, done at New York, 23 October 1956, in force 29 July 1957, art Ⅱ.

② Robert L Brown, *Nuclear Authority: The IAEA and the Absolute Weapon* (Georgetown UP 2015) 55-61.

③ Treaty on the Non-Proliferation of Nuclear Weapons, done at Washington, London, and Moscow, 1 July 1968, in force 5 March 1970, art Ⅲ.

④ Ibid., art Ⅵ.

⑤ David Fischer, *History of the International Atomic Energy Agency: The First Forty Years* (IAEA 1997) 10.

⑥ IAEA Statute, art Ⅲ (A) (6); Paul C Szasz, *The Law and Practices of the International Atomic Energy Agency* (International Atomic Energy Agency 1970).

实施核能立法和标准。① 1986 年切尔诺贝利灾难暴露了这种安排的重大缺陷。审查小组建议，要加强信息交流，制定额外的安全标准和指南，并提高执行评估能力。其他条约得以缔结，将软法硬化为规则。②

如果设立国际人工智能机构，则其可以从三个方面吸取核能国际规制方面的经验，包括鼓励加入的协议、权限范围以及组织结构。

（a）协议

明确的协议可以弥合人工智能最先进的国家（如美国、中国）的中期利益和其他国家的短期需求之间的差距。国际原子能机构和防扩散制度是在核大国垄断享有核能破坏力的时候进行的，核大国知道这种垄断不会持续下去。那些当今拥有最先进致命性自主武器系统的国家可能发现：如果这种武器广泛分布于世界各处，那么，这个世界将非常不稳定；如果通用人工智能进步表明或显现超级智能的危险性，那些希望该技术能够保密的人们，请回想一下费米的警告，即地球不会停止围绕太阳运动。

尽管之前似乎没有建立过这种联系，但自 2017 年以来国际电信联盟在其全球人工智能会议上使用的"人工智能造福人类"（AI for Good）的措辞，与艾森豪威尔 64 年前的"原子为和平服

---

① Philippe Sands and Jacqueline Peel, *Principles of Environmental Law* (4th edn, Cambridge University Press 2018) 595.

② Convention on Early Notification of a Nuclear Accident, done at Vienna, 26 September 1986, in force 27 October 1986; Convention on Assistance in the Case of a Nuclear Accident or Radiological Emergency, done at Vienna, 26 September 1986, in force 26 February 1987; Convention on Nuclear Safety, 17 June 1994, in force 24 October 1996; Joint Convention on the Safety of Spent Fuel Management and on the Safety of Radioactive Waste Management, done at Vienna, 5 September 1997, in force 18 June 2001.

务"(Atoms for Peace)讲话有相似之处。① 艾森豪威尔曾谈及核能有潜力成为"造福全人类的巨大福音","人工智能造福人类峰会"则强调人工智能创新将是实现联合国可持续发展目标的核心支柱。② 值得注意的是,艾森豪威尔的提议花了一段时间才被苏联接受,并被美国参议员道格拉斯·麦卡锡斥为"疯狂"。③ 国际原子能机构的创设及其相对成功,与人们对于和平使用核技术与不扩散核武器方面的国际合作呼吁密不可分,也与其作为新机构的明晰、确定的角色相关。④

当然,目前尚不清楚在当今条件下是否会出现类似的情况,特别是在全球公共机构的合法性受到质疑的时候,而美国和中国出于不同的原因特别警惕外部机构的约束。⑤ 如何在不损害组织机构合法性的前提下管理强大国家的特权,是国际制度建设中最棘手的方面之一。接受一个国家是有核国家并同时在联合国安理会拥有否决权,是对基于军事力量的特权作出的最明目张胆的让步之一。人工智能领域在这一点上并没有直接的可比性,但可以从流行病方面得出另一种类比。1980年天花最终被消灭后,所有已知的病毒库存均被销毁,但有两个例外。美国和俄罗斯保留了少量病毒:官方原因是美国和俄罗斯拥有两个最高安全存储设

---

① Address by Mr Dwight D Eisenhower, President of the United States of America, to the 470th Plenary Meeting of the United Nations General Assembly (Atoms for Peace) (United Nations, 8 December 1953); Robert L Brown, *Nuclear Authority: The IAEA and the Absolute Weapon* (Georgetown UP 2015) 41-50. 到1953年,苏联和英国两国都成功地进行了自己的核试验。

② See, eg, AI for Good Global Summit 2017 (ITU, 7-9 June 2017).

③ 'McCarthy Scorches Plan of Giving Atom Materials', *The News-Review* (Roseburg, OR, 9 February 1957).

④ Robert L Brown, *Nuclear Authority: The IAEA and the Absolute Weapon* (Georgetown UP 2015) 64-65.

⑤ See Simon Chesterman, 'Can International Law Survive a Rising China?' (2021) 31 *European Journal of International Law* 1507.

施的世界卫生组织参考实验室；非官方原因则是冷战的政治现实。①

（b）权限范围

可以从国际原子能机构吸取的第二个教训是制定明确且有限的规范议程，同时采取渐进的执行方法。这里所提出的主要"红线"是人工智能的军事化，狭义上可将其理解为开发缺乏"有意义的人类控制"的致命性自主武器系统，广义上可将其理解为开发可能存在不可控制或无法遏制风险的人工智能系统。②

从更狭义的理解来看，人们可能询问国家是否愿意放弃那些可以提供军事优势的武器。然而，除了限制核武器之外，各国也限制化学和生物武器，以及最近限制致盲武器。③ 假如可以以互惠方式进行限制，那么，没有理由认为禁止致命性自主武器系统是无法实现的。实际上，国际人道法的大部分内容均包含限制国家在武装冲突中可能使用武器方法的规则，国际人道法之所以被接受，是因为人们知道类似限制也适用于一个国家的潜在对手。尽管这是一个相对较新的补充，但今天的核心正当性在于此类法

---

① Resolution WHA33.4 (World Health Assembly, 1980), recommendations 9 and 10; Smallpox Eradication: Destruction of Variola Virus Stocks (World Health Organization, A52/5, 15 April 1999).

② 参见本书第 5 章第 5.3 节。比照参见 Draft Report with Recommendations to the Commission on a Civil liability regime for Artificial Intelligence [EU Parliament Committee on Legal Affairs, 2020/2014 (INL), 27 April 2020]（对人工智能的"高风险"与其他人工智能应用作出区分）。

③ Convention on the Prohibition of the Development, Production and Stockpiling of Bacteriological (Biological) and Toxin Weapons and on Their Destruction, done at Washington, London, and Moscow, 10 April 1972, in force 26 March 1975; Convention on the Prohibition of the Development, Production, Stockpiling, and Use of Chemical Weapons and on Their Destruction, done at Paris, 13 January 1993, in force 29 April 1997. 参见本书第 2 章第 2.2.2 节。

律"在战争中保持了一定的人性"。①

从更广泛的理解来看,第 5 章讨论的超级智能相关问题更具有争议性。从第 7 章可以得出,人们普遍同意人工智能系统应当在人类控制之下。② 短期内还不能创造具有感知能力且不受控制的人工智能,目前貌似不存在迫近的危险。③ 然而,已有大量不受控制的计算机病毒的例子。④ 最现实的前景可能是:国家同意人工智能控制的原则,定期审查通用人工智能的发展进程,并重新考虑是否需要限制进一步的研究。⑤

就像国际原子能机构随着时间推移制定安全标准一样,这些可能成为拟议"国际人工智能机构"的一项附加职能。人工智能标准可能借鉴第 7 章讨论的各项原则加以制定,其中应当优先制定的是人类控制和透明度原则。人类控制原则适用于上文所讨论的自主武器和通用人工智能。对于透明度原则,不同政治制度将以自己的方式作出回应。⑥ 就国际层面的"红线"而言,要求各国防止以不能追踪到可以识别的所有者、运营者或生产者的方式部署人工智能系统。⑦ 例如,与航空领域飞行数据记录器的作用

---

① Robert Kolb,'The Protection of the Individual in Times of War and Peace' in Bardo Fassbender and Anne Peters (eds), *The Oxford Handbook of the History of International Law* (Oxford University Press 2012) 317 at 321.

② 参见本书第 7 章第 7.3.2 节。

③ 参见本书第 5 章第 5.3 节。

④ See, eg, Danny Palmer,'MyDoom:The 15-Year-Old Malware That's Still Being Used in Phishing Attacks in 2019', *Wired* (26 July 2019).

⑤ Cf Stephan Guttinger,'Trust in Science:CRISPR-Cas9 and the Ban on Human Germline Editing' (2018) 24 *Science Engineering Ethics* 1077.

⑥ 参见本书第 6 章相关内容。

⑦ 这将包括海上船只(如十多年前谷歌的模拟船只。该模拟船只是由四层货柜堆叠而成的建筑,可以漂浮在水上,形状似于平底船。——译者注),这些船只仍在领土边界的国家的管辖之下。参见 Steven R Swanson,'Google Sets Sail:Ocean-Based Server Farms and International Law' (2011) 43 *Connecticut Law Review* 709。

相比，电气和电子工程师协会强调错误可追踪的重要性。① 这个类比对于分析故障很重要，但更重要的等效技术是使用雷达反射器来跟踪飞机并首先识别它们。

　　这样的要求对人工智能来说并不新鲜。正如我们在第 1 章中所看到的，欧盟要求高频交易算法具有可识别性。② 人们越来越认识到，人工智能系统不应假装自己是人类，或者应该被要求明确表明自己不是人类。③ 过去曾有维持自主代理人登记注册的提议，该提议借鉴了诸如国家保有公司登记注册等现有实践。④ 事实上，芬兰赫尔辛基和荷兰阿姆斯特丹于 2020 年 9 月推出了人工智能登记注册制度，作为城市使用人工智能系统的"窗口"。⑤ 作为公共机构使用人工智能系统情况的一种披露形式，这是值得称赞的。但是，考虑到人工智能系统可能的扩散性和普遍性，大规模登记注册是行不通的，因为这可能要求"登记注册"每个计算机程序。对此，也许可以尝试其中某些方面的自动化，如通过分

---

　　① Ethically Aligned Design：A Vision for Prioritizing Human Well-being with Autonomous and Intelligent Systems (IEEE，2019) 137.
　　② 参见本书第 1 章第 1.2 节。
　　③ 参见本书第 7 章第 7.4 节。
　　④ See，eg，Curtis EA Karnow，'Liability for Distributed Artificial Intelligences' (1996) 11 *Berkeley Technology Law Journal* 147，193-96；European Parliament Resolution with Recommendations to the Commission on Civil Law Rules on Robotics［2015/2103（INL）］(European Parliament，16 February 2017)，paras 2，59. 参见本书第 5 章第 5.1 节。建立原子能机构核材料数据库的提议遭到各国的抵制，原因是各国担心商业信息泄露，或者担心在其材料被用于恐怖事件时可能被追究责任。参见 Robert L Brown，*Nuclear Authority*：*The IAEA and the Absolute Weapon* (Georgetown UP 2015) 162. 相反，各国被鼓励保留自己的国家资料来源登记册。参见 David Fischer，*History of the International Atomic Energy Agency*：*The First Forty Years* (IAEA 1997) 204。
　　⑤ Sarah Wray，'Helsinki and Amsterdam Launch AI Registers to Detail City Systems'，*ITU News Magazine* (30 September 2020).

布式账本制度促成交易。① 可以要求人工智能系统通过诸如通知的方式主动识别自己，或者以在代码中包含数字签名并禁止删除的方式进行身份识别。

没有哪种制度是完美的，或者对高深玩家的恶作剧行为完全免疫。它需要辅以具有取证能力的主体来识别那些应对"流氓"人工智能系统负责的人。这可能是一项具有挑战或不能完成的任务。② 但是，国际人工智能机构可以作为收集并共享人工智能系统信息的中心——国际原子能机构也有类似设计。为便于追踪"脱离监管控制"的核原料，国际原子能机构于1995年建立了非法交易数据库。③

国际人工智能机构的最后一个职能是应对紧急情况。尽管国家是处理紧急情况的首要主体，但国际人工智能机构可以作为联络点，通报具有跨境危害的紧急情况并协调相应行动。对于不受控制或不可遏制的人工智能，不应对国家积极发出相关警报抱有幻想，特别是该国有可能被识别为相关的人工智能来源国的情况。事实上，这是苏联对1986年切尔诺贝利核灾难的最初反应。后来，各国通过了一项条约，要求缔约方将其管辖或控制范围内的任何可能发生放射性物质释放并可能具有"辐射安全重要性"

---

① Cf Jacob Turner, *Robot Rules: Regulating Artificial Intelligence* (Palgrave Macmillan 2019) 197-201; Kelvin Low and Eliza Mik, 'Pause the Blockchain Legal Revolution' (2020) 69 *International and Comparative Law Quarterly* 135.

② Cf Edwin Dauber, *et al*, 'Git Blame Who? Stylistic Authorship Attribution of Small, Incomplete Source Code Fragments' (2017) 1701.05681v3 *arXiv*.

③ IAEA Incident and Trafficking Database (ITDB) (IAEA, 2020); Klaus Mayer, Maria Wallenius, and Ian Ray, 'Tracing the Origin of Diverted or Stolen Nuclear Material through Nuclear Forensic Investigations' in Rudolf Avenhaus, *et al* (eds), *Verifying Treaty Compliance: Limiting Weapons of Mass Destruction and Monitoring Kyoto Protocol Provisions* (Springer 2006) 389 at 402.

的事故通知原子能机构或受影响国家。① 假如在第一次真正的人工智能紧急情况发生之前国家不接受类似义务,那么它们可能在紧急情况发生后不久接受此等义务。

(c) 组织结构

可以从国际原子能机构学习的第三点是其平凡但重要的结构。多数国际机构在设计方面存在不足,即治理权力由成员国牢牢把持,日常管理则由秘书处执行。联合国是这方面最明显的例子,统领的"秘书长"职位在该组织创始文件中被称为"首席行政官"。② 联合国安理会则是个例外,该机构拥有"真正牙齿"般的执行权力,包括施加经济制裁和使用军事力量的权力。然而,安理会的职权范围限于威胁国际和平与安全方面的事务,其权力牢牢掌握在成员国手中。即便人工智能紧急情况可能上升到需要安理会采取行动的程度,安理会采取行动也一直依赖专家机构。例如,在防止核扩散方面,安理会吸取了国际原子能机构所拥有的朝鲜、伊拉克、伊朗相关问题上的专业知识和资源。

就政府间国际组织而言,国际原子能机构也是一个例外,其理事会作为由部分成员国组成的机构,每年举行五次会议,负责持续监督国际原子能机构的运作、任命行政长官、评估章程的遵守情况,这些事务并非由所有成员国每年举行一次会议的成员国大会负责。③ 这

---

① Convention on Early Notification of a Nuclear Accident, arts 1, 2. See also IAEA Response and Assistance Network (IAEA, 2018).

② 《联合国宪章》第 97 条。参见 Simon Chesterman (ed), Secretary or General? The UN Secretary-General in World Politics (Cambridge University Press 2007)。

③ Robert L Brown, Nuclear Authority: The IAEA and the Absolute Weapon (Georgetown UP 2015) 55. Cf Simon Chesterman, 'Executive Heads' in Jacob Katz Cogan, Ian Hurd, and Ian Johnstone (eds), The Oxford Handbook of International Organizations (Oxford University Press 2016) 822 at 824.

使得国际原子能机构能够更有效地发挥职能，但它也要求成员国派遣更多的人员作为国家代表参与其中。实际上，国际原子能机构的历史反映了其职能的转变，从早年鼓吹核能的核机构首脑转变为更关心核不扩散和预算方面的外交人员。[1]

就构想的国际人工智能机构而言，将其定位为拥有附加机制的专家机构，让行业、学术界和活动家参与其中，将增加该机构的合法性和相关性。然而，如果想让该机构拥有实质权力作为"牙齿"，则需要国家的公共权威作为基础。

8.3　国家责任

国际原子能机构的任务是促进核技术的安全、可靠与和平使用，但从整体上看，该机构规模很小。国际原子能机构的预算为7亿美元，拥有约2500名员工，规模相当于一个小镇的地方政府，不到东京消防局规模的1/4。国际原子能机构由于自身缺乏执行权力，在极端情况下依赖联合国安理会。但与大多数国际法一样，遵守情况取决于成员国的行为和态度。

本书认为，现有国家机构和规范能够规制大多数人工智能应用程序。几乎所有国家的立法机构、执法机构、司法机构事实上都可以适应快速、自主且不透明的人工智能系统。这些机构适应的有效性与国家层面公共机构的独特合法性紧密相关，这要求这些权力由对公众负责的官员行使，而不是外包给机器。[2] 本节将简要讨论政府不同部门的作用和局限。为了确定并填补监管生态

---

[1]　David Fischer, *History of the International Atomic Energy Agency: The First Forty Years* (IAEA 1997) 425.

[2]　参见本书第4章第4.3节。

系统中的空白，拥有广泛授权的独立机构或官员将是重要补充。此处提供的示例是人工智能监察员。

8.3.1 立法机构

尽管全球各国立法机构一直对过度监管人工智能系统表示警惕，但为了解决时代变迁所带来的问题，如假定所有车辆均由"司机"驾驶这般的过时问题，他们不得不制定或修改法律。[①] 除了确保不因人工智能系统的发展速度、自主性和不透明而产生规避法律行为外，可能还需要额外的新法律来确保人类控制和透明度。[②]

立法机构具有民主正当性方面的优势，很多法域倾向于将其作为基本社会政策或涉及有争议的价值选择作出决策的机构。决策由政治代表而非专业人士作出，而这些决策具有法律效力与普遍适用性。同时，立法机构的审议速度可能很慢，而且他们制定的法令也很难撤销。正如第 7 章所讨论的，这使国家陷入两难境地：一方面，新技术相关风险具有不确定性；另一方面，国家对不必要的限制创新保持警惕。当人们一致认为需要明确规则和强有力的执行时，立法是最合法、最有效的途径。在法律制定之前，国家可能更倾向于"巧妙的不作为"。[③]

8.3.2 执法机构

法律的实施由执法机构负责。负责执法的机构可能发展执行方面的专业知识且其监管手段更为灵活。然而，就专业知识而言，公共机构难以追赶上私营部门的步伐。正如我们在第 1 章中

[①] 参见本书第 2 章第 2.1 节。
[②] 参见本书第 6 章第 6.3 节、第 7 章第 7.3 节。同时，可能还需要立法保护"社交机器人"免受伤害。另参见本书第 7 章第 7.3.2 节。
[③] 参见本书第 7 章第 7.2 节。

所看到的，这种情况在证券监管、竞争法或反垄断法领域是真实存在的，同样也存在于更普遍的技术监管领域。① 灵活性和快速反应能力可能引发问责问题，因为执法机构可能面临民主正当性方面的合法性问题。问题可能表现在过度监管或监管不足方面，以及可能发生监管俘获问题。这些问题可以通过监控和审查策略来减缓。②

在世界各地，许可机构、产品安全监管机构、证券监管机构、交通运输机构、警察机构、国家安全机构和数据保护机构将处于是否以及如何监管人工智能系统的最前线。在法律制定得宽泛或模糊的情况下，这些实体将拥有相当大的自由裁量权。它们有能力提前采取行动、发布指导材料以及主动与开发商、制造商和消费者接触，这使它们有别于其他政府部门。当它们未能采取行动时，假如公司回避冒险行为或将这些风险推给消费者，则不确定性可能让它们付出代价。③

8.3.3 司法机构

当发生损害或产生争议时，人们可能请求法院介入其中。④ 司法造法的优点和缺点在于对不断变化的情况作出回应。这使得法官在解释法律或运用先例时可以发挥一定的创造性，但这也意味着法官需要对摆在面前的案件负责。在大多数法域，法院无法对假设情况发表意见；当他们按照普通法传统这样做时，他们的

---

① 参见本书第 1 章第 1.2 节、第 1.3 节。

② Robert Baldwin, Martin Cave, and Martin Lodge, *Understanding Regulation: Theory, Strategy, and Practice* (2nd edn, Oxford University Press 2011) 343-44。另参见本书第 8 章第 8.1.2 节。

③ Nathan Cortez, 'Regulating Disruptive Innovation' (2014) 29 *Berkeley Technology Law Journal* 175, 203-4. 另参见本书第 7 章第 7.2 节。

④ 参见本书第 7 章第 7.2.2 节。

意见是附随意见，这些意见对其他法庭没有约束力。同时，法院在争议发生后所发挥的作用也可能具有经过较长时间之后的滞后性：上诉程序可能需要数年时间，这意味着法院在相关技术过时后才能作出最终判决。①

正如奥利弗·温德尔·霍姆斯法官（Oliver Wendell Holmes）一个世纪前所作出的著名警告那样，"疑难案件会产生糟糕的法律"。然而，这种陈腔滥调的背景通常使这一观察变得更加微妙。因为疑难案件通常是重大案件：

> 像疑难案件这样的重大案件会产生糟糕的法律。重大案件之所以称为"重大"，并不是因为它们对塑造未来法律具有真正重要性，而是因为一些直接的压倒性利益的偶然事件诉诸了感情并扭曲了判断。这些直接利益产生了一种动态压力，使先前的明确之处变得令人怀疑，在这种压力面前，即使是良好的既定法律原则也会屈服。②

人工智能是否将对既定规范造成"动态压力"？同样，法院在很大程度上已能够作出调试。在缺乏新形式的法律主体的情况下，③假定人工智能行为可以归因于传统法律主体④且举证责任得以满足，⑤那么，人工智能的快速发展、自主性和不透明所带来的问题虽然艰难，但并不是不可克服的挑战。

---

① Mark R Patterson, *Antitrust Law in the New Economy* (Harvard University Press 2017).
② *Northern Securities Company v. United States*, 193 US 197, 400-1 (1904).
③ 参见本书第 5 章相关内容。
④ 参见本书第 4 章相关内容。
⑤ 参见本书第 6 章相关内容。

在多数情况下，人工智能系统会产生边缘性风险或相关行为不完全属于现有风险类别。尽管有进取心的法官将努力明智地适用法律，就像相关机构和立法机构努力确保这些法律及其实施的相关性一样，但谨慎的做法还是增加一个专门机构负责识别和解决这些法律主体缺位问题。

8.3.4 人工智能监察员？

尽管各个法域长期以来一直有类似官员，但"监察员"（ombudsperson）一词起源于斯堪的纳维亚。一般来说，"监察员"是指由国家任命的代表公众利益的个人。监察员通常在其职责范围内享有一定程度的独立性和灵活性，有时被视为维护行政正义、人权或法治的化身。除了对投诉作出答复外，监察员的职责还包括代表公共利益处理系统性问题。①

监察员的执行权可能是有限的，通常其权限仅限于调查、建议、报告方面的"软"权力。尽管存在这些局限，20世纪后半叶"监察员之风"盛行，人们将监察机构视为解决各种问责问题的工具。20世纪80年代，监察机构与人权话语相重叠；20世纪90年代中期开始，监察机构与全球治理相关联。如今，国际监察员协会（International Ombudsman Institute）在120多个国家拥有成员机构。②

---

① See Varda Bondy and Margaret Doyle, 'What's in a Name? A Discussion Paper on Ombud Terminology' in Marc Hertogh and Richard Kirkham (eds), *Research Handbook on the Ombudsman* (Edward Elgar 2018) 485; Richard Kirkham and Chris Gill (eds), *A Manifesto for Ombudsman Reform* (Palgrave Macmillan 2020). 参见 'Algorithms, Artificial Intelligence, and the Law' (2020) 25 *Judicial Review* 46, 54-57（提议成立一个专家算法委员会）。

② Charles S Ascher, 'The Grievance Man or Ombudsmania' (1967) 27 *Public Administration Review* 174; Chris Gill, 'The Evolving Role of the Ombudsman: A Conceptual and Constitutional Analysis of the "Scottish Solution" to Administrative Justice' (2014) *Public Law* 662; Tero Erkkilä, *Ombudsman as a Global Institution: Transnational Governance and Accountability* (Palgrave Macmillan 2020).

尽管公共部门或其他领域存在许多类似职责的办公室，但在传统监管不足领域，事实证明设立专门的监察员机构是有用的。例如，就国际安全相关问题而言，以某种非正式形式解决投诉有时比司法程序更有效。①

有些国家可能更愿意采用"专员"（commissioner）、"监察长"（inspector-general）、"人民代言人"（people's advocate）这些表述。与这些职位的独立性、职权、权力和资源相比，职位的准确称呼并不重要。如果要认真对待这些职位，那么这些职位独立于政府和行业是至关重要的。除了避免监管俘获，监察机构有助于跨越行政障碍。应当广泛设置监察员职权，对于人工智能所引发的不能通过现有规范和机制进行预防或解决的损害和不公，可以让监察员进行识别并解决。监察员职权应包括启动调查以及对申诉作出回应的能力。正如第 6 章所强调的，将透明度限制在可解释性方面，需要个人"知道"其遭受损害并自行发起调查，对个人而言意味着不适当的负担。②

为了发挥效用，监察员有权要求合作并获得相关文件，包括那些本可免于披露的文件。尽管相关程序具有保密性，但至关重要的是可以选择结果公开。监察员所出具的报告不应局限于解决争议，也应包含提出更广泛的建议来改变实践、政策和立法。这些建议无须具有强制约束力，最佳做法是要求立法机构或其他相

---

① Simon Chesterman, *One Nation under Surveillance: A New Social Contract to Defend Freedom without Sacrificing Liberty* (Oxford University Press 2011) 218.

② Cf Lilian Edwards and Michael Veale, 'Slave to the Algorithm? Why a "Right to an Explanation" Is Probably Not the Remedy You Are Looking For' (2017) 16 *Duke Law & Technology Review* 18, 83-84.

关主体就不接受建议给出理由。①

人工智能监察员的大部分工作可能是将案件转移给适当的政府机构或法律系统的相关机构。然而，监察员的作用不应只是确保合法性和合规性，其价值在于促进人权和良好的行政管理。②在欧盟，数据保护当局履行了其中一些职能。③ 现有的监察机构也可能承担一些职能。实际上，2020年3月，国际监察员协会与加泰罗尼亚监察员组织了一次研讨会，探讨监察机构在人工职能领域保护和捍卫人权方面的作用。④ 鉴于人工职能所呈现的陡峭的学习曲线及其带来的影响可能扩大，设立专门的人工智能办公室，无论是独立办公室还是作为更大实体的组成部分，均能够给予人工职能问题适当关注以及防止重复工作。

8.4 机构前景

艾森豪威尔的"和平利用原子能"演讲所带来的一个结果是全球见证了最大规模的科学论坛。1955年，由美国提议、联合国大会召开的第一届和平利用原子能国际会议（后来被称为第一届日内瓦会议）汇聚了来自38个国家的约1500名代表，收到1000多篇论文。1958年举行的第二届日内瓦会议规模几乎是第一届的

---

① Developing and Reforming Ombudsman Institutions (International Ombudsman Institute, June 2017).

② P Nikiforos Diamandouros, 'From Maladministration to Good Administration: Retrospective Reflections on a Ten-Year Journey' in Herwig CH Hofmann and Jacques Ziller (eds), *Accountability in the EU: The Role of the European Ombudsman* (Edward Elgar 2017) 217.

③ General Data Protection Regulation 2016/679 (GDPR) 2016 (EU), art 57.

④ Ombudsmen Alert about Artificial Intelligence and Human Rights (International Ombudsman Institute, 11 March 2020).

两倍。那是一个欣喜且乐观的时期,许多国家在起草和批准《国际原子能机构规约》,同时制订了本国核研究和开发计划。①

人工智能与核能相类比的局限是显而易见的。核能是指分配不均的特定物质所产生的具有明确界定的反应程序;人工智能则是一个没有固定含义的词语,其应用范围非常广泛。国际原子能机构的重大谈判要点是那些制造成本高昂且难以隐藏的武器;人工智能武器化则可能既不昂贵,也并非难以隐藏。

如果要有效地监管人工智能,在全球层面建立某种机制是必不可少的。本章认为,行业标准对于管理风险是非常重要的,国家将成为执法的重要组成部分,国家层面的人工智能监察员或类似机构将填补监管空白。然而,在互联世界,以领土为基础的主权国家作为监管的前提并不符合人工智能的监管目的。此处提议设立的国际人工智能机构是解决结构问题的一种方案。

然而,20世纪50年代控制核能的尝试与今天监管人工智能的最大区别在于:当艾森豪威尔在联合国发表演讲时,日本广岛和长崎核爆炸的影响仍然存在。② 艾森豪威尔警告说,这些武器的"可怕秘密"不再局限于美国。苏联已经测试了自己的设备,并且可能与其他一些国家或所有其他国家分享核能知识。什么都不做则意味着接受绝望的结局,"两个原子巨头注定要恶意地在一个颤抖的世界中无限期地注视着对方"。③

---

① Robert A Charpie, 'The Geneva Conference', (1955) 193 (4) *Scientific American* 27; David Fischer, *History of the International Atomic Energy Agency: The First Forty Years* (IAEA 1997) 31.

② Lesley MM Blume, *Fallout: The Hiroshima Cover-Up and the Reporter Who Revealed It to the World* (Scribe 2020).

③ Address by Mr Dwight D Eisenhower, President of the United States of America, to the 470th Plenary Meeting of the United Nations General Assembly (Atoms for Peace) (United Nations, 8 December 1953).

人工智能目前不存在这样的威胁，当然也没有相对明显的证据证明其破坏力。在缺乏这种威胁的情况下，很难在全球层面对人工智能进行有意义的监管达成一致。联合国安理会之所以享有其前身国际联盟所缺乏的权力，其中一个原因在于：成员国就《联合国宪章》谈判之时，第二次世界大战的炸弹仍在降落。最终文件以充满抱负且心照不宣的语言书写，承诺"免后世再遭今代人类两度身历惨不堪言之战祸"。①

正如下一章所讨论的，人工智能本身可能能够帮助解决此处提及的问题。如果不能，则需在第一次人工智能紧急情况发生之后，立即建立这样一个全球机构，避免再次发生人工智能紧急情况。

---

① 《联合国宪章》序言。

第 9 章
由人工智能进行监管？

中国法官的法袍是象征着理性的黑色,其红色前襟、装饰性金黄色领扣与法庭墙上悬挂的国徽相得益彰。红色象征革命;天安门城楼上空冉冉升起的金色星星象征着人民在党的领导下团结一致。直到世纪之交,中国司法官员都穿着类似于军装的制服;最高人民法院位于法律体系的顶端,处于共产党领导之下。

在杭州互联网法院2019年年底发布的预审会议视频中,从外表来看,这位"法官"当时可能还没有上过法学院。当然,外表可能具有欺骗性,因为"她"的大众脸和简单发型是由计算机科学家设计的。头像的嘴唇动了动,合成的声音用普通话问道:"被告对原告提交的司法区块链证据的性质有什么异议吗?""没有异议",作为人类的被告回答。

这在某种程度上既是宣传,也是福音。在中国《新一代人工智能发展规划》中,法院系统被确定为有待改进的领域之一。在社会治理部分,《新一代人工智能发展规划》要求建立智慧法庭。① 像杭州这样的试点是在全国诉讼数字化和标准化举措基础

---

① 《国务院关于印发新一代人工智能发展规划的通知》(国发〔2017〕35号,2017年7月20日)。

之上实施的，为进一步推广智慧法院铺平了道路。网上法庭可处理在线商事纠纷、版权案件、电子商务产品责任诉讼。① 选择杭州作为试点的原因是阿里巴巴总部坐落在杭州，可以与淘宝等交易平台进行集成，以收集证据和获得"技术支持"。②

在线争议解决并不新鲜。易贝（eBay）长期以来在线帮助各方累计解决数千万起纠纷。③ 在中国背景下，有趣的是技术渗透到法院层级的程度，即技术不仅用于以调解方式解决小额索赔，而且一直渗透到最高人民法院。

司法责任制最初是一场促进判决一致性而发起的运动。④ 中国过去在促进判决一致方面的努力依赖于上级审查，但这种做法被认为是不现实的，同时也会损害受理案件的法官的权威。⑤ 人工智能系统现在会在作出判决前将类似案件推送给法官，如果判决结果严重背离过去的数据，人工智能系统则会发出"异常判决

---

① 《最高人民法院关于互联网法院审理案件若干问题的规定》（最高人民法院法释［2018］16号）；Chuanman You, 'Law and Policy of Platform Economy in China' (2020) 39 *Computer Law & Security Review* 1.

② Du Guodong and Yu Meng, 'A Close Look at Hangzhou Internet Court', *China Justice Observer* (3 November 2019).

③ Pablo Cortés, *The Law of Consumer Redress in an Evolving Digital Market: Upgrading from Alternative to Online Dispute Resolution* (Cambridge University Press 2017) 8; Ethan Katsh and Orna Rabinovich-Einy, *Digital Justice: Technology and the Internet of Disputes* (Oxford University Press 2017).

④ 《最高人民法院关于统一法律适用加强类案检索的指导意见（试行）》（法发［2020］24号）。

⑤ Cf Margaret YK Woo, 'Court Reform with Chinese Characteristics' (2017) 27 *Washington International Law Journal* 241; Junfeng Li, *et al*, 'Artificial Intelligence Governed by Laws and Regulations' in Donghan Jin (ed), *Reconstructing Our Orders: Artificial Intelligence and Human Society* (Springer 2018) 61 at 67-71.

警告"。① 这是已采取的一系列技术中的一部分，受到中国科技公司的技术供给影响，也受到复杂且不断发展的法律体系需求的影响。苏州市吴江区人民法院试点采用简易判决"一键生成"，自动生成带有判决理由的建议。② 其他法院也纷纷效仿。③

新加坡大法官表示，中国的发展正在使"机器辅助法庭裁决成为现实"。同时，该大法官注意到，人工智能在司法系统的使用引发了"一系列独特的伦理关注，包括可信度、透明度和问责制方面的关注"。④ 除此之外，还应考虑司法公正性，因为推动更高程度的自动化是由财力雄厚的客户和与之更密切相关的科技公司所主导的，这给未来司法行政带来了不确定的后果。⑤

人工智能对司法实践的影响远远超过本书所讨论的范围。⑥

---

① Yu Meng and Du Guodong, 'Why Are Chinese Courts Turning to AI?', The Diplomat (19 January 2019).

② 《苏州法院刑案简易判决一键生成》，载《法制日报》2017 年 6 月 19 日。

③ 《中国法院的互联网司法》，人民法院出版社 2019 年版，第 63-65 页；Yadong Cui, *Artificial Intelligence and Judicial Modernization* (Springer 2020).

④ Sundaresh Menon, 'Opening of the Legal Year' (Supreme Court, Singapore, 7 January 2019).

⑤ Seth Katsuya Endo, 'Technological Opacity & Procedural Injustice' (2018) 59 *Boston College Law Review* 821.

⑥ See, eg, Richard Susskind, *The Future of Law: Facing the Challenges of Information Technology* (OUP 1996); Richard Susskind, *The End of Lawyers? Rethinking the Nature of Legal Services* (OUP 2008); Dory Reiling, *Technology for Justice: How Information Technology Can Support Judicial Reform* (Leiden UP 2010); Richard Susskind, *Tomorrow's Lawyers: An Introduction to Your Future* (OUP 2013); Kevin D Ashley, *Artificial Intelligence and Legal Analytics: New Tools for Law Practice in the Digital Age* (CUP 2017); Richard Susskind, *Online Courts and the Future of Justice* (OUP 2019); Simon Deakin and Christopher Markou (eds), *Is Law Computable? Critical Perspectives on Law and Artificial Intelligence* (Hart 2020).

本章考虑的是一个比较狭窄的问题，即人工智能系统本身是否以及如何支持人工智能监管。就快速、自治且不透明的系统所揭示的规制空白而言，除了制定新规则并创立新机构，是否还需要以人工智能监管者和法官的形式引入新的法律主体补充进行规制？

本章第 1 节简述过去为实现法律自动化所作的努力。尽管人工智能法官是最具争议的示例，① 但是人们认为法律实践和监管的许多领域的自动化时机已成熟。尽管人工智能在简单和重复性的任务中取得了成功，但人工智能法官方面的努力往往会因为对法律的误解而失败，即误认为法律仅仅是将明确的规则应用于大家所同意的事实。实际上，规则很少如此明确，事实分歧是法律纠纷的重要组成部分。

更有前景的做法是放弃"像律师一样"思考的目标，将法律分析作为数据而不是规则对事实的应用进行处理。本章第 2 节讨论自下而上的法律分析方法，这些分析将揭示人工智能存在的局限性，与其说是技术局限，不如说是社会和政治方面的明显局限。尽管人工智能系统在预测监管结果方面变得越来越好，但法律系统拥抱人工智能则意味着根本性的转变，由作出判决转变为预测判决。

即使由人工智能进行一般监管是可行的，也并不是可取的。然而，由人工智能系统本身进行监管是否可以成为一个特例？如果反对人工智能监管者或反对人工智能法官的理由是人工智能无法理解法律裁决发生的社会环境，或者人类命运由统计数据决定所涉及的合法性问题，那么其中一种回应是这种做法不适用于人

---

① See, eg, Tania Sourdin, 'Judge v. Robot? Artificial Intelligence and Judicial Decision-Making' (2018) 41 *UNSW Law Journal* 1114; Eugene Volokh, 'Chief Justice Robots' (2019) 68 *Duke Law Journal* 1135.

工智能监管。本章第 3 节讨论系统如何实现"自我监管"（self-policing）。正如我们所看到的，人工智能的优点之一是相对透明，因为它可以运行带有少许变化的模拟以寻找偏差。同时，不同于人类，机器更有可能承认自己的错误。①

就提高人工智能系统的透明度和人类控制而言，这些发展可能是有用的。但是，由人工智能进行自我监管最终会面临着类似于行业自我监管的局限。尽管确立标准和最佳实践是有益的，但必须画定红线，并由政治上合法且可问责的行为者进行最终监管。同时，如果不允许将固有的政府职能外包给快速、自主且不透明的机器，那么该禁令的执行本身就不能交给这些机器。

9.1 法律自动化

在有关人工智能和法律的文献中，早期研究主题为法律实践是实现法律自动化的重要备选选项，认为法律实践本质上是将规则有逻辑地适用于既定事实。尽管最初限于理论层面，② 20 世纪 80 年代，研究人员开发了雏形系统，该系统基于手动创建的规则符号具有机器可读性。③ 这种热情是那个时代的特征，就像也会有"人工智能冬天"那样，人们会周期性地看到过高的期望与现实相冲突。④

---

① 参见本书第 3 章第 3.2.2 节。

② See, eg, L Thorne McCarty, 'Reflections on TAXMAN: An Experiment in Artificial Intelligence and Legal Reasoning' (1977) 90 *Harvard Law Review* 837.

③ See, eg, MJ Sergot, *et al*, 'The British Nationality Act as a Logic Program' (1986) 29 *Communications of the ACM* 370.

④ Anja Oskamp and Marc Lauritsen, 'AI in Law Practice? So Far, Not Much' (2002) 10 *Artificial Intelligence and Law* 227.

接下来的几十年，时代见证了法律研究与文件管理方面的变革。这些变革提高了律师获取信息的机会以及使用和共享信息的效率，但并没有从根本上改变其角色。即使那些鼓励采用技术的人也认为，人工智能无法模仿人类特质限制了其承担律师所承担的更高职能的范围，尤其是法官的角色。[①] 然而，正如我们在其他领域所看到的，模仿人类的方法可能不是获得人工智能优势的正确方法或最佳方法。举一个明显的例子，自动驾驶汽车并不是由类人机器人驾驶，而是由代替"驾驶员"的机械手和脚来控制速度和方向。

DoNotPay 聊天机器人于 2015 年推出，为未来发展提供了线索。该聊天机器人是斯坦福大学一名 17 岁的学生编写的，它遵循一系列规则就停车罚款提起诉讼。类似技术目前可以用于执行其他简单任务，从立遗嘱到新闻报道涉嫌歧视，这不仅提高效率，也为更广泛的公众提供了获得基础法律服务的机会。[②] 对于受监管行业而言，这引发人们重新评估法律实践意味着什么。如果提供法律意见的主体必须具有法律执业证书或律师协会会员资格，那么自动化系统何时越过这条线呢？基于规则运行的聊天机器人貌似没什么问题，这类似于一本带有流程图的教科书，指示法律如何处理各种假设情况。但是，如果人工智能系统引入新信息，对其进行分析，并以超出程序员专业知识的方式推荐行动方案，那

---

① Richard Susskind, 'Detmold's Refutation of Positivism and the Computer Judge' (1986) 49 *Modern Law Review* 125.

② Paul Gowder, 'Transformative Legal Technology and the Rule of Law' (2018) 68 \ (Supplement 1) *University of Toronto Law Journal* 82; Frank Pasquale, 'A Rule of Persons, Not Machines: The Limits of Legal Automation' (2019) 87 *George Washington Law Review* 1, 7-17. 然而，将某些法律程序的自动化称为任何意义上的"人工智能"都有些牵强。

么这会成为法律建议吗？人工智能系统是否应该像律师一样受到监管？①

这些是法律技术在法律实践扩展领域所引发的一些问题。② 当前的解决方案是由律师签署法律意见，就像律所合伙人批准实习生起草备忘录的重要内容那样。③ 在另一个技术进入法律职业的备受关注的例子中，美国贝克·豪斯勒律师事务所（Baker & Hostetler）宣布 IBM 的罗斯（Ross）加入该所破产法律执业。④ 尽管罗斯通常被称为"机器人律师"，但它并不是两者之一：它是一种缺乏任何物理形式（当然不是类人形态的）的订阅服务，而且它本身不提供法律建议。然而，罗斯擅长从大量文件中筛选

---

① 例如，2019 年 10 月，德国汉堡汉萨律师协会在科隆地区法院成功挑战了 Wolters Kluwer 运营的机器人 Smartlaw，因为其运营不符合德国《法律服务法》[Rechtsdienstleistungsgesgesetz]。更多内容参见 Michael Stockdale and Rebecca Mitchell, 'Legal Advice Privilege and Artificial Legal Intelligence: Can Robots Give Privileged Legal Advice?' (2019) 23 *International Journal of Evidence & Proof* 422; Polly Botsford, Future of Law: Courts Debate Legality of Legal 'Bots' (International Bar Association, 11 March 2020)。

② Sanda Erdelez and Sheila O'Hare, 'Legal Informatics: Application of Information Technology in Law' (1997) 32 *Annual Review of Information Science and Technology* 367; Jens Frankenreiter and Michael A Livermore, 'Computational Methods in Legal Analysis' (2020) 16 *Annual Review of Law and Social Science* 39.

③ See, eg, Model Rules of Professional Conduct (American Bar Association, 2020), rule 5.3（关于非律师协助的责任，尽管该规则的语言明确假设此类协助来自"个人"）。参见 Ed Walters, 'The Model Rules of Autonomous Conduct: Ethical Responsibilities of Lawyers and Artificial Intelligence' (2019) 35 *Georgia State University Law Review* 1073; Anthony E Davis, 'The Future of Law Firms (and Lawyers) in the Age of Artificial Intelligence' (2020) 27 (1) *The Professional Lawyer* 3。

④ Michal Addady, 'Meet Ross, the World's First Robot Lawyer', *Forbes* (12 May 2016).

支持公司案件的相关信息。①

　　许多律师长期以来认为诉讼将是法律实践中最后被自动化的部分,尽管本章开头提到的中国示例表明中国也正在取得进展。对于小额诉讼而言,在线争议解决具有长久历史,不仅受到易贝和贝宝(PayPal)这些在线交易商的青睐,而且也为加拿大和英国的法律体系所采用。②

　　然而,长期以来理查德·萨斯坎德(Richard Susskind)等人预测的变革海啸尚未发生。③

　　第一个原因是制度阻力。律师们一直在捍卫自己的领域免受会计师事务所和其他主体的侵犯;有些人将计算机视为下一个需要击退的乌合之众。④ 作为一种职业,律师也以保守著称。尽管交易律师必须适应业务需求,但法庭程序仍然保留着一些烦琐和古老的元素。2020年暴发的新冠病毒感染疫情迫使人们重新评估

---

① See, eg, Dena Dervanovi?, 'I, Inhuman Lawyer: Developing Artificial Intelligence in the Legal Profession' in Marcelo Corrales, Mark Fenwick, and Nikolaus Forgó (eds), *Robotics, AI and the Future of Law* (Springer 2018) 209 at 226-27; Sergio Alberto Gramitto Ricci, 'Artificial Agents in Corporate Boardrooms' (2020) 105 *Cornell Law Review* 869, 876。ROSS Intelligence 公司于 2020 年 12 月宣布关闭失败的业务,不是因为其程序的局限性或法律的开放性,而是因为竞争对手的诉讼。参见 Rhys Dipshan, 'ROSS Shuts Down Operations, Citing Financial Burden from Thomson Reuters Lawsuit', *Law.com* (11 December 2020)。

② Richard Susskind, *Online Courts and the Future of Justice* (Oxford University Press 2019).

③ See, eg, Richard Susskind, *The Future of Law: Facing the Challenges of Information Technology* (Oxford University Press 1996); Richard Susskind, *The End of Lawyers? Rethinking the Nature of Legal Services* (Oxford University Press 2008).

④ Chay Brooks, Cristian Gherhes, and Tim Vorley, 'Artificial Intelligence in the Legal Sector: Pressures and Challenges of Transformation' (2020) 13 *Cambridge Journal of Regions, Economy, and Society* 135, 148.

律所和法院对于信息技术的使用。① 然而，正如学校和大学课堂使用 Zoom 等视频会议服务一样，这只是媒介的改变，而不是法律实践方式的转变。

法律行业抵制激进变革并且可能一直如此的第二个原因，是一个不那么自私的理由。因为事实证明，人们希望法律行业广泛自动化的两个前提都经不起审查，即法律是一个内在逻辑系统和事实可以得到明确确立这两个前提均经不起审查。

9.1.1 法律的内在不合逻辑

一个初步的问题是，法律规则通常以自然语言表达，计算机可能难以解析。这是语言学中的一个常见问题：人类常常一致地解释语言，但却不合逻辑。例如，想象一下一个带有下述要求的购物指令："请买一份报纸；如果商店有香蕉，请买六（份/个）。"对这个指令的天真且字面解释可能导致"自主主体"（autonomous agent）带着六份报纸返回。同样，"我和我妻子一起猎杀熊"和"我用我的刀猎杀了熊"这两句话，其含义对一个人而言是显而易见的，但对自主主体而言却需要额外信息才能理解。② 语言有时候可能是内在模糊的。"I saw the girl with the telescope"这句表述，既可以表示说话者通过望远镜看到女孩，也可以表示女孩拿着一个望远镜。

自然语言处理的进步已经克服了许多困难，尽管法规和判例

---

① Julie Marie Baldwin, John M Eassey, and Erika J Brooke, 'Court Operations During the COVID-19 Pandemic' (2020) 45 *American Journal of Criminal Justice* 743. Cf Daphne Yong, 'The Courtroom Performance' (1985) 10 (3) *The Cambridge Journal of Anthropology* 74.

② Ian McEwan, *Machines Like Me* (Vintage 2019) 178.

法可能比普通文本更具挑战性。① 实际上，法律职业依赖于向客户提供建议并收取费用的能力，法律执业者就客户如何安排活动以符合法律提供建议，并代表客户主张以支持其利益。给定的文本甚或精心起草的文本可能有多种看似合理的解释。在法规和判决以可以使用形式逻辑表示的方式编写之前，权威文本是原始文本。②

这指向了一个更基础的问题，即很多法律不能简化为逻辑表示。③当然，有些法律可能可以。例如，道路交通法规定，超过特定速度限制即构成违法。许多法域都使用测速摄像头来自动记录违法行为并处以罚款。然而，值得注意的是，这些法律，即对于大多数人来说是最常经历的法律，正因为其如此清晰，很少出现在法学院课程中。④

其他则不然。例如，第4章中讨论的过失侵权，不能将其表

---

① See, eg, Livio Robaldo, et al, 'Introduction for Artificial Intelligence and Law: Special Issue "Natural Language Processing for Legal Texts"' (2019) 27 *Artificial Intelligence and Law* 113; Loïc Vial, Benjamin Lecouteux, and Didier Schwab, 'Sense Vocabulary Compression through the Semantic Knowledge of WordNet for Neural Word Sense Disambiguation' (2019) *arXiv* 1905.05677v3; Boon Peng Yap, Andrew Koh, and Eng Siong Chng, 'Adapting BERT for Word Sense Disambiguation with Gloss Selection Objective and Example Sentences' (2020) *arXiv* 2009.11795v2; Zakaria Kaddari, et al, 'Natural Language Processing: Challenges and Future Directions' in Tawfik Masrour, Ibtissam El Hassani, and Anass Cherrafi (eds), *Artificial Intelligence and Industrial Applications* (Springer 2021) 236.

② L Karl Branting, 'Artificial Intelligence and the Law from a Research Perspective' (2018) 14 (3) *Scitech Lawyer* 32.

③ Cf H Patrick Glenn and Lionel D Smith (eds), *Law and the New Logics* (Cambridge University Press 2017).

④ 请注意，许多法域允许以"合理理由"作为辩护，因此，即使是这个例子也可能没那么简单。

示为注意义务＋违约＋因果关系－抗辩＝责任。过失侵权中著名的"克拉彭公共汽车上的人"①和合理性概念，明确结合了以人类经验为基础的判断。在其他法律领域，诸如"善意"或"不合情理"等术语很难使用对机器有用的术语来定义。②如果假装以其他方式进行处理，则是将法官的解释任务委托给机器，而不是确立参数的程序员。③更正式地说，人们有时认为，由于法律系统及所有类似系统存在必然的不完备，像对待易于自动化的逻辑系统那样对待法律的努力将会失败。④

在任何情况下，今天很少有法学家坚持严格的形式主义立场，即法律可以或应当被机械地解释。例如，罗纳德·德沃金（Ronald Dworkin）确实认为法律问题（即使是困难的问题）有一个正确答案，但他明确拒绝这意味着计算机设计师可以通过"电子魔术师"得出这个答案。⑤相反，适用法律的困难在于，法律始终是一种政治道德的实践，解释法律的最好方式是代表共同体为国家强制行为寻找正当理由。⑥约瑟夫·拉兹（Joseph Raz）反对德沃金关于法律正确答案的观点，认为法官在这种情况下类

---

① *McQuire v. Western Morning News* [1903] 2 KB 100, 109 (Collins MR).

② See, eg, Mindy Chen-Wishart and Victoria Dixon, 'Humble Good Faith: 3 x 4' in Paul Miller and John Oberdiek (eds), *Oxford Studies in Private Law Theory* (Oxford University Press 2020) 187.

③ Francesco Contini, 'Artificial Intelligence and the Transformation of Humans, Law and Technology Interactions in Judicial Proceedings' (2020) 2 (1) *Law, Technology, and Humans* 4, 7.

④ CF Huws and JC Finnis, 'On Computable Numbers with an Application to the AlanTuringproblem' (2017) 25 *Artificial Intelligence and Law* 181, 183.

⑤ Ronald Dworkin, *Law's Empire* (Harvard University Press 1986) 412.

⑥ Brian Sheppard, 'Warming Up to Inscrutability: How Technology Could Challenge Our Concept of Law' (2018) 68 (Supplement 1) *University of Toronto Law Journal* 36, 60.

似于下级立法者,具有制定特定规则的法律义务。① 实证主义传统通常被认为最支持法律程序自动化,但即使是哈特,也认为法官必须在现有法律未能规定何种裁决"正确"时作出选择。② 强调法官的角色和权力对社会秩序产生影响的法律现实主义者和批判法学家则认为,法律自动化问题如此荒谬,不值得认真对待。③

9.1.2 事实

在美国参议院的确认听证会上,首席大法官约翰·罗伯茨(John Roberts)打趣说他的工作只是"判定坏球和好球",不偏不倚,以此反驳别人对他的党派偏见。考虑到法庭的政治化性质,这个答案是不诚实的,并且罗伯茨也低估了大联盟体育运动的自动化趋势。特别是在棒球领域,很多人呼吁裁判员需要由电脑控制的好球区协助或完全由电脑取代。如果法官的角色就像确定一个皮革包裹的球是否在三平方英尺区域内一样简单,那么,法官应由机器取代,这样会更有效率,也更一致。④

即使一项法律字面表达清晰明确,然而,如何在实践中应用这项法律则可能并非如此,哈特就此列举的第一个知名示例是

---

① Joseph Raz, *Ethics in the Public Domain: Essays in the Morality of Law and Politics* (Clarendon Press 1995) 249-50.

② HLA Hart, *The Concept of Law* (3rd edn, Clarendon Press 2012) 273. Cf Abdul Paliwala, 'Rediscovering Artificial Intelligence and Law: An Inadequate Jurisprudence?' (2016) 30 *International Review of Law, Computers & Technology* 107.

③ Cf Sangchul Park and Haksoo Ko, 'Machine Learning and Law and Economics: A Preliminary Overview' (202) 11 (2) *Asian Journal of Law and Economics* 15 (采用法律经济学分析可得出结论,这种系统可以被视为专家证人,但不能取代人类法官).

④ Jennifer Walker Elrod, 'Trial by Siri: AI Comes to the Courtroom' (2020) 57 *Houston Law Review* 1085.

我们，机器人？
人工智能监管及其法律局限

"公园内禁止车辆"。我们也许同意该示例中的"车辆"涵盖汽车，但是否涵盖自行车、滑板、玩具汽车呢？① 是否涵盖婴儿车呢？或者是否涵盖二战坦克雕像呢？②

根本问题是语言的优点和缺点在于其结构开放，这种想法可以追溯到维特根斯坦（Wittgenstein）。③ 即使人们对法律适用的许多方面可能达成近乎普遍的一致意见，边缘案例也会出现。语言和法律的开放性本质与时间有着重要的联系，因为未来可能出现规则起草者无法预知的情况。例如，20 世纪的立法者可能无法预料到禁止进入公园的车辆是否包括无人机，这是情有可原的。④

法律运用于特定事实需要灵活性，这并非假设。19 世纪末，美国纽约州上诉法院审理了一起案件，其中遗嘱通俗易懂的语言和相关立法都清楚表明弗朗西斯·B. 帕尔默的孙子应该继承他的遗产。然而，年轻的帕尔默先生毒死了他的祖父，这一事实让法官犹豫了。德沃金用这个例子来论证，几乎普遍认可的正义原则甚至可能需要背离明确的文本规则（谋杀者没有得到他的遗产）。⑤

也许法律服务市场最能就法律运用于事实的困难给出说明，

---

① HLA Hart,'Positivism and the Separation of Law and Morals'(1958) 71 *Harvard Law Review* 593, 607.

② Pierre Schlag, 'No Vehicles in the Park' (1999) 23 *Seattle University Law Review* 381; Frederick Schauer, 'A Critical Guide to Vehicles in the Park' (2008) 83 *New York University Law Review* 1109.

③ HLA Hart, *The Concept of Law* (3rd edn, Clarendon Press 2012) 124; Ralf Poscher, 'Ambiguity and Vagueness in Legal Interpretation' in Lawrence M Solan and Peter M Tiersma (eds), *The Oxford Handbook of Language and Law* (Oxford University Press 2012) 128.

④ Michael A Livermore, 'Rules by Rules' in Ryan Whalen (ed), *Computational Legal Studies: The Promise and Challenge of Data-Driven Research* (Edward Elgar 2020) 238 at 246-47.

⑤ Ronald Dworkin, *Taking Rights Seriously* (Harvard University Press 1977) 23, citing *Riggs v. Palmer*, 115 NY 506 (1889).

特别是诉讼市场。倘若法律起草得清晰明确且易于适用,那么,很少有争议需要由法院解决,因为理性、博识的行为主体可以自己得出正确结论。这将无须上诉法院。案件由法院解决的原因很少是因为一方当事人客观上存在明显"错误"。这一点在实践中得到证实。例如,假设民事诉讼中潜在的诉讼当事人对审判结果有理性的估计,则意味着其胜诉率接近 50%,无论实体法律如何规定。① 这个数字只适用于有限情况,随着决策标准更加明确、各方对自己案件的估计更加准确、双方的利益具有相似的价值,该数字才得以实现。这得到了实证支持。②

9.2 法律作为数据

关于人工智能和法律监管的许多争论,本质上是对法律的理解存在根本差异,而不是对人工智能的理解存在差异。如果以狭隘的形式主义方式理解法律,将规则盲目地应用于无争议的事实,那么,通过算法进行处理是有意义的,否则就像让监管者或法官进行手工长除法而不是使用计算器一样效率低下。③ 但是,显而易见的是,法律不是长除法。除了最简单的案例之外,行为规范和争议解决本质上是一项论争性事业,必然涉及争议的价值

---

① George L Priest and Benjamin Klein,'The Selection of Disputes for Litigation'(1984) 13 *Journal of Legal Studies* 1.

② Simon Chesterman,'Do Better Lawyers Win More Often? Measures of Advocate Quality and Their Impact in Singapore's Supreme Court'(2020) 15 *Asian Journal of Comparative Law* 250.

③ Mireille Hildebrandt,'Law as Information in the Era of Data-Driven Agency'(2016) 79 *Modern Law Review* 1. 关于使用人工智能重新思考法律逻辑概念的例子,参见 Douglas Walton,*Argumentation Methods for Artificial Intelligence in Law*(Springer 2005).

观和意义。① 正如霍姆斯法官的名言："法律的生命不在于逻辑，而在于经验。"②

然而，计算机科学家可能作出回应。当今，经验正是机器可以学习且复制的。

事实上，最近的创新反映了法律方法的转变，类似于人工智能研究向机器学习的转变。与其尝试将法律规则编码至固定系统，然后将其应用于经过净化的事实（可以说是自上而下），不如说是在自下而上分析大量数据方面取得了关键成就。这种方法并非寻求对个案作出答复，但可以基于过去的经验就裁决结果作出预测。③ 正如米雷耶·希尔德布兰特（Mireille Hildebrandt）所观察到的，这代表着"从理性到统计、从论证到模拟"的转变。④

事实证明，人工智能对于识别法律研究、合同审查和事实发现的相关性方面是有用的。⑤ 但如果将人工智能扩展至监管和裁决，则在根本上改变任务的本质，从作出裁决转变为预测裁决。⑥

---

① Jeremy Waldron, 'The Rule of Law and the Importance of Procedure' in James E Fleming (ed), *Nomos L: Getting to the Rule of Law* (New York University Press 2011) 3 at 22.

② Oliver Wendell Holmes, Jr, *The Common Law* (Little, Brown 1881) 1.

③ Maxi Scherer, 'Artificial Intelligence and Legal Decision-Making: The Wide Open?' (2019) 36 *Journal of International Arbitration* 539, 569-71. See, eg, Nikolaos Aletras, et al, 'Predicting Judicial Decisions of the European Court of Human Rights: A Natural Language Processing Perspective' (2016) 2: e93 *PeerJ Computer Science*.

④ Mireille Hildebrandt, 'Law as Computation in the Era of Artificial Legal Intelligence: Speaking Law to the Power of Statistics' (2018) 68 (Supplement 1) *University of Toronto Law Journal* 12, 29.

⑤ See Robert Dale, 'Law and Word Order: NLP in Legal Tech' (2019) 25 *Natural Language Engineering* 211.

⑥ Cf Oliver Wendell Holmes, Jr, 'The Path of the Law' (1897) 10 *Harvard Law Review* 457, 461（"我所说的法律是对法院事实上将采取的行动的预言，而非更多自命不凡的东西"）。

这种裁决更像是预测天气，而不是法律发展中的社会进程的一部分。① 分析可以为争议各方提供更多信息，促进争议的有效解决，同时减少偏见和错误，② 但分析不能取代司法职能本身。③

实际上，这种方法在一些法域遭到公然的敌意。法国 2019 年就颁布法律，禁止发布揭示或预测特定法官如何判决案件的数据分析，违者最高处五年监禁。④ 尽管法国可能仍然是一个例外，但人工智能系统在短期内不会取代律师或法官。更可能的情况是越来越多地使用人工智能系统作为法律服务的一部分，有时这种伙伴关系被比作人类和机器配对下高级国际象棋，也被称为"半人马"或"机器人国际象棋"。⑤

在这种情况下，通常会对帮助获取信息的技术和帮助作出判决的技术进行区分。⑥ 前者与使用计算器相类似，被认为是没有问题的；后者则引发了令人不安的问题，即谁在行使裁量权。但是，当获取的"信息"成为案件裁决的核心要素时，前述区分则

---

① Frank Pasquale and Glyn Cashwell,'Prediction, Persuasion, and the Jurisprudence of Behaviourism'(2018) 68 (Supplement 1) *University of Toronto Law Journal* 63, 64-65.

② Daniel L Chen,'Judicial Analytics and the Great Transformation of American Law'(2019) 27 *Artificial Intelligence and Law* 15.

③ 另参见本书第 3 章引言中关于医学研究与法律研究的对比讨论。

④ 参见本书第 3 章第 3.3.2 节。

⑤ See, eg, Rebecca Crootof,'"Cyborg Justice" and the Risk of Technological-Legal Lock-In'(2019) 119 *Columbia Law Review Forum* 233, 243; John Morison and Adam Harkens,'Re-engineering Justice? Robot Judges, Computerised Courts and (Semi) Automated Legal Decision-Making'(2019) 39 *Legal Studies* 618, 634-35.

⑥ Zihuan Xu, *et al*,'Case Facts Analysis Method Based on Deep Learning' in Weiwei Ni, *et al* (eds), *Web Information Systems and Applications* (Springer 2020) 92.

可能是矫揉造作的。正如我们在第 3 章所看到的，依赖不透明系统就判决等事项提供建议，实则放弃了司法功能，这并非因为这些建议可能不正确，而是因为这样做是不合法的。更为普遍的是，自动化偏见所引发的忧虑在于：人类代理可能减少，人们更倾向于依赖机器。① 即使对于经验丰富的决策者来说，也很难判断算法的"推动"在哪里结束以及责任人的选择从哪里开始。②

就当前目的而言，可以得出的结论是人工智能将继续转变法律职业和律师角色，但不是完全取代后者。这些局限与其说是技术性的，不如说是法律本质所固有的，以及大多数秩序良好的社会通过政治结构赋予法律的合法性。

9.3　法律作为编码

然而，是否存在特殊情况，可以使人工智能在监管人工智能本身方面发挥更大作用？

人工智能系统的速度、自主性及其不透明性确实偶尔会在实践和理念层面给人类监管者带来困难。就某些情况而言，解决方案是降低人工智能系统的速度，就像应对高频交易那样。③ 就其他一些情况而言，已采取的方案是确保实施问责的可能性，要求相关行为可追溯至所有者、运营者或生产者等传统法律主体。④

---

① 参见本书第 3 章第 3.1 节。

② Mariano-Florentino Cuéllar, 'Cyberdelegation and the Administrative State' in Nicholas R Parrillo (ed), *Administrative Law from the Inside Out: Essays on Themes in the Work of Jerry L Mashaw* (Cambridge University Press 2017) 134 at 159.

③ 参见本书第 1 章第 1.2 节。

④ 参见本书第 4 章第 4.1.1 节。

就另外一些情况而言,已采取的方案是呼吁完全禁止某些行为,最突出的是禁止使用致命性武力。①

尽管人工智能确实提供了支持人工智能监管的媒介,但正如第5章所讨论的,传统的监管正当性无法简单融入人工智能系统。特别是人工智能缺少法律人格的背景下,监管对象不是人工智能系统本身,而是拥有、运营或制造这些系统的人。话虽如此,人工智能的独特特点提供了两种自我监管途径。第一,可以将监管目标植入软件。类似于将隐私价值植入获取个人数据的软件,这可以称为"通过设计进行监管"(regulation by design)。第二,人工智能系统允许以传统法律行为者不可能的方式询问错误和不良结果。这应该能够提高有关错误的透明度,但后果也应与传统法律主体有所不同。这里将其描述为"通过调试进行监管"(regulation by debugging)。

9.3.1 通过设计进行监管

将合规行为植入人工智能系统的想法,貌似不证自明。例如,自动驾驶交通工具应当遵守交通法;分配社会利益或推荐贷款的算法不应基于性别或种族进行歧视。但就人工智能而言,也许可以走得更远些。

通过设计实现监管的理念并不新鲜。尽管法律学者经常关注"命令与控制"方法,但设计标准可以收集信息、制定标准并为监管目的塑造监管行为。② 常用的监管工具是命令、激励、影响,

---

① 另参见本书第2章第2.2节。

② Karen Yeung, '"Hypernudge": Big Data as a Mode of Regulation by Design' (2017) 20 *Information, Communication & Society* 118, 120. See generally Lawrence Lessig, *Code: Version 2.0* (Basic Books 2006); Mireille Hildebrandt, 'Saved by Design? The Case of Legal Protection by Design' (2017) 11 *Nanoethics* 307; Nynke Tromp and Paul Hekkert, *Designing for Society: Products and Services for a Better World* (Bloomsbury Visual Arts 2019).

即假定需要强迫或说服人类行为者（或其公司代理人）采取或不采取某些行动。① 可用于编程的设备和系统（包括本书中考虑的大多数人工智能应用）提供了将监管标准直接植入其代码的可能性。

这里存在局限。正如第 7 章所述，类似于阿西莫夫机器人三定律的提议误解了法律本质，永远不会成为解决人工智能系统带来的监管挑战的完整解决方案。但作为对此类系统功能的限制，它们指出了一条充满希望的前进道路。正如第 8 章所强调的，在某些情况下，有效的标准制定需要全球规则。这些规则的实施不应仅依赖于国家执法，在可能的范围内，它们应该被编码到人工智能系统中。就这些规则的内容而言，大多数与适用于产品或服务的规则相同。例如，与其要求机器人不得谋杀人类，禁止生产商制造能够谋杀人类的机器人才更为切实。

更有趣的是，通过设计实施监管可能支持第 7 章所述的两个潜在规制空白：人类控制和透明度。

在人类控制方面，建立能力限制和"终止开关"可能听起来像是显而易见的设计解决方案。就目前而言，第 8 章提议设立全球机构来支持禁止创建不可控制或不可遏制的人工智能，这是正确的。然而，正如第 5 章所讨论的，在超级智能的出现变得更加现实的情况下，前述限制可能产生人们试图避免的邪恶；更审慎的做法可能是将人类价值观植入超级智能。②

在透明度方面，根据争议决策或争议行为的类型确定不同程度的透明度是适宜的。然而，一般而言，人工智能系统的设计应

---

① 参见本书第 7 章第 7.3 节。
② 参见本书第 5 章第 5.3 节。

当使其能够识别自身，也使其能够识别其所有者、运营者或生产者。① 另外，系统应保持最低程度的审计追踪，可以追查决策是如何制定的。② 这指向了人工智能辅助自身监管的第二条路径，即故障调查。

9.3.2 通过调试进行监管

当一人杀害另一人时，可能引发刑事指控和法律诉讼，这些都是需要解决的法律问题。当机器杀害某人时，可能需要调查机器的所有者、运营者或生产者。但就机器本身而言，这更有可能被视为机器操纵问题。就像使用飞行数据记录器的信息来研究飞机失事一样，人工智能系统中的审计追踪为审查错误发生的方式和原因提供了机会。如果审计追踪揭示人工智能所有者、运营者或生产者存在过失，接下来则可能采取法律救济措施。然而，对于人工智能系统本身而言，因犯错而受罚实际上毫无道理，就像因引擎故障而惩罚飞机那样没有意义。③

如果一个系统被认定为不安全，则它可能从市场上下架；但更可能的情况是它会得到改进。就像软件随着错误和漏洞的发现而不断更新补丁一样，世界上运行的人工智能系统应当随着环境的变化而不断发展。市场压力会鼓励此等更新，但它们也可能成为监管对象或法院命令的对象。④

以这种方式进行调试可以以更小代价满足监管目的。假设这些改进不会引入其他错误，人工智能系统也不再次受到诱惑而出

---

① 参见本书第 8 章第 8.2.2（b）节。
② 参见本书第 6 章第 6.2.2（b）节。
③ 参见本书第 5 章第 5.1.2（b）节。
④ Mark A Lemley and Bryan Casey, 'Remedies for Robots' (2019) 86 *University of Chicago Law Review* 1311, 1386-89.

现偏差，那么这种方法可能比传统的监管工具更可靠。当然，它假定人工智能领域存在传统监管环境中无法实现的一定程度的透明度。如果有人问一位人类驾驶员是否闯红灯，或者询问一位人类经理是否存在种族歧视，答案可能不可靠。适当的审计日志应该可以避免人工智能系统出现这方面的问题。

这种得出直接答案的能力指向人工智能系统的另一个潜在优势，即自我监督。正如第 6 章所描述的，监督的两大知名理论是"警察巡逻"和"火灾报警"，具体取决于监督是通过定期调查还是等待问题升级来进行。① 人工智能系统提供了第三种调查的可行性，即自我调查。这不仅仅是一种自我监管机制，因为它不依赖于有背叛动机的行为者的善意。② 只要指令是清晰的，系统就可以报告其对规则和政策的遵守情况，包括人类不可能坦诚相告的行为偏见审查情况。通过这种方式披露的问题还将指向重新考虑可用补救措施的必要性——不是作为要惩罚的罪行，而是作为需要纠正的错误。③

9.4 监管前景

在虚拟法官与当事人互动结束后，庆祝杭州互联网法院成立

---

① 参见本书第 6 章第 6.1.2 节。
② 参见本书第 8 章第 8.1 节。另参见 Casey Chu, Andrey Zhmoginov, and Mark Sandler, 'CycleGAN, a Master of Steganography' (2017) 1712.02950v2 arXiv; Joel Lehman, et al, 'The Surprising Creativity of Digital Evolution: A Collection of Anecdotes from the Evolutionary Computation and Artificial Life Research Communities' (2018) arXiv 1803.03453v1; Tom Simonite, 'When Bots Teach Themselves to Cheat', Wired (8 August 2018)（描述了学会"作弊"的人工智能系统）。
③ 参见本书第 3 章第 3.2.2 节。

的视频播放了有关副院长倪德锋的访谈。倪副院长兴奋地说:"我们现在所做的事情,你不能将其仅仅理解为提高效率。它还触及法律正义问题。快速,是正义的一种,因为迟到的正义就是被剥夺的正义。"

对效率和一致性的追求推动着中国法院系统数字化,并得到政府、司法部门和行业的大力支持。尽管法官本身在很大程度上仍由人类担任,但上海法院正在用人工智能系统取代书记员来进行基础法律研究,这是利用技术推动司法系统现代化的又一步。① 这些发展与中国法学界对计算法学研究的接受相匹配。过去十年,中国对于实证法研究的转向比美国更为广泛。现在,在中国顶级综合性法学期刊发表的文章经常使用计算方法。②

计算方法在理论和实践层面对中国具有更大吸引力的部分解释是,与西方国家相比,中国更拥护法治的工具属性。③ 中国法官将法律解释和裁量权运用称为"裁判尺度","裁判尺度"在西方传统中没有精确的对应表达,但中国法官为统一司法标准常常引用这一表述。④ 中国基层法院和中级法院的判决往往较为简短,包括用几个段落来陈述事实、概述适用的法律、对各方观点作出

---

① Sarah Dai,'Shanghai Judicial Courts Start to Replace Clerks with AI Assistants', *South China Morning Post* (1 April 2020).

② Yingmao Tang and John Zhuang Liu,'Computational Legal Studies in China: Progress, Challenges, and Future' in Ryan Whalen (ed), *Computational Legal Studies: The Promise and Challenge of Data-Driven Research* (Edward Elgar 2020) 124.

③ Randall Peerenboom, *China's Long March Toward Rule of Law* (Cambridge University Press 2002) 280-330; Cong-rui Qiao,'Jurisprudent Shift in China: A Functional Interpretation'(2017) 8 (1) *Asian Journal of Law and Economics*; Simon Chesterman,'Can International Law Survive a Rising China?'(2020) 31 *European Journal of International Law* 1507.

④ 《统一裁判尺度规范法律适用》(最高人民法院 2018 年 1 月 12 日)。参见 Jiang Na,'Old Wine in New Bottles? New Strategies for Judicial Accountability in China'(2018) 52 *International Journal of Law, Crime and Justice* 74.

回应以及阐明判决。

尽管如此,中国法官也对"黑箱"决策表示谨慎。① 部分原因在于担心判决结果的准确性。例如,最初就计算机对谋杀案件训练的努力不得不搁置,因为案件数量不足,而且每个案件的事实差异很大。② 不过,这也取决于支撑法律体系和法治本身的信任程度。

中国是否代表人工智能监管的未来或仅是有限意义上的个案,还有待观察。本章认为,人工智能系统的某些特性使其难以通过传统流程进行监管,但它可能为新流程监管提供工具。通过设计进行监管和通过调试进行监管表明,可以将人工智能系统打造得符合法律,也可以让人工智能系统以大多数人类可能感觉不舒服或不可能的方式调查其自身偏见与故障。

然而,人工智能的这一角色也存在局限。尽管人工智能系统比人类监管者和法官更高效率、更具有一致性,但这不能证明更广泛地移交权力是正当的。

法律权威不仅在形式上而且在实质上取决于程序。监管、法律裁决不仅仅是图灵测试,我们不应借此推测公众能否猜出监管者或法官是一个人还是一个机器人。合法性存在于过程本身,即行使自由裁量权应当与有能力权衡不确定价值并支持行使自由裁量权相关联。接受其他方式将意味着接受法律推理不是教义、规

---

① 郭富民:《人工智能无法取代法官的审慎艺术》,载《人民法院报》2017年5月12日。Jie-jing Yao and Peng Hui, 'Research on the Application of Artificial Intelligence in Judicial Trial: Experience from China' (2020) 1487 *Journal of Physics: Conference Series* 012013, 4.

② Jinting Deng, 'Should the Common Law System Welcome Artificial Intelligence: A Case Study of China's Same-Type Case Reference System' (2019) 3 *Georgetown Law Technology Review* 223, 275.

范和跨学科学术的综合，而是一种历史——强调对过去实践的适当分类，而不是参与前瞻性的社会项目。①

正如另一位美国最高法院法官罗伯特·H. 杰克逊（Robert H. Jackson）曾经指出的那样："并非因为我们绝不犯错，所以我们的判决是终局的，而是因为我们的判决是终局的，所以我们绝不犯错。"② 因此，很多判决也许适合被合理地移交给机器。但是，就自由裁量权的最终行使而言，即关于我国与周围世界互动的法律程序的公共控制，仅当我们就移交政治控制做好准备，也就是当我们放弃投票而选择机器投票时，才应移交最终自由裁量权。

---

① Cf Michael A Livermore (ed), *Law as Data: Computation, Text, and the Future of Legal Analysis* (Santa Fe Institute Press 2019).
② *Brown v. Allen*, 344 US 443, 540 (1953) (Jackson, J concurring).

结　论
我们，机器人？

一百多年前，随着卡雷尔·恰佩克（Karel Čapek）的戏剧《罗萨姆的万能机器人》在布拉格国家剧院首演，"机器人"一词进入现代词汇。《罗萨姆的万能机器人》以"我们星球上某个地方"的一座岛屿为背景，讲述了机器人的创造过程。与其说它们是作为人类精简版的机械生物，不如说它们是被创造出的强大且聪明的生物实体，但没有灵魂。

尽管这个戏剧在很多方面都过时了，有限的幽默源自岛上的六个男人争夺唯一女人的手的情节，但该剧在世界的愿景方面却具有先见之明——机器人被托付越来越多的人类需求，最终为人类进行战争。对于捷克观众而言，标题中的政治暗示很明显："罗伯特"（robota）是一个术语，意思是"强迫劳动"，是农奴曾经在主人的土地上进行的那种劳动。以防有人忽略这一点，公司总经理在戏剧开场就称赞其新员工的主要优点：新员工的廉价和可替代性。关于该剧，1922年纽约制作的一篇评论称为"对我们机械化文明的绝妙讽刺；对我们所称之当今工业社会的这种奇怪、疯狂的事物的最严肃而微妙的控诉"。①

一个世纪后,关于人工智能的社会地位之争与该剧主题相呼应:如何利用科技所带来的好处,同时又不承担不可接受的风险;对于那些至少可以模仿以及具备人类品质的实体,它们可以拥有哪些权利;如果我们的创造物超越我们,或当我们的创造物超越我们之时,人类将处在什么位置。

本书探讨了快速、自主性且不透明的人工智能系统出现所带来的监管问题。就此而言,恰佩克对于终将爆发的机器人革命的看法,并不比阿西莫夫对于内省机器人的描述更有帮助,阿西莫夫书中的机器人对旨在控制它们的三大定律感到痛苦。许多关于这一主题的更严肃的后续写作,同样以一种极端情况之下的通用人工智能的未来前景为写作重点,或者以另一极端的特定技术发展为写作重点。比较而言,本书讨论的重点是监管本身,即人工智能在监管层面所面临的挑战、可以采用的监管工具、监管所呈现的可能性,本书增加了过去一直缺少的公法和国际法视角。

本书第一部分阐述了现代人工智能的速度、自主性和不透明性,并从实用性、伦理性和正当性三个视角入手提出对待监管困境的三种路径。有一些风险是可以管理的,如高频交易造成的经济损失或自动驾驶汽车造成的人身危险。其他风险,如在战场上作出生死决定的自主武器、无法控制或无法遏制的人工智能,则应予以禁止。还有一些风险,特别是法官和其他公职人员行使自由裁量权,不应外包给机器或其他任何人。

在多数情况下,现有的法律和机构可以应对这些挑战。本书

---

① Karel Čapek, R. U. R. (*Rossum's Universal Robots*) (Paul Selver tr, Doubleday 1923) 10 quoting Maida Castellum in *The Call*).

第二部分以责任、个性和透明度三种形式提出了可采用的方法。短期问题是确保人工智能的有害行为可以归因于传统的法律主体，强制保险可用来避免出现效率低下或不公平的情况。另一种方法是赋予人工智能一定形式的法律地位。随着此类系统接近人类智能，承担越来越多的责任，创造美丽和有价值的事物，我们是否应该承认它们在法律面前是人？答案是否定的，或者至少现在还不行。尽管基于工具理性方面的考虑，应当将人类法律和伦理原则灌输给人工智能系统，但在可预见的未来，这并不需要我们对道德或法律义务的看法进行根本性改变。然而，维持这一立场的核心是透明度，这不仅仅意味着要求就不利决定作出解释的有限权利。

本书第三部分概述三个方面的发展：规则、机构、人工智能自我监管可以发挥的角色。制定伦理指南、框架和原则所投入的创造力和精力是巨大的。本书的目的不是增加这种指南、框架和原则，而是锁定实际缺失的东西。可以证明的是，在程序上保障透明度以及在实体规范上保持人类控制，可以约束人工智能活动并使人类持续对人工智能行为负责。对于监管而言，为了继续对人工智能进行公共控制，国家的积极参与至关重要。尽管自我监管和国际协调对于制定标准和监管红线非常重要，但占主导地位的政治问责治理机构仍然是国家。委托给国家机构的权力不应外包给人工智能，就像不应外包给私人或其他参与者一样。然而，鉴于信息技术的全球化，对此需要采取全球方案。为鼓励人工智能的积极应用，为帮助维持红线来防止人类创造物被用作武器或受到迫害，本书提出设立一个拟议的国际人工智能机构。

在《罗萨姆的万能机器人》中，机器人既是受害者，也是杀戮者。该剧以公司总裁女儿溜进工厂、作为理想主义的"人类联盟"代表为机器人辩护为开幕；以机器人奋起反抗，杀害一名制造者之外的所有人为结局。幸免于难的是建筑主管阿尔奎斯特先生，因为机器人看到他"像机器人一样"用手劳作。当他问机器人是什么促使它们对人类实施种族灭绝时，机器人感到难以置信。机器人解释说，这是必须的；机器人已经学会了人类所能提供的一切。"如果你想像人一样，你就必须杀戮和统治。读一读历史！读一读人类的书籍！如果你想成为人类，你就必须征服并杀戮。"在第一个英文翻译版本中删掉了一句台词，阿尔奎斯特无助地回答："对于一个人来说，没有比自己的形象更异化的东西了。"①

实际上，这是恰佩克戏剧中最失败的：放弃了机器人所拥有的不同于其创造者所持有的念头。通过戏剧性的手法，机器人与人类之间的差异被抹除了，机器人发展出灵魂和繁殖的能力。最后，机器人没有反叛：一群人只是被另一群人推翻。② 帷幕落下，新的亚当和夏娃步入落日余晖中。

法治是人类中心主义的缩影：人类是人类创造、解释和执行规范的首要主体和客体，这体现在政府的民有、民治、民享之中。尽管诸如公司之类的法律构造可能拥有权利和义务，但这些

---

① Karel Čapek, *R. U. R. Rossum's Universal Robots*; *Kolektivní Drama v Vstupní Komedii a Tech Aktech* (Aventinum 1920) 85. Cf Karel Čapek, 'R. U. R. (Rossum's Universal Robots)' in Peter Kussi (ed), *Toward the Radical Center: A Karel Čapek Reader* (Claudia Novack-Jones tr, Catbird 1990) at 99. See further Merritt Abrash, 'R. U. R. Restored and Reconsidered' (1991) 32 *Extrapolation* 184.

② René Wellek, 'Karel Čapek' (1936) 15 *Slavonic and East European Review* 191, 196.

权利和义务反过来又可以追溯到其创造行为的人类代理，并且这些法律构造的日常行为在不同程度上受到人类代理人的监督。即使是规范国家间关系的国际法，其基本文本也以"我们人民……"这句话开头。① 快速、自主且不透明的人工智能系统的出现，迫使我们质疑以人类为中心的假设，尽管现在还不是放弃这一假设的时候。

---

① 《联合国宪章》(1945年6月26日在旧金山订立，1945年10月24日生效)，序言。

参考文献

Abate RS, *Climate Change and the Voiceless: Protecting Future Generations, Wildlife, and Natural Resources* (Cambridge University Press 2019).

Abbott R, 'I Think, Therefore I Invent: Creative Computers and the Future of Patent Law' (2016) 57 *Boston College Law Review* 1079.

— 'The Reasonable Computer: Disrupting the Paradigm of Tort Liability' (2018) 86 *George Washington Law Review* 1.

— *The Reasonable Robot: Artificial Intelligence and the Law* (Cambridge University Press 2020).

Abraham KS and Rabin RL, 'Automated Vehicles and Manufacturer Responsibility for Accidents: A New Legal Regime for a New Era' (2019) 105 *Virginia Law Review* 127.

Abrash M, 'R. U. R. Restored and Reconsidered' (1991) 32 *Extrapolation* 184.

Aguiar L, Claussen J, and Peukert C, 'Catch Me If You Can: Effectiveness and Consequences of Online Copyright Enforcement' (2018) 29 *Information Systems Research* 656.

Ajunwa I, 'The Paradox of Automation as Anti-bias Intervention' (2020) 41 *Cardozo Law Review* 1671.

Aldridge I and Krawciw S, *Real-Time Risk: What Investors Should Know about FinTech, High-Frequency Trading, and Flash Crashes* (Wiley 2017).

Aletras N et al, 'Predicting Judicial Decisions of the European Court of Human Rights: A Natural Language Processing Perspective' (2016) 2:

e93 *PeerJ Computer Science*.

Alfonsi C, 'Taming Tech Giants Requires Fixing the Revolving Door' (2019) 19 *Kennedy School Review* 166.

Allain J (ed), *The Legal Understanding of Slavery: From the Historical to the Contemporary* (Oxford University Press 2013).

Allen HJ, 'Regulatory Sandboxes' (2019) 87 *George Washington Law Review* 579.

Alschuler AW, 'The Changing Purposes of Criminal Punishment: A Retrospective on the Past Century and Some Thoughts about the Next' (2003) 70 *University of Chicago Law Review* 1.

Amirthalingam K, 'The Non-delegable Duty: Some Clarifications, Some Questions' (2017) 29 *Singapore Academy of Law Journal* 500.

Amsler CE, Bartlett RL, and Bolton CJ, 'Thoughts of Some British Economists on Early Limited Liability and Corporate Legislation' (1981) 13 *History of Political Economy* 774.

Ananny M, 'Toward an Ethics of Algorithms: Convening, Observation, Probability, and Timeliness' (2016) 41 *Science, Technology, & Human Values* 93.

Ananny M and Crawford K, 'Seeing without Knowing: Limitations of the Transparency Ideal and Its Application to Algorithmic Accountability' (2018) 20 *New Media & Society* 973.

Anderson JM et al, *Autonomous Vehicle Technology: A Guide for Policymakers* (RAND 2014).

Anderson K, Reisner D, and Waxman M, 'Adapting the Law of Armed Conflict to Autonomous Weapon Systems' (2014) 90 *International Law Studies* 386.

Anderson SL, 'Asimov's "Three Laws of Robotics" and Machine Metaethics' (2008) 22 *AI & Society* 477.

Angel JJ and McCabe DM, 'Insider Trading 2.0? The Ethics of Information Sales' (2018) 147 *Journal of Business Ethics* 747.

Anshar M and Williams M-A, 'Simplified Pain Matrix Method for Artificial Pain Activation Embedded into Robot Framework' (2021) 13 *International Journal of Social Robotics* 187.

Aquinas T, *Summa Theologica* (Fathers of the English Dominican Province trs, first published 1265-74, Benziger Brothers 1911).

Arkin RC, 'The Case for Ethical Autonomy in Unmanned Systems' (2010) 9 *Journal of Military Ethics* 332.

Armstrong MJ, 'Modeling Short-Range Ballistic Missile Defense and Israel's Iron Dome System' (2014) 62 *Operations Research* 1028.

Ascher CS, 'The Grievance Man or Ombudsmania' (1967) 27 *Public Administration Review* 174.

Ashley KD, *Artificial Intelligence and Legal Analytics: New Tools for Law Practice in the Digital Age* (Cambridge University Press 2017).

Ashrafian H, 'Artificial Intelligence and Robot Responsibilities: Innovating Beyond Rights' (2015) 21 *Science and Engineering Ethics* 317.

'Can Artificial Intelligences Suffer from Mental Illness? A Philosophical Matter to Consider' (2017) 23 *Science and Engineering Ethics* 403.

Asimov I, 'Runaround', *Astounding Science Fiction* (March 1942).

The Complete Robot (Doubleday 1982).

Foundation and Earth (Doubleday 1986).

Auletta K, *Googled: The End of the World as We Know It* (Penguin 2009).

Austin J, *The Province of Jurisprudence Determined* (first published 1832, Cambridge University Press 1995).

Avant D, 'From Mercenary to Citizen Armies: Explaining Change in the Practice of War' (2000) 54 *International Organization* 41.

The Market for Force: The Consequences of Privatizing Security (Cambridge University Press 2005).

Aven T, 'On Different Types of Uncertainties in the Context of the Precautionary Principle' (2011) 31 *Risk Analysis* 1515.

Awad E *et al*, 'The Moral Machine Experiment' (2018) 563 *Nature* 59.

Ayres I and Braithwaite J, *Responsive Regulation: Transcending the Deregulation Debate* (Oxford University Press 1992).

Babbage C, *Passages from the Life of a Philosopher* (Longman 1864).

Baird HS, Coates AL, and Fateman RJ, 'PessimalPrint: A Reverse Turing Test' (2003) 5 *International Journal on Document Analysis and Recognition* 158.

Baldwin JM, Eassey JM, and Brooke EJ, 'Court Operations during the COVID-19 Pandemic' (2020) 45 *American Journal of Criminal Justice* 743.

Baldwin R and Black J, 'Driving Priorities in Risk-Based Regulation: What's the Problem?' (2016) 43 *Journal of Law and Society* 565.

Baldwin R, Cave M, and Lodge M, *Understanding Regulation: Theory, Strategy, and Practice* (2nd edn, Oxford University Press 2011).

—— (eds), *The Oxford Handbook of Regulation* (Oxford University Press 2010).

Balkin JM, 'The Three Laws of Robotics in the Age of Big Data' (2017) 78 *Ohio State Law Journal* 1217.

Balp G and Strampelli G, 'Preserving Capital Markets Efficiency in the High-Frequency Trading Era' (2018) *University of Illinois Journal of Law, Technology & Policy* 349.

Banteka N, 'Artificially Intelligent Persons' (2021) 58 *Houston Law Review* 537.

Barabas C et al, 'Interventions over Predictions: Reframing the Ethical Debate for Actuarial Risk Assessment' (2018) 81 *Proceedings of Machine Learning Research* 1.

Barfield W and Pagallo U (eds), *Research Handbook on the Law of Artificial Intelligence* (Edward Elgar 2018).

Barocas S and Selbst AD, 'Big Data's Disparate Impact' (2016) 104 *California Law Review* 671.

Barocas S, Selbst AD, and Raghavan M, 'The Hidden Assumptions Behind Counterfactual Explanations and Principal Reasons' (2020) *ACM Conference on Fairness, Accountability, and Transparency* (FAT*) 80.

Barredo Arrieta A et al, 'Explainable Artificial Intelligence (XAI): Concepts, Taxonomies, Opportunities, and Challenges Toward Responsible AI' (2020) 58 *Information Fusion* 82.

Baudrillard J, *The Gulf War Never Happened* (Polity Press 1995).

Bayern S, 'Of Bitcoins, Independently Wealthy Software, and the Zero-Member LLC' (2014) 108 *Northwestern University Law Review* 1485.

—— 'The Implications of Modern Business-Entity Law for the Regulation of

Autonomous Systems' (2015) 19 *Stanford Technology Law Review* 93.

Beard JM, 'Autonomous Weapons and Human Responsibilities' (2014) 45 *Georgetown Journal of International Law* 617.

Becker M, 'When Public Principals Give Up Control over Private Agents: The New Independence of ICANN in Internet Governance' (2019) 13 *Regulation & Governance* 561.

Benvenisti E, 'Upholding Democracy amid the Challenges of New Technology: What Role for the Law of Global Governance?' (2018) 29 *European Journal of International Law* 9.

'The WHO—Destined to Fail? Political Cooperation and the Covid-19 Pandemic' (2020) 114 *American Journal of International Law* 588.

Berg P, 'Asilomar 1975: DNA Modification Secured' (2008) 455 *Nature* 290.

Berg P *et al*, 'Summary Statement of the Asilomar Conference on Recombinant DNA Molecules' (1975) 72 *Proceedings of the National Academy of Sciences* 1981.

Berk R, *Machine Learning Risk Assessments in Criminal Justice Settings* (Springer 2019).

Bethel EW *et al*, 'Federal Market Information Technology in the Post Flash Crash Era: Roles for Supercomputing' (2012) 7 (2) *The Journal of Trading* 9.

Bhatt U *et al*, 'Explainable Machine Learning in Deployment' (2020) 1909. 06342v4 *arXiv*.

Bhuta N *et al* (eds), *Autonomous Weapons Systems: Law, Ethics, Policy* (Cambridge University Press 2016).

Birnie P, A Boyle, and C Redgwell, *International Law and the Environment* (3rd edn, Oxford 2009).

Blanco-Justicia A *et al*, 'Machine Learning Explainability via Microaggregation and Shallow Decision Trees' (2020) 194 *Knowledge-Based Systems* 105532.

Blume LMM, *Fallout: The Hiroshima Cover-Up and the Reporter Who Revealed It to the World* (Scribe 2020).

Bonnefon J-F, A Shariff, and I Rahwan, 'The Social Dilemma of Autonomous Vehicles' (2016) 352 (6293) *Science* 1573.

Bostrom N, 'Ethical Issues in Advanced Artificial Intelligence' in I Smit and GE Lasker (eds), *Cognitive, Emotive and Ethical Aspects of Decision Making in Humans and in Artificial Intelligence* (International Institute for Advanced Studies in Systems Research 2003) vol 2, 12.

— *Superintelligence: Paths, Dangers, Strategies* (Oxford University Press 2014).

Bovis CH, *EU Public Procurement Law* (Edward Elgar 2007).

Box GEP and NR Draper, *Empirical Model-Building and Response Surfaces* (Wiley 1987).

Boyer-Kassem T, 'Is the Precautionary Principle Really Incoherent?' (2017) 37 *Risk Analysis* 2026.

Bradley P, 'Risk Management Standards and the Active Management of Malicious Intent in Artificial Superintelligence' (2019) 35 *AI & Society* 319.

Branting LK, 'Artificial Intelligence and the Law from a Research Perspective' (2018) 14 (3) *Scitech Lawyer* 32.

Brauneis R and EP Goodman, 'Algorithmic Transparency for the Smart City' (2018) 20 *Yale Journal of Law & Technology* 103.

Brin D, *The Transparent Society: Will Technology Force Us to Choose between Privacy and Freedom?* (Addison-Wesley 1998).

Brogaarda J et al, 'High Frequency Trading and Extreme Price Movements' (2018) 128 *Journal of Financial Economics* 253.

Broockman D, GF Ferenstein, and N Malhotra, 'Predispositions and the Political Behavior of American Economic Elites: Evidence from Technology Entrepreneurs' (2019) 63 *American Journal of Political Science* 212.

Brooks C, C Gherhes, and T Vorley, 'Artificial Intelligence in the Legal Sector: Pressures and Challenges of Transformation' (2020) 13 *Cambridge Journal of Regions, Economy, and Society* 135.

Brown A et al, *Contemporary Intellectual Property: Law and Policy* (5th edn, Oxford University Press 2019).

Brown RL, *Nuclear Authority: The IAEA and the Absolute Weapon* (Georgetown University Press 2015).

Brownsword R, E Scotford, and K Yeung (eds), *The Oxford Handbook of Law, Regulation, and Technology* (Oxford University Press 2017).

Bryson JJ, ME Diamantis, and TD Grant, 'Of, for, and by the People: The Legal Lacuna of Synthetic Persons' (2017) 25 *Artificial Intelligence and Law* 273.

Budish E, P Cramton, and J Shim, 'The High-Frequency Trading Arms Race: Frequent Batch Auctions as a Market Design Response' (2015) 130 *Quarterly Journal of Economics* 1547.

Burrell J, 'How the Machine "Thinks": Understanding Opacity in Machine Learning Algorithms' (2016) 3 (1) *Big Data & Society*.

Buyers J, *Artificial Intelligence: The Practical Legal Issues* (Law Brief 2018).

Bygrave LA, 'Automated Profiling: Minding the Machine—Article 15 of the EC Data Protection Directive and Automated Profiling' (2001) 17 *Computer Law & Security Review* 17.

Calo MR, 'Open Robotics' (2011) 70 *Maryland Law Review* 571.

Calo R, AM Froomkin, and I Kerr (eds), *Robot Law* (Edward Elgar 2016).

Capek K, *RU. R. Rossum's Universal Robots; Kolektivní Drama v Vstupní Komedii a Tech Aktech* (Aventinum 1920).

— *R. U. R. (Rossum's Universal Robots)* (Paul Selver tr, Doubleday 1923).

— 'R. U. R. (Rossum's Universal Robots)' in P Kussi (ed), *Toward the Radical Center: A Karel Capek Reader* (C Novack-Jones tr, Catbird 1990).

Carozza PG, 'Subsidiarity as a Structural Principle of International Human Rights Law' (2003) 97 *American Journal of International Law* 38.

Carson HL, 'The Trial of Animals and Insects: A Little Known Chapter of Mediæval Jurisprudence' (1917) 56 *Proceedings of the American Philosophical Society* 410.

Cartwright J, 'Unilateral Mistake in the English Courts: Reasserting the Traditional Approach' (2009) *Singapore Journal of Legal Studies* 226.

Casey-Maslen S et al, *Drones and Other Unmanned Weapons Systems under*

International Law (Brill 2018).

Casey B, 'Robot Ipsa Loquitur' (2019) 108 *Georgetown Law Journal* 225.

Casey B, A Farhangi, and R Vogl, 'Rethinking Explainable Machines: The GDPR's "Right to Explanation" Debate and the Rise of Algorithmic Audits in Enterprise' (2019) 34 *Berkeley Technology Law Journal* 145.

Cassese A, 'The Martens Clause: Half a Loaf or Simply Pie in the Sky?' (2000) 11 *European Journal of International Law* 187.

Cassese's International Criminal Law (3rd edn, Oxford University Press 2013).

Cathcart T, *The Trolley Problem; or, Would You Throw the Fat Guy Off the Bridge? A Philosophical Conundrum* (Workman 2013).

Chagal-Feferkorn KA, 'Am I an Algorithm or a Product? When Products Liability Should Apply to Algorithmic Decision-Makers' (2019) 30 *Stanford Law & Policy Review* 61.

Chalmers D, G Davies, and G Monti, *European Union Law: Text and Materials* (4th edn, Cambridge University Press 2019).

Chalmers DJ, 'The Singularity: A Philosophical Analysis' (2010) 17 (9-10) *Journal of Consciousness Studies* 7.

Chander A, 'The Racist Algorithm?' (2017) 115 *Michigan Law Review* 1023. Chander A and UP Lê, 'Data Nationalism' (2015) 64 *Emory Law Journal* 677.

Charpie RA, 'The Geneva Conference' (1955) 193 (4) *Scientific American* 27.

Chen DL, 'Judicial Analytics and the Great Transformation of American Law' (2019) 27 *Artificial Intelligence and Law* 15.

Chen JH and SM Asch, 'Machine Learning and Prediction in Medicine—Beyond the Peak of Inflated Expectations' (2017) 376 (26) *New England Journal of Medicine* 2507.

Chen M, 'Beijing Internet Court Denies Copyright to Works Created Solely by Artificial Intelligence' (2019) 14 *Journal of Intellectual Property Law & Practice* 593.

Chesterman S, *Just War or Just Peace? Humanitarian Intervention and In-*

ternational Law (Oxford University Press 2001).

You, the People: The United Nations, Transitional Administration, and State-Building (Oxford University Press 2004).

'An International Rule of Law?' (2008) 56 *American Journal of Comparative Law* 331.

'The Turn to Ethics: Disinvestment from Multinational Corporations for Human Rights Violations—The Case of Norway's Sovereign Wealth Fund' (2008) 23 *American University International Law Review* 577.

One Nation under Surveillance: A New Social Contract to Defend Freedom without Sacrificing Liberty (Oxford University Press 2011).

(ed), *Data Protection Law in Singapore: Privacy and Sovereignty in an Interconnected World* (2nd edn, Academy 2018).

'Can International Law Survive a Rising China?' (2021) *European Journal of International Law* 1507.

Chesterman S and A Fisher (eds), *Private Security, Public Order: The Outsourcing of Public Services and Its Limits* (Oxford University Press 2009).

Chesterman S and C Lehnardt (eds), *From Mercenaries to Market: The Rise and Regulation of Private Military Companies* (Oxford University Press 2007).

Chinen M, *Law and Autonomous Machines: The Co-evolution of Legal Responsibility and Technology* (Edward Elgar 2019).

Chopra S and LF White, *A Legal Theory for Autonomous Artificial Agents* (University of Michigan Press 2011).

Chouldechova A, 'Fair Prediction with Disparate Impact: A Study of Bias in Recidivism Prediction Instruments' (2017) 5 *Big Data* 153.

Chu C, A Zhmoginov, and M Sandler, 'CycleGAN, a Master of Steganography' (2017) 1712. 02950v2 *arXiv*.

Citron DK, 'Technological Due Process' (2008) 85 *Washington University Law Review* 1249.

Clarke AC, *2001: A Space Odyssey* (Hutchinson 1968).

Coase R, 'The Nature of the Firm' (1937) 4 *Economica* 386.

Cobbe J, 'Administrative Law and the Machines of Government: Judicial Review of Automated Public-Sector Decision-Making' (2019) 39 *Legal Studies* 636.

Coca-Vila I, 'Self-Driving Cars in Dilemmatic Situations: An Approach Based on the Theory of Justification in Criminal Law' (2018) 12 *Criminal Law and Philosophy* 59.

Coffee JC, Jr, ' "No Soul to Damn: No Body to Kick": An Unscandalized Inquiry into the Problem of Corporate Punishment' (1981) 79 *Michigan Law Review* 386.

Cofone IN, 'Algorithmic Discrimination Is an Information Problem' (2019) 70 *Hastings Law Journal* 1389.

Cohen E, 'Law, Folklore, and Animal Lore' (1986) 110 *Past & Present* 6.

Cohen JE, *Between Truth and Power: The Legal Constructions of Informational Capitalism* (Oxford University Press 2019).

Cohen M, 'When Judges Have Reasons Not to Give Reasons: A Comparative Law Approach' (2015) 72 *Washington & Lee Law Review* 483.

Collingridge D, *The Social Control of Technology* (Frances Pinter 1980).

Contini F, 'Artificial Intelligence and the Transformation of Humans, Law and Technology Interactions in Judicial Proceedings' (2020) 2 (1) *Law, Technology, and Humans* 4.

Coombs N, 'What Is an Algorithm? Financial Regulation in the Era of High-Frequency Trading' (2016) 45 *Economy and Society* 278.

Corrales M, M Fenwick, and N Forgó (eds), *Robotics, AI and the Future of Law* (Springer 2018).

Cortés P, *The Law of Consumer Redress in an Evolving Digital Market: Upgrading from Alternative to Online Dispute Resolution* (Cambridge University Press 2017).

Cortez N, 'Regulating Disruptive Innovation' (2014) 29 *Berkeley Technology Law Journal* 175.

Craik N, *The International Law of Environmental Impact Assessment: Process, Substance and Integration* (Cambridge University Press 2008).

Crane DA, KD Logue, and BC Pilz, 'A Survey of Legal Issues Arising from the Deployment of Autonomous and Connected Vehicles' (2017) 23

Michigan Telecommunications and Technology Law Review 191.

Crawford J, *The International Law Commission's Articles on State Responsibility: Introduction, Text and Commentaries* (Cambridge University Press 2002).

Crootof R, 'War Torts: Accountability for Autonomous Weapons' (2016) 164 *University of Pennsylvania Law Review* 1347.

' "Cyborg Justice" and the Risk of Technological—Legal Lock-In' (2019) 119 *Columbia Law Review Forum* 233.

Cuéllar M-F, 'Cyberdelegation and the Administrative State' in NR Parrillo (ed), *Administrative Law from the Inside Out: Essays on Themes in the Work of Jerry L Mashaw* (Cambridge University Press 2017) 134.

Cui Y, *Artificial Intelligence and Judicial Modernization* (Springer 2020).

Cuk T and A van Waeyenberge, 'European Legal Framework for Algorithmic and High Frequency Trading (Mifid 2 and MAR): A Global Approach to Managing the Risks of the Modern Trading Paradigm' (2018) 9 *European Journal of Risk Regulation* 146.

Cullen FT and KE Gilbert, *Reaffirming Rehabilitation* (2nd edn, Anderson 2013). Cunningham S, *Driving Offences: Law, Policy and Practice* (Routledge 2008).

Dal Bó E, 'Regulatory Capture: A Review' (2006) 22 *Oxford Review of Economic Policy* 203.

Dale R, 'Law and Word Order: NLP in Legal Tech' (2019) 25 *Natural Language Engineering* 211.

Damiano L and P Dumouchel, 'Anthropomorphism in Human—Robot Co-evolution' (2018) 9 *Frontiers in Psychology* 468.

Danaher J, 'Why AI Doomsayers Are Like Sceptical Theists and Why It Matters' (2015) 25 *Mind and Machines* 231.

'Regulating Child Sex Robots: Restriction or Experimentation?' (2019) 27 *Medical Law Review* 553.

Danchin PG et al, 'The Pandemic Paradox in International Law' (2020) 114 *American Journal of International Law* 598.

Dari-Mattiacci G et al, 'The Emergence of the Corporate Form' (2017) 33 *Journal of Law, Economics and Organization* 193.

Datta A, MC Tschantz, and A Datta, 'Automated Experiments on Ad Privacy Settings: A Tale of Opacity, Choice, and Discrimination' (2015) 1 *Proceedings on Privacy Enhancing Technologies* 92.

Datta A, S Sen, and Y Zick, 'Algorithmic Transparency via Quantitative Input Influence: Theory and Experiments with Learning Systems' (2016) *IEEE Symposium on Security and Privacy* (SP) 598.

Dauber E *et al*, 'Git Blame Who? Stylistic Authorship Attribution of Small, Incomplete Source Code Fragments' (2017) 1701. 05681v3 *arXiv*.

Davis AE, 'The Future of Law Firms (and Lawyers) in the Age of Artificial Intelligence' (2020) 27 (1) *The Professional Lawyer* 3.

Dawes J, 'Speculative Human Rights: Artificial Intelligence and the Future of the Human' (2020) 42 *Human Rights Quarterly* 573.

de Fine Licht K and J de Fine Licht, 'Artificial Intelligence, Transparency, and Public Decision-Making: Why Explanations Are Key When Trying to Produce Perceived Legitimacy' (2020) 35 *AI & Society* 917.

de Laat PB, 'Algorithmic Decision-Making Based on Machine Learning from Big Data: Can Transparency Restore Accountability?' (2018) 31 *Philosophy & Technology* 525.

Deakin S, 'Organisational Torts: Vicarious Liability versus Non-delegable Duty' (2018) *Cambridge Law Journal* 15.

Deakin S and Z Adams, *Markesinis and Deakin's Tort Law* (8th edn, Oxford University Press 2019).

Deakin S and C Markou (eds), *Is Law Computable? Critical Perspectives on Law and Artificial Intelligence* (Hart 2020).

Deeks A, 'The Judicial Demand for Explainable Artificial Intelligence' (2019) 119 *Columbia Law Review* 1829.

Deng J, 'Should the Common Law System Welcome Artificial Intelligence: A Case Study of China's Same-Type Case Reference System' (2019) 3 *Georgetown Law Technology Review* 223.

Dennerley JA, 'State Liability for Space Object Collisions: The Proper Interpretation of "Fault" for the Purposes of International Space Law' (2018) 29 *European Journal of International Law* 281.

Dewey J, 'The Historic Background of Corporate Legal Personality' (1926)

35 *Yale Law Journal* 655.

Diamantis ME, 'Clockwork Corporations: A Character Theory of Corporate Punishment' (2018) 103 *Iowa Law Review* 507.

Dick PK, *Do Androids Dream of Electric Sheep?* (Doubleday 1968).

Domingos P, *The Master Algorithm: How the Quest for the Ultimate Learning Machine Will Remake Our World* (Basic Books 2015).

Downes L, *The Laws of Disruption: Harnessing the New Forces that Govern Life and Business in the Digital Age* (Basic Books 2009).

du Sautoy M, *The Creativity Code: Art and Innovation in the Age of AI* (Harvard University Press 2019).

Dubber MD, F Pasquale, and S Das (eds), *The Oxford Handbook of Ethics of AI* (Oxford University Press 2020).

Duffy SH and JP Hopkins, 'Sit, Stay, Drive: The Future of Autonomous Car Liability' (2013) 16 *SMU Science and Technology Law Review* 453.

Dunlap CJ, Jr, 'Accountability and Autonomous Weapons: Much Ado about Nothing' (2016) 30 *Temple International & Comparative Law Journal* 63.

Duwe G and KD Kim, 'Sacrificing Accuracy for Transparency in Recidivism Risk Assessment: The Impact of Classification Method on Predictive Performance' (2016) 1 *Corrections* 155.

Dworkin R, *Taking Rights Seriously* (Harvard University Press 1977).

Law's Empire (Harvard University Press 1986).

Dyson M, *Comparing Tort and Crime: Learning from across and within Legal Systems* (Cambridge University Press 2015).

Easterbrook FH and DR Fischel, 'Limited Liability and the Corporation' (1985) 52 *University of Chicago Law Review* 89.

Ebers M and S Navas (eds), *Algorithms and Law* (Cambridge University Press 2020).

Edmonds D, *Would You Kill the Fat Man? The Trolley Problem and What Your Answer Tells Us about Right and Wrong* (Princeton University Press 2013).

Edwards L (ed), *Law, Policy, and the Internet* (Hart 2019).

Edwards L and M Veale, 'Slave to the Algorithm? Why a "Right to an Explanation" Is Probably Not the Remedy You Are Looking For' (2017) 16 *Duke Law & Technology Review* 18.

'Enslaving the Algorithm: From a "Right to an Explanation" to a "Right to Better Decisions"?' (2018) 16 (3) *IEEE Security & Privacy* 46.

Egloff FJ, 'Public Attribution of Cyber Intrusions' (2021) 6 *Journal of Cybersecurity* 1.

Elrod JW, 'Trial by Siri: AI Comes to the Courtroom' (2020) 57 *Houston Law Review* 1085.

Endo SK, 'Technological Opacity & Procedural Injustice' (2018) 59 *Boston College Law Review* 821.

Engstrom NF, 'When Cars Crash: The Automobile's Tort Law Legacy' (2018) 53 *Wake Forest Law Review* 293.

Enough B and T Mussweiler, 'Sentencing under Uncertainty: Anchoring Effects in the Courtroom' (2001) 31 *Journal of Applied Social Psychology* 1535.

Epstein R, G Roberts, and G Beber (eds), *Parsing the Turing Test: Philosophical and Methodological Issues in the Quest for the Thinking Computer* (Springer 2009).

Erdelez S and S O'Hare, 'Legal Informatics: Application of Information Technology in Law' (1997) 32 *Annual Review of Information Science and Technology* 367.

Erdélyi OJ and J Goldsmith, 'Regulating Artificial Intelligence: Proposal for a Global Solution' (2018) *AAAI/ACM Conference on AI, Ethics, and Society* (AIES'18) 95.

Erkkilä T, *Ombudsman as a Global Institution: Transnational Governance and Accountability* (Palgrave Macmillan 2020).

Etzioni A and O Etzioni, 'Pros and Cons of Autonomous Weapons Systems', *Military Review* (May—June 2017) 71.

Eubanks V, *Automating Inequality: How High-Tech Tools Profile, Police, and Punish the Poor* (St Martin's 2017).

Evans EP, *The Criminal Prosecution and Capital Punishment of Animals* (EP Dutton 1906).

Ezrachi A and ME Stucke, *Virtual Competition: The Promise and Perils of the Algorithm-Driven Economy* (Harvard University Press 2016).

'Artificial Intelligence & Collusion: When Computers Inhibit Competition' (2017) *University of Illinois Law Review* 1775.

Fairgrieve D, *Product Liability in Comparative Perspective* (Cambridge University Press 2005).

Farjama M and O Kirchkampb, 'Bubbles in Hybrid Markets: How Expectations about Algorithmic Trading Affect Human Trading' (2018) 146 *Journal of Economic Behavior & Organization* 248.

Feeley MM and J Simon, 'The New Penology: Notes on the Emerging Strategy of Corrections and Its Implications' (1992) 30 *Criminology* 449.

Feldman RC, E Aldana, and K Stein, 'Artificial Intelligence in the Health Care Space: How We Can Trust What We Cannot Know' (2019) 30 *Stanford Law & Policy Review* 399.

Fellous J-M and MA Arbib, *Who Needs Emotions? The Brain Meets the Robot* (Oxford University Press 2005).

Fenwick M, WA Kaal, and EPM Vermeulen, 'Regulation Tomorrow: What Happens When Technology Is Faster than the Law?' (2017) 6 *American University Business Law Review* 561.

Fermi E, 'Atomic Energy for Power' in AV Hill (ed), *Science and Civilization: The Future of Atomic Energy* (McGraw-Hill 1946) 93.

Fifield W, 'Pablo Picasso: A Composite Interview' (1964) 32 *Paris Review* 37.

Finch J, S Geiger, and E Reid, 'Captured by Technology? How Material Agency Sustains Interaction between Regulators and Industry Actors' (2017) 46 *Research Policy* 160.

Firth-Butterfield K, 'Artificial Intelligence and the Law: More Questions than Answers?' (2017) 14 (1) *Scitech Lawyer* 28.

Fischer D, *History of the International Atomic Energy Agency: The First Forty Years* (IAEA 1997).

Flores AW, K Bechtel, and CT Lowenkamp, 'False Positives, False Negatives, and False Analyses: A Rejoinder to "Machine Bias: There's Software Used across the Country to Predict Future Criminals. And It's Biased against Blacks"' (2016) 80 (2) *Federal Probation* 38.

Floridi L, 'Robots, Jobs, Taxes, and Responsibilities' (2017) 30 *Philosophy & Technology* 1.

Follesdal A, 'The Principle of Subsidiarity as a Constitutional Principle in International Law' (2013) 2 *Global Constitutionalism* 37.

Fosch-Villaronga E, *Robots, Healthcare, and the Law: Regulating Automation in Personal Care* (Routledge 2019).

Frank X, 'Is Watson for Oncology per se Unreasonably Dangerous? Making a Case for How to Prove Products Liability Based on a Flawed Artificial Intelligence Design' (2019) 45 *American Journal of Law & Medicine* 273.

Frankenreiter J and MA Livermore, 'Computational Methods in Legal Analysis' (2020) 16 *Annual Review of Law and Social Science* 39.

Franklin S and AC Graesser, 'Is It an Agent, or Just a Program?: A Taxonomy for Autonomous Agents' in JP Müller, MJ Wooldridge, and NR Jennings (eds), *Intelligent Agents III: Agent Theories, Architectures, and Languages* (Springer 1997) 21.

French P, 'The Corporation as a Moral Person' (1979) 16 *American Philosophical Quarterly* 207.

Gandy OH, Jr, 'Engaging Rational Discrimination: Exploring Reasons for Placing Regulatory Constraints on Decision Support Systems' (2010) 12 *Ethics and Information Technology* 29.

Gebru T et al, 'Datasheets for Datasets' (2020) *arXiv* 1803.09010v7.

Gehl RW, *Weaving the Dark Web: Legitimacy on Freenet, Tor, and I2P* (MIT Press 2018).

Geistfeld MA, 'A Roadmap for Autonomous Vehicles: State Tort Liability, Automobile Insurance, and Federal Safety Regulation' (2017) 105 *California Law Review* 1611.

'The Regulatory Sweet Spot for Autonomous Vehicles' (2018) 53 *Wake Forest Law Review* 101.

Gelman A and J Hill, *Data Analysis Using Regression and Multilevel/Hierarchical Models* (Cambridge University Press 2007).

Gerber LG, 'The Baruch Plan and the Origins of the Cold War' (1982) 6 (4) *Diplomatic History* 69.

Gervais DJ, 'The Machine as Author' (2020) 105 *Iowa Law Review* 2053.

Gill C, 'The Evolving Role of the Ombudsman: A Conceptual and Constitutional Analysis of the "Scottish Solution" to Administrative Justice' (2014) *Public Law* 662.

Gilligan B, *Practical Horse Law: A Guide for Owners and Riders* (Blackwell Science 2002).

Glenn HP and LD Smith (eds), *Law and the New Logics* (Cambridge University Press 2017).

Goel S et al, 'Combatting Police Discrimination in the Age of Big Data' (2017) 20 *New Criminal Law Review* 181.

Good IJ, 'Speculations Concerning the First Ultraintelligent Machine' in FL Alt and M Rubinoff (eds), *Advances in Computers* (Academic 1965) vol 6, 31.

Goodman B and S Flaxman, 'European Union Regulations on Algorithmic Decision Making and a "Right to Explanation"' (2017) 38 (3) *AI Magazine* 50.

Gottesman O et al, 'Guidelines for Reinforcement Learning in Healthcare' (2019) 25 *Nature Medicine* 16.

Goudkamp J and D Nolan, 'Contributory Negligence in the Twenty-First Century: An Empirical Study of First Instance Decisions' (2016) 79 *Modern Law Review* 575.

Gowder P, 'Transformative Legal Technology and the Rule of Law' (2018) 68 (Supplement1) *University of Toronto Law Journal* 82.

Grabiner Lord A, 'Sex, Scandal and Super-Injunctions—The Controversies Surrounding the Protection of Privacy' (2012) 45 *Israel Law Review* 537.

Gramitto Ricci SA, 'Artificial Agents in Corporate Boardrooms' (2020) 105 *Cornell Law Review* 869.

Gravanis G et al, 'Behind the Cues: A Benchmarking Study for Fake News Detection' (2019) 128 *Expert Systems with Applications* 201.

Griffiths J, *The Great Firewall of China: How to Build and Control an Alternative Version of the Internet* (Zed Books 2019).

Grimmelmann J, 'There's No Such Thing as a Computer-Authored Work—

and It's a Good Thing, Too' (2016) 39 *Columbia Journal of Law & the Arts* 403.

Guidotti R *et al*, 'A Survey of Methods for Explaining Black Box Models' (2018) *arXiv* 1802. 01933v3.

Guihot M, AF Matthew, and NP Suzor, 'Nudging Robots: Innovative Solutions to Regulate Artificial Intelligence' (2017) 20 *Vanderbilt Journal of Entertainment & Technology Law* 385.

Guihot M and LB Moses, *Artificial Intelligence, Robots and the Law* (LexisNexis 2020).

Guiora AN, 'Accountability and Decision Making in Autonomous Warfare: Who Is Responsible?' (2017) *Utah Law Review* 393.

Gunningham N and P Grabosky, *Smart Regulation: Designing Environmental Policy* (Clarendon Press 1998).

Gunkel DJ, *Robot Rights* (MIT Press 2018).

郭富民:《人工智能无法取代法官的审慎艺术》, 载《中国法院报》2017 年 5 月 12 日。

Guo L, 'Regulating Investment Robo-Advisors in China: Problems and Prospects' (2020) 21 *European Business Organization Law Review* 69.

Guttinger S, 'Trust in Science: CRISPR-Cas9 and the Ban on Human Germline Editing' (2018) 24 *Science Engineering Ethics* 1077.

Hacker P and B Petkova, 'Reining in the Big Promise of Big Data: Transparency, Inequality, and New Regulatory Frontiers' (2017) 15 *Northwestern Journal of Technology and Intellectual Property* 1.

Hagendorff T, 'The Ethics of AI Ethics: An Evaluation of Guidelines' (2020) 30 *Minds & Machines* 99.

Häggström O, 'Challenges to the Omohundro—Bostrom Framework for AI Motivations' (2019) 21 *Foresight* 153.

Hallevy G, *When Robots Kill: Artificial Intelligence under Criminal Law* (Northeastern University Press 2013).

Liability for Crimes Involving Artificial Intelligence Systems (Springer 2015).

Hamdani A and A Klement, 'Corporate Crime and Deterrence' (2008) 61 *Stanford Law Review* 271.

Hancox-Li L, 'Robustness in Machine Learning Explanations: Does It Matter?' (2020) *ACM Conference on Fairness, Accountability, and Transparency* (FAT*) 640.

Hannah-Moffat K, 'Sacrosanct or Flawed: Risk, Accountability and Gender-Responsive Penal Politics' (2011) 22 *Current Issues in Criminal Justice* 193.

— 'The Uncertainties of Risk Assessment: Partiality, Transparency, and Just Decisions' (2015) 27 *Federal Sentencing Reporter* 244.

Hansmann H and R Kraakman, 'The Essential Role of Organizational Law' (2000) 110 *Yale Law Journal* 387.

Harasimiuk DE and T Braun, *Regulating Artificial Intelligence: Binary Ethics and the Law* (Routledge 2021).

Harlow C and R Rawlings, *Law and Administration* (3rd edn, Cambridge University Press 2009).

Harrington A, *Mind Fixers: Psychiatry's Troubled Search for the Biology of Mental Illness* (Norton 2019).

Harrison H, *War with the Robots* (Grafton 1962).

Hart HLA, 'Positivism and the Separation of Law and Morals' (1958) 71 *Harvard Law Review* 593.

— *The Concept of Law* (3rd edn, Clarendon Press 2012).

He J et al, 'The Practical Implementation of Artificial Intelligence Technologies in Medicine' (2019) 25 *Nature Medicine* 30.

Heald D, 'Varieties of Transparency' in C Hood and D Heald (eds), *Transparency: The Key to Better Governance?* (Oxford University Press 2006) 25.

Henderson DA, *Smallpox: The Death of a Disease* (Prometheus 2009).

Henkin L, *How Nations Behave: Law and Foreign Policy* (2nd edn, Columbia University Press 1979).

Henrich J, SJ Heine, and A Norenzayan, 'The Weirdest People in the World?' (2010) 33 *Behavioral and Brain Sciences* 61.

Henry N and A Powell, 'Sexual Violence in the Digital Age: The Scope and Limits of Criminal Law' (2016) 25 *Social & Legal Studies* 397.

Herings PJ-J, R Peeters, and MS Yang, 'Piracy on the Internet: Accommodate It or Fight It? A Dynamic Approach' (2018) 266 *European Journal of Operational Research* 328.

Hertogh M and R Kirkham (eds), *Research Handbook on the Ombudsman* (Edward Elgar 2018).

Hildebrandt M, 'Law as Information in the Era of Data-Driven Agency' (2016) 79 *Modern Law Review* 1.

'Saved by Design? The Case of Legal Protection by Design' (2017) 11 *Nanoethics* 307.

'Law as Computation in the Era of Artificial Legal Intelligence: Speaking Law to the Power of Statistics' (2018) 68 (Supplement1) *University of Toronto Law Journal* 12.

Hildt E, 'Artificial Intelligence: Does Consciousness Matter?' (2019) 10 (1535) *Frontiers in Psychology*.

Hoffman RR et al, 'Metrics for Explainable AI: Challenges and Prospects' (2019) *arXiv* 1812. 04608v2.

Hofmann J, C Katzenbach, and K Gollatz, 'Between Coordination and Regulation: Finding the Governance in Internet Governance' (2017) 19 *New Media & Society* 1406.

Hofstadter DR, *Gödel, Escher, Bach: An Eternal Golden Braid* (Basic Books 1979).

Holcombe L, *Wives and Property: Reform of the Married Women's Property Law in Nineteenth-Century England* (Martin Robertson 1983).

Holmes OW, Jr, *The Common Law* (Little, Brown 1881).

'The Path of the Law' (1897) 10 *Harvard Law Review* 457.

Hu Y, 'Robot Criminals' (2019) 52 *University of Michigan Journal of Law Reform* 487.

Huang R and X Sun, 'Weibo Network, Information Diffusion and Implications for Collective Action in China' (2014) 17 *Information, Communication & Society* 86.

Hughes J, 'The Law of Armed Conflict Issues Created by Programming Automatic Target Recognition Systems Using Deep Learning Methods' (2019) *Yearbook of International Humanitarian Law* 99.

Humphreys P, 'The Philosophical Novelty of Computer Simulation Methods'

(2009) 169 *Synthese* 615.

Huws CF and JC Finnis, 'On Computable Numbers with an Application to the AlanTuringproblem' (2017) 25 *Artificial Intelligence and Law* 181.

Imbens GW and DB Rubin, *Causal Inference for Statistics, Social, and Biomedical Sciences: An Introduction* (Cambridge University Press 2015).

Iuliano J, 'Jury Voting Paradoxes' (2014) 113 *Michigan Law Review* 405.

Iwai K, 'Persons, Things and Corporations: The Corporate Personality Controversy and Comparative Corporate Governance' (1999) 47 *American Journal of Comparative Law* 583.

Jiang N, 'Old Wine in New Bottles? New Strategies for Judicial Accountability in China' (2018) 52 *International Journal of Law, Crime and Justice* 74.

Jin D (ed), *Reconstructing Our Orders: Artificial Intelligence and Human Society* (Springer 2018).

Jobin A, M Ienca, and E Vayena, 'The Global Landscape of AI Ethics Guidelines' (2019) 1 *Nature Machine Intelligence* 389.

Johnston S, 'The Practice of UN Treaty-Making Concerning Science' in S Chesterman, DM Malone, and S Villalpando (eds), *The Oxford Handbook of United Nations Treaties* (Oxford University Press 2019) 321.

Jones CAG, *Expert Witnesses: Science, Medicine, and the Practice of Law* (Clarendon Press 1994).

Jordan P *et al*, 'Exploring the Referral and Usage of Science Fiction in HCI Literature' (2018) *arXiv* 1803.08395v2.

Kaddari Z *et al*, 'Natural Language Processing: Challenges and Future Directions' in T Masrour, I El Hassani, and A Cherrafi (eds), *Artificial Intelligence and Industrial Applications* (Springer 2021) 236.

Kaminski ME, 'Binary Governance: Lessons from the GDPR's Approach to Algorithmic Accountability' (2019) 92 *Southern California Law Review* 1529.

Kaminski ME and G Malgieri, 'Multi-layered Explanations from Algorithmic

Impact Assessments in the GDPR' (2020) *ACM Conference on Fairness, Accountability, and Transparency* (FAT*) 68.

Karnow CEA, 'Liability for Distributed Artificial Intelligences' (1996) 11 *Berkeley Technology Law Journal* 147.

Katsh E and O Rabinovich-Einy, *Digital Justice: Technology and the Internet of Disputes* (Oxford University Press 2017).

Katz A, 'Intelligent Agents and Internet Commerce in Ancient Rome' (2008) 20 *Society for Computers and Law* 35.

Kazis NM, 'Tort Concepts in Traffic Crimes' (2016) 125 *Yale Law Journal* 1131.

Keating GC, 'Products Liability as Enterprise Liability' (2017) 10 *Tort Law Journal* 41.

Kehrer T, 'Closing the Liability Loophole: The Liability Convention and the Future of Conflict in Space' (2019) 20 *Chicago Journal of International Law* 178.

Kerr I and K Szilagyi, 'Evitable Conflicts, Inevitable Technologies? The Science and Fiction of Robotic Warfare and IHL' (2018) 14 *Law, Culture and the Humanities* 45.

Khaitan T, *A Theory of Discrimination Law* (Oxford University Press 2015). Khanna VS, 'Corporate Criminal Liability: What Purpose Does It Serve?' (1996) 109 *Harvard Law Review* 1477.

Khoo K and J Soh, 'The Inefficiency of Quasi—Per Se Rules: Regulating Information Exchange in EU and US Antitrust Law' (2020) 57 *American Business Law Journal* 45.

Kim YH and JJ Yang, 'What Makes Circuit Breakers Attractive to Financial Markets? A Survey' (2004) 13 *Financial Markets, Institutions & Instruments* 109.

King BA, T Hammond, and J Harrington, 'Disruptive Technology: Economic Consequences of Artificial Intelligence and the Robotics Revolution' (2017) 12 (2) *Journal of Strategic Innovation and Sustainability* 53.

King MA, *Public Policy and the Corporation* (Chapman and Hall 1977).

Kirilenko A *et al*, 'The Flash Crash: High-Frequency Trading in an Electronic Market' (2017) 72 *Journal of Finance* 967.

Kirkham R and C Gill (eds), *A Manifesto for Ombudsman Reform* (Palgrave Macmillan 2020).

Kirkwood WT, 'Inherently Governmental Functions, Organizational Conflicts of Interest, and the Outsourcing of the United Kingdom's MOD Defense Acquisition Function: Lessons Learned from the US Experience' (2015) 44 *Public Contract Law Journal* 443.

Klein H, 'ICANN and Internet Governance: Leveraging Technical Coordination to Realize Global Public Policy' (2002) 18 *The Information Society* 193.

Kleinberg J et al, 'Discrimination in the Age of Algorithms' (2018) 10 *Journal of Legal Analysis* 113.

Ko H et al, 'Human-Machine Interaction: A Case Study on Fake News Detection Using a Backtracking Based on a Cognitive System' (2019) 55 *Cognitive Systems Research* 77.

Koppell JGS, 'Pathologies of Accountability: ICANN and the Challenge of "Multiple Accountabilities Disorder"' (2005) 65 *Public Administration Review* 94.

Krisch N and B Kingsbury, 'Global Governance and Global Administrative Law in the International Legal Order' (2006) 17 *European Journal of International Law* 1.

Kroll JA et al, 'Accountable Algorithms' (2017) 165 *University of Pennsylvania Law Review* 633.

Krupiy T, 'Regulating a Game Changer: Using a Distributed Approach to Develop an Accountability Framework for Lethal Autonomous Weapon Systems' (2018) 50 *Georgetown Journal of International Law* 45.

Kucherbaev P, A Bozzon, and G-J Houben, 'Human-Aided Bots' (2018) 22 (6) *IEEE Internet Computing* 36.

Kurki VAJ, *A Theory of Legal Personhood* (Oxford University Press 2019).

Kurki VAJ and T Pietrzykowski (eds), *Legal Personhood: Animals, Artificial Intelligence and the Unborn* (Springer 2017).

Kurzweil R, *The Singularity Is Near: When Humans Transcend Biology* (Viking 2005).

Laffont J-J and J Tirole, 'The Politics of Government Decision-Making: A Theory of Regulatory Capture' (1991) 106 *Quarterly Journal of Economics* 1089.

Lalive R et al, 'Parental Leave and Mothers' Careers: The Relative Importance of Job Protection and Cash Benefits' (2014) 81 *Review of Economic Studies* 219.

Lambert P, *Gringras: The Laws of the Internet* (5th edn, Bloomsbury 2018).

Lang RD and LE Benessere, 'Alexa, Siri, Bixby, Google's Assistant, and Cortana Testifying in Court: Novel Use of Emerging Technology in Litigation' (2018) 35 (7) *Computer and Internet Lawyer* 16.

Lange A-C, M Lenglet, and R Seyfert, 'Cultures of High-Frequency Trading: Mapping the Landscape of Algorithmic Developments in Contemporary Financial Markets' (2016) 45 *Economy and Society* 149.

Lannetti DW, 'Toward a Revised Definition of "Product" under the Restatement (Third) of Torts: Products Liability' (2000) 35 *Tort & Insurance Law Journal* 845.

Lastowka FG, *Virtual Justice: The New Laws of Online Worlds* (Yale University Press 2010).

Laubacher TJ, 'Simplifying Inherently Governmental Functions: Creating a Principled Approach from Its ad hoc Beginnings' (2017) 46 *Public Contract Law Journal* 791.

Lavy M and M Hervey, *The Law of Artificial Intelligence* (Sweet & Maxwell 2020).

Le Moli G, PS Vishvanathan, and A Aeri, 'Whither the Proof? The Progressive Reversal of the Burden of Proof in Environmental Cases before International Courts and Tribunals' (2017) 8 *Journal of International Dispute Settlement* 644.

Lee HCB, JM Cruz, and R Shankar, 'Corporate Social Responsibility (CSR) Issues in Supply Chain Competition: Should Greenwashing Be Regulated?' (2018) 49 *Decision Sciences* 1088.

Lee KF, *AI Superpowers: China, Silicon Valley, and the New World Order* (Houghton Mifflin Harcourt 2018).

Legge D and S Brooman, *Law Relating to Animals* (Cavendish 2000).

Lehman-Wilzig SN, 'Frankenstein Unbound: Towards a Legal Definition of Artificial Intelligence' (1981) 13 *Futures* 442.

Lehman J et al, 'The Surprising Creativity of Digital Evolution: A Collection of Anecdotes from the Evolutionary Computation and Artificial Life Research Communities' (2018) arXiv 1803. 03453v1.

Lemley MA and B Casey, 'Remedies for Robots' (2019) 86 *University of Chicago Law Review* 1311.

Lenglet M and J Mol, 'Squaring the Speed of Light? Regulating Market Access in Algorithmic Finance' (2016) 45 *Economy and Society* 201.

Lessig L, *Code: Version 2. 0* (Basic Books 2006).

Levendowski A, 'How Copyright Law Can Fix Artificial Intelligence's Implicit Bias Problem' (2018) 93 *Washington Law Review* 579.

Leveringhaus A, *Ethics and Autonomous Weapons* (Palgrave Macmillan 2016).

Levine ME and JL Forrence, 'Regulatory Capture, Public Interest, and the Public Agenda: Toward a Synthesis' (1990) 6 (Special Issue) *Journal of Law, Economics, and Organization* 167.

Levine SS and MJ Prietula, 'Open Collaboration for Innovation: Principles and Performance' (2014) 25 *Organization Science* 1287.

Levy D and AT Young, ' "The Real Thing": Nominal Price Rigidity of the Nickel Coke, 1886-1959' (2004) 36 *Journal of Money, Credit, and Banking* 765.

Levy S, *In the Plex: How Google Thinks, Works, and Shapes Our Lives* (New York 2011).

Lewis M, *Flash Boys: A Wall Street Revolt* (WW Norton 2014).

Lim D, 'AI & IP: Innovation & Creativity in an Age of Accelerated Change' (2018) 52 *Akron Law Review* 813.

Lim HYF, *Autonomous Vehicles and the Law: Technology, Algorithms, and Ethics* (Edward Elgar 2018).

Lin P, K Abney, and R Jenkins (eds), *Robot Ethics 2. 0: From Autonomous Cars to Artificial Intelligence* (Oxford University Press 2017).

Lipton J, *Rethinking Cyberlaw: A New Vision for Internet Law* (Edward Elgar 2015).

Liu J, 'China's Data Localization' (2020) 13 *Chinese Journal of Communication* 84.

Liu Y-H et al, 'Reduction Measures for Air Pollutants and Greenhouse Gas in the Transportation Sector: A Cost-Benefit Analysis' (2019) 207 *Journal of Cleaner Production* 1023.

(ed), *Law as Data: Computation, Text, and the Future of Legal Analysis* (Santa Fe Institute Press 2019).

Livingston S and M Risse, 'The Future Impact of Artificial Intelligence on Humans and Human Rights' (2019) 33 *Ethics and International Affairs* 141.

London AJ and J Kimmelman, 'Why Clinical Translation Cannot Succeed without Failure' (2015) 4 *eLife* e12844.

Loughnan A, *Manifest Madness: Mental Incapacity in the Criminal Law* (Oxford University Press 2012).

Low K and E Mik, 'Pause the Blockchain Legal Revolution' (2020) 69 *International and Comparative Law Quarterly* 135.

Luciano F et al, 'AI4People—An Ethical Framework for a Good AI Society: Opportunities, Risks, Principles, and Recommendations' (2018) 28 *Minds and Machines* 689.

Ludsin H, *Preventive Detention and the Democratic State* (Cambridge University Press 2016).

Luetge C, 'The German Ethics Code for Automated and Connected Driving' (2017) 30 *Philosophy & Technology* 547.

Maas MM, 'Regulating for "Normal AI Accidents": Operational Lessons for the Responsible Governance of Artificial Intelligence Deployment' (2018) Proceedings of 2018 *AAAI/ACM Conference on AI, Ethics, and Society* (AIES'18) 223.

Mac Sithigh D and M Siems, 'The Chinese Social Credit System: A Model for Other Countries?' (2019) 82 *Modern Law Review* 1034.

MacKenzie D, '"Making", "Taking", and the Material Political Economy of Algorithmic Trading' (2018) 47 *Economy and Society* 501.

Magnuson WJ, *Blockchain Democracy: Technology, Law, and the Rule of the Crowd* (Cambridge University Press 2020).

Manheim K and L Kaplan, 'Artificial Intelligence: Risks to Privacy and Democracy' (2019) 21 *Yale Journal of Law & Technology* 106.

Mantelero A, 'AI and Big Data: A Blueprint for a Human Rights, Social, and Ethical Impact Assessment' (2018) 34 *Computer Law & Security Review* 754.

Mantrov V, 'A Victim of a Road Traffic Accident Not Fastened by a Seat Belt and Contributory Negligence in the EU Motor Insurance Law' (2014) 5 *European Journal of Risk Regulation* 115.

Margulies P, 'Sovereignty and Cyber Attacks: Technology's Challenge to the Law of State Responsibility' (2013) 14 *Melbourne Journal of International Law* 496.

Marmura SME, *The WikiLeaks Paradigm: Paradoxes and Revelations* (Palgrave 2018).

Mattli W, *Darkness by Design: The Hidden Power in Global Capital Markets* (Princeton University Press 2019).

Maurer M et al (eds), *Autonomous Driving: Technical, Legal and Social Aspects* (Springer 2016).

Maurer SM, *Self-Governance in Science: Community-Based Strategies for Managing Dangerous Knowledge* (Cambridge University Press 2017).

Maurutto P and K Hannah-Moffat, 'Assembling Risk and the Restructuring of Penal Control' (2006) 46 *British Journal of Criminology* 438.

McBride NJ and R Bagshaw, *Tort Law* (6th edn, Pearson 2018).

McCarty LT, 'Reflections on TAXMAN: An Experiment in Artificial Intelligence and Legal Reasoning' (1977) 90 *Harvard Law Review* 837.

McCormack TLH and GJ Simpson, 'A New International Criminal Law Regime?' (1995) 42 *Netherlands International Law Review* 177.

McCubbins MD and T Schwartz, 'Congressional Oversight Overlooked: Police Patrols versus Fire Alarms' (1984) 28 *American Journal of Political Science* 165.

McDougall C, 'Autonomous Weapon Systems and Accountability: Putting the Cart before the Horse' (2019) 20 *Melbourne Journal of International Law* 58.

McEwan I, *Machines Like Me* (Vintage 2019).

McFarland T and T McCormack, 'Mind the Gap: Can Developers of Autonomous Weapons Systems Be Liable for War Crimes?' (2014) 90 *International Studies* 361.

McKelvey F and M MacDonald, 'Artificial Intelligence Policy Innovations at the Canadian Federal Government' (2019) 44 (2) *Canadian Journal of Communication* 43.

McNair B, *Fake News: Falsehood, Fabrication and Fantasy in Journalism* (Routledge 2018).

McNamara SR, 'The Law and Ethics of High-Frequency Trading' (2016) 17 *Minnesota Journal of Law, Science & Technology* 71.

McWilliams A et al (eds), *The Oxford Handbook of Corporate Social Responsibility: Psychological and Organizational Perspectives* (Oxford University Press 2019).

Meissner G, 'Artificial Intelligence: Consciousness and Conscience' (2020) 35 *AI & Society* 225.

Meloni C, 'Command Responsibility: Mode of Liability for the Crimes of Subordinates or Separate Offence of the Superior?' (2007) 5 *Journal of International Criminal Justice* 618.

Menn J, *All the Rave: The Rise and Fall of Shawn Fanning's Napster* (Crown 2003).

Merat N et al, 'The "Out-of-the-Loop" Concept in Automated Driving: Proposed Definition, Measures and Implications' (2019) 21 *Cognition, Technology & Work* 87.

Merkin R and J Steele, *Insurance and the Law of Obligations* (Oxford University Press 2013).

Merkin RM and J Stuart-Smith, *The Law of Motor Insurance* (Sweet & Maxwell 2004).

Mettraux G, *The Law of Command Responsibility* (Oxford University Press 2009).

Meyer DR and G Guernsey, 'Hong Kong and Singapore Exchanges Confront High Frequency Trading' (2017) 23 *Asia Pacific Business Review* 63.

Miller T, 'Explanation in Artificial Intelligence: Insights from the Social Sciences' (2019) 267 *Artificial Intelligence* 1.

Millon D, 'Piercing the Corporate Veil, Financial Responsibility, and the Limits of Limited Liability' (2007) 56 *Emory Law Journal* 1305.

Mitchell M et al, 'Model Cards for Model Reporting' (2019) *ACM Conference on Fairness, Accountability, and Transparency* (FAT*) 220.

Mitnick BM, *The Political Economy of Regulation: Creating, Designing, and Removing Regulatory Forms* (Columbia University Press 1980).

Mittelstadt BD et al, 'The Ethics of Algorithms: Mapping the Debate' (2016) 3 (2) *Big Data & Society*.

Mittelstadt B, C Russell, and S Wachter, 'Explaining Explanations in AI' (2018) *arXiv* 1811.01439v1.

Mohseni S, N Zarei, and ED Ragan, 'A Multidisciplinary Survey and Framework for Design and Evaluation of Explainable AI Systems' (2020) *arXiv* 1811.11839v4.

Molnar C, *Interpretable Machine Learning* (Lulu 2019).

Montavon G et al, 'Explaining Nonlinear Classification Decisions with Deep Taylor Decomposition' (2017) 65 *Pattern Recognition* 211.

Morawetz V, *A Treatise on the Law of Private Corporations* (Little, Brown 1886).

Morison J and A Harkens, 'Re-engineering Justice? Robot Judges, Computerised Courts and (Semi) Automated Legal Decision-Making' (2019) 39 *Legal Studies* 618.

Mothilal RK, A Sharma, and C Tan, 'Explaining Machine Learning Classifiers Through Diverse Counterfactual Explanations' (2020) *ACM Conference on Fairness, Accountability, and Transparency* (FAT*) 607.

Mulligan C, 'Revenge Against Robots' (2018) 69 *South Carolina Law Review* 579.

Munday R, *Agency: Law and Principles* (3rd edn, Oxford University Press 2016).

Murphy J, 'The Liability Bases of Common Law Non-delegable Duties: A Reply to Christian Witting' (2007) 30 *UNSW Law Journal* 86.

Murphy KP, *Machine Learning: A Probabilistic Perspective* (MIT Press

2012).

Murray A, *Information Technology Law: The Law and Society* (3rd edn, Oxford University Press 2016).

Murugan V, 'Embryonic Stem Cell Research: A Decade of Debate from Bush to Obama' (2009) 82 *Yale Journal of Biology and Medicine* 101.

Naffine N, 'Who Are Law's Persons? From Cheshire Cats to Responsible Subjects' (2003) 66 *Modern Law Review* 346.

Nasarre-Aznar S, 'Ownership at Stake (Once Again): Housing, Digital Contents, Animals, and Robots' (2018) 10 *Journal of Property, Planning, and Environmental Law* 69.

Nissenbaum H, 'Protecting Privacy in an Information Age: The Problem of Privacy in Public' (1998) 17 *Law and Philosophy* 559.

Nwana HS, 'Software Agents: An Overview' (1996) 21 *Knowledge Engineering Review* 205.

O'Carroll F, 'Inherently Governmental: A Legal Argument for Ending Private Federal Prisons and Detention Centers' (2017) 67 *Emory Law Journal* 293.

O'Connell M, *To Be a Machine: Adventures among Cyborgs, Utopians, Hackers, and the Futurists Solving the Modest Problem of Death* (Granta 2017).

O'Neil C, *Weapons of Math Destruction: How Big Data Increases Inequality and Threatens Democracy* (Broadway Books 2016).

O'Sullivan T and K Tokeley, 'Consumer Product Failure Causing Personal Injury under the No-Fault Accident Compensation Scheme in New Zealand— A Let-Off for Manufacturers?' (2018) 41 *Journal of Consumer Policy* 211.

Ogus A, *Regulation: Legal Form and Economic Theory* (Hart 2004).

Ohlin JD, 'The Combatant's Stance: Autonomous Weapons on the Battlefield' (2016) 92 *International Law Studies* 1.

Ohlin JD (ed), *Research Handbook on Remote Warfare* (Edward Elgar 2017).

Omohundro S, 'Autonomous Technology and the Greater Human Good' (2014) 26 *Journal of Experimental & Theoretical Artificial Intelli-*

gence 303.

Oskamp A and M Lauritsen, 'AI in Law Practice? So Far, Not Much' (2002) 10 *Artificial Intelligence and Law* 227.

Pagallo U, *The Laws of Robots: Crimes, Contracts, and Torts* (Springer 2013).

Page LL, 'Write This Down: A Model Market-Share Liability Statute' (2019) 68 *Duke Law Journal* 1469.

Page WH, 'The Gary Dinners and the Meaning of Concerted Action' (2009) 62 *Southern Methodist University Law Review* 597.

Paliwala A, 'Rediscovering Artificial Intelligence and Law: An Inadequate Jurisprudence?' (2016) 30 *International Review of Law, Computers & Technology* 107.

Parasuraman R and D Manzey, 'Complacency and Bias in Human Use of Automation: An Attentional Integration' (2010) 52 *Human Factors* 381.

Park S and Haksoo Ko, 'Machine Learning and Law and Economics: A Preliminary Overview' (2020) 11 (2) *Asian Journal of Law and Economics*.

Parkin J, 'Adaptable Due Process' (2012) 160 *University of Pennsylvania Law Review* 1309.

Pasquale F, *The Black Box Society: The Secret Algorithms That Control Money and Information* (Harvard University Press 2015).

'A Rule of Persons, Not Machines: The Limits of Legal Automation' (2019) 87 *George Washington Law Review* 1.

New Laws of Robotics: Defending Human Expertise in the Age of AI (Belknap Press 2020).

Pasquale F and G Cashwell, 'Prediction, Persuasion, and the Jurisprudence of Behaviourism' (2018) 68 (Supplement1) *University of Toronto Law Journal* 63.

Patterson FD and K Neailey, 'A Risk Register Database System to Aid the Management of Project Risk' (2002) 20 *International Journal of Project Management* 365.

Patterson MR, *Antitrust Law in the New Economy* (Harvard University Press 2017).

Pearl TH, 'Fast & Furious: The Misregulation of Driverless Cars' (2017) 73 *New York University Annual Survey of American Law* 24.

Peerenboom R, *China's Long March Toward Rule of Law* (Cambridge University Press 2002).

Peloso C, 'Crafting an International Climate Change Protocol: Applying the Lessons Learned from the Success of the Montreal Protocol and the Ozone Depletion Problem' (2010) 25 *Journal of Land Use & Environmental Law* 305.

Percy S, *Mercenaries: The History of a Norm in International Relations* (Oxford University Press 2007).

Peters B (ed), *Digital Keywords: A Vocabulary of Information Society and Culture* (Princeton University Press 2016) 18.

Petit N, 'Antitrust and Artificial Intelligence: A Research Agenda' (2017) 8 *Journal of European Competition Law & Practice* 361.

Poitras R, 'Article 36 Weapons Reviews & Autonomous Weapons Systems: Supporting an International Review Standard' (2018) 34 *American University International Law Review* 465.

Poscher R, 'Ambiguity and Vagueness in Legal Interpretation' in LM Solan and PM Tiersma (eds), *The Oxford Handbook of Language and Law* (Oxford University Press 2012) 128.

Powell TW, 'Command Responsibility: How the International Criminal Court's Jean-Pierre Bemba Gombo Conviction Exposes the Uniform Code of Military Justice' (2017) 225 *Military Law Review* 837.

Prassl J, *Humans as a Service: The Promise and Perils of Work in the Gig Economy* (Oxford University Press 2018).

Press M, 'Of Robots and Rules: Autonomous Weapon Systems in the Law of Armed Conflict' (2017) 48 *Georgetown Journal of International Law* 1337.

Priest GL and B Klein, 'The Selection of Disputes for Litigation' (1984) 13 *Journal of Legal Studies* 1.

Prins SJ and A Reich, 'Can We Avoid Reductionism in Risk Reduction?' (2018) 22 *Theoretical Criminology* 258.

Prosser T, 'Regulation and Social Solidarity' (2006) 33 *Journal of Law and*

Society 364.

The Regulatory Enterprise: Government, Regulation, and Legitimacy (Oxford University Press 2010).

Qiao C-r, 'Jurisprudent Shift in China: A Functional Interpretation' (2017) 8(1) Asian Journal of Law and Economics.

Radu R, Negotiating Internet Governance (Oxford University Press 2019).

Raji ID et al, 'Closing the AI Accountability Gap: Defining an End-to-End Framework for Internal Algorithmic Auditing' (2020) 2001. 00973v1 arXiv.

Raustiala K and CJ Sprigman, 'The Second Digital Disruption: Streaming and the Dawn of Datadriven Creativity' (2019) 94 New York University Law Review 1555.

Rawls J, Political Liberalism (Columbia University Press 1996).

Raz J, Ethics in the Public Domain: Essays in the Morality of Law and Politics (Clarendon Press 1995).

Reiling D, Technology for Justice: How Information Technology Can Support Judicial Reform (Leiden University Press 2010).

Rhodes R, The Making of the Atomic Bomb (Simon & Schuster 1986).

Richardson R, JM Schultz, and K Crawford, 'Dirty Data, Bad Predictions: How Civil Rights Violations Impact Police Data, Predictive Policing Systems, and Justice' (2019) 94 New York University Law Review 192.

Richelson JT, Spying on the Bomb: American Nuclear Intelligence from Nazi Germany to Iran and North Korea (Norton 2006).

Rifkin J, The Zero Marginal Cost Society: The Internet of Things, the Collaborative Commons, and the Eclipse of Capitalism (St Martin's Press 2014).

Robaldo L et al, 'Introduction for Artificial Intelligence and Law: Special Issue "Natural Language Processing for Legal Texts"' (2019) 27 Artificial Intelligence and Law 113.

Roberts H et al, 'The Chinese Approach to Artificial Intelligence: An Analysis of Policy, Ethics, and Regulation' (2021) 36 AI & Society 59.

Rodgers C, 'A New Approach to Protecting Ecosystems' (2017) 19 Environmental Law Review 266.

Roig A, 'Safeguards for the Right Not to Be Subject to a Decision Based Solely on Automated Processing (Article 22 GDPR)' (2017) 8 (3) *European Journal of Law and Technology*.

Rose SPR and H Rose, '"Do Not Adjust Your Mind, There Is a Fault in Reality"—Ideology in Neurobiology' (1973) 2 *Cognition* 479.

Rosenberg A, 'Strict Liability: Imagining a Legal Framework for Autonomous Vehicles' (2017) 20 *Tulane Journal of Technology and Intellectual Property* 205.

Rousseau J-J, *The Social Contract* (GDH Cole tr, first published 1762, JM Dent 1923).

Roy K, *War and Society in Afghanistan: From the Mughals to the Americans, 1500-2013* (Oxford University Press 2015).

Rudin C, 'Stop Explaining Black Box Machine Learning Models for High Stakes Decisions and Use Interpretable Models Instead' (2019) 1 *Nature Machine Intelligence* 206.

Ruggie JG, Guiding Principles on Business and Human Rights: Implementing the United Nations 'Protect, Respect and Remedy' Framework, UN Doc A/HRC/17/31 (2011).

Russell SJ, *Human Compatible: Artificial Intelligence and the Problem of Control* (Viking 2019).

Russell SJ and P Norvig, *Artificial Intelligence: A Modern Approach* (3rd edn, Prentice Hall 2010).

Sadat LN, 'Prosecutor v Jean-Pierre Bemba Gombo' (2019) 113 *American Journal of International Law* 353.

Sales Lord, 'Algorithms, Artificial Intelligence, and the Law' (2020) 25 *Judicial Review* 46.

Samek W et al, 'Evaluating the Visualization of What a Deep Neural Network Has Learned' (2017) 28 (11) *IEEE Transactions on Neural Networks and Learning Systems* 2660.

Samuelson P, 'Allocating Ownership Rights in Computer-Generated Works' (1986) 47 *University of Pittsburgh Law Review* 1185.

Sands P and J Peel, *Principles of Environmental Law* (4th edn, Cambridge

University Press 2018).

Santoni de Sio, F, 'Killing by Autonomous Vehicles and the Legal Doctrine of Necessity' (2017) 20 *Ethical Theory and Moral Practice* 411.

Schär F and A Berentsen, *Bitcoin, Blockchain, and Cryptoassets* (MIT Press 2020).

Schauer F, 'A Critical Guide to Vehicles in the Park' (2008) 83 *New York University Law Review* 1109.

Schellekens M, 'No-Fault Compensation Schemes for Self-Driving Vehicles' (2018) 10 *Law, Innovation and Technology* 314.

Scherer MU, 'Regulating Artificial Intelligence Systems: Risks, Challenges, Competencies, and Strategies' (2016) 29 *Harvard Journal of Law & Technology* 353.

Scherer M, 'Artificial Intelligence and Legal Decision-Making: The Wide Open?' (2019) 36 *Journal of International Arbitration* 539.

Schlag P, 'No Vehicles in the Park' (1999) 23 *Seattle University Law Review* 381.

Schneewind JB, *The Invention of Autonomy: A History of Modern Moral Philosophy* (Cambridge University Press 1997).

Schwab K, *The Fourth Industrial Revolution* (Crown 2017).

Searle JR, 'Minds, Brains, and Programs' (1980) 3 *Behavioral and Brain Sciences* 417.

Selbst A and S Barocas, 'The Intuitive Appeal of Explainable Machines' (2018) 87 *Fordham Law Review* 1085.

Selbst AD, 'Disparate Impact in Big Data Policing' (2017) 52 *Georgia Law Review* 109.

Selbst AD *et al*, 'Fairness and Abstraction in Sociotechnical Systems' (2019) *ACM Conference on Fairness, Accountability, and Transparency* (FAT*) 59.

Selby J, 'Data Localization Laws: Trade Barriers or Legitimate Responses to Cybersecurity Risks, or Both?' (2017) 25 *International Journal of Law and Information Technology* 213.

Selznick P, 'Focusing Organizational Research on Regulation' in R Noll (ed), *Regulatory Policy and the Social Sciences* (University of California

Press 1985) 363.

Seng D, 'The State of the Discordant Union: An Empirical Analysis of DMCA Takedown Notices' (2014) 18 *Virginia Journal of Law & Technology* 369.

Sergot MJ et al, 'The British Nationality Act as a Logic Program' (1986) 29 *Communications of the ACM* 370.

Service RF, 'Chipmakers Look Past Moore's Law, and Silicon' (2018) 361 (6400) *Science* 321.

Shearer D, *Private Armies and Military Intervention* (Oxford University Press 1998).

Sheiner N, 'DES and a Proposed Theory of Enterprise Liability' (1978) 46 *Fordham Law Review* 963.

Sheppard B, 'Warming Up to Inscrutability: How Technology Could Challenge Our Concept of Law' (2018) 68 (Supplement1) *University of Toronto Law Journal* 36.

Shils EA, *The Torment of Secrecy: The Background and Consequences of American Security Policies* (Heinemann 1956).

Shokri R, M Strobel, and Y Zick, 'On the Privacy Risks of Model Explanations' (2020) *arXiv* 1907. 00164v5.

Siciliani P, 'Tackling Algorithmic-Facilitated Tacit Collusion in a Proportionate Way' (2019) 10 *Journal of European Competition Law & Practice* 31.

Silver D et al, 'Mastering the Game of Go without Human Knowledge' (2017) 550 *Nature* 354.

Silver N, *The Signal and the Noise: Why So Many Predictions Fail—But Some Don't* (Penguin 2012).

Singer P, 'Speciesism and Moral Status' (2009) 40 *Metaphilosophy* 567.

Soares N and B Fallenstein, 'Agent Foundations for Aligning Machine Intelligence with Human Interests: A Technical Research Agenda' in V Callaghan et al (eds), *The Technological Singularity: Managing the Journey* (Springer 2017) 103.

Solaiman SM, 'Legal Personality of Robots, Corporations, Idols and Chimpanzees: A Quest for Legitimacy' (2017) 25 *Artificial Intelligence and Law* 155.

Solove DJ, 'Privacy and Power: Computer Databases and Metaphors for Information Privacy' (2001) 53 *Stanford Law Review* 1393.

Solum LB, 'Legal Personhood for Artificial Intelligences' (1992) 70 *North Carolina Law Review* 1231.

Sourdin T, 'Judge v Robot? Artificial Intelligence and Judicial Decision-Making' (2018) 41 *UNSW Law Journal* 1114.

Sparrow A, *The Law of Virtual Worlds and Internet Social Networks* (Gower 2010).

Sparrow MK, *The Regulatory Craft: Controlling Risks, Solving Problems, and Managing Compliance* (Brookings Institution 2000).

Stapleton J, *Product Liability* (Butterworths 1994).

Steiner C, *Automate This: How Algorithms Came to Rule Our World* (Penguin 2012).

Stockdale M and R Mitchell, 'Legal Advice Privilege and Artificial Legal Intelligence: Can Robots Give Privileged Legal Advice?' (2019) 23 *International Journal of Evidence & Proof* 422.

Stone CD, 'Should Trees Have Standing? Towards Legal Rights for Natural Objects' (1972) 45 *Southern California Law Review* 450.

Strandburg KJ, 'Rulemaking and Inscrutable Automated Decision Tools' (2019) 119 *Columbia Law Review* 1851.

Stucki S, 'Towards a Theory of Legal Animal Rights: Simple and Fundamental Rights' (2020) 40 *Oxford Journal of Legal Studies* 533.

Sullivan LA, WS Grimes, and CL Sagers, *The Law of Antitrust, An Integrated Handbook* (3rd edn, West 2014).

Sunstein C, *Laws of Fear: Beyond the Precautionary Principle* (Cambridge University Press 2005).

Susskind R, 'Detmold's Refutation of Positivism and the Computer Judge' (1986) 49 *Modern Law Review* 125.

The Future of Law: Facing the Challenges of Information Technology (Oxford University Press 1996).

Transforming the Law: Essays on Technology, Justice, and the Legal Marketplace (Oxford University Press 2000).

The End of Lawyers? Rethinking the Nature of Legal Services (Oxford University Press 2008).

Tomorrow's Lawyers: An Introduction to Your Future (Oxford University Press 2013).

Online Courts and the Future of Justice (Oxford University Press 2019).

Susskind R and D Susskind, *The Future of the Professions: How Technology Will Transform the Work of Human Experts* (Oxford University Press 2015).

Swanson SR, 'Google Sets Sail: Ocean-Based Server Farms and International Law' (2011) 43 *Connecticut Law Review* 709.

Sykes K, 'Human Drama, Animal Trials: What the Medieval Animal Trials Can Teach Us about Justice for Animals' (2011) 17 *Animal Law* 273.

Szasz PC, *The Law and Practices of the International Atomic Energy Agency* (International Atomic Energy Agency 1970).

Taeihagh A and HSM Lim, 'Governing Autonomous Vehicles: Emerging Responses for Safety, Liability, Privacy, Cybersecurity, and Industry Risks' (2019) 39 *Transport Reviews* 103.

Take I, 'Regulating the Internet Infrastructure: A Comparative Appraisal of the Legitimacy of ICANN, ITU, and the WSIS' (2012) 6 *Regulation & Governance* 499.

Tan D, 'Fair Use and Transformative Play in the Digital Age' in M Richardson and S Ricketson (eds), *Research Handbook on Intellectual Property in Media and Entertainment* (Edward Elgar 2017) 102.

Taplin J, *Move Fast and Break Things: How Facebook, Google, and Amazon Cornered Culture and Undermined Democracy* (Little, Brown 2017).

Taylor PM, *A Commentary on the International Covenant on Civil and Political Rights* (Cambridge University Press 2020).

腾讯研究院、中国信通院互联网法律研究中心:《人工智能:国家人工智能战略行动抓手》,中国人民大学出版社2017年版。

Thomas WR, 'Incapacitating Criminal Corporations' (2019) 72 *Vanderbilt Law Review* 905.

Tjio H, 'Lifting the Veil on Piercing the Veil' (2014) *Lloyd's Maritime and*

Commercial Law Quarterly 19.

Tomsett R et al, 'Interpretable to Whom? A Role-Based Model for Analyzing Interpretable Machine Learning Systems' (2018) *arXiv* 1806.07552.

Totschnig W, 'The Problem of Superintelligence: Political, Not Technological' (2019) 34 *AI & Society* 907.

Trainor SA, 'A Comparative Analysis of a Corporation's Right Against Self-Incrimination' (1994) 18 *Fordham International Law Journal* 2139.

Tromp N and P Hekkert, *Designing for Society: Products and Services for a Better World* (Bloomsbury Visual Arts 2019).

Turchin A and D Denkenberger, 'Classification of Global Catastrophic Risks Connected with Artificial Intelligence' (2020) 35 *AI & Society* 147.

Turilli M and L Floridi, 'The Ethics of Information Transparency' (2009) 11 *Ethics and Information Technology* 105.

Turing AM, 'Computing Machinery and Intelligence' (1950) 59 *Mind* 433.

Intelligent Machinery, a Heretical Theory (lecture given to the '51 Society' at Manchester) (Turing Digital Archive, AMT/B/4, 1951).

'Intelligent Machinery, A Heretical Theory' (1996) 4 *Philosophia Mathematica* 256.

Turing D, *Prof Alan Turing Decoded: A Biography* (History Press 2015).

Turner J, *Robot Rules: Regulating Artificial Intelligence* (Palgrave Macmillan 2019).

Ugur M (ed), *Governance, Regulation, and Innovation: Theory and Evidence from Firms and Nations* (Edward Elgar 2013).

Upson J and RA Van Ness, 'Multiple Markets, Algorithmic Trading, and Market Liquidity' (2017) 32 *Journal of Financial Markets* 49.

Valentine S, 'Impoverished Algorithms: Misguided Governments, Flawed Technologies, and Social Control' (2019) 46 *Fordham Urban Law Journal* 364.

Veal R and M Tsimplis, 'The Integration of Unmanned Ships into the Lex Maritima' (2017) *Lloyd's Maritime and Commercial Law Quarterly* 303.

Veale M and L Edwards, 'Clarity, Surprises, and Further Questions in the Article 29 Working Party Draft Guidance on Automated Decision-Making and Profiling' (2018) 34 *Computer Law & Security Review* 398.

Vial L, B Lecouteux, and D Schwab, 'Sense Vocabulary Compression through the Semantic Knowledge of WordNet for Neural Word Sense Disambiguation' (2019) *arXiv* 1905. 05677v3.

Vladeck DC, 'Machines without Principals: Liability Rules and Artificial Intelligence' (2014) 89 *Washington Law Review* 117.

Volokh E, 'Chief Justice Robots' (2019) 68 *Duke Law Journal* 1135.

Von Ahn L et al, 'CAPTCHA: Using Hard AI Problems for Security' in E Biham (ed), *Advances in Cryptology—EUROCRYPT 2003* (Springer 2003) 294.

von Heinegg WH, R Frau, and T Singer (eds), *Dehumanization of Warfare: Legal Implications of New Weapon Technologies* (Springer 2018).

Vosoughi S, D Roy, and S Aral, 'The Spread of True and False News Online' (2018) 359 (6380) *Science* 1146.

Wachter S and B Mittelstadt, 'A Right to Reasonable Inferences: Re-thinking Data Protection Law in the Age of Big Data and AI' (2019) *Columbia Business Law Review* 494.

Wachter S, B Mittelstadt, and L Floridi, 'Why a Right to Explanation of Automated Decision-Making Does Not Exist in the General Data Protection Regulation' (2017) 7 *International Data Privacy Law* 76.

Wachter S, B Mittelstadt, and C Russell, 'Counterfactual Explanations without Opening the Black Box: Automated Decisions and the GDPR' (2018) 31 *Harvard Journal of Law & Technology* 841.

Wagner B, 'Liable, but Not in Control? Ensuring Meaningful Human Agency in Automated Decision-Making Systems' (2019) 11 *Policy & Internet* 104.

Waldron J, 'Theoretical Foundations of Liberalism' (1987) 37 (147) *The Philosophical Quarterly* 127.

'The Rule of Law and the Importance of Procedure' in JE Fleming (ed), *Nomos L: Getting to the Rule of Law* (New York University Press 2011) 3.

Wallach W, *A Dangerous Master: How to Keep Technology from Slipping*

Beyond Our Control (Basic Books 2015).

Wallach W and C Allen, *Moral Machines: Teaching Robots Right from Wrong* (Oxford University Press 2009).

Walsh T, *Android Dreams: The Past, Present, and Future of Artificial Intelligence* (Hurst 2017).

Walters E, 'The Model Rules of Autonomous Conduct: Ethical Responsibilities of Lawyers and Artificial Intelligence' (2019) 35 *Georgia State University Law Review* 1073.

Walton D, *Argumentation Methods for Artificial Intelligence in Law* (Springer 2005).

Waltz K, The Spread of Nuclear Weapons: More May Better (International Institute for Strategic Studies, Adelphi Papers, Number 171, 1981).

Walzer M, *Just and Unjust Wars: A Moral Argument with Historical Illustrations* (3rd edn, Basic Books 2000).

Wang D *et al*, 'Designing Theory-Driven User-Centric Explainable AI' (2019) CHI '19: Proceedings of the 2019 CHI Conference on Human Factors in Computing Systems Paper No 601.

Wang FF, *Law of Electronic Commercial Transactions: Contemporary Issues in the EU, US and China* (2nd edn, Routledge 2014).

Ward T and S Maruna, *Rehabilitation* (Routledge 2007).

Watson SM, 'The Corporate Legal Person' (2019) 19 *Journal of Corporate Law Studies* 137.

Watts P and FMB Reynolds, *Bowstead and Reynolds on Agency* (21st edn, Sweet & Maxwell 2018).

Weaver JF, *Robots Are People Too: How Siri, Google Car, and Artificial Intelligence Will Force Us to Change Our Laws* (Praeger 2014).

Wechsler H, 'Toward Neutral Principles of Constitutional Law' (1959) 73 *Harvard Law Review* 1.

Weinrib EJ, 'Causal Uncertainty' (2016) 36 *Oxford Journal of Legal Studies* 135.

Wellek R, 'Karel Capek' (1936) 15 *Slavonic and East European Review* 191.

Weller BM, 'Does Algorithmic Trading Reduce Information Acquisition?'

(2018) 31 *Review of Financial Studies* 2184.

Wessel RA, 'Regulating Technological Innovation through Informal International Law: The Exercise of International Public Authority by Transnational Actors', in MA Heldeweg and E Kica (eds), *Regulating Technological Innovation* (Palgrave Macmillan 2011) 77.

Wexler R, 'Life, Liberty, and Trade Secrets: Intellectual Property in the Criminal Justice System' (2018) 70 *Stanford Law Review* 1343.

Whalen R (ed), *Computational Legal Studies: The Promise and Challenge of Data-Driven Research* (Edward Elgar 2020).

Wilson G, 'Minimizing Global Catastrophic and Existential Risks from Emerging Technologies through International Law' (2013) 31 *Virginia Environmental Law Journal* 307.

Wischmeyer T and T Rademacher (eds), *Regulating Artificial Intelligence* (Springer 2020).

Witting C, 'Breach of the Non-delegable Duty: Defending Limited Strict Liability in Tort' (2006) 29 *UNSW Law Journal* 33.

Street on Torts (15th edn, Oxford University Press 2018).

Wong P-H, 'Democratizing Algorithmic Fairness' (2020) 33 *Philosophy & Technology* 225.

Woo MYK, 'Court Reform with Chinese Characteristics' (2017) 27 *Washington International Law Journal* 241.

Woodward M, 'The Need for Speed: Regulatory Approaches to High Frequency Trading in the United States and the European Union' (2011) 50 *Vanderbilt Journal of Transnational Law* 1359.

Wright P, *Spycatcher: The Candid Autobiography of a Senior Intelligence Officer* (Viking 1987).

Wringe B, *An Expressive Theory of Punishment* (Palgrave Macmillan 2016).

Wu T, 'Agency Threats' (2011) 60 *Duke Law Journal* 1841.

Xu X and F Chiang-Ku, 'Autonomous Vehicles, Risk Perceptions and Insurance Demand: An Individual Survey in China' (2019) 124 (C) *Transportation Research Part A: Policy and Practice* 549.

Xu Z *et al*, 'Case Facts Analysis Method Based on Deep Learning' in Weiwei

Ni *et al* (eds), *Web Information Systems and Applications* (Springer 2020) 92.

Yao J-j and P Hui, 'Research on the Application of Artificial Intelligence in Judicial Trial: Experience from China' (2020) 1487 *Journal of Physics: Conference Series* 012013.

Yap BP, A Koh, and ES Chng, 'Adapting BERT for Word Sense Disambiguation with Gloss Selection Objective and Example Sentences' (2020) *arXiv* 2009. 11795v2.

Yeo TM, 'Unilateral Mistake in Contract: Five Degrees of Fusion of Common Law and Equity' (2004) *Singapore Journal of Legal Studies* 227.

Yeung K, ' "Hypernudge": Big Data as a Mode of Regulation by Design' (2017) 20 *Information, Communication & Society* 118.

—— 'Algorithmic Regulation: A Critical Interrogation' (2018) 12 *Regulation & Governance* 505.

Yong D, 'The Courtroom Performance' (1985) 10 (3) *The Cambridge Journal of Anthropology* 74.

You C, 'Law and Policy of Platform Economy in China' (2020) 39 *Computer Law & Security Review* 1.

Yudkowsky E, 'Complex Value Systems in Friendly AI' in J Schmidhuber, KR Thórisson, and M Looks (eds), *Artificial General Intelligence* (Springer 2011) 388.

Zalnieriute M, LB Moses, and G Williams, 'The Rule of Law and Automation of Government Decision-Making' (2019) 82 *Modern Law Review* 425.

Zarsky TZ, 'Transparent Predictions' (2013) *University of Illinois Law Review* 1503.

Zerilli J *et al*, 'Transparency in Algorithmic and Human Decision-Making: Is There a Double Standard?' (2019) 32 *Philosophy & Technology* 661.

Zetzsche DA *et al*, 'Regulating a Revolution: From Regulatory Sandboxes to Smart Regulation' (2017) 23 *Fordham Journal of Corporate & Financial Law* 31.

Zhang M and S Jian, 'Outsourcing in Municipal Governments: Experiences from the United States and China' (2012) 35 *Public Performance &*

Management Review 696.

Zhang X, *Legislation of Tort Liability Law in China* (Springer 2018).

Zhou H and PS Kalev, 'Algorithmic and High Frequency Trading in Asia-Pacific, Now and the Future' (2019) 53 *Pacific-Basin Finance Journal* 186.

Zhou H and Q Pan, 'Information, Community, and Action on Sina-Weibo: How Chinese Philanthropic NGOs Use Social Media Authors' (2016) 27 *VOLUNTAS: International Journal of Voluntary and Nonprofit Organizations* 2433.

Zuboff S, *The Age of Surveillance Capitalism: The Fight for a Human Future at the New Frontier of Power* (Public Affairs 2019).

索 引

A

阿尔法狗 ii
阿什利·麦迪逊数据泄露事件 163
阿西洛马原则 174
阿西洛马重组 DNA 会议 238
埃里克·卢米斯 062
艾伦·图灵 123
艾萨克·阿西莫夫 157
艾森豪威尔的"和平利用原子能"演讲 230
爱德华·希尔斯 078
安德鲁·卡茨 142
安理会 251
安娜莉·纽维茨 163
奥利弗·温德尔·霍姆斯 260
澳大利亚 036
澳大利亚《人工智能伦理原则》190

B

保密性 078

保险 091，103
贝克·豪斯律师事务所 272
被定义 iii，166
被起诉 121，131
本质上危险活动 109
比尔·盖茨 133
B2C2/Quoine 案例 054
比例原则 111
边界 120
波动率指数 003
剥夺犯罪分子的作案能力 136
补救措施 020
不合规的后果 245
不合逻辑 274
不可接受的决策 070
不可取 192
不可委托职责 208
《不扩散核武器条约》249
不透明性 062

不透明性带来的问题 084

不作为或未能实施的行为 116

部分自动化 028

C

裁判尺度 287

查尔斯·巴比奇 068

差别待遇 071

差别影响 072

产品责任 030

《产品责任指令》101

超过人类 154

超级智能 154

乘客 039

惩罚 136

惩戒 135

穿透公司面纱 132

创新 xiii

从犯责任 114

错误 054

D

戴维·科林格里奇 211

大卫·斯莱特 147

代理 094

代理责任 108

单方面错误 054

弹道导弹防御系统 041

道德机器 038

道路交通法 036

德国 009

德怀特·艾森豪威尔 230

第零个定律 226

第一届和平利用原子能国际会议（第一届日内瓦会议）263

蒂姆·吴 218

电车难题 038

电气和电子工程师协会 174

定价 017

定期审核 170

定义 ii

董事会成员 134

动态定价 017

动物 012

对动物进行审判 090

E

厄瓜多尔 128

2010年"闪电崩盘" 005

恩里科·费米 229

F

发明 153

罚款 135

法国 009

法莱兹猪杀人案 089

法律改革 012

法律建议 272

法律人格 123

法律责任 089

法律职业 275

法律自动化 270

法律作为编码 282

法律作为数据 279

法人人格 128

法人人格集合论 128

法人人格虚构论和特许论 129

法人身份 132

反垄断法（竞争法）259

反事实 175

反向图灵测试 196

方法 173

非代表性数据 072

非洲裔美国人 072

风险评估工具 069

风险管控 092

风险评估 072

弗兰克·帕斯奎尔 064

弗朗茨·卡夫卡 194

负责使用的用户 035

G

高度自动化 028

高级目标定位和致命自动化系统 042

高频交易 011

高频交易员 005

高速率的人工智能 ix

个人身份识别数据 075

《关于在自动处理个人数据方面保护个人的公约》186

公共产品 241

公共控制 xii

公共权力 xiii

公司 018

公司登记注册 254

共同过失 032

谷歌 044

谷歌被罚案 185

固定式杀伤武器 041

雇佣兵 048

雇佣作品 149

关联非因果 73

观望 216

规范 242

规模 257

国际标准化组织 237

国际电信联盟 241

国际法委员会 244

国际红十字会 041

国际人道主义法 042

国际人工智能机构 xii

国际人工智能小组 247

国际原子能机构 231

国家责任 257

过失 030

H

哈特 277

韩国 203

行业标准 232

好处 070

合法性 051

何时披露 169

黑箱社会 064

黑猩猩 144

红线 220

互联网 237

互联网法院 266

互联网名称与数字地址分配机构 237

环境影响评估 177

回归模型 074

豁免 189

火灾报警 169

J

《机器人伦理宪章》202

机器学习 280

基因切割 235

基于实例的解释 168

激励创新 148

集体行动 xii

加拿大 069

加拿大的《自动化决策指令》189

家庭财产 143

假新闻 006

价格操纵 018

驾驶辅助技术 028

驾驶员 028

监察员 258

监管前景 028

监管"沙盒" 220

监管俘获 238

监管的市场合理性 207

监管时机 213

减速带 013

剑桥分析公司丑闻 234

交易数据 013

交易算法 005

矫正 137

揭示面纱机制 132

杰里米·边沁 084

结构开放 278

结构性挑战 240

解释权 183

金融工具市场指令二 013

金融市场 003

近程武器系统 041

警察巡逻 169

警惕性克制 216

竞争法 016

局限性 159

举证责任 100

K

卡雷尔·恰佩克 290

卡斯·桑斯坦 214

开放源码运动 070

科林格里奇困境 239

可分解性 173

可解释性 172

克里斯托弗·拉塞尔 164

刻板印象 075

《空间物体所造成损害的责任公约》243

恐慌指数 004

跨境损害 240

L

拉斐尔·瓦斯克斯 025

赖兰兹诉弗莱彻案 096

了解他们是否在与另一个人互动 164

类人机器人谬误 140

《里约宣言》213

理论 128

立场 131

立法机构 257

联合国 230

脸书 xiv

聊天机器人 053

劣质决策 067

伦理问题 040

伦理学家 038

罗伯特·H. 杰克逊 289

罗纳德·德沃金 276

《罗萨姆的万能机器人》290

罗斯 272

M

麻文项目 044

马顿斯条款 043

迈克尔·沃尔泽 046

美国 v

美国商业圆桌会议 235

美国《算法问责法案》188

《蒙特勒文件》050

米尔顿·弗里德曼 235

米雷耶·希尔德布兰特 280

面部识别技术 075

民法 031

民事责任 030

模糊 274

模拟技术 007

模型卡 181

摩尔定律 005

N

纳温德·辛格·萨拉奥 022

尼尔·理查兹 140

倪德锋 287

拟人化 140

拟人化的谬论 xi

奴隶制 142

O

欧盟《数据保护指令》079

欧盟《通用数据保护条例》069

欧盟《通用数据保护条例》非约束性的

序言第 71 条 183

欧盟 069

欧洲数据保护委员会（第 29 工作组）184

欧洲委员会 186

P

帕梅拉·塞缪尔森 148

陪审团 082

披露什么 167

偏见 073

普通法 108

Q

欺诈 022

汽车工程师协会 028

契约论 128

乔治·博克斯 166

巧妙的不作为 215

侵权法 090

全球化 007

全自动化 028

R

让-皮埃尔·贝姆巴 115

人工智能的冬天 xiv

人工智能造福人类峰会 251

人工智能伙伴关系组织 203

人类控制 040

人类中心主义困境 064

《日内瓦公约第一附加议定书》043

软件是否应被认定为产品 101

软件则被视为服务 101

软件代理 094

瑞安·阿博特 226

瑞安·卡洛 102

S

筛选决策 070

设计缺陷 099

社交媒体平台 010

深度伪造 009

《神学大全》122

审计追踪 285

审判 082

生命未来研究所 203

实质性隐藏 008

《世界人权宣言》142

世界知识产权组织 150

市场份额责任 100

疏忽行为 096

术语 002

数据保护法 vii

数据（或隐私）保护影响评估 177

数据表 181

数据共享 018

《数字共和国法》187

输入垃圾，输出垃圾 068

司法机构 257

司法责任制 268

司法职能 057

私营军事和安全公司 049

私有化 118

算法决策 051

算法审计 179

算法透明度 173

算法影响评估 177

随机暗网购物者 055

T

替代性制裁犯罪矫正管理剖析软件 062

替代责任 094

调试 037

条约 223

通谋 020

通用人工智能 ix

透明度谬论 192

透明性 163

图灵测试 124

推特 010

托比·沃尔什 227

托马斯·阿奎那 122

W

网络安全问题 031

危险物种 096

威廉·斯马特 140

威慑 107

围棋 ii

维萨·库尔基 155

问责和监督 066

问责制 059

乌戈·帕加洛 094

无过错责任制度 105

无人驾驶飞行器 041

武器审查 047

误伤友军 044

外包服务的伦理问题 040

X

习惯国际法 242

狭义人工智能 005

先进技术外部咨询委员会 239

现实主义 129

响应式监管 218

象征论 128

《像我一样的机器》161

新加坡 vii

新机构 229

新西兰 106

新西兰《算法宪章》191

信任 191

信息不对称 014

信息全球化 021

刑法 032

刑事惩罚 136

行政法 081

行政长官 256

虚幻的透明度 192

虚拟沙盒 220

训练数据 071

Y

延迟危险 020

严格责任 096

验证码 196

伊恩·麦克尤恩 161

伊奎文特公司 063

伊丽莎程序 123

伊莱恩·赫茨伯格 024

以模型为中心的可解释性 167

以主体为中心的可解释性 168

隐私 viii

隐私影响评估 177

英国 003

英国《2018 年自动驾驶和电动汽车法案》104

英国《税收管理法》056

影响评估 xi

拥有财产 133

用户投诉成本 172

由人工智能进行监管 266

有条件自动化 028

有意义的信息 184

语言 274

预防性拘留 075

预防原则 213

原子能 230

远程反舰导弹 040

约翰·杜威 127

约翰·罗伯茨 277

约翰·麦卡锡 xv

约瑟夫·拉兹 276

Z

在线争议解决 267

责任归属 244

债务 003

征税 133

正义原则 278

证明责任 066

政府固有职能 092

政府职能 vi

知识产权 006

指导原则 111

指挥责任 091

智慧监管 217

中国 vi

中国《新一代人工智能发展规划》210

中国《新一代人工智能治理原则——发展负责任的人工智能》191

注意标准 096

著作权保护 149

专利保护 152

专利法 150

自动化 268

自动化决策过程所产生的不可接受的决策 070

自动化偏见 068

自动化处理 056

自动驾驶汽车 027

自动债务索偿系统 052

自然人格 141

自然语言处理 274

自我调查 286

自相矛盾 081

自治 235

自主武器 iv

自主性 024

组织结构 256

译 后 记

"人是万物的尺度",古希腊哲学家、智者普罗泰戈拉(Protagoras)两千多年前如是说。

但是,碳基生物可以为硅基生物立法吗?在这个以大数据算法技术为核心的信息时代,渊源于农业纪元和工业纪元的人类社会法律范式,能在多大维度上应对迅猛迭代的人工智能带来的治理挑战,以平衡人类世界的安全与发展,增进人类文明的公平、公正、公开呢?

感谢陈西文教授,给予我们宝贵的机会向中文读者引介这部关于人工智能治理规范的系统性、前瞻性论著。本书贯通古今、融汇东西,不仅回顾了从14世纪法莱兹母猪杀人案到21世纪印尼大猩猩版权案等古今案例,还涵盖了从中国的人工智能发展规划到欧盟的人工智能立法等东西方政策、法律。本书系统地讨论了现有制度和判例等规范工具对于当前的弱人工智能治理的有效性与局限性,为将来规训通用人工智能甚至超级人工智能提出了国际协作与机器自我监管的路径指导。

本书的翻译工作,主要由游传满翻译开篇至第6章,由费秀艳翻译第7章至结论。我们的翻译工作得到了陈芳姝、马淑娴、徐乐、杨禹韬、赵婧怡等同学的大力协助,他们对专有名词的核对、中英文脚注的整理等工作极大地提高了我们翻译工作的效率性、准确性与愉悦性。在此,我们向他们表示特别的感谢!当然,囿于时间仓促,加上才识有限,翻译中的不足之处皆是译者的责任,恳请读者不吝批评指正。

我们要特别感谢北京大学出版社的孙维玲女士以及剑桥大学出版社的Joe Ng先生。他们是本书得以在一年左右的时间迅速完成审批立项、版权引进、付印出版的幕后功臣!也特别感谢北京大学法学院院长郭雳教授,阅读本书后应邀为此中译本作序推荐。我们还要感谢新加坡国立大学,为本书的出版提供经费支持。

最后,我们要感谢家人和组织[香港中文大学(深圳)国际事务研究院、华东政法大学国际法学院]对我们追求学术初心的包容、理解与支持。毕竟,在当前"数字化""指标化""结构化"的高校科研评估体系里,译著成果的智慧成本"输入"(input)与考评绩效"输出"(output),或许并不是"最优路径算法"。

借由本书的付梓,我们也由衷地期待有机会与更多的学界同侪、产业同道以及政府有司探讨如何在尊重个体价值、保障个人权利的同时,发挥人工智能在提高效率、促进创新方面的社会潜力,以构建更加公平、公正、公开的人类文明新纪元!

游传满
2024甲辰年孟夏于鹏城神仙湖畔